D0003119

MARGARET JOAN ANSTEE

Never Learn to Type

A WOMAN AT THE UNITED NATIONS

WILEY

Published in the UK in 2004 by   John Wiley & Sons Ltd, The Atrium, Southern Gate,
Chichester, West Sussex PO19 8SQ, England
Telephone (+44) 1243 779777

Email (for orders and customer service enquiries): cs-books@wiley.co.uk
Visit our Home Page on www.wileyeurope.com or www.wiley.com

Copyright © 2003 Dame Margaret Joan Anstee

Reprinted May 2003

First published in March 2003
This paperback edition published April 2004

All Rights Reserved. No part of this publication may be reproduced, stored in a
retrieval system or transmitted in any form or by any means, electronic, mechanical,
photocopying, recording, scanning or otherwise, except under the terms of the
Copyright, Designs and Patents Act 1988 or under the terms of a licence issued by
the Copyright Licensing Agency Ltd, 90 Tottenham Court Road, London W1T 4LP,
UK, without the permission in writing of the Publisher. Requests to the Publisher
should be addressed to the Permissions Department, John Wiley & Sons Ltd, The
Atrium, Southern Gate, Chichester, West Sussex PO19 8SQ, England, or emailed to
permreq@wiley.co.uk, or faxed to (+44) 1243 770571.

Dame Margaret Joan Anstee has asserted her right under the Copyright, Designs and
Patents Act 1988, to be identified as the author of this work.

Other Wiley Editorial Offices

John Wiley & Sons Inc., 111 River Street, Hoboken, NJ 07030, USA

Jossey-Bass, 989 Market Street, San Francisco, CA 94103-1741, USA

Wiley-VCH Verlag GmbH, Boschstr. 12, D-69469 Weinheim, Germany

John Wiley & Sons Australia Ltd, 33 Park Road, Milton, Queensland 4064, Australia

John Wiley & Sons (Asia) Pte Ltd, 2 Clementi Loop #02-01, Jin Xing Distripark,
Singapore 129809

John Wiley & Sons Canada Ltd, 22 Worcester Road, Etobicoke, Ontario, Canada
M9W 1L1

Wiley also publishes its books in a variety of electronic formats. Some content that
appears in print may not be available in electronic books.

British Library Cataloguing in Publication Data

A catalogue record for this book is available from the British Library

ISBN 0-470-85431-6

Typeset in 9.5/13pt Melior by Mathematical Composition Setters Ltd, Salisbury,
Wiltshire
Printed and bound in Great Britain by Biddles Ltd, Guildford and King's Lynn
This book is printed on acid-free paper responsibly manufactured from sustainable
forestry in which at least two trees are planted for each one used for paper
production.

10 9 8 7 6 5 4 3 2 1

PROPERTY OF LIBRARY

Photo of Margaret Anstee: Robert Michael Schuster

Dame Margaret Anstee served the United Nations (UN) for over four decades (1952–93), and, in 1987, was the first woman to achieve the rank of Under Secretary-General. She worked on operational programmes of economic and social development in all regions of the world, mostly with the United Nations Development Programme (UNDP). From 1987–92 she served as Director-General of the UN at Vienna, Head of the Centre for Social Development and Humanitarian Affairs and Co-ordinator of all UN narcotic drug control programmes. From 1992–3 she was the Secretary-General's Special Representative to Angola, the first woman to head a UN peacekeeping mission including its military component.

Dame Margaret served successively as Resident Representative of UNDP in eight countries, in Asia, Latin America and Africa. From 1974–87 she occupied senior positions at UN headquarters in New York and was also given special responsibility for a number of disaster relief programmes, including the Chernobyl nuclear disaster, the Mexican earthquake of 1985 and the Kuwait oil wells of 1991.

From 1967–8 Dame Margaret served as Senior Economic Adviser to Harold Wilson in the Prime Minister's Office of the Government of the United Kingdom.

Dame Margaret was educated at Newnham College, Cambridge, of which she is an Honorary Fellow. She continues to work *ad honorem* for the UN and for the President and Government of Bolivia. Amongst other activities she is a member of Jimmy Carter's International Council for Conflict Resolution.

Previous books by the same author

The Administration of International Development Aid, The Maxwell School of Citizenship and Public Affairs, Syracuse University, New York, 1969.

Gate of the Sun: A Prospect of Bolivia, Longman, London, 1970.

Bolivia: Gate of the Sun, Erikson, New York, 1971 (American edition).

Africa and the World, A Haile Selassie Prize Trust Symposium, edited jointly with R.K.A. Gardiner and C.L. Patterson, Oxford University Press, 1970.

Orphan of the Cold War: The Inside Story of the Angolan Peace Process, 1992–3, Macmillan Press, London, 1996.
(American edition of same name, St. Martin's Press, New York, 1996. Portuguese edition, *Orfão da Guerra Fría: Radiografía do Colapso do Processo de Paz Angolano 1992–3*, Campo das Letras, Oporto, 1997).

'What a life! She strode – and occasionally stumbled – across Development, the UN and the men in her life with a style, intelligence and curiosity reminiscent of those extraordinary Victorian women explorers. She is one of those redoubtable Englishwomen for whom England was always a size too small.'
Mark Malloch Brown, Administrator, United Nations Development Programme

'As a leading international civil servant, Margaret Anstee has lived with the great themes of post-war history: poverty, conflict and the unending difficulty of limiting either. But she also writes of romance and travel, friendship and daily incident – even about making herself a ball-gown out of a parachute and dancing the night away.'
Onora O'Neill, Principal, Newnham College, Cambridge

'An intelligent and courageous human being, Dame Margaret Anstee is also a wonderful writer. She vividly presents for us the adventures she has experienced, the battles she has won and lost and the fascinating people she has encountered along the way.'
Gerald J. Bender, Professor (and former Director), School of International Relations, University of Southern California, and former President of the African Studies Association

'The preamble of the UN Charter announces the commitment of the Peoples of the United Nations to, among other things, "reaffirm the faith in the fundamental dignity and worth of the human person" and "promote social progress and better standards of life in larger freedom". No one has lived for these principles more selflessly or diligently than Margaret Anstee. Her life of service to the global community is inspirational, and her story is highly recommended to anyone interested in the remarkable development of the UN since 1945.'
Jimmy Carter, former President of the United States of America

'Margaret Joan Anstee is a true pioneer of the international community. Her career spans more than half a century's service across four continents. The first woman to be appointed Special Representative of the Secretary-General of the United Nations, she has made an enormous and enduring contribution to the UN family – and continues to do so to this day. With this memoir, she offers an account of a rich and fascinating life, as well as the kind of insight only the insider can provide into the nature of conflict, development and the work for peace.'
Kofi A. Annan, Secretary-General of the United Nations

'Margaret Anstee's memoir provides insight into the problems women face in the man's world of the United Nations. Yet the real world is at least half a woman's world. Women, as she says, have a great deal to contribute.'
Rt Hon. Shirley Williams, leader of the Liberal Democrats in the House of Lords

'To succeed as a woman in the upper reaches of the UN you need to be intelligent and rather stubborn. As Foreign Secretary I knew that [Margaret] Joan Anstee was both. I could guess at the difficulties with which she wrestled in the labyrinth of UN Headquarters and later as she struggled on behalf of us all to bring peace to Angola. But until I read this dramatic book I had no notion of the earlier struggles which brought her from a village green in Essex through Cambridge, the Foreign Office, the Labour Party and Downing Street, to the centre of international life in the UN.'
The Rt Hon. Lord Hurd of Westwell CH CBE PC (Douglas Hurd, former UK Secretary of State for Foreign and Commonwealth Affairs)

'[Margaret] Joan Anstee's varied and exciting career in national and international service has been primarily a search for the economic and social sources of greater

security and equity in the world. Her book also provides an unusual, and refreshingly specific, account of the United Nations in action and of its unsung but significant achievements as well as its better known shortcomings.'
Sir Brian Urquhart, former Under Secretary-General of the United Nations

'An engrossing story, told with deep conviction as well as a sharp eye for describing a wide range of societies and people. A personal – as well as a political – adventure story, Dame Margaret's memoir paints a revealing portrait of life on the frontlines of the engagement between the developed and developing worlds.'
Chester A. Crocker, Professor at the Institute for the Study of Diplomacy, Georgetown University, Washington, and former US Assistant Secretary of State for African Affairs

'During 41 years of UN service Margaret Anstee visited 130 member states and always her strong sense of adventure comes through. Not for her the stuffiness of maps and reference books, this is a writer who sets off up rivers, into the plains, mountains and deserts to get to the heart of a country. This is a remarkable story told by a remarkable lady.'
Rt. Hon Peter Hain, MP, Secretary of State for Wales (Minister of State, Foreign and Commonwealth Office, 1999–2002)

'Dame Margaret Anstee has made an outstanding contribution to development, peace-keeping and conflict resolution over four decades. Her achievements are truly inspirational.'
The Rt Hon. Jack Straw MP, Secretary of State for Foreign and Commonwealth Affairs

'A truly absorbing account of achievement and adventure, by a remarkable woman trail-blazing in the once pinstriped world of international diplomacy. Margaret Anstee wisely never learned to type – but she certainly knows how to write in a way that engages and holds the reader's attention from beginning to end.'
The Rt Hon. The Lord Howe of Aberavon CH QC (Geoffrey Howe, former UK Secretary of State for Foreign and Commonwealth Affairs, Chancellor of the Exchequer and Deputy Prime Minister)

'Dame Margaret Anstee's story begins in rural England and describes the breaking down of the barriers of gender discrimination in a man's world, of facing the challenges of development in the third world, especially in Bolivia, and of conflict resolution and peace-keeping in the globalised world. A story written with wit, charm and affection about a life devoted to the evolution of the United Nations where she achieved the position of Under Secretary-General.'
Gonzalo Sánchez de Lozada, President of Bolivia

'Margaret Joan Anstee is the first woman to have headed a United Nations peace-keeping mission and her experience for over four decades in the UN is unique. Her book *Never Learn to Type* is a remarkable and entertaining account of her adventures in many parts of the world.'
Boutros Boutros-Ghali, former Secretary-General of the United Nations

'I am very pleased to have a new opportunity to express my gratitude to Margaret for the remarkable services she rendered for 41 years to the United Nations. In my 10 years as Secretary-General, my experience with her was extraordinary. Her affection, intelligence and strength to achieve her goals always had my admiration and support. On many occasions her actions as Secretary-General's Special Representative were very successful and helpful for different countries.'
Javier Pérez de Cuéllar, former Secretary-General of the United Nations

Contents

PROPERTY OF
ROYAL OAKS LIBRARY

For my beloved parents, and for Christina, my aunt,
without whose love and constant support and
encouragement none of the rest would have been
possible.

The United Nations System

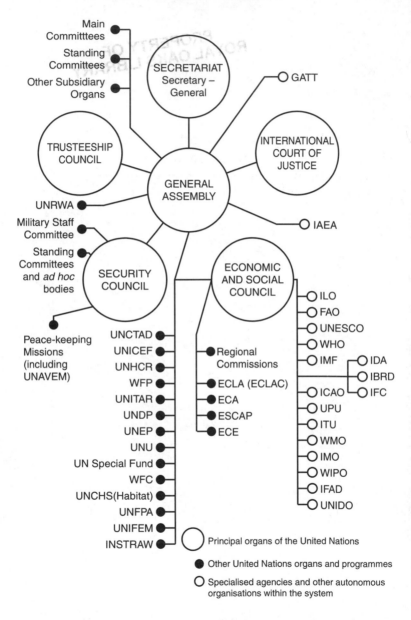

This is a simplified chart of the United Nations System designed to assist the readers of this book. The full titles of the organisations mentioned in the text are given in the List of Acronyms on page 520.

Preface

As a child I dreamed of roaming the world, a wild ambition for a small girl in an English country village, likely to leave school at 14 and whose career horizon might have been expected to be limited to a job in the nearest town and marriage to a local boy. Even my wildest dreams could not foresee that I would live in a dozen countries, visit over 130 more, and wander in some of the remotest places in the world. Now, as I write in my home in Bolivia, looking out over the vivid blue waters of Lake Titicaca to the shimmering white peaks of the Cordillera Real of the Andes that girdle this magical world, I realise once again how extraordinarily lucky I have been.

I was given the opportunity to surmount barriers that women had never previously been allowed to cross and eventually became the first woman to rise through the ranks of the United Nations to the highest level under the Secretary-General, that of Under Secretary-General. During my 41 years service I was involved in some of the major events of my lifetime – processes of profound social change, wars, revolutions and catastrophes, both natural and man-made.

Along the years many people have asked me to write my experiences. I was always too busy. I still am, but in this book have at last tried to do so, conscious, in the evocative words of Gabriel García Márquez, at the beginning of his own memoirs, that '*La vida no es la que uno vivió, sino la que recuerda, y cómo la recuerda para contarla*' – 'Life is not the one you lived, but the one you remember, and how you remember it when you tell the tale.'

Memory is selective, mine evidently not sufficiently so, for many incidents and anecdotes have had to be excised from this book, for reasons of space, and in order not to try the reader's patience excessively.

There have been many challenges along the way and, inevitably, setbacks and disappointments as well as successes, sadness and sometimes tragedy, as well as moments of great happiness. Through it all I have been buoyed up by my mother's favourite dictum, relentlessly drilled into me during my childhood: 'Never say your mother had a jibber.' I would have liked it to be the title of this book but was advised that no one would understand it. For me the meaning has always been crystal-clear. A jibber is a horse that jibs at a fence and my dear mother was determined that I should take my fences head-on. Her words have echoed throughout my life, long after she was dead. As this volume may show, I have continued to charge at fences, when it might have been more prudent to walk round the side, sometimes knocking off the top rail, often falling into the water on the other side.

The title that now adorns this book is a dictum that I invented for myself and have also stuck to throughout my career. I was lucky enough to study at one of the most prestigious universities in the world at a time when places for women were severely limited. Subsequent career openings for women with arts degrees, even those with first-class honours, were sparse indeed, apart from teaching. Many of my peers had to take secretarial courses and became high-powered assistants to men often not as bright or as qualified as themselves. I decided very early on that I would never learn to type, in order to avoid a similar fate. Nowadays, in our computer-dominated world, everyone has to learn to type to some degree, including men. But in my day the dictum served me well.

When you reach a 'certain age', especially in a life as varied as mine, you feel the need to assess whether it has all been haphazard and a matter of chance and coincidence, or whether some pattern has informed it. That is what I have tried to do in these pages. Three main streams seem to run through them, sometimes on the surface, sometimes as barely discernible undercurrents.

Conflict and war have certainly been recurrent themes. My coming into the world was the result of a chance encounter brought about by the circumstances of the 1914–18 Great War. My early childhood was overshadowed by the intense fear of war and was then very nearly brought to an untimely end by the Second

World War. Fears of an even more deadly conflagration loomed over my four decades with the United Nations and, although that fortunately did not happen, the Cold War effectively blocked many endeavours to improve world security in its widest sense. After that came to an end, I finished my formal career leading a doomed peace-keeping mission, trying to resolve a vicious civil war in Angola. Many activities relating to the resolution of conflicts continue to occupy me to this day.

It is not surprising, then, that so much of my life has been taken up by the United Nations, the second continuous element. I joined it when both the organisation and I were very young, as a local field staff member in a programme that was only just beginning. It was a heady period when, fired by the optimism of youth and the ideals enshrined in the United Nations Charter, many of us thought, perhaps naively, that together we might really help to change the world. That vision was to be tempered by sober experience. Yet many years of fieldwork in all developing regions, and my subsequent senior posts at Headquarters, allowed me to take part in many rewarding areas of the United Nations work: political, economic, social and humanitarian. I was also able to follow the many vicissitudes that dogged the organisation, as well as the changes that have enabled it to survive to this day.

The third stream reflects the perspective of a woman who, by chance, found herself challenging deeply rooted beliefs and traditions that had hitherto circumscribed a woman's role in international affairs. In my tomboy childhood I bitterly resented the disadvantages that I perceived the female condition to entail. Later I learned to hold my own in what was then very much a man's world and took part in the evolution of woman's place in that world, as I hope this book will also show.

I could not have done all these things without the love, friendship and support of many people all over the world, first and foremost my beloved parents and my Aunt Christina. I am sad that they are no longer here to read this tribute to them. Neither is Jacko (Commander Sir Robert Jackson, a much admired United Nations official with a legendary capacity for troubleshooting and successfully managing large-scale operations in the most adverse circumstances imaginable), with whom I shared many years of personal and professional companionship. Many others too numerous to mention, and not only those in high positions, have helped me along the way, especially in its stony places. Many of them too are gone, but I do not forget them. Among them were several men who encouraged and supported me academically and professionally at a time when it was far from the norm for women to have careers such as mine. Their names figure in these pages.

Now that I no longer have an office or a secretary but still travel the world and am as busy as ever, the dictum that saved me from becoming a secretary myself has caught up with me. I am accordingly immensely grateful to Kristina Thompson who patiently typed two of the much longer earlier versions of this book, and to Margaret Fry who, at short notice, undertook the arduous task of producing the final text. My gratitude goes also to my editor, Sally Smith, who was invaluable in advising me how to cut and shape the narrative of a very varied life.

Villa Margarita
Lake Titicaca   March 2003

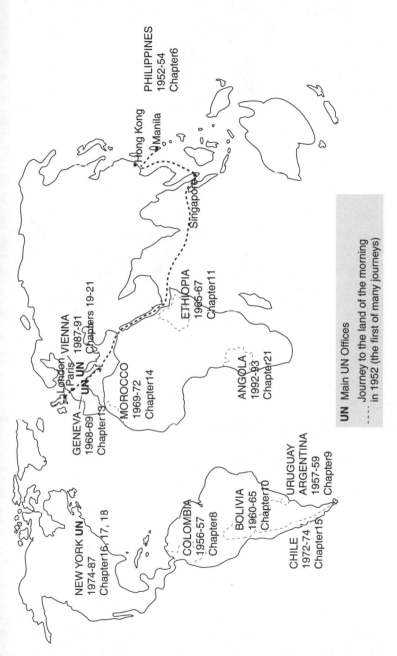

Map 1 Map references relating to the text.

Map 2   Latin America.

PART ONE

The Early Years

1

Prelude

One Sunday evening in 1915 a young soldier, invalided home from Gallipoli, shyly greeted a pretty young girl after church in Kington, a small market town in north-west Herefordshire, where he had been sent to recuperate. Had it not been for the vagaries of war my parents would never have met. In those days there was small chance for country-folk, born into straitened circumstances on the opposite sides of England, to move away from their place of origin.

Many years later, as an Under Secretary-General of the United Nations, I caused some consternation when, responding to the Turkish Foreign Minister's speech at a dinner given in my honour in Istanbul, I regretted that I had not been taken to the Dardanelles. My hosts relaxed visibly when I explained that, but for Gallipoli (where my father, a private soldier in the Fifth Essex Regiment, had narrowly escaped death), I would not have been at that dinner table, would not have existed at all.

Eleven years were to elapse after that chance encounter before I appeared on the scene. The young couple were able to 'walk out' together for only a brief few weeks before my father was sent back to the Middle East, first to Alexandria and then to join Allenby's campaign through Palestine. They could correspond only in the stark multichoice options allowed by army postcards and did not meet again until after the war. On 16 September 1921 they became engaged and on 9 September 1922, they were married.

The Herefordshire Line

My mother's parents came from farming stock in Radnorshire, and my grandmother's family name, Probert, is Welsh, a modification of Ap-Robert, or 'son of Robert'. An orphan at three years old, she nonetheless had a comfortable childhood; she had her own pony, and went to boarding-school, spending the holidays with uncles and aunts who farmed the rich dairying country round Hereford at Bishopstone and Yazor Court, still solid farmhouses today, with an air of prosperity about them. She was barely eighteen when she married John Mills, at Penybont. He, too, came from a comfortable background, but the story of their marriage was, in the material sense, one of progressive decline. As their children increased, they moved to ever smaller and remoter hill farms, graduating downwards from ownership to tenancies.

According to my mother, my grandfather's troubles were caused by a ne'er-do-well nephew who either embezzled money from him, or failed to repay him a large loan, absconding, so the story goes, to Australia. The family fortunes were not helped by my grandfather's way of life. An accomplished horseman, frequently riding off to sheep fairs as far away as mid-Wales, he was of an outgoing and gregarious nature, and there was no lack of people prepared to take advantage of his generosity. He was also a handsome man, with that irresistible Celtic combination of dark, almost black hair, deep blue eyes and a ruddy complexion. A faded sepia photograph shows him in the saddle, clad in well-cut riding clothes and impeccably polished boots, looking quite splendid.

My grandmother was also a personality to be reckoned with. Of her I can speak directly, for she lived past 90, dying in 1964. She had an infectious sense of humour, and an almost mordant wit, softened by her Herefordshire accent, verging on a Welsh lilt. She was also a good-looking woman with large brown eyes and the high cheekbones that defy the onslaught of the years. Even in advanced old age she retained not only her beauty but also the imperceptibly imperious aura that goes with it. Life had done its best to defeat her but in the end one felt that it was she who had been the victor.

My mother was the fourth of the nine children, and the second girl. She was born on 12th February 1898 and christened Annie Adaliza, a Welsh name, after a great-aunt. To her eternal chagrin, it was spelt out as two words on her birth certificate, owing to a mistake by the registrar and the inattention of her father.

She was born at Heywood Common, outside Kington, on a small farm on the edge of Hergest Ridge, one of the tawny, bracken-covered hills that formed the natural bourne of the Welsh Marches long before King Offa of Mercia built his dyke. Her childhood memories were of the family's next home, the Bower, a hill farm of some two hundred acres. The poetic-sounding name must have been given by someone with a bent for wishful thinking. At the turn of the century it was a cold, grey stone house standing bleakly in its farmyard, surrounded by its granaries and barns, on the side of Rushock Hill, another bastion of the Welsh Marches. A more inclement and lonely location can scarcely be imagined. Yet it had, and still retains today, a compelling wild beauty that weaves its own spell.

My mother's childhood was hard but she recalled a happy time. She ran wild with her brothers about the hills and in the plocks (meadows) and paddocks around the farm. Jim, the one nearest to her in age and affection, was not much more than a year older and they were inseparable, almost like twins. He was killed at Ypres, in 1917, when barely 20, and my mother never quite recovered from his death.

Every morning my mother walked miles to the school in Kington in the valley below, climbing back up the hills in the evening, winter and summer. She was awarded a prize for never missing a day, whatever the weather. Her prize could hardly be called romantic, but was certainly suitable: it was a pair of boots.

The family moved to Oatcroft, a farm on the other side of the hill, a pleasant, large house with a lovely view over rolling countryside. The move also meant a new school for my mother, in the village of Titley, where she was very happy, for the school-master taught not only the regulation three R's but even the elements of shorthand and Latin, as well as appreciation of poetry and literature. But my grandfather's health, like his finances, was flagging. Perhaps as a result of those long rides over bleak hills in all weathers, arthritis now confined him to bed. At the age of 12, in 1910, my mother had to leave school to care for him. This was a sorrow to her all her life, for she had been a good scholar, much addicted to 'book-learning'.

When, in 1914, my grandfather died – at the age of 49, leaving his widow only debts and nine children, the youngest only three – my mother was sent into domestic service. The family had to move out of the spacious farmhouse into a tiny, dour cottage, reached only by a rough track high on the hill above, with the appropriately bleak name of Gorsty Doles.

Yet my childhood memories of Gorsty are imbued with a fairy-like aura, as of a castle guarding remote hills, high over the sunlit plain. The saving grace of Gorsty Doles was the view. A vast panoply of English countryside lay spread below, an intricate and enchanting mosaic of fields and woodlands, threaded with rivers, roads and hedgerows – a marvellous, composite picture, illumin-ated variously into changing images by shifting cloud shadows, one feature now thrown into relief by a shaft of sunlight while another was tantalisingly masked in shade.

My indomitable grandmother lived there for 20 years, hauling water from a well at the bottom of the hill, and cauldrons to pools in the valley to heat water over a wood fire to wash the family's clothes. She never lost her sense of humour and transformed the dreariest of activities into fun. With the help of the older siblings she even managed to educate two of her daughters to become teachers. There was a special, wholesome smell about her kitchen – where a sooty kettle, suspended on a hook over the old black grate, was always singing quietly away with the promise of a cup of tea – a smell compounded of wood smoke and the salty tang of whole sides of bacon hung from the blackened rafters. Despite the cold floor of enormous granite slabs, it was a warm, friendly place, where the family gathered at mealtimes at the old round table, lit at night by the soft glow of candles and oil lamps, and the fire in the hearth. At the risk of idealising a very hard existence, there must also have been compensations of a kind little known today.

My mother's life at her first 'place', Hergest Croft, just outside Kington, was not easy either. Aged barely 16, she earned £10 a year, most of which went home. Yet old photos show her always neatly and even fashionably turned out, for she sewed all her own clothes, adding finishing touches of embroidery, pin tucks and lace.

She showed enterprise in other directions too. Through an agency, she acquired a series of positions as parlour-maid to titled and high-society families, with whom she moved around: to London for the 'season' (where she frequently opened the door to Lady Elizabeth Bowes-Lyon, then a young debutante, later Queen, and ultimately Queen Mother); summers in Scotland; and visits to large country estates. During my childhood she regaled me with hilarious tales of life below stairs in grand establishments. I particularly relished those about a rumbustious cook, keen on her tipple, who on one occasion threw a pan of fish over the butler, already formally attired for dinner, and then picked up the pieces from the floor to serve to the guests; and who, on another, dumped the same unfortunate man in the sink in his own butler's pantry, and turned the tap on him.

The Essex Line

My father, Edward Curtis Anstee, was born on 26 November 1894. His family had deep roots in rural Essex, centred on the village of Writtle, in those far-gone days – and still in my own childhood – a self-contained community where the same families lived on for generations.

From mediaeval times Writtle clustered round a traditional green, surrounded by flat countryside of arable land and pastures, where the winds swept in unimpeded from the North Sea, a landscape very different from the hills that enfolded my mother's childhood homes. My paternal great-grandfather was the village tailor, William Collicott. My grandmother, Alice Ellen Collicott, was born in 1863. In 1887 she married her cousin, George Frederick William Anstee, then resident in Lambeth. He was born in Barnet, Hertfordshire, in 1862, the son of William Austin Anstee, a prosperous butcher who had expanded his business to Lambeth (there is still an 'Anstee's Yard' in Barnet).

One thing my parents' families had in common was declining fortunes. My grandfather was a total misfit as a butcher and businessman. By inclination he was a born scholar and intellectual. He had been sent away to school, and it seems had passed an entrance examination to Cambridge, which explains why he was so pleased when I got there two generations later. But his father died and he was thrust into the family business. He never recovered from this cruel change in his destiny. Not many years after their marriage my grandparents moved back to Writtle, probably because my grandfather had little taste for regular work, and particularly not the butchering kind.

For nearly 50 years my grandparents rented a solid stone house called Heroffs, fronting on Writtle Green. My grandfather occasionally worked for the village butcher, but mainly devoted himself to his intellectual interests. This unusual way of life was facilitated by a windfall, on his mother's death in 1905, of one or two properties which provided small rents.

My grandparents had aspirations to higher social status, an illusion to which my grandfather's life of leisure was no doubt considered to give credence. He read a lot, and dabbled in history and poetry. His reputation as an educated man led him to acquire the role of village wise man, filling in forms for people and counselling them on various matters. He was a big man, with a drooping walrus moustache in the Victorian mode, and always wore the stiff, celluloid shirt fronts of the same era. Early in life he became crippled, a mixture of arthritis and gout (no doubt hastened by his predilection for good drink and mountainous breakfasts of steak, as well as bacon and eggs). I cannot remember a time when he was not heaving himself awkwardly around, cross-legged, on creaking crutches. In summer he would station himself in a chair at the front gate, which gave him a commanding position for watching cricket on the village green, as well as for intercepting passers-by and harvesting village gossip.

To us children he was a gruff and intimidating figure, though in my later schooldays I had no hesitation in soliciting his help before history or Latin examinations. He had a remarkable memory, knowing all the dates, declensions and conjugations off pat, and I still cherish a tattered Latin dictionary bearing on its flyleaf the signature 'G. F. W. Anstee 1876' followed by my own, with the date 1942.

My grandmother was tiny but probably the more formidable personality. She must have had a hard time bringing up a brood of children (several died in babyhood but eventually there were seven extant) and trying to keep up appearances (she continued to have one or two maids while the children were growing up). She had a ferocious temper, which put the fear of God into everyone – including, I suspect, my grandfather – and ruled the household with a rod of iron. She was also a very good cook, producing gargantuan meals for large numbers of people.

Despite his own intellectual cast of mind, my grandfather did little to encourage his children's education. All of them left the village school at 14. The eldest, George, was something of a dare-devil but his adventurous spirit did not survive long. He was killed on the Somme, about the same time as my mother's brother, Jim, lost his life. The other boys were apprenticed to local factories in Chelmsford. My father was the one who most deeply felt the lack of further education. He had been top of his class, and won many prizes (mostly bloodthirsty annals of patriotism and Empire, which I still have). He went into the employ of a local printer in Chelmsford and trained as a compositor, the nearest he could get to indulging his love of books, literature and learning. Dorothy, the youngest, and the only girl, became a lady's maid.

After the war my father went back to his old job and spent the next 30 years painstakingly composing type with little metal letter blocks, coming home each night with fingers stained black with printer's ink. As subsequent events showed, he was capable of much more, but he seemed to lack both confidence and ambition. Whether this was the result of an innate gentleness of character or of being brought up in an authoritarian household, it is hard to say. Perhaps it was a bit of both. My mother, in contrast, was full of energy and initiative, determined to overcome all obstacles.

The Wedding

My parents were married from Gorsty Doles in Titley Church, a couple of miles down the hill, whither the wedding party descended on foot. The letters that my father sent my mother in the weeks beforehand make touching reading, concerned with the presents they were to give one another, arrangements for the wedding and for their life together. 'Dearest' was the strongest expression that my father allowed himself, but the depth of love and commitment comes through all the more because of the lack of superficial endearments.

Their presents to one another were severely practical. That of my father to my mother, a Singer sewing-machine, is still functioning 80 years later. For himself he requested a badger shaving brush, and was precise, if chauvinistic, about the specifications: 'Get them to guarantee that it is English-made, for there have been a lot of foreign ones about infected with anthrax, and one cannot be too careful.' Fortunately, no such catastrophe occurred, and the shaving brush, no doubt on account of being made of solid British materials, saw long years of service.

To her mother's consternation, the bride did not wear white but a navy blue suit, in the latest style, with a white lacy blouse and a becomingly large and fashionable hat. She prudently wanted to spend her money on something she could wear afterwards. Because of distance and cost my father's family could not attend, except for his youngest brother, Bob, who combined best man functions with a week's holiday.

My father's last letter before the wedding ends with a surprising enquiry. Had she made any arrangements with the vicar about the wedding? What time does she 'contemplate having it?' And this, only a week before the fateful date! My mother, ever-efficient, had of course made all the arrangements. It was the vicar who forgot. He was digging his garden and, while the wedding party cooled its heels, he was hastily summoned, and struggled into appropriate attire. My mother loved to recount how his muddy boots could be seen under the lacy hem of his surplice as he conducted the service.

The honeymoon was a family affair. The newly-weds and their best man stayed at one of the lodges guarding the entrance to the Eywood estate and every day walked up to Gorsty Doles. It was a week of glorious September weather, spent in family picnics in the old quarry behind Gorsty Doles, and in wandering over sunlit hills and harvest fields. It was a happy time for everyone.

My parents' first home in Writtle was the cottage that my great-grandfather had left to his youngest daughter who, being often abroad working as a 'lady's companion' to wealthy families, offered it to them at a low rent. It still had its tailoring workshop built on. My mother found it hard to adjust. An independent spirit, she did not get on easily with her temperamental mother-in-law, who wanted a finger in everything. Villages were then tightly knit communities, made up of families who intermarried locally. My mother still felt a 'foreigner' after 20 years in Writtle.

After a year or so my parents moved to 2 Albert Villas, a little further from the centre of the village, in Oxney Green. In 1924 my mother's youngest sister, Christina, came to live with them, there being better opportunities for employment (other than domestic service) in eastern England. My mother found an office job for her at Crompton's factory in Chelmsford.

2

A Rural Childhood

It was in the front bedroom of 2 Albert Villas that I came into the world on 25 June 1926, most inconveniently at four o'clock in the morning; even more inconveniently in the middle of the General Strike. Undaunted, my maternal grandmother left her remote fastness at Gorsty Doles and struggled across England by such trains as there were and a most circuitous route, in order to be present at the birth of her first grandchild.

She had her sleeves rolled up and was elbow-deep in soapy water, washing nappies, when my Writtle grandmother turned up, dressed for a social occasion and (in my maternal grandmother's vivid and cutting phrase) 'tossing a pair of gloves'. Although each had shown fortitude in the face of hardship, there was no empathy between them.

My parents, who had both had to look after younger siblings, and whose education had been curtailed, determined to have only one child, and to ensure it the best education they could manage. I did not know until her last illness that my mother had not wanted to have children at all. I was flying back to Africa, and it was in a farewell telephone conversation from Heathrow Airport that she told me this, adding, 'I am so glad your father persuaded me to have you.' It was one of the most moving moments of my life.

Coaxed reluctantly into motherhood, my mother entered into the part with zeal and dedication. I became the focus of all her frustrated dreams and unrealised capabilities.

Writtle Life

Albert Villas was one of a pair of semi-detached houses, built in 1898, the other couple being inevitably named, with patriotic fervour, Victoria Villas. With their red brick and bay front windows they were a cut above neighbouring cottages, but there was no bathroom, and the lavatory, though equipped with cistern and chain, was outside. The only heating was a coal fire downstairs. My bedroom, the smallest of three, faced north, and in winter the window would be patterned with a lacework of hoar frost, and sometimes even lined with sheets of ice. But I do not remember ever feeling cold, and loved my little room so much that when our landlord tried to persuade my mother to move, for the same rent, to a detached villa with a bathroom, I cried so forlornly that we stayed where we were.

When my parents first moved to Oxney Green the road was simply a gravelled track. I do not remember it being asphalted, but I do recall gas being laid on, and the transition from oil lamps and candles to electric light. Friday night was bath night and a major performance. Rainwater, captured in two large water butts, was heated in the old stone copper in the scullery. The bath was a long, narrow, zinc affair, customarily hung outside the coalshed door. This must have been hard work for my mother, but I remember those Friday evenings as warm, companionable family occasions, when our bleak scullery became a genial welcoming place, with the steam rising from the bath and misting the window. Until I was too large for it, I had a smaller bath in the sitting-room. I have known many well-appointed bathrooms since but, for sheer Sybaritic luxury, there was nothing to compare with that small tin bath before a glowing fire. The lack of a bathroom was not without its embarrassments later when school and university friends came to stay. Once, our form mistress, blissfully unaware of the circumstances in which a few of us lived in outlying villages, lectured us on the need to have a daily bath. Such was the social slur of not having a bathroom that I did not dare say that such a regime was totally impractical for my family − or point out that we did keep ourselves clean by daily washing!

Behind the house was a long, narrow garden, boasting two handkerchief-sized lawns, flower-beds, rose bushes and several fruit trees. In addition my father rented an allotment, on which he grew all our vegetables.

As my father earned only £3 a week there was no money to spare for even minor luxuries. Yet we ate well and I was always well dressed for my mother made my clothes. Often she would cut down her old dresses, not always with success; on one occasion, aged about six, I trotted off to the village school, arrogantly flaunting a navy-and-white spotted dress, adorned with a lacy jabot, then the latest fashion. I soon had my comeuppance: by lunch-time, no doubt as a result of over-exertion in the playground, my 'new' dress had split right down the back. I can still feel the shame of that moment, and my poor mother's chagrin when I returned home half-naked and sobbing.

There were some advantages unknown today: the baker and the milkman called every day and the butcher several times a week. The milkman – a large young man called George Hitch – arrived every morning, clad in a white coat, with his churns fresh from the milking sheds of his parents' farm in the next village, Highwood. He would know from the jugs my mother had put out on the windowsill how much milk he had to ladle out. Such practices would be deemed dangerous to health nowadays, but the milk was creamy and delicious. George also brought us freshly laid eggs and rich farmhouse butter. During the war, poor George, then engaged to a Land Army girl working on the farm, hanged himself in the milking shed. The tragic end of this apparently placid, contented man shook the village, and showed that rural life was not without stress even then.

My childhood, despite limitations that would be considered privations today, was a very happy one. We enjoyed a rare privilege: the last vestiges of traditional English village life, before the influx of commuters en masse. Although the social pattern of Writtle was changing, enough remained of the old life for us to feel linked with our forebears. My grandparents, the patriarchs, remained surrounded by their surviving sons. The village was still made up of families who, like ours, could trace their presence for several generations. Everyone knew everyone else and their place in a strictly stratified rural society.

We children roamed the surrounding fields and meadows at will and knew every footpath, stream and hedgerow, and where every wild flower or bird's nest could be found. My cousin John and I were inseparable companions, getting into innumerable scrapes, which were the despair of our parents. I was the only girl in the neighbourhood and moved around in a gang of small boys. There was, of course, another gang, of sworn enemies. We went for long sorties, making camps in hollow trees, fishing for tadpoles, bird's-nesting, following the course of the stream that lay at the bottom of the Alley Fields, exploring the mysteries of the old gravel pit and climbing trees. Exchanging 'dares' was an integral part of our ritual and led to many risky escapades. Once a widow with a son (whom we children privately considered an effeminate mother's boy) exclaimed to my mother how lucky she was, as girls did not get up to devilish pranks. My mother grimly produced a pair of shorts, with the seat clean torn out, the result of my falling from an oak tree through a hawthorn hedge, and coming home with lacerated legs and arms. The great taboo was wet feet, thought to cause colds and illness. If you had the misfortune to fall into a stream or pond you were put straight to bed. So, if the worst happened, you went to enormous lengths to conceal the fact. I still remember the heartbreak when my mother, discovering wet clothes under the bed, cancelled a long-anticipated picnic. Rashly accepting a dare from John, I had clambered out on a bough over a pond, and promptly fallen in.

Our childhood entertainments were geared to the seasons and rural pursuits. In spring there were excursions further afield to woods with glades of primroses and, later, bluebells. Nearer at hand was a magical place called the Paigle Mead, a lush, marshy meadow, carpeted with golden yellow cowslips – 'paigles' in the Essex dialect. Alas, they were ploughed up long ago. On Mothering Sunday, we would make a pilgrimage to Tuppenny Pond and Green Lane, where the hedgerows were purple with periwinkles, the traditional offering to our mothers. Every spot where some special fruit or blossom could be found had its place in our rural calendar. In autumn we bicycled out at dawn to collect fresh mushrooms for breakfast, and went with walking sticks to pick blackberries and wild crab-apples for jams and jellies. My grandmother was a great wine-maker and produced gallons of all varieties – with which, much to my mother's annoyance, she plied her grandchildren when we did her Saturday shopping for sixpence. My father also tried his hand at wine-making. One night – before the war made nocturnal bangs common – I was awakened by a terrific explosion, followed by loud expletives from my father (a man not given to raise his voice in anger, much less swear). A cask of fermenting blackberry wine had blown its lid off and liberally coloured the scullery walls, which he had just painted a pristine white, with deep magenta scrolls.

Village life was self-contained, and centred round the green where cricket was played in almost idyllic conditions, though often to the danger of passing traffic. My father and his brothers made up the core of the team. The green was also the site of a centuries-old Whitsuntide fair, an event anticipated with great excitement by us children; there were roundabouts, and swings on which we dared one another to pull the swingboats to ever more dizzy and perilous heights, dodgems, all kinds of stalls with tawdry prizes for shooting bull's-eyes or lifting weights, fortune-tellers, sideshows and – my favourite – women boxers who called male challengers from the crowd and knocked them out cold. My fastidious Writtle grandmother was appalled when she injudiciously (and certainly prematurely) enquired of me, aged six, what I wanted to be when I grew up, and received the unhesitating reply, 'A lady boxer in a fair.' For one day the green was transformed into a magic scene, vibrant with colour and the noise of discordant music blaring stridently forth from a dozen sources. The fairs were the unchallenged domain of gypsy families, whose caravans processed from village to village. During the war, when the fair was suspended, a solitary gypsy and his horse would appear on the green each Whitsuntide to maintain the mediaeval right to hold it. One year's absence would have meant it lapsed forever.

On Empire Day – 24 May – the green was the scene of village festivities: children's races and more boisterous activities, such as walking the greasy pole over the Wear Pond, fringed by its graceful weeping willow trees. There was a good deal of pomp and circumstance: 'Land of hope and glory' and 'Rule Britannia' were sung with a degree of patriotic and imperial fervour that seems quaint today, and the local gentry and sometimes the Member of Parliament harangued the populace on their civic duty from the unstable vantage point of a swaying hay wagon.

The Flower Show, in July, occasioned enormous rivalry between cottagers and allotment holders. In our household we all competed – my mother with jams, cakes and flower arrangements; my father with vegetables and cut flowers, I with wild flowers and grasses. In memory it always seems to have been a fine hot Saturday, and I can still smell the dizzying aroma inside the white marquees dotted all over the football meadow, a heady mixture of massed flowers, vegetables and trampled grass.

Rural produce also figured large at the Harvest Festival in September. On Harvest Sunday the altar in Writtle Church would be piled high with the gifts that we children presented, which were later donated to Chelmsford Hospital. My father groomed his chrysanthemums especially for this event. There being no other cool place, the chosen blooms were hung in great swathes in the outside lavatory. I can never smell chrysanthemums today without being spirited back to that place, which became a favourite, if idiosyncratic, sanctuary for me, especially on frosty moonlit nights.

The commemoration, each 11 November, of Armistice Day, and of the villagers who had given their lives in the 1914–18 War, was a sadder ceremony. The village memorial bore a tragically long list of the names of the fallen, among them my Uncle George. We schoolchildren marched there in ragged crocodiles and formed up alongside British Legion contingents all bearing banners. Everyone wore red poppies, and the grey stone of the memorial was awash with scarlet wreaths. The vicar conducted the service of remembrance, a mournful band played, we sang 'O God, our help in ages past' and the last post was sounded. Even a child could not fail to be moved by the solemnity and pathos of that homespun ceremony.

The village hall buzzed with communal activities throughout the year – whist drives (where my parents bore off many prizes), concerts, Women's Institute meetings and the like. Cards were a major source of entertainment during those pre-television days. We played dominoes too, and every Saturday night bridge, with my Uncle Dick and his wife, and the milkman, George. Those smoke-filled evenings of my bridge-playing days, between the ages of seven and 12, successfully insulated me against any temptation to take up the game in later life. Village concerts were unsophisticated affairs – piano pieces, songs of the 'Seated one day at the organ' variety and children's recitations. I gave one such performance with a burn from the hairdresser's curling iron on my face and eyes red-rimmed from tears, a well-meaning aunt having paid for my very straight fair hair to be crimped into a 'Marcel wave'. 'Alexander's ragtime band' performed by the Women's Institute (among them my mother) on combs and tissue paper was considered a daring innovation. My mother also took an active part in a village amateur dramatics group. *Rookery Nook* was one of their hits, but scandalised the more conservative elements of village opinion when my Aunt Janet appeared on a balcony clad only in a lacy camisole and French knickers. My mother, accoutred in borrowed riding clothes and boots so tight she could not bend her knees, had to be bodily pushed up the steps onto the stage by her leading man.

On summer Sundays, after tea, whole families would sally forth along well-trodden paths through fields of lush grass mingled with poppies, buttercups, daisies, cornflowers and scabious, and bordered by flowering hedgerows still gloriously unrestrained by herbicides. Everyone dressed in their best for the many encounters with their neighbours and, like the fat white woman whom Francis Cornford saw from a train, the women walked 'through the fields in gloves', though, unlike her, none missed much of their surroundings. Quaint as the custom seems now, the ritual Sunday walk was a marvellous vehicle for maintaining family cohesion and social communication. In winter, Sunday walks took place after lunch, brisk outings along country roads, which lacked the relaxed aura of warm summer evenings in the blossoming meadows.

Several public houses were also a focus of social life, mainly for men. My father rarely frequented them, saying he had seen enough drink in his parents' home. Money was another factor. Only at Christmas was there any drink in our house and then only one bottle of British port, and another of British sherry (the cheapest variety). That was the only time also, apart from birthdays, that we ate chicken, then an expensive delicacy. But how we enjoyed it, because it was such a rare treat.

The seasons in those pre-refrigeration days also dictated our menu. For my birthday in June my mother would produce a huge bowl of strawberries or raspberries, with lashings of cream, and insist we gorge ourselves to surfeit because we would not enjoy the taste again for another year. That made the pleasure all the sharper. Plums and damsons were bottled, as were tomatoes; onions from the garden were pickled; and eggs preserved in isinglass in a huge earthenware crock so that we would not go hungry during winter months.

The Village School

My parents taught me to read and write long before I entered the village school in 1931, and I soon moved up two classes to join the seven-year-olds. Suddenly I began to act very oddly, obsessively touching everything with one hand and then the other. The village doctor warned my alarmed parents that it could be the onset of St Vitus's Dance. Then my teacher told them that I was naturally left-handed but that the headmistress was forcing me to use my right hand, caning me with a ruler when I disobeyed. A worthy lady, but of Victorian cast of mind, the headmistress never tired of drumming into us that country children were not as intelligent as our town counterparts and that those of us who had the misfortune to be female were even less so. That myth took longer to disprove, but the immediate problem was resolved by a doctor's certificate warning that persistent efforts to correct my left-handedness would have calamitous effects.

The school for infants and girls crouched in the lee of the church, alongside the graveyard. The playground was a rough place where the boys bullied the girls but, although initially terrified, I soon gave as good as I got. Goaded into action by one persistent tormentor, I thwacked him round the head with the wooden handles of my skipping rope, which had ball-bearings in the handles. I never had any more trouble with him.

I walked a mile to and from school four times a day. Sometimes Christina collected me. 'Your sister has come for you', the other children would chorus and she seemed more like an older sister than an aunt in my eyes too. Through another happy initiative of my mother's she had obtained a position as a laboratory assistant at the Essex Institute of Agriculture in Chelmsford. When she was barely 22, she landed the job of bacteriologist in the Liverpool Cooperative Society's Dairy, an amazing feat in 1932 for a woman, especially one so young and without a university degree. Beautiful as well as clever, she became my glamorous fairy godmother and a role model.

At school I acquired a bosom girl friend for the first time. We went to Sunday school (where the teacher, noting my early fascination with foreign parts, suggested I might become a missionary ...!). I joined the Brownies and a children's religious group known as 'the King's Messengers'. Neither activity lasted long. When it came time to graduate to the Girl Guides my mother could not afford the uniform. As for the King's Messengers, after spending weeks knitting a muffler for a Zulu, I resigned of my own accord when she showed me a picture of a Zulu wearing very little indeed.

Most of the village children finished their schooling at 14. Only a very few escaped to further education in Chelmsford, through competitive examinations that admitted you either at age 11 to the girls' high school or the boys' grammar school or at 13 to the technical college.

The village schools were housed in old buildings to which little had been done since my father and grandmother had attended them. The infants' and girls' school was particularly dark, cold and insalubrious. My mother was forever muttering darkly that much else besides water drained down from the churchyard, and all sorts of sick humours must pervade the classrooms because of unhealthy proximity to the dead. She was fortified in this view by the fact that her child, on whom every care was lavished, nonetheless fell prey, in monotonous succession, to whooping cough, chicken pox, measles, German measles, mumps and septic tonsils. Whenever I pricked my finger picking a wild rose, it went septic, and once I narrowly escaped septicaemia. I was a great runner, winning all the races (largely because my legs were longer than those of my peers) until my toes went septic too, and put a stop to all that.

The climax came when scarlet fever at age nine was followed, a year later, by diphtheria. Both required me to be whisked to the 'isolation hospital' in Chelmsford, where my parents could only wave through a window that no sound could penetrate. The diphtheria nearly put an end to any hope of educational advancement as well as my days, since it struck in September 1936, only six months before I was to sit the crucial examination for the high school. Our GP, a gruff, 'no-nonsense' man who had looked after me since I was a baby, initially diagnosed a flare-up of my troublesome tonsils, whose extraction, however, he resolutely opposed. I appeared to recover, but a week later had a relapse. The doctor declared that I was shamming and should be taken out for a brisk walk. My parents obediently did so, but were less convinced by his verdict when I fainted clean away and repeated the performance next morning. This time the doctor took swabs of my throat. Within four hours he was back, looking pale, with an ambulance. My poor mother, usually so strong, broke down and wept. She was not allowed to come with me and, worst of all, all my treasured books and playthings were to be burned. I think she really believed the end had come.

The treatment for diphtheria then was an agonisingly painful injection into the spine, which affected the heart, and I was ordered to stay in bed for six months. For an active child this was purgatory, and worse for my mother who had to keep some kind of control over me. My bed was brought downstairs and squeezed into our little sitting-room. It was there, on 10 December 1936, that I listened, with tears in my eyes, to the abdication speech of Edward VIII.

I could not go back to school until just before the examination on which my future depended. I was advanced for my age, and top of the class, but my mother left nothing to chance. She engaged a Welsh schoolteacher at the boys' school to come round several evenings a week to put me through my paces. There was also the BBC *Schools Programme* on the wireless. Although one of Writtle's few claims to fame was that the first broadcast ever had been made from a Marconi shed there in 1921 (Dame Nelly Melba once sang from there), the wireless had not become available to most village folk until the early 1930s. Now it proved a great boon, the only problem being that the schools programme included irresistible dancing classes, and more than once I was caught tripping the light fantastic and hustled smartly back into bed.

In March 1937 I went back to school but Nemesis had another trick up her sleeve. I was put next to a girl who had a mysterious infection all over her head and a week later was afflicted with the same disease. Within 24 hours my head was covered with huge sores, as large as half-crowns. On the day before the examination my mother, sobbing, had to cut off my hair close to the scalp. She was in despair. Next morning she walked to the village school but the Dickensian headmistress gave her no comfort: there was only one day for the exam and no second chance. My mother could not accept that fate could be so cruel. She put on her best coat and hat, took the bus to Chelmsford and sought out the Chief Education Officer for Essex. She did not know his name, much less have an appointment, but he was a kindly man, and put her fears at rest: there was a second date in May for children who had been ill. I have often reflected how extraordinary it was that a country-woman should have doubted the word of no less a pundit than the headmistress of the village school and taken the law into her own hands – and how different my life would have been had she not done so.

The second examination was held on Empire Day, 24 May 1937. On my return I jumped off the bus at the village green just in time to win the 100 yards race. My head was better, thanks to daily dressings by my mother, which took two hours and often made me faint with pain, but I still wore a white handkerchief round my scarred scalp, which made me the butt of other children. Because the doctor feared that this unknown disease could return, my hair was cut short like a boy's until I was 16. That suited my tomboy habits, but secretly I envied the plaits and curls of other girls.

It was about this time that our doctor was at last persuaded that tonsillectomy might cure my frequent illnesses. My friend was also to have her tonsils removed, and we were cajoled by assurances that we would live on nothing but ice cream for days afterwards. The operations were carried out in our house, on our old deal table, scrubbed and put in the front room. In a gesture of bravado I opted to go first, but my heroic pose evaporated when the chloroform mask was clapped on my face. I thought I was being suffocated and the doctors had difficulty in holding me down. My next memory is of waking up in my parents' bed, and catching the doctor showing my infected tonsils to my mother.

In September 1937 I started a new life at Chelmsford County High School for Girls. I threw myself enthusiastically into games and gym, but developed an excruciatingly painful bony lump on my left knee. Doctors declared themselves baffled until a Harley Street specialist, visiting Chelmsford Hospital, diagnosed the condition as one usually found only in boys, and called 'rugby knee'. The lump was growing and could be malignant. I was to undergo surgery in a small orthopaedic hospital in Epping Forest, in the summer of 1938, but Hitler's armies entered Czechoslovakia, war seemed imminent, and the operation was postponed until after the Munich agreement. The hospital, tucked away in the woods, consisted of one large ward, with 20 boys and girls up to age 14, and a babies' annexe. Most were long-term cases, and rudimentary tuition was provided. I was to miss a whole term, and my teachers armed me with books and study programmes. To my delight, when I returned I was further ahead than the rest of the class.

That hospital stay was educational in other ways. My defect was corrected by a single operation. The others were cruelly deformed, and had been there for years. One 14-year-old boy had had 20 operations following polio, and was still a mangled mess, but the most cheery soul imaginable. A six-year-old, Henry, deformed from birth, knew no world other than the hospital. His mother had refused to see him since the day he was born. Not surprisingly, Henry was obstreperous. The punishment when his tantrums became too extreme was to shut him in a hall outside the ward where, alone in the dark, he would scream with terror for hours.

The regime was strict. Fresh air was considered essential. Every morning at 7.30 a.m. our beds were wheeled outside although the autumn mist would sometimes be lapping the blankets. We stayed out until four o'clock, and had lessons, breakfast and lunch outside. Visitors were allowed only every other Sunday. My parents spent most of the day on the long bus journey from Writtle. They came laden with home-made cakes, eggs, fruit and vegetables, which were whisked away and never seen again. Mary, the Irish ward maid, who became a bosom friend in that dreary place, whispered to me that Cook had most of the treats that families brought for the children. This was all too plausible; Cook was vastly fat and both double doors at the end of the ward had to be opened to make way for her heaving mounds of flesh.

I left with an acute sense of my own good fortune: I could go back to home and family while those other children, whose lives I had shared for two months, were doomed to stay for years. I was lucky in other respects too. The bony growth proved non-malignant, and the fear that I might be left with a straight leg proved unfounded when, several weeks later, it was forcibly bent by the surgeon. He had promised there would be no scar, little realising that a 12-year-old tomboy would want something to show for her ordeal. I need not have worried; I was left with a prominent scar that has frequently led people to point out supposed ladders in my stocking.

Herefordshire Holidays

There was little money for holidays. When I was very small my parents took me once to Felixstowe, where we stayed in a seaside boarding-house. There is a faded snapshot of the three of us bound for the beach, me clutching bucket and spade, all of us incredibly overdressed, my mother even sporting a large, rather modish hat, my father the cap he always favoured.

After that we invariably went to my Herefordshire grandmother for the long summer school holidays. My father joined us for his scant annual week of holiday. The journey took all day, and was a great excitement. We took a bus to Chelmsford, a train to Liverpool Street, and then crossed London to Paddington where the steaming

GWR train to Hereford stood waiting. The names of the stations along the way sang in my ears, like a refrain spelling happiness and freedom, growing ever louder after Oxford was passed: Kingham, Charlbury, Moreton-in-the-Marsh, Evesham, Pershore, Worcester, the two Malverns ... By this time the train's eager pace had dwindled to a contented dawdle, but each of the remembered names had a magical quality, a blend of memories and anticipation, as the landscape softened into gently rolling hills and verdant valleys, so different from the monotonous Essex flatlands. At Hereford we changed into a smaller train bound for Leominster, where in one still smaller, we chugged onwards to the Welsh Marches, stopping at every tiny station until, at Titley, the Eywood gamekeeper would be waiting with a pony and trap to whisk us (for a consideration) away up into sunny uplands and Gorsty Doles.

Distractions were few, but the sheer bliss of being in that enchanted place was more than enough. With three cousins, who lived in the cottage next door, we roamed the hills and meadows. Low-slung branches of beech trees were our swings; we rolled down grassy slopes to see who could go fastest; and played houses, using whatever we could lay hands on – dock seed provided a convincing simulation of tea. One meadow was called the Haresfield, because in late summer it was blue with harebells (alas, long gone, victims of intensive farming). There sprawled an ancient fallen oak, on which we played for hours. All the fields around had names redolent of their use and history – the Long Field, the Horse Field, Wheels Field, the Eleven Acres, the Eighteen Acres. Halfway up Rushock Hill, with no road to it, was Old House Field where a woman had perished in childbirth because no doctor could reach her; neither her grief-stricken husband, nor anyone else, had ever wanted to live there again. All that remained of that grim tale was a heap of stones, a gnarled apple tree, and a goodly crop of nettles. Burnt House Field also told its own story of past tragedy.

At harvest time everyone turned out to help. We took picnics to the field where the wheat, oats or barley was being cut by the old-fashioned binder, whirring round like a Ferris wheel, drawn by two statuesque cart-horses. As the cut grain fell, men bound the long stalks in stooks, and stood them in groups, like yellow wigwams scattered over the field. Evening shadows would already be laying long fingers across the landscape when the last square of corn was left standing in the middle of the field, the ultimate redoubt of the rabbits and other small animals driven there by the inexorable advance of the binder. Then men with sticks would beat them out and dogs chase them in their terrified dash across the stubble to the safety of the hedgerow. Some would escape, but everyone would go home with a rabbit for next day's dinner. It was a cruel sport, but the extra food was welcome to households with many mouths to feed.

I loved this place so much that I never envied other children their seaside holidays. We could go only once a year; my mother saved up for 12 months to make even that possible and during the remaining 11 I pined with homesickness for Gorsty Doles. Once, I dreamt in mid-winter that I was in the Haresfield, surrounded by a haze of blue, and wept when I woke to find it all illusion.

In 1931 my mother left me there at Easter, and collected me just before I first started school in September. I remember an idyllic summer. I helped my grandmother with her chickens, and had a pet pullet, whom I put to bed every night on the doorstep, draped in a yellow duster. There were cats and kittens to play with, milk to be collected in cans from Oatcroft at the bottom of the hill (an adventurous excursion, since a garrison of geese, commanded by a very fierce gander, had to be circumnavigated) and water from far-off Kennel Well. In mid-summer, the hay in the Big Meadow just below Gorsty Doles was cut, and I rode aloft the hay waggon all day with my Uncle Henry.

There were less pleasurable moments. One day, the son of the family farming Oatcroft was counting sheep out of the old stone sheepfold. I, the ringleader, had inveigled my cousins to join with me in shouting different numbers to confuse the poor boy. I never knew what hit me; a human tornado, my otherwise loving grandmother, hurtled out of the cottage, grabbed me by the scruff of the neck and bore me indoors to a severe scolding.

My mother, when she came to collect me, was nonplussed to find me enquiring belligerently, with a strong Herefordshire accent, 'And what have you come for, then?'

In 1933 my grandmother moved to another cottage on the Eywood estate, lower down and nearer the village. Whitewashed, with roses wreathed round the door, The Green nestled in the lee of a wood, with the large expanse of Eywood Pool nearby. Its sheltered position made for more comfortable living than bleak Gorsty Doles, but I missed those wild, gorse-covered hills and the view that stretched to eternity. There were several acres of land so that Henry could keep a few sheep, and my grandmother increase the number of her chickens.

Henry recruited me as an apprentice shepherdess. I learnt to deal with footrot, maggoty tails and dipping. In Herefordshire they used a coloured dip before the sheep went to market, and the rosy pink sheep scattered over the green plocks and pastures made a pretty sight. We children adored Henry and longed for his good opinion, but it was hard to come by. The harshest criticism for me was to be called 'a townie', a term I considered unjust, since we too lived in the country although less remotely.

Sentiment, as well as economics, guided the management of the small flock: some sheep had pet names and were allowed to live out their mortal lives. Once such was Tiddy, so-called because she had been a 'tiddling lamb' (bottle-fed), who became the leader of the flock. One evening, I was helping to drive the sheep to a neighbouring pasture. Henry had no dog, and I had received severe training on how to shepherd sheep through gates and keep them together. To my consternation, as we crossed a large open space, I saw another flock being driven towards us. Worse still, my uncle and the other drover engaged in lengthy conversation while I watched in horror as the two flocks merged. I ran helplessly hither and thither, anticipating his cutting comments. Henry was enjoying this spectacle hugely, and endlessly prolonged the conversation. When at last the confabulation ended, he simply called Tiddy's name, and she emerged serenely from the heaving throng and with stately gait led out her fellows. Small wonder that I loved Tiddy, who was the recipient of many childish confidences. On the dreaded evening before we returned to Essex, I would seek her out on some grassy bank under the oak and beech trees, and weep silently into her fleece while she, calmly chewing the cud, seemed to understand. Years later, on leave from some far-off country where I headed a sizeable UN staff, I would still dash around through hedgerows and under barbed wire fences, obeying Henry's every command and anxious for his approval.

My pursuits were solitary. The wood became an African jungle, which I intrepidly explored, being early imbued with a lust for adventure and travel. It was a most beautiful English wood, with primroses, bluebells and the delicate wild anemone or windflower. One warm summer evening, I heard my mother come whistling through the wood, and realised with a great surge of empathy, that she too was happy. Eywood Pool, another source of adventure and imagination, was a beautiful artificial lake – the grounds had been laid out by Capability Brown – from the far end of which one could see the shimmering rosy reflection of the great house. I was forbidden to swim there, but there were fallen trees on which I scrambled precariously over its muddy waters to observe the then rare great-crested grebe.

My head fizzed with romantic notions culled from my teacher aunts' library; I was enormously affected by *Elizabeth and Her German Garden*, which I first encountered at age ten. I would spend hours reading, sometimes hiding in the hay barn, where my grandmother's beautiful white cat, Snowy, invariably had a litter of racially mixed kittens, or poring over a book by candlelight in bed, when I was supposed to be asleep. That nearly ended in disaster one balmy summer night, when my mother, walking in the garden, spotted the faint flicker of light, and called up through the open window that I must blow it out. My response was to lower the book over the flame to hide its glow, with the inevitable result that the book caught fire, all pandemonium broke out and I was severely chastised.

There were only two bedrooms. Henry had one, which my father shared on his brief holiday, and the womenfolk – sometimes as many as five, when my aunts were home – shared two double beds in the other. The bedrooms were quaintly shaped, with sloping ceilings, beams and unexpected abutments in the rough whitewashed walls. The cosy intimacy·of those summer nights when we all lay chatting, I the only child among the grown-ups, epitomises those halcyon days of childhood.

So do days spent picnicking with my parents on Rushock Hill and Knill Garraway. From there we had superb views down country to Hereford and counties east; to the Black Mountains and Hay Bluff; to the gentle prospect of the Hindwell Valley immediately below, and then the gaunt battlements of Radnor Forest, leading the eye onward into Wales and the farthest horizon. Before the war, gorse and bracken higher than a man covered both hills, interspersed with sheep paths. For a child it was like roaming through a vast primeval forest. There were other stimuli for a burgeoning romantic imagination, for this was the ancient border, the scene of strife between marauding foreign armies and the Celtic fringe, driven back into the mountain fastnesses of Wales. Offa's Dyke, the fortified ditch that King Offa of Mercia built to keep Wales isolated, runs over these hills. In my mind's eye, I peopled them with ghostly rival armies, heard the clash of steel, the thundering hooves of horses and the battle cries of warriors. My history was confused. In my imagination, untrammelled by facts, the Romans figured large, but Offa's Dyke was not built until the eighth century. Nor does history record any major battles fought hereabouts. But these hilltops must have thronged with men when a vast army of labourers worked on King Offa's grandiose enterprise; and there must have been sporadic skirmishes in the ancient woodlands that clothed them in mediaeval times.

In my childhood there were still remnants of those woodlands on Knill Garraway, that falls down into the Hindwell Valley and the tiny hamlet of Knill and on the escarpment of Bron Scar, pocked with disused stone quarries. Sometimes our walks took us down the old bridle way, between gnarled oak trees and stately beech, to the ford through the Hindwell Brook. One Eastertide, just after the war, my mother and I walked across 'the Top' and watched an otter hunt in full cry along the banks of the Hindwell far below. But then the old woods were felled, and the Forestry Commission planted serried rows of conifers, and all the plant life that had enriched those idyllic glades was extinguished under monotonous evergreen shade. But the cruel sport of otter hunting also disappeared, and otters have returned to the Hindwell.

In the 1930s you encountered country-folk in the remotest spots: men tending sheep, cutting bracken or mending fences. I became fast friends with Bill Bufton and Bill Bullock, hedgers and ditchers. They were characters in their own right. There were many such to be found, not always of impeccable rectitude. Tom the Filer, so-called because he went from village to village sharpening knives (no one knew his real name; rumour had it that he was the black sheep of a well-to-do family), was wont to drink hard once he had money in his pockets and became legendary for his protest, on being carried from a ditch after one such bout: 'Oim orl roight but me legs be gorn.'

The woods on the estate were beautifully tended, the pathways, gates and stiles in perfect order, so that the gentry could hunt, shoot, ride and walk without let or hindrance. Eywood must have given employment and shelter to some 50 families between the domestic staff, gardeners, gamekeepers and woodmen. There was a definite hierarchy, both within the ranks of the servants and between the servants and the gentry. A graceful semi-circular drive swept up to the imposing front portico of the house; in which Byron had slept and reputedly seduced the lady of the house; where a bloodstain on the stairs marked the spot on which a murder was supposed to have been committed; and where a famous Hungarian general, hero of the abortive revolution of 1848, had taken refuge and ultimately died. We were not supposed to use that drive but one evening, late for supper, and fearing a wigging, I took a short cut along it. Alas, I was seen by Mrs Gwyer, the lady of the house, who innocently asked Edward (the handsome footman, whom I hero-worshipped), 'who the little girl in the red blazer was'. Edward spilt the beans at home and I did receive a wigging, for something other than anticipated. When Henry became head gardener in 1939 and my grandmother moved with him and my aunts to the Garden House, I was always told to disappear whenever one of 'the family' appeared, including a grandson around my age. Ironically, we were later undergraduates in Cambridge at the same time.

The Garden House, a pleasant double-fronted Georgian cottage, had two attics as well as four large bedrooms, but still no bathroom or inside lavatory. An orchard and plock went with it, on which Henry could continue to keep sheep and my grandmother chickens. There were two huge walled kitchen gardens, with acres of interconnected greenhouses along the south-facing walls, heated by antediluvian steam pipes, where peaches, figs and grapes were grown, as well as hothouse flowers and plants. Across the length of the main kitchen garden ran a double herbaceous border, with a fountain in the centre. There were potting-houses, potato sheds, storage sheds, bothies – a maze of intriguing places to explore.

The old style of life that all this represented was dying before our eyes with the coming of the Second World War. Mr Gwyer had died, and Eywood was let to an evacuated girls' public school. Tragically two of Mr Gwyer's sons were killed in the First World War, and the grandson who should have inherited perished in the second. There being no male heir to carry on the estate, Eywood was sold. A terrible desecration followed. The main house was pulled down, and Adam's fireplaces, the main staircase, even the bricks, were auctioned off. The destruction of such a beautiful and historic stately home would never be allowed today, but in the aftermath of war it was ruthlessly perpetrated, jagged walls left open to the sky, the huge portico still standing desolately today, a sad monument to a senseless sacrifice. Money, not the conservation of beauty, was the sole concern of the main purchasers. The stable block was turned into cheap flats; even the magnificent woods of ancient beech and oak were cut down, and replaced by ugly conifers.

There was a brighter side. My uncle was able to buy the Garden House, and 17 acres of land, comprising the walled kitchen gardens and the surrounding plock and orchard. The sweeping formal gardens around the mansion decayed into a wilderness, but so long as Henry and his sister Margaret lived, the kitchen gardens, operating as a market garden, were impeccably maintained.

3

Wartime Schooldays

The only shadow over my early childhood was the fear of war. I suffered from insomnia, kept awake by this dread, long before I was old enough to have any conception of what war was about. I can remember, at age six, calling for my mother and pleading, 'There isn't going to be another war, is there?' This was not so strange, since both my parents had lost brothers in the 1914–18 War, and the grown-ups were always talking about the ominous clouds again gathering in Europe.

There was much interest in current events in our household. Through the pages of the *Children's Newspaper* I became aware of the changes taking place in Germany, the Japanese invasion of Manchuria, the Spanish Civil War, the Italian entry into Ethiopia, and then the rearming of Germany and its progressive encroachment on neighbouring countries. I even wrote a letter to the editor, defending the role of His Majesty's Loyal Opposition, and was not amused to receive a bland reply, merely celebrating the fact that we bought their publication!

When war came, my reaction was one of sheer terror. I remember exactly where I was standing in our small living-room as we listened to Prime Minister Chamberlain's broadcast at 11 o'clock on the morning of 3 September 1939. I was trembling with fright, though it was a lovely day, with the faintest tinge of autumn in the breeze, the kind of day when it normally feels good to be alive.

My father, too old for active service, was on duty that night as an air-raid warden, and my mother and I were alone. When I started awake to find her shaking me – 'The air-raid warning has sounded!' – my heart leapt with fear and I felt physically sick.

No one knew quite how to behave. Everyone was leaning out of their bedroom windows or chatting in the road below, waiting for something to happen. Fortunately for us, nothing did, nor was there any explanation as to why the alarm had sounded. There followed the long months of the 'phoney war'.

The high school was very vulnerable, its playing fields adjacent to Hoffman's munitions factory. One air-raid trench had been hurriedly constructed but there was room in it for only one form. For the rest of 1939, we went to school for half a day each week, and were given work to do at home. I got through it in a day or so and spent a lot of time walking alone around the countryside. I took up bird-watching, kept rather pretentious nature journals and started writing several novels and stories, never finished. At an early age I learned to live by myself and find my own interests and amusements.

By the new year, trenches had been dug for the whole school. They were damp earth tunnels, in the furthest playing-field, very near the prime bombing target of Hoffman's factory. School returned to its normal course, intermittently interrupted by air-raid practices.

The End of the 'Phoney War'

Within a few months, the charade became reality. One day in early June 1940 we saw the summer sky obliterated by palls of smoke as the Allied armies burnt fuel depots in their retreat to the beachheads of Dunkirk. Then the air-raid sirens began to wail in earnest. Sometimes the all-clear did not sound for 24 hours and there was an ominous blackout on news. We were in the front line of coastal air defence and on a direct flight path to London. Now we were constantly herded into the trenches, sometimes for a whole school day. Down there it was cold, damp, muddy and very uncomfortable – we sat on benches of slatted wood, clutching the battered cardboard boxes containing our gas masks, often ankle-deep in water. We sang lustily to keep our spirits up. Secretly we rejoiced at being liberated from a lesson. Better still was to be interrupted in the middle of a dreaded test, until one day the test was continued underground. Our teachers had realised that, at this rate, we would never get an education and classes resumed in the trenches. Public examinations – what was then called School Certificate (at 16) and Higher School Certificate (at 18) – posed a special problem. A colonnade in the main building was fortified as a shelter, to which we were whisked, under oath of silence, if the siren sounded in the middle of an exam. By the time I had reached those two decisive stages – in 1942 and 1944 – we were all so blasé about air-raids that we almost wished for a warning during an exam, in the hope of being marked more leniently.

During the summer and early autumn of 1940 we had a front-row seat at the Battle of Britain. In a daily aerobatic display Spitfires, Hurricanes and Messerschmitts careered across the skies above us, twisting and turning in spins and rolls, locked in a lethal dance of death. Dark smoke trails traced the intricate steps of this deadly ballet and every so often smoke broke into flame, and a plane crashed to earth in a ball of fire. We watched from our fields and country lanes, cheering on the gallant young RAF pilots, though the Germans were no less courageous, and equally young. Despite the tragedy of war brought close to home, the pungent smell of the fires of defeat wafting over from France, and the imminent threat of German invasion, a heady atmosphere gripped the whole country that I shall never forget, and have never since experienced. It was the sense of a community fighting single-mindedly for its survival. We really did believe that the Germans would land at any moment, and that those of us who lived near the eastern coasts would be the first to face them. The bells of the village church, fallen silent on the outbreak of war, would announce their coming. Signposts were torn down, so as to give the enemy no help; any stranger in our midst was regarded with utmost suspicion for Fifth Column infiltrators, we were warned, could appear anywhere and at any time; and 'careless talk costs lives' was our watchword. We really did keep pitchforks, and a motley array of other rustic implements readily to hand, with the firm intention of wielding them against the invaders. Now our conviction that we could make a stand with such paltry weapons seems wild fantasy, but then it was very real. The nation was truly galvanised. I, who had so long dreaded war, no longer felt fear.

Fortunately, thanks to the rash courage of those Battle of Britain pilots, our resolution was never put to the test. The church bells never rang out, and the threat of invasion receded. But as autumn progressed the Luftwaffe's blitz began to batter London and other major cities, rising to a crescendo during that dreadful winter, and calling for a different kind of resolve. Being under a direct flight path to the capital we heard the bomber squadrons lumber over every night, and saw the sky over London refulgent with the criss-crossed beams of searchlights and exploding bombs. The nightly cacophony of gunfire was ear-splitting for we were surrounded by anti-aircraft batteries trying to down German planes before they reached London, or prevent them getting home. As the air-raid siren in Chelmsford could be heard only when the wind was in the right direction my father had to go round blowing a whistle to announce a raid, and ringing a bell when the all-clear sounded. Often he had not finished his round with the bell when a new warning sounded. He also had a rattle, to announce a gas attack, luckily never used.

When I came home from school one day in October 1940 my mother broke the news that my uncle, Cyril Hicks, had been killed. Cyril and my mother's sister, Mary, had been sweethearts since grammar school and had married barely a year before. Mary was a teacher, and Cyril had entered the Royal Air Force, rising through the ranks to Wing Commander. He was dashing and handsome, an irresistible icon for a small girl to idolise. He was a superb pilot and, when stationed in Essex before the war, would fly low over our garden, looping the loop and executing all sorts of aerobatics. The cachet that this gave me with other children was priceless. Once he had picked me up in Writtle in his old jalopy, and we had driven through the night across England to my grandmother's. I adored him and had been delighted when he and my aunt married. Now he was dead, and for the stupidest of reasons.

Cyril was beyond the age for a fighter pilot, and was training others in Wales. He and his commanding officer, the latter at the controls, were flying to London for a meeting when their plane crashed near Reading. It was rumoured that they had run into German fighter planes, but a more mundane explanation prevailed – they had flown into a tangled network of barrage balloons. We naturally thought that, had Cyril been piloting, the accident would never have occurred.

Cyril was given a hero's funeral in the little cemetery on a quiet hillside above Kington. Very little of him could be found to place in the coffin. We were not able to go, but that Christmas my mother and I made the difficult trek across England to be with Mary and my grandmother. We had to travel by night, crossing London in the blitz. The train was crammed with servicemen and we stopped at every station, and sometimes in between. When we at last got seats, an exhausted sailor fell asleep on my shoulder.

It was a sad Christmas in the Garden House where Mary and Cyril had spent their brief honeymoon only a year before. She and I wept together over photos of Cyril and his RAF insignia and medals.

My aunt, Christina was also facing great risks, nightly patrolling the shattered streets of Liverpool as an air-raid warden, while working by day. We seldom saw her, for a wide swathe of the east coast had been cordoned off as a defence zone. That aside, the slogan, 'Is your journey really necessary?' was blazoned everywhere. Because of its munitions factories and anti-aircraft batteries, Chelmsford was sometimes a target. One night Hoffman's received a direct hit. Among those killed was a girl with whom I had gone to Writtle School. That brought the sense of danger very close.

During raids my mother and I crouched in the pantry under the stairs, or under the kitchen table. Towards the end of the war the Government tardily issued us with a table shelter, a massive structure of solid iron. One night, lying there alone, I heard the unmistakable hiss of a falling bomb. I remember thinking, quite calmly, that my last moments had come. There was an almighty thud, the floor heaved and the windows shook. But there was no reverberating explosion. My father donned his helmet and, armed only with a torch, set out across the fields, nearly falling into a crater 30 feet deep and as much across. At the bottom was a massive, unexploded, 1,000-ton land-mine. Had it gone off, our chances of survival would have been slight.

One gloriously fine September Saturday, my father and I were in the fields picking blackberries when, with a thunderous roar, wave after wave of heavy RAF planes droned low overhead, making for the coast. Because of the news clampdown it was only much later that we realised that the planes had been carrying paratroopers to the ill-fated venture at Arnhem. Many who set out on that lovely autumn morning, when the English countryside they were defending was at its shimmering best, never came back.

With the advent of the V-1 (the 'doodlebug' or 'buzz bomb') and the V-2 (the rocket) no advance warnings were possible. The V-1 was an automated small plane, which, when the fuel ran out, fell like a stone and exploded. The engine made a hideously sinister noise, a psychological terror in itself, for you knew that the moment it stopped the 'doodlebug' would fall. The not-very-comforting theory was that, if it stopped overhead, you had nothing to fear. We were all suffering from lack of sleep and, obsessed with exams, I refused to spend nights in the table shelter. I became adept at sleeping through doodlebug attacks unless the sound stopped, in which case in a trice I was out of bed and downstairs. With the V-2s, fired from across the Channel, the first notification was the monumental explosion as they landed. One evening a V-2 exploded very near home, seemingly in the village, through which my father's bus from work passed at that hour. My mother and I waited anxiously to hear his brisk step in the passage, but it did not come. We were beside ourselves with worry but felt helpless since it was winter and dark, and the village was half a mile away. Thirty minutes late, my father appeared. The V-2 had fallen just short of the village, blowing a great crater in uninhabited fields. My father's bus had merely been detained by the incident which, but for sheer luck, would have cost many lives, including his.

In 1940, under a government scheme to take children to safety abroad, my parents applied to send me to Australia, where my maternal great-uncle had emigrated at the end of the nineteenth century. I therefore penned a letter to him, announcing my imminent arrival and giving a description of myself. We never had a reply, but the letter was received, for some 40 years later, when I visited Tasmania, this self-conscious teenage epistle was handed back to me by Uncle Tom's descendants. Because of German submarine activity, travel arrangements were top secret.

You received a message to present your child, with a few hours' notice, at a particular railway station in London. My trunk was packed in readiness, and I was caught between excitement at a new adventure and consternation at the thought of leaving my parents to an uncertain fate and for a long time. One day the summons came. By then one or two ships loaded with children had been sunk by enemy action. I learned afterwards that my parents sat up all night, weighing up the comparative risks for their only child. It was an agonising decision but, character-istically, the argument that finally swayed them was not the danger of a boat going down, but that further education was not guaranteed. Soon afterwards, with the loss of another shipload of children, the scheme was abandoned. My parents often wondered whether that was the boat on which I would have embarked. I wonder how different my life would have been had I spent the next five years in Australia.

My First Jobs

Even with scholarships my schooling was expensive and we had to augment our income. My mother began cleaning other peoples' houses and doing their washing. In those pre-labour-saving days that meant brutally hard work, scrubbing floors on your knees. She earned one shilling an hour. She also arranged for me, aged 11, to work in the market garden of one of her employers, an eccentric widower, for sixpence an hour. This work was also quite hard, involving daily watering of three or four large greenhouses with watering cans (the budget did not, evidently, run to a hosepipe). One fine Saturday, I received my first earnings ever in the grand sum of 2s. 6d. With the half-a-crown piece tucked into the pocket of my shorts I proudly set off home on my bicycle. Alas, an ominous tinkle revealed that my pocket had a hole. I searched everywhere to no avail, and arrived home in floods of tears. My father (who could ill spare such an amount) offered to replace the half-crown but nothing but the original coin would do. So my father, dear soul that he was, walked all the way back, to renew the search. But my first wages were lost forever.

My employer, like my grandfather, was an *intellectuel manqué*, with a particular predilection for anthropology, a subject on which he was never loath to hold forth, to the detriment of our gardening endeavours. One dilapidated garden shed was piled high with mouldering books on the subject, which he urged me to read. Thus, as well as earning some money, I received education on a number of esoteric subjects, such as the initiation rites of strange tribes in the jungles of New Guinea or North Borneo, that I am sure my mother (had she known) would have much preferred me to do without. A more physical hazard came from numerous beehives. Angry bees would get entangled in my short Eton crop and I would get stung on either the head or the finger with which I tried to extract them. I was terrified of them. Assurances that these unsolicited bee-stings would free me from rheumatism and arthritis in later life not only failed to console me then but have proved unfounded since.

We also took in lodgers: first evacuated teachers and land-girls; then an office worker, a rather strange man, terrified of air-raids who committed suicide after the war; and, later, a man rather grander than the rest, who my mother was convinced was the scion of a 'good family' – another black sheep. He certainly dressed the part but he too had a clerical job, and seemed hard put to it to stump up the meagre rent.

A year or two after the war started the Essex War Agriculture Committee set up its headquarters in Writtle. My mother, with customary initiative, applied for a job as a clerk, passed the test with flying colours and became a civil servant. For someone who had left school at 12, that was not bad. For the first time in her life she was in her element, interviewing farmers and keeping books and records with exceptional efficiency, as testified by her superiors. She was very popular and her incisive manner, and initials A. A. A., led to her becoming affectionately known as 'Ack-Ack' after the anti-aircraft batteries!

I loved school, and did well, getting straight A grades. The headmistress, a formidable Quaker lady, Miss Geraldine Cadbury, once told my parents that their daughter was 'not very bright, but works very hard'. It was true that I did prodigious hours of homework and was probably quite insufferable.

Our excellent teachers were mostly middle-aged maiden ladies. Rumour had it that they had lost fiancés in the carnage of the First World War, and the almost limitless romantic possibilities of such conjectures led to much wild surmise among adolescent school-girls. We also had our own schoolgirl crushes. One rather shy younger mistress, Miss Shand, inspired us with her own love of English literature, and was a particular idol.

Miss Jackson, the biology mistress, was a kind, elderly lady with white hair scraped back into a bun. There were clear limits to our biology tuition. We did the rabbit rather thoroughly, including its reproductive system, this last rather more sketchily. When it came to human reproduction Miss Jackson, very red in the face, said hastily, 'It's just like in rabbits', and passed on. That left us, as 13-year-olds, deeply mystified, and gave free rein to our fertile imaginations. It was all the sex education we ever received, apart from a homily from the headmistress when we reached age 16 and the Upper Fifth, another embarrassing occasion for all concerned. The message was succinctly summed up in a single phrase, 'Don't let boys mess about with you!'

At age 14 we had to choose between arts and science. I was an all-rounder, and my inclination was for science, until the Latin mistress argued otherwise, since Latin was a prerequisite for a place at Oxford or Cambridge. I had never dreamed that I might get to university at all, much less Oxbridge, which was a remote ambition for our school anyway. It meant staying on in the Sixth Form, and my scholarship ended at age 16. There was much discussion at home. My father, usually supportive, but in whom the fires of will and ambition had somehow been quenched, said sadly that he did not see how we could afford it. My mother rose to the challenge. 'I don't know either but we've got to try. We just all have to work very hard.'

We certainly did that, all of us to earn money and I to pass exams. The only way to finance my two years in the Sixth Form was to sign a commitment to go on to teacher training college and become a teacher. The idea did not appeal. The only alternative was the Ashdown Scholarship, awarded for the best School Certificate result in the whole of the County of Essex. It was a pipe dream, but I worked like blazes for my School Certificate, taken in July 1942.

In the two months before the results came out, my commitment obliged me to do a month's 'pupil teaching'. In marvellous September weather I set off on my bicycle to Highwood village school, three miles from Writtle. The school boasted only two classrooms, and about 70 pupils, ranging between the ages of five and 15. It was run by two gentle spinster sisters, but it could more accurately be said that the school ran them. Indiscipline was rife, the ringleader being a gypsy boy whom I shall call Dan, as big as me, and only one year younger. The school was difficult to manage anyway, with several different age levels in each classroom and one family of children who were mentally defective. As one of the sisters was ill, I found myself coping with the junior classroom on my own, rather than being taught on the job.

At lunchtime I escaped across the fields to eat my sandwiches on a grassy spot under a tree, where I had a soothing view of golden stubble fields, shimmering in autumn mist. I did not remain soothed for long. When my day was finished, I was bent on testing my grandfather's theory that one could freewheel all the way downhill from Highwood to Oxney Green. But there was a puncture in my back tyre and I had to push my bicycle all the way home. The next day, when I went to enjoy my picnic lunch on the same grassy knoll, I found it desecrated by turds. The two occurrences were obviously connected, and I deduced that the culprit was Dan.

The educational authorities sent in a supply teacher who was the exact antithesis of the two resident teachers – a large energetic lady, with a booming voice and a rod of iron. When the remaining sister retired to look after her ailing sibling, we ran the school together and I grew up fast. I was completely outsmarted by a five-year-old, notorious for missing school without reason or explanatory note who, when I asked why he had been absent, turned up limpid blue eyes and, with an air of injured innocence, lisped, 'Coz not, miss.' One Saturday, blackberrying with my parents along the Highwood Road, we saw some children scuttling to hide behind some bushes, hissing apprehensively, 'Look out, there's *Miss*' – a description that reduced my parents to paroxysms of mirth. But the most astonishing thing of all was that Dan became my faithful slave and protector, and rode half the way home with me every afternoon.

While this interlude increased my self-confidence, I am not sure that it did much to develop whatever aptitude I might have had for elementary schoolteaching. Fortunately for countless children, it was never put to the test. To the surprise of myself and everyone else, I won the Ashdown Scholarship. My two years in the Sixth Form were assured, and I was released from the teaching commitment.

The Village Hierarchy

In our village I was considered something of a freak and my parents ill-advised. 'Educate a girl?' they scoffed. 'She'll only get married!' There were even darker mutterings that my parents forced me to study. No one could imagine that I enjoyed it.

In any case my life was not all work and no play. I had a close school friend in Chelmsford, with parents who were very culturally and politically aware, and a glamorous, artistic older brother, who once rode me home on his tandem bicycle. Another friend lived at Sturgeons Farm, two miles outside the village. We bicycled to school together, leaving coded messages in pebbles on a convenient bridge. At the farm we played games among the barns and haystacks and explored the walled-up cellars under the old house.

Within the village things were more difficult. In that then strictly hierarchical rural society, a child from an ordinary family going to secondary school ended up in social limbo. Inevitably I grew apart from my peers in the village school who by then were out working. The few other young people of my own age who shared my interests and studies were at boarding-school. Their families were well-off and belonged to a different social stratum.

Miss Usborne, the last remaining member of a family who had made money from brewing, lived in a large house opposite us. A tall lady of dourly severe mien and imponderable age, she rode sidesaddle to hounds and, when not engaged in the hunt, in an attire and style that looked remarkably similar, on an ancient 'sit-up-and-beg' bicycle, bearing aloft a big black umbrella. She never smiled and spoke to no one. She was a Justice of the Peace and in

1946 refused to sign my first passport application, saying she did not know me. Expressing surprise that I was actually at university, and Cambridge to boot, she unbent sufficiently to enquire what I intended to do. When I rashly ventured that I would like to go into the Foreign Service, if it became open to women, she snorted, 'Hrrmph – far too ambitious.' It was the only conversation we ever had.

The 'upper crust' of village society was mainly composed of well-to-do professional families to whom a bridge was provided to me by a family who came to live in a lovely old Georgian house on Writtle Green. The Cantelos were intelligent, cultivated and liberal in their views. They had one daughter, April. At the onset of the war, they offered a home to a German Jewish refugee, Tilly Cahn, who had escaped by the skin of her teeth from Cologne, where her father was a lawyer. The two girls were sent to the high school, and Tilly was placed in my form. Tilly brought an aura of continental sophistication with her; her family was highly cultured, and she had interests in music, arts and literature beyond the bounds of the school syllabus, as well as an amazing talent for languages and for wicked mimicry. The latter gift, applied injudiciously to some of our teachers, several times ended in grief all round. Tilly and I became bosom friends. We went on long walks, reciting poetry and exchanging romantic adolescent yearnings and confidences about the latest crush of the moment, which could vary from the adored English mistress (whose own love prospects also engaged our earnest preoccupation) to unobtainable idols such as handsome young army officers whom we glimpsed at dances in the village hall (where I was the resident wallflower) or the cello-playing scion of a musical family in Writtle, an austere and melancholy bachelor.

Tilly also brought the horrors of the Holocaust very near. In 1943 her older brother, an engineer, wrote from Australia that he had received the briefest of cards from their parents, saying that they were going away and would not be heard from for a long while. The ominous implications of this cryptic message were all too plain. In 1945, after the German surrender, I shared six weeks of horrendous suspense with Tilly during which she was told she might receive news of her parents. But they had perished at Auschwitz.

I was accepted into the Cantelo household with the same warmth as Tilly. Reg and Eve Cantelo had an enormously positive and broadening impact on my life, providing my introduction into a dynamic circle of cultural activity in Writtle. There was even a small orchestra in which Tilly and April played. I did not (there was no money for music lessons) but I enjoyed being in the audience and my musical horizons widened greatly.

Through the Cantelos I was included in parties held with other young people away at boarding school. These were innocent but enjoyable affairs; we played charades, 'murder' and 'sardines' in winter, and tennis in summer. My access to these events was not without upsets. One summer the vicar's eldest son, who had taken rather a shine to me (not reciprocated) had a birthday party, which I attended. I was by that time a senior prefect at school, and captain of a house. A day or two later, my helper at the school dinner table over which I presided was the vicar's daughter, a notoriously tactless child, who loudly announced that there had been a terrible row in her family before the party. Her parents had said I could not be invited as I did not belong to the same social class and they 'could not invite (my) parents to the house'. Her brother had insisted that if I was not invited he would not have a party at all and, after a monumental argument, had won the day. The effects of these words on the junior girls present, who had previously held me in some awe, can be imagined. My main emotions were mortification that I had unknowingly attended the party and rage on my parents' behalf. They found the episode uproariously funny, pointing out that they had no desire to be invited to the vicarage anyway.

I stopped going to church. Up to then I had attended every Sunday, and Tilly and I had just been confirmed. It was not just my family pride that was hurt. My religious faith received a fatal blow from this discovery that a man of God should act in such a manifestly unchristian way. The vicar was clearly perturbed. One day as I cycled home from school he came pedalling furiously behind me in a vain attempt to give me an explanation and perhaps an apology. I suspected that his wife was more at fault, but I rode stolidly on, telling him that if I and my parents were not welcome in his home, then we were not welcome in his church.

Privately, I am ashamed to say, I wished vengeance on him and his wife. A few years later I had reason to feel guilty, for the vicar died at a prematurely early age.

Our young group contained an extraordinary amount of talent for a small village. One did very well in science. Another, who had dark, matinée-idol good looks, had a promising theatrical career that was cut tragically short when he died of kidney failure at 26, when working with Laurence Olivier in the direction of Christopher Fry's play, *The Lady's not for Burning*. He had been my first schoolgirl love, unrequited, except by friendship, for he was in love with April Cantelo. April was very pretty and had a magnificent soprano voice. She went on to study music and so met Colin Davis. April was already making a name for herself as a singer when they married very young, their wedding celebrated by a performance of *Cosi Fan Tutte* with the village orchestra. For a number of years April was the main breadwinner and by far the better known of the two. Her support then was vital in making Colin's dream of becoming a conductor come true, and he went on to win international acclaim. It was all the sadder, then, for those of us who had participated in its fairytale beginning, when their marriage came to an end.

A Defining Year

Normally, then, if you hoped to go to university, you spent three years in the Sixth Form. At the end of the second you took your Higher School Certificate, aiming to qualify for the few coveted state and county major scholarships that would cover the bulk of tuition and lodging fees. The third year was devoted to the punishing round of university entrance and scholarship exams.

In wartime there was no place for such luxuries. At age 18 you were called up for service in the armed forces. If you had a university place, you were allowed to follow a shortened two-year course first. There was thus no time to lose, and so Higher School Certificate and university entrance and scholarship exams were telescoped into two years. In addition Chelmsford High School was not geared to cram students for university entrance in the same way as elite girls' boarding-schools. My teachers were helpful, but I had to do a lot of work on my own.

I have always been dubbed a workaholic, but I never remember working as hard as in the year between my seventeenth and eighteenth birthdays. The competition for Oxford and Cambridge was tremendous because of the severely restricted intake for girls – for the two Cambridge colleges a total of about 160 each year. I was applying both to Somerville College, Oxford, and Newnham College, Cambridge, but my preference was for the former. As a fall-back position I applied to King's College, London.

No one had advised me as to what I should read at university, or what I might do afterwards. After my involuntary break with science at age 14, I was left with a motley group of arts subjects for Higher School Certificate: English, French and Latin, with history as a subsidiary. I suddenly realised that I would probably end up teaching, the very thing I had worked so hard to avoid. Languages offered wider prospects, but only French had been taught at school. I wrote to Somerville and Newnham enquiring about the possibilities of reading for a modern languages degree. The best Somerville could offer was a combined degree in French and Latin (teaching again! I thought). Newnham offered a daunting alternative. Provided I learned enough Italian or Spanish in the next three months to pass the entrance examination in November 1943, I could be admitted to the Modern and Mediaeval Languages Tripos.

By one of those quirks of fate that determine the rest of your life, Chelmsford Technical College offered no Italian course. Since I had only three months, there was no alternative to paying for the private services of the Spanish teacher, an engineer at one of the local factories, who had been born in Gibraltar. His knowledge of grammar was rudimentary; I had to teach him what a subjunctive was but he served the purpose. He lived in a house called Calpe (the Spanish name for Gibraltar), with an extremely large and highly-strung wife (he was very small). It was a time of fierce air-raids and the señora huddled under their table shelter punctuating our lessons with heartfelt, 'A...a...ay...ays'. Such was my anxiety to learn fast that I would not allow her husband to join her, and we plodded on as the world about reverberated with noise. The lessons took place at night, and I used to cycle back to Writtle under skies riven with searchlight beams and the flashes of exploding anti-aircraft shells from batteries all around.

I also had to study three different syllabuses in English, French and Latin for Newnham in November, and Somerville and King's College in January and February, as well as yet another, plus history, for the Higher School Certificate in July. Unbeknown to my parents I was starting work at 4.30 every morning in my icy little bedroom, and continuing late at night. I rejoiced when I had a cold, because I could stay in bed and get on with my own priorities, rather than waste time in classes that I found irrelevant. I knew that I was overstretched and it seemed sensible to substitute Spanish for history in Higher School Certificate. It did not seem sensible to my headmistress. My parents were summoned, first together and then separately, to be told I had gone out of my mind. Not only would I fail the Newnham entrance, but I would ruin my chances of winning state and county scholarships and thus of going to university at all. I have never loved or admired my parents more than at that moment. They firmly said that I obviously knew what I was doing and would not be budged. It still remains a wonder to me that a country couple – intelligent certainly, but unversed in higher education – should back their 17-year-old daughter, equally ignorant on the subject, against the superior wisdom of her school.

Their backing made me work all the harder. I passed the written examination for Newnham, including Spanish, and those for Somerville and King's. Then came nerve-racking interviews at all three places, One of my interviews at Somerville is an especially embarrassing recollection. I had become besotted with Baudelaire, one of the many subjects on which I had worked without guidance. I had developed my own theory which I expounded in the written exam. At Somerville I found myself facing the formidable figure of Enid Starkie. Such was my state of blissful ignorance that I had no idea that she was *the* authority on Baudelaire and had written a seminal book on him! Encouraged by her questions, I enthusiastically outlined my doubtless outlandish and immature ideas, without reference to her own work, of which I was so blithely unaware. She did not even blink. Perhaps I got points for imagination, for I was offered a place at Somerville, notwithstanding. I was also offered a scholarship at King's College, London.

Despite my original predilection for Oxford, I accepted the place offered at Newnham, since the Modern and Mediaeval Languages Tripos at Cambridge offered the best way forward. And there had been a moment, as I stood in Newnham's lovely garden, listening to a thrush singing on a sparkling spring morning, when it came to me in a flash of almost blinding happiness, that this was going to be my home for the next three years.

There was still the financial hurdle and the Higher School Certificate to be surmounted in July. The results were announced in September, only a few weeks before I was due to go up to Cambridge; I had obtained distinction in all subjects, including Spanish, and had been awarded both state and county major scholarships. Suddenly, several girls at school were being encouraged to follow my example and 'do Spanish on the side'. My Gibraltarian teacher acquired more pupils, and put up his fees. He had, after all, improved his grammatical skills through teaching me. But I had good reason to be grateful to him.

So my schooldays came to an end. Amid the euphoria that autumn of having achieved what had seemed unattainable was mingled a sensation tantamount to anticlimax, as well as some trepidation. Cambridge would be a venture into the unknown. And the war was not over. I would now be exempted from national service, but only for two years.

Figure 1 My mother when she was young.

Figure 2 My father, about the time of his marriage.

Figure 3 Family photo taken at my parents' wedding in September 1922 at Titley, Herefordshire. Christina, my aunt, is on the left in the front row, my grandmother next to the bridegroom in the second row.

Figure 4 Playing cricket on Writtle Green in the 1930s, as seen from the church tower.

Figure 5 At Gorsty Doles with my mother and my Uncle Henry, who always claimed he taught me to walk!

Figure 6 With my grandmother at The Green, Titley. Taken during the summer holidays.

Figure 7 Feeding my grandmother's chickens at The Green.

Figure 8 At Writtle with my uncle (by marriage), Cyril Hicks, who was killed in the Battle of Britain.

Figure 9 With Christina, my aunt, in the garden at 2 Albert Villas.

Figure 10 A summer tea party at The Green with my parents and my aunts, Margaret and Mary, who were both schoolteachers.

Figure 11 In 1937, my first year at Chelmsford County High School for Girls, with white cat – and Eton crop!

Figure 12 A proud graduate in 1947, taken at 2 Albert Villas.

Figure 13 The love scene from García Lorca's *Mariana Pineda*, which Mrs Camille Prior tried to 'hot up'. Performed in 1947 by Cambridge University Spanish Society at the ADC Theatre.

Figure 14 My best friend, Mary Gibson (née Beveridge) with my goddaughter Charlotte, taken in 1961.

Figure 15 Dancing with President Victor Paz Estenssoro in La Paz, Bolivia, about 1963.

Figure 16 Dancing the Bolivian *Diablada* (Devil Dance) on the shores of Lake Titicaca, 1978. (I am on the left!)

Figure 17 Precarious Bolivian welcome to Otavi, in the Department of Potosi.

Figure 18 Fiesta at the Margaret Anstee rural hospital in Otavi.

Figure 19 Joining in the fiesta at the Otavi hospital.

PART TWO

Fresh Fields and Pastures New

4

The Groves of Academe

Cambridge

Cambridge opened a magic door into a world I had hardly dared to contemplate. Books and examinations continued to loom large but I discovered an exciting life of culture, art, theatre and lively debate on every subject under the sun, as well as more frivolous activities hitherto unknown to me. This heady combination was not only intellectually stimulating but also gave a much-needed boost to my self-confidence. For the first time in my life I found myself in the midst of a social whirl, instead of hovering nervously on the fringes. My three years at Newnham were among the happiest I have known.

They also saw the start of the closest friendship of my life. My journey had taken me across country, bicycle and trunk in the guard's van, first from Chelmsford to Marks Tey, and then on a branch-line, on which we ambled across the gently undulating landscape of Essex and Suffolk, behind a contentedly puffing steam engine, stopping frequently at ancient villages of thatched cottages and steepled churches.

I had only just entered my small bed-sitting-room in Sidgwick Hall when there was a knock at the door. Outside stood a girl in a blue dressing-gown, who introduced herself as my neighbour, Mary Beveridge. It turned out that we were both reading French and Spanish. Our backgrounds were very different. Mary came from a well-to-do family in Edinburgh and had been educated at the élite Scottish boarding-school, St Leonard's. Notwithstanding, the empathy was immediate and we became inseparable companions.

When we went down three years later, the principal, Dame Myra Curtis, previously a formidable and unapproachable figure, disarmed us by saying, 'Well, you two have been hunting in pairs for three years now ...' And it was true that we had for some time gone out in a foursome with army officers following the special Russian course. Our friendship remained unimpaired by time or distance until Mary's tragic death from cancer in 1994.

Stocking up for Cambridge had been a problem at a time of severe clothes rationing. Until then I had always worn school uniform and I had also to take sheets and towels. Under my mother's guidance, I had become quite a good dressmaker. I had one good coat, in a splendid green, black and white check, and I made myself a green suit, complete with matching fur hat, from some remnants of my grandmother's. Having the right contacts was even more important. My mother's leading man in the village amateur dramatics was the shopwalker in the main store in Chelmsford. Through him we obtained 'utility' wartime sheets, and blue velvet curtain material (not on coupons), which was transformed into an elegant housecoat. It was also warm, a very necessary quality in those pre-central-heating days when we were allowed only two scuttles of coal a week. We would take it in turns to make a fire in the evenings, and then huddle around it, drinking NAMCO (National Milk Cocoa), discussing the state of the world, philosophising and dreaming until the late hour and the dying embers of the fire brought us back to the cold chill of reality.

In my third year I moved to Fawcett Building, which had gas fires. Heat was still rationed, but there was no fireplace to clean. Our counterparts in the men's colleges still had their 'bedmakers', who attended to their every want. We had not only to keep our rooms clean, but also to undertake general cleaning and gardening duties, as domestic staff and gardeners were hard to come by.

The discrimination did not stop there. Not only was the total number of women undergraduates strictly limited to 500 for both Girton and Newnham over the whole three years, but women were not admitted as full members of the university. Although we attended the same lectures and supervisions, and sat the same examinations, marked by the same examiners, we only received a 'title to a degree', which was sent through the post instead of being conferred in a Senate House ceremony. This had the same validity in the workplace as a man's degree, but was still an astonishing anachronism. It was revoked in 1948, a year too late for me to receive my BA degree with due ceremony, but I had the satisfaction of receiving my MA at the Senate House in 1955. There were some advantages: we did not have to wear gowns, and were not subject to the discipline of the proctors and their bulldogs.

Unlike our earlier sisters, we no longer had chaperones but we were subjected to rules that seem antediluvian today. No men were allowed in your room, or indeed the college, after 10 p.m. (it seemed to be assumed that nothing untoward could occur before that watershed hour) and you had to be in college by then unless you had a late pass to 11 p.m. or midnight; in that case you had to ring at the Porter's Lodge and sign your name. Exceptions were made for May Balls, when you danced all night, had a champagne breakfast on the river, and did not get back to college until mid-morning. If you had too many late passes, your hall tutor would call your attention to the dangers of burning the candle at both ends and flunking your exams – if that awful event happened, you were sent down without ado or chance of return. Needless to say, a lot of wall-climbing went on. Male undergraduates also considered it smart to belong to the Newnham Bath Club, which entailed having a bath in Nownham. This was considered incredibly daring, and one would often come across an anxious young woman biting her nails outside a locked bathroom door.

In my first year, I acquired a Mexican admirer – a postgraduate law student – who announced his intention of climbing into the college garden and serenading me with his guitar. I begged him to abandon such a disaster-prone exercise, which could end in my being sent down, or rusticated for a term. He was very Mexican, complete with black mustachios and enormous sombrero, and was indignant that the British customs had obliged him to surrender the pistols he carried at his waist. Salvador (nicknamed Chendis) used to take me to tea dances, an innocent and rather delightful pastime of the day. One afternoon I invited him to tea in my room. To my amazed embarrassment, in the midst of the toasted crumpets, he fell to his knees, poured out a lyrically eloquent declaration of love and proposed marriage. This had never happened to me before but I did my best to refuse him gently without hurting his pride. In this I was singularly unsuccessful – perhaps through inadequate grasp of the finer points of the Spanish language – for he leapt haughtily to his feet and strode out of the room. At least, that was his intention, but he unfortunately mistook the door and marched into the wardrobe, whence I had to extricate him from the tangle of my clothes. Perhaps I should not have been surprised when, visiting Mexico years later, I phoned his office (he was by then a prosperous lawyer) and found he did not wish to renew the acquaintance ...

Cambridge wrought a change in my language priorities, greatly influencing the course of my life. The French Faculty was large and impersonal while the Spanish Faculty was tiny. The Head of the Spanish Faculty, Professor J. B. Trend, was an extraordinary eccentric who inspired great enthusiasm in his students. Not very tall, rosy-cheeked, and with an equally pink bald pate surrounded by an unruly halo of grey hair, he looked like a merry, mediaeval monk who had strayed into the twentieth century. He had the liveliest, twinkling eyes I have ever seen, forever darting hither and thither to pounce on intellectual titbits, as a robin might pounce on a worm. His mind was always several steps ahead of his speech, and he stammered and stuttered as his tongue strove vainly to catch up with his thought. This often rendered him almost inarticulate, as the words tumbled out pell-mell. An affectionate joke went the rounds, in Spanish doggerel, that J. B., or 'Prof' as he was known by all and sundry, never finished a sentence until he left the lecture room.

> *Al terminar la frase,*
> *Ya está fuera de la clase.*

In contrast, J. B.'s written style was clarity itself, painstakingly set down in a large, square, almost childish hand. His numerous books were all leavened by this deceptively simple language. His work was not held in high regard by some other scholars, perhaps because of this, but also because his interests were so broad. It was not his style to spend years researching, say, seventeenth-century Spanish chapbooks, and churning over convoluted theories or obscure textual interpretations. Prof's interests were chiefly mediaeval, in keeping with his monastic appearance, but he knew Spanish literature through and through, and could put everything into context. It was extraordinarily stimulating for a young undergraduate exploring new ground, to get illuminating (if not always coherent) answers to every question. J. B. always had the relevant book in the well-filled shelves of his rooms that had once been Darwin's in Christ's College, and the required tome was usually on the top shelf. His physical movements were as impetuous and unpredictable as his speech. Hardly had you finished the question when he would leap onto the back of the sofa and, poised perilously on one leg, arms at full stretch, would extract the reference that would help you on your way.

J. B.'s favourite accolade for anything worthwhile was that it was '*alive*'. He applied it equally to works of authors dead for centuries and to all sorts of contemporary events. Many is the time that I found a postcard from J. B. in my pigeonhole at Newnham, beseeching me not to miss the play at the arts theatre, or film at the arts cinema, because it was 'alive'.

J. B.'s eclectic tastes stemmed from the twists and turns of his career. He had read mathematics at the beginning of the century, as a contemporary of Rupert Brooke, which lent him a certain glamour in our eyes. After the First World War he became onamoured of Spain and its culture. In the 1920s Spain was in a state of intellectual and political effervescence. J. B. became caught up in exciting and fast-moving events, which certainly met his criteria of being 'alive'. He became a close friend of Manuel de Falla and Federico García Lorca, and had riveting tales of gypsy festivals they organised to revive Spanish folklore and the essence of Spanish culture. He also knew all the giants of the so-called 'Generation of 1898' – Unamuno, Ortega y Gasset, Azorín – who aimed to bring about a renaissance in Spanish political thinking, social attitudes and cultural heritage.

All that reached its apotheosis in the Spanish Republic of the early 1930s when J. B. was appointed to the Chair of Spanish in Cambridge, only its second incumbent. He was in his element and was made a *Comendador de la República*, one of the highest honours in the ill-fated Republic. Then came the dreadful tragedy of the Spanish Civil War, which changed the face of Europe, and set the stage for the greater war to follow. Cambridge became the refuge of Basque children, and of many luminaries from the Republic's brief heyday, some of whom came to teach us.

J. B.'s world also fell apart. He vowed never to return to Spain until Franco was overthrown and, dying before that happened, he never did. In later years he spent holidays in Portugal, wistfully looking over the frontier, and in his sixties learned Portuguese. Arguably, Salazar, the Portuguese dictator, was no better, but Prof had not become so identified with that country. He made it his mission to bring Spanish and Spanish culture 'alive' in Cambridge. Paradoxically, one of the things that made it so was the ideological split in the Spanish Faculty. Not all its members shared J. B.'s republican sympathies. The opposing faction was led by Dr Bullock, a less appealing personality. Nearly a decade after the civil war ended in Spain, it was still being waged by proxy in the lecture halls and common rooms of Cambridge. It added a certain spice to life and topical relevance to our studies.

Salazar Chapela, a Republican stalwart, taught us in an impeccable Castilian accent but we could not understand the former Catalan Minister, Dr Batista i Roca, either in Spanish or English. He insisted on dictating prose translations in his decidedly obfuscated English. One day, in a sentence of which we could make neither head nor tail, he included the word 'sward', which we variously translated as *césped* (lawn) or *pasto* (grass), only to be soundly lambasted when our papers returned – the word was 'sword'! Luis Cernuda, a magical lyrical poet, was an abysmal lecturer. A shy, introverted dreamer, he overcame his phobia for lecturing by gazing into the eyes of one of the female undergraduates, fixing her with an unswerving stare from his lambent brown eyes for the whole hour. It was an unnerving experience. Inez Macdonald was the Spanish tutor in Newnham, specialising in the mediaeval period and the Golden Age of the Renaissance. She was very musical and sang Spanish folk-songs in a full-bodied voice. In our second year Helen Grant came into our lives. She inculcated into us a tremendous enthusiasm for the Generation of '98 and for modern Spanish literature, poetry and culture generally.

J. B. was one of the first British academics to appreciate the immense interest and potential of Latin America, perhaps because he had visited Spanish Republican friends exiled in Mexico, and written a book about that country. Whenever someone notable from Spain or Latin America visited London, J. B. invited them to speak at the University Spanish Society of which I was the secretary during my second and third years, a double ordeal initially. J. B. always took the guest out to dinner and, since he was a bachelor, I, who had rarely been in a restaurant, was expected to be his hostess. How glad I was that my mother had been a parlour-maid in great houses and had taught me which knife, spoon and fork to use when! My first meeting, when I had to introduce the speaker in Spanish, was disastrous. My predecessor, a male undergraduate, had read haltingly from a trembling piece of paper and I was determined to do better. Pride went before a fall. The first speaker was a distinguished Colombian writer and historian. I had laboriously learned my introduction by rote and began well enough. Then suddenly my mind went totally blank. 'Say it in English,' the kindly speaker said, taking pity on this nervous 19-year-old. But I couldn't say it in any language, and just stood there, mouth open, eyes glazed. I thought I would never recover from the shame. But of course I did, and years later in New York the same distinguished gentleman immediately remembered me, which he would not have done had I produced a seamless performance. Latin American ambassadors were also invited, and I received invitations to lunch at Claridge's or national day receptions which, in my innocence, I considered the height of glamour.

J. B. was the British expert on Manuel de Falla, about whom the BBC came to interview him, during a Spanish Society meeting. I can still see him, rosy with irrepressible excitement, sitting cross-legged on the floor, hugging a cushion to his chest, eyes cast ceiling-ward as the strains of the *Three Cornered Hat* throbbed through the ancient turrets and staircases of Christ's College. In 1947 J. B. was to broadcast a seventieth birthday tribute to de Falla. As usual, the words were impeccably written on small cards, and he recited them to himself on the train to London, to the considerable alarm of other passengers. When he got there, the BBC told him that de Falla had suddenly died, in his exile in

Argentina. Poor J. B., overcome with emotion at the death of his dear and long unseen friend, had to improvise a very different tribute.

The war made it impossible to pursue our linguistic studies abroad and vacation courses were arranged in England. One Spanish course was held in the Instituto Español in London, staffed by distinguished exiles, some of them former ministers, and financed by Republican government funds that had been taken abroad. The Franco Government retaliated by setting up a rival institution in London, confusingly called 'Instituto de España' but J. B., of course, recognised only the Instituto Español, and we remained faithful to it also. Even when foreign travel became possible, I refused to visit Spain while Franco was in power. Our Republican mentors in Cambridge and at the Instituto Español were at first buoyed up by the hope that he too must fall in the wake of his German and Italian allies, and it was painful to see their growing despair that the rest of their lives might be condemned to exile. In 1951 I succumbed and went to Spain, realising that Franco might be around for a very long time.

I harboured a secret desire to become an actress, but knew that my parents would be appalled if I embraced such an uncertain career. At Cambridge I joined the Mummers, and appeared in several productions in my first two years but later concentrated on French and Spanish plays. In 1947 the Spanish Society ambitiously produced Federico García Lorca's *Mariana Pineda*. Donald Beves of King's College, and Camille Prior, widow of the former Professor of French, coached us for both French and Spanish plays. Mrs Prior hardly understood a word of Spanish, but threw herself into Lorca with passion. Tiny and by no means young, she exuded a verve and energy in inverse relation to her size. I played the name part, and at one point had to fling myself into the arms of my lover (a good-looking but wooden young man from Trinity Hall) on whose account I was to be led off to my execution, still spouting reams of deliciously lyrical verse. Camille was appalled at our performance of this touching scene. 'Not like *that*, you two,' she fumed. 'Like this ...' So saying she flung herself passionately, and with evident enjoyment, at the young man who, crimson with embarrassment, very nearly collapsed under the impact. We played to a packed audience in the ADC Theatre and won praise in the *Cambridge Review* but it was a tremendous amount of work for a one-night stand.

I loved dancing also. There were tea dances at the Dorothy Café, and Mary and I joined the Highland Dance Society, practising every week for the culminating event of the Highland Ball. The May Balls (held, naturally, in June!) were all-night affairs, after which, if one's energies and the weather held up, boat parties would punt to Grantchester and breakfast on the river. On one occasion Mary and I, with our partners, inveigled 17 couples into the Trinity May Ball on two tickets. I am ashamed of this now, but it seemed a good lark at the time, especially as we were short of money and had been long starved of such entertainment.

Mary and I celebrated both VE day (the victory in Europe) and VJ day (the victory over Japan) together; the first in Cambridge, where a great bonfire was set alight in Market Square, and the second in Edinburgh where, with her twin sister Cara, John Coleridge, a fellow undergraduate on leave from the navy, and other friends we joined the delirious crowds that thronged Princes Street.

Peace released us from our obligation to join the armed forces, and travel abroad became possible again, albeit in precarious circumstances, as Mary and I found when, in the long vac of 1946, we went on a French course at St Servan-sur-Mer, in Brittany. Mary had been staying with me in Writtle and we spent the last night in London, to be up betimes for the boat-train. There was one snag: our passports had not arrived. Quite how we managed to embark without them, I can't recall, but embark we did. We were on the deck of the Channel steamer bound for Calais when our names were called over the loudhailer. Fearing the worst we duly presented ourselves ... and received our first passports! They had arrived that morning and my ever resourceful mother had dashed up to London, arriving at Victoria as the boat-train was leaving. She just had time to thrust the passports into the guard's hands before it moved off.

One year after victory, France still bore the scars of war. In Paris we made our way with difficulty by underground to the YWCA, a gloomy place where we each had to share a tiny cubicle with strangers. There was a long queue for supper, the only visible food a bowl of wilting lettuce. In the train dining-car from Calais we had made the disconcerting discovery that you could not get food without a French ration card. The YWCA cheerily informed us that we could not even have one of the dejected lettuce leaves without one. We were rescued by Mary's diplomat cousin, James Marjoribanks, who was in Paris with Ernest Bevin, then Foreign Secretary, for discussions about the peace settlement. From the sordid squalor of the YWCA we were transported to the splendour of the Hotel George V, horribly conscious, among the glittering diplomatic entourage, of our travel-stained appearance. There, for the first time, I tasted the delights of *Turbot bonne femme*. It was all that was on the menu, even in that grand hotel. On the day-long train journey next day we ate lunch in the dining-car, only revealing at the end that we had no food coupons. The waiter was furious, but could do little about food already in our stomachs!

In St Servan Mary and I shared a room in a small hotel overlooking the sea. The bathroom was kept locked, you paid for the one bath allowed every week and the lavatory was unsavoury, while the lady proprietor scolded us on our pronunciation and grammatical errors. A battered tram took us to our class along the seafront, clearing the way ahead with a jaunty horn blaring forth a tune reminiscent of the opening bars of Mendelssohn's 'Italian' Symphony. We ate omelettes at Mont St Michel, swam and once even skinny-dipped at midnight. We visited Rennes and, more sombrely, the bleak ruins of Caen, its shell-pocked cathedral standing like some tragic monument in the rubble that was all that remained after the Normandy battles of two summers before.

There were touching gestures from French people who had witnessed the Allied invasion. On the boat-train back to Calais, a workman, seeing our ravenous eyes fixed on his ham-filled baguette, broke it in two and gave us half. Once on the Channel steamer we tucked hungrily into bacon and eggs ...

Our last year at Cambridge was one of intense swotting for Part Two of the Modern and Mediaeval Languages Tripos. Sometimes Mary and I were up all night, finishing essays, meeting at intervals to imbibe 'Russian' tea, with lemon, which we considered very chic. We were also imbibing the special delights of Cambridge to the maximum, burning the candle at both ends, until I had a return of heart trouble, a legacy of diphtheria a decade earlier, and had to follow a strict routine.

I had obtained a first in Part One, in 1945, and Newnham awarded me the Mary Sparke Scholarship. Nonetheless, I remained anxious that my studies were preparing me for little other than teaching. Even at Newnham there was little advice to be had. Curiously I never thought of economics, but I opted for agricultural science for Part Two. My grandfather had been a farmer, I had had a rural upbringing, so it seemed appropriate. My tutor was appalled, telling me that I was expected to get a first in Part Two also and persuaded me to continue with modern languages.

The 1945 election, in which, much to our disgust, we 19-year-olds had no vote, returned a Labour Government and marked the beginning of a new era. Our lecture rooms filled up with older men, discharged from military service, who returned to complete degree courses truncated by the war. 1946–47 was a cruel winter. Snow lay thick on the ground for weeks. We still had the same exiguous coal rations and huddled over our books with fingers encased in mittens. In the spring, Newnham held its first Ball since the onset of the war. Mary invited an old family friend, from Scotland, I a beau from Oxford, met during the previous summer at St Servan-sur-Mer, whom I had encountered only through ardent correspondence since. We invested jointly in a bottle of sherry, four sherry glasses (of which I still have my two) and a packet of cigarettes. We felt very racy. So much for bright hopes! A sudden thaw and torrential rains inundated the British Isles, Cambridge became a floating island in the Fens, and all train services were suspended. My partner managed to struggle through from Oxford, but Mary's never made it. A friend of a friend from Gonville and Caius was hurriedly recruited into the breach. He, James Gibson, became her husband five years later.

It was the end of term, and I returned to Oxford with my partner for a few days. We had a nightmare journey, arriving late at night at his digs to find the front garden thigh-deep in water. Gallantly, he carried me over the threshold, a very romantic gesture.

Then the final run-up to Part Two of the Tripos gathered momentum in earnest. I went through those exams in a complete haze. Then, suddenly, there were the May Balls and all the things that had to be done before going down for the last time, the fond farewells to people with whom one had lived closely for three years and might not see again for many years, if ever.

Just before term ended, J. B. came to tea. On a sunny June afternoon we sat on a bench in Newnham garden, surrounded by summer fragrances, and he indiscreetly, and against all the rules, told me that I had indeed got a First, almost a Starred First, but for one French paper. Mary had a very good 2.1.

J. B. and other members of the Spanish Faculty played a pivotal role in directing my future life, inculcating in me a great love of Hispanic culture. I was already fired with desire to get to Latin America, but that was long before cheap airfares permitted students to wander the world. When I did get to Colombia a decade later, as the first woman UN field officer anywhere, I found that, though my work was technical and political, the understanding of Spanish literature and culture and of Latin America acquired at Cambridge greatly helped me steer a path through a 'macho' jungle, where women did not even have the vote.

I kept in touch with J. B. by letter and occasional visits. It was a joy to learn, in 1957, that he was to give lectures in Chile and at last fulfil his ambition of travelling farther south than Mexico. I was head of the UN programme in Uruguay and arranged for him to be invited there also. Alas, it was not to be. J. B. was smitten with a massive stroke and lay prone in his college rooms over a weekend until a bedmaker discovered him. He was still alive, but past saving. He was just 70, the same age at which his friend Manuel de Falla had died. When the news reached me in Montevideo I put on all my de Falla records, and wept.

J. B.'s books were distributed among his students and colleagues. I got a dull volume, which did not at all reflect the interests that had cemented our relationship. Years later, at a lunch party in New York given by a Sierra Leonean colleague, Davidson Nichol, I learned that he had been a Fellow of Christ's with rooms above J. B.'s. When I told him I had been one of J. B.'s students, he said, 'You must see my most prized possession', and produced the book he had received on J. B.'s death. It was the first edition of the *Oxford Book of Spanish Verse*, compiled by J. B.'s predecessor, with all J. B.'s carefully inscribed annotations for the second edition. I was green with envy.

My host went on to remark, 'One of intriguing things is a note on separate paper and in another hand, unsigned but obviously from some learned classical scholar.' He showed me the note, which made a rather pretentious comparison between a verse of Juvenal's and some lines of a mediaeval Spanish poet. It was a moment before I realised, with shock, that the note was from me, and not from some learned don. I remembered that J. B. was wont to begin sentences with 'you as a classical scholar will know that ... ' It was a wild exaggeration, even in those days, but I was ashamed that I no longer understood the Latin verses I had priggishly penned three decades earlier. The fact that J. B. had used my note made me want the book all the more. My host gave me a photocopy of the note, but it was not the same ...

Acquiring my degree did not solve the problem of what to do next. One possibility was to study for a doctorate but, much as I loved Cambridge, I felt I owed it to my parents to start earning right away. For a woman with an arts degree, job opportunities were not enticing. Many of my peers, including Mary, learned to type and became overqualified secretaries to male executives, often less able than themselves.

I was amazingly lucky. Just before I was due to go down, my director of studies, Dr Mary Beare, called me in. The Professor of Spanish at Queen's University, Belfast, had asked her to find a lecturer to assist him. Would I be interested? Though inwardly nervous, I jumped at it. I was to work on a doctorate at the same time, a first rung of the academic ladder. Even for those days, when everything was topsy-turvy in the aftermath of war, it was an extraordinary opportunity for a new graduate without experience.

That summer I had my twenty-first birthday. There was no question of my parents giving a party – there was no money for such frills. Yet I had the most wonderful celebration anyone could wish for. My birth date coincided with the Ball of Brasenose

College, where my Oxford beau was completing his own under-graduate career. Clothes rationing being still severe, my dress was made from a surplus military parachute of white nylon, then a totally new fabric. The parachute was huge, and also provided undies for the female members of the family. The dress had a tight bodice and a full skirt, and was liberally adorned with ruffles and violet velvet ribbon (the only colour available). I thought it beautiful. I was also in love, and deliriously danced the summer night away. One of my partners was Lord Goddard, then Lord Chief Justice, who waltzed fast, if erratically, to the 'Eton boating song', carolling loudly the while 'We'll all swing together', a refrain with a decidedly sinister ring since hanging was still legal. Another was the Master of Brasenose. He seemed a jovial character, but soon after fell to his death from a train in mysterious circumstances.

As morning broke it was decided that I should punt everyone up the river, where we would cook sausages for breakfast on an island. Loath to spoil my parachute dress, I was kitted out in a borrowed male shirt and cricketing flannels. Everyone was sleepy, and there was only the faintest protest from the Oxford men that I punted from the Cambridge end. At 11 o'clock in the morning we were back in the High, drinking coffee, everyone except me still in evening dress.

The idyll did not last. Before the summer was over, my beau and I had broken up. I spent much of the Long Vac not with him but in the Cambridge University Library, desperately preparing lectures.

Queen's University, Belfast

Queen's was a salutary return to earth after Cambridge, a redbrick university, in a large, industrial city. We were only two in the Spanish Faculty, and the teaching load was heavy. Professor Llubera was a Catalan, who looked eerily like Dr Batista i Roca, the Cambridge lecturer, who was our outside examiner. Small rotund figures trotting round the quad together, with their black suits, black Homburgs and black moustaches, they looked like Twee-dledum and Tweedledee. Professor Llubera insisted on speaking English but, like his compatriot's, it was decidedly idiosyncratic.

This gave rise to numerous misunderstandings, until I managed to persuade him, tactfully, to address me in Spanish.

I earned the princely salary of £300 a year, paid quarterly in arrears, so I had to survive the first term virtually on air. Professor Llubera and his charming French wife had arranged accommodation for me in a genteel guest-house, which, in their kindly old-fashioned way, they considered eminently suitable for a young, single lady. The snag was that it cost six guineas a week – more than my salary. Instead the mother of a school-friend fixed me up with lodgings in a friend's family. But her friend had died, and her daughter now ran the household for her father and two adolescent brothers. The house was dark and gloomy, located in a dingy street. The family was constantly rowing, and my concentration when preparing lectures was shattered by loud arguments and fearsome oaths. I had never heard such language in my life. I became depressed and searched for somewhere pleasanter to live. This was some years before open violence broke out between Protestant and Catholic communities, but at every door on which I knocked, the first question was, 'What is your religion?' I was affronted at this intrusion into a private matter but soon realised that, if I wanted somewhere decent to live, I had to rediscover my christening and confirmation into the Church of England.

Eventually, Jean Sidebotham, a lecturer just appointed to the Geography Department, and I rented what was euphemistically called a 'flat' in a house owned by two elderly ladies. This consisted of a sitting-room, a share of a tiny kitchen and bathroom with a constantly rowing couple, and a bedroom on the floor below. There was only a large double bed so we placed a rolled eiderdown down the middle to give the semblance of two single beds. With some reason we christened it 'the Slum'. It became renowned for some lively parties but was not tolerable for long, and the following spring we moved to a basement flat in an eighteenth-century square. Our departure from 'the Slum' was dramatic. We meticulously cleaned everything, scrubbing floors on our hands and knees, but the old ladies demanded payment for more cleaning, which we refused. They retaliated by locking the front door and holding us hostage! It was a Saturday, and we were expected to lunch by our respective professors but, though we banged on the glass panels of the door and shouted, no one heard. It was not until two o'clock that a policeman appeared. He advised the ladies that they could not imprison us against our will and we were released. Our ordeal caused furore in the otherwise quiet backwater of Queen's University.

My confidence as a fledgling lecturer was not much bolstered when, on my first appearance, a cocky youth took me for a first-year student and pontificated about Ortega y Gasset, but his discomfiture was greater than mine when he discovered, from the back row of the elementary class, that I was the new lecturer! More disconcerting still was to find that I had a brilliant third-year student, Brian Tate, just returned from the army, who was several years older and probably knew more than I did about Spanish language and literature. His first-class degree at the end of the year gave me as much pleasure as my own. Later, I was even prouder to learn of his appointment to the Chair of Spanish at Nottingham University. A more troubling student was a religious fanatic, obsessed with the Spanish mystical poets. Convinced that I was bound for hell-fire he determined to convert me to Catholicism, plied me with books and tracts and could sometimes be seen standing in the street below 'the Slum', on a cold winter's night, gazing up at our windows.

I had a punishing schedule of 12 lectures a week, all of which had to be prepared from scratch. It proved impossible to write each lecture in full and, as my confidence grew, I resorted to brief guidelines. Before long I found I actually enjoyed lecturing, instead of being paralysed with nerves. To eke out my salary I gave private Spanish lessons. All this slowed progress on my doctoral thesis on the poetry of Juan Ramón Jiménez, further deterred by a sharp letter from the poet's wife, who did not want his work to be written about.

Two young women lecturers were rare in a still male-dominated university and Jean and I had a lively social life At times this led to awkward situations, as when the Dean of the Faculty of Science and one of his research graduates arrived on the doorstep simultaneously to take me out. Our contacts extended beyond the university. There were groups where poets declaimed their own poetry, and Saturday night ceilidhs spent dancing wild Irish jigs. Such events were attended by Catholic and Protestant alike and I was not conscious of tension, nor had I any inkling of the appalling civil strife that would break out later, though even then you would think twice before walking down the Falls Road at night if you were a Protestant, still less sing 'The sash my father wore' – the Orangemen's song about the Battle of the Boyne – at any hour.

A Catholic friend outside the university, a dairy bacteriologist doing similar work to my Aunt Christina's, was a tremendous asset because of his contacts over the border. Rationing was still in full swing in the UK but not in Eire. When we had a party he and an associate, a leery little man who worked in a garage, would drive down and buy all the food. On the way back the associate would drop off before the border, and carry the purchases along some hidden path, later rejoining the driver, who had meanwhile negotiated customs and border formalities. Much of our crockery, linen and utensils was obtained in this way. So were my 1947 Christmas presents, though the process was more complicated. In Dublin I bought shirts for my father and fur boots for my mother and mailed them to the postmistress in a border village. The go-between, who lived on the Ulster side, then invited the postmistress to dinner, the parcels were carried over, and posted to Belfast. The only financial charge involved was the cost of the dinner! It was a very Irish solution – they had a good night out, and I got my presents. The day before I sailed to Liverpool for the Christmas holiday I bought a huge turkey. I spent the night with this unlikely companion hanging in my cabin, and so all the way on the long train journey to Essex. Other passengers were distinctly unimpressed but I was given a heroine's welcome when I arrived home, loaded with goodies not seen for many a year.

Jean's thesis was on transhumance, and I sometimes accompanied her on field trips to remote places where this ancient tradition was still practised. Once we rented a primitive stone cottage in a rocky cove on the north coast, ten miles from Ballycastle. An ancient taxi dropped us on the cliffs above, where the driver swore upon all the gods of Ireland that he would come back on a certain day, at a certain time. An idyllic few days followed. The sea almost lapped the doorstep of the cottage. We bathed in its chilly waters, wandered over the hills looking for traces of transhumance, and ate huge high teas, Irish style – big fry-ups, with all those delicious breads and bannocks – by a roaring fire of driftwood collected on the shore. That was before the cholesterol ogre appeared. It was also before the sexual revolution. Two young men from Queen's accompanied us, but their most daring exploit was to appear outside our bedroom window at midnight, moaning and draped in sheets to scare us into believing the farmer's wife's tale that the cottage was haunted. At the appointed day and hour, we toiled back but no taxi appeared. The farmhouse had no telephone or car. There was no help for it but to walk, lugging our cases. The road was deserted and we trudged five or six miles before a farmer appeared and drove us into Ballycastle. We never did know what happened to our taxi. Perhaps he went on another day. Perhaps he is still waiting now ... It was another very Irish story.

My plan had been to return to Cambridge after three years at Queen's and embark on a full academic career but none of that happened. The Foreign Service had just been opened to women and I applied, though not very seriously as competition was fierce, only four or five candidates, male or female, making the grade. First there was a written exam, after which those who passed muster attended a 'country house weekend' at a mansion in Stoke d'Abernon, under strict observation from morning to night. The tests included governing an imaginary island, beset with problems; undertaking a complex diplomatic negotiation; chairing a committee; giving a serious lecture or a humorous talk; and undergoing psychological tests and individual interviews. It was even rumoured that one's table manners and general conversation were monitored, as well as one's ability to imbibe three Martinis before dinner and still remain coherent, such attributes still then considered essential for a successful diplomatic career. The final hurdle was an even more intimidating interview at the Civil Service Commission, when a dozen distinguished people fired catch questions, on any subject whatsoever.

No one was more surprised than I when I received a letter instructing me to report for work at the Foreign Office on 26 July 1948. I left Queen's University with genuine sadness. My 'academic career' had lasted barely one year but I had made many friends, and it had been a maturing experience.

5

The Foreign Office

When I timidly entered the Foreign Office on 26 July 1948 I was delighted to be assigned to the South American Department because of my knowledge of Spanish, then a rare commodity. My enchantment faded when I learned that it was Foreign Office policy *never* to send a woman diplomat to Latin America. The reasoning (if that is the correct word) was that a female diplomat would swiftly suffer 'a fate worse than death' at the hands of some passionate Latino, and become unreliable. I felt that the powers who decreed this policy would have done well to read an article that appeared in *Esquire* about that time, entitled 'Latins are Lousy Lovers'.

Our 'Third Room', where third and second secretaries sat, was Room 101, which looked directly down on to Downing Street and the Prime Minister's residence. There being only four or five women with diplomatic rank (albeit, as first entrants, at the lowest level) it was surprising that the South American Department boasted two. Caroline Petrie, a few years older than me, was efficient, pretty and glamorous, and I was overawed, but we nonetheless became good friends. The men in the department were welcoming, with the exception of one misanthrope, who thawed later. The head of department, Evelyn Shuckburgh, and the assistant head, Robin Cecil, both men of intellectual stature, as well as good-looking and charming – the epitome of one's idea of the perfect diplomat – could not have been kinder or more tolerant of my early gaffes.

Nonetheless, the Foreign Office was not an easy bastion for an inexperienced 22-year-old girl to penetrate. Women had not been allowed to darken its doors, even as secretaries, until 1917. The term 'sexual harassment' had not yet been coined, but I was never aware of being subjected to it. The negative reactions were subtler, more in the way of discrimination, another term not yet current. There was the salary to start with. Female third secretaries began at £360, their male counterparts higher, the argument being that they might have a wife to support, or would have to take girlfriends out at their expense (though our male colleagues invariably expected us to 'go Dutch'!) Women diplomats who married had to resign immediately. This was the fate of several of the first entrants and a factor that inexorably trimmed the ranks of women diplomats until the rule was relaxed over 20 years later.

In day-to-day relations, negative reactions ranged from openly hostile to (sometimes involuntarily) patronising. I came back almost in tears one day from a glacial encounter with a senior officer dealing with the Middle East. More amusing was Caroline's experience when she took a draft for clearance to the Vice-Marshal of the Diplomatic Corps, Marcus Cheke who, quill pen poised to pounce and finding no error, enquired with unintentional irony, 'Did *you* do this?' and when she modestly admitted authorship, insisted, in clear disbelief, 'What, *all* of it?'

Such incidents apart, I found the Foreign Office a stimulating place, for the intellectual calibre was very high, though under-stated. It was also awesome from a social point of view. Although diplomats were no longer expected to have a private income, the majority were not only Oxbridge, but from privileged families and public school backgrounds. To be female *and* of working-class and grammar-school origins was a double and dubious distinction, even though a Labour government was in power, and the Foreign Secretary was Ernest Bevin, a man of impeccable trade union and working-class background. In practice, it was assumed that because you were there, you were automatically 'one of us'.

The old standards were becoming more difficult to sustain, however, even for those who had the means. I was once invited by a senior colleague to spend a weekend with him and his wife, at their country manor. 'Bring something loose' he admonished me. Baffled, and too shy to enquire further, I plumped for a pair of slacks, which indeed came in handy, as I spent the Saturday digging their vegetable garden. On Sunday evening, our host again uttered this mystifying phrase. 'Let's change into something loose!' This time I had no option but to ask my hostess for clarification. 'Oh, any long skirt will do,' she said airily. I had packed all sorts of things, but a long skirt was not among them. The only possibility was a flowered dressing-gown I had just made, but it was open from the waist down. With difficulty I sewed myself into it. My host turned up resplendent in monkey-jacket and cummerbund, which did not look loose at all, the other guest in dinner jacket and black tie. In the face of such splendour the supper was an anticlimax; the Italian domestics had the evening off, and had left sardines and salad. Afterwards, the gramophone came into action and we were pressed into Scottish dances ... When I recounted this story at home, 'Wear something loose' became a favourite family joke.

My salary was higher than in Belfast, but the difference was more than swallowed up by London's higher cost of living. I lived in a bed-sitter in Hampstead; and at weekends went home to my parents, and our bathroomless house with its outside lavatory.

The Foreign Office was still the home of long-cherished tradition. Our files were paper folders bound together by the red tape (in actual fact, pink) inherited from the Mogul Empire. Every night these dog-eared bundles had to be stowed away in steel cupboards, and the last to leave put the keys in the safe. Security rounds were made later, and woe betide the person who forgot to lock the safe, or left a file out. Frock-coated messengers, elderly and avuncular, carried red leather boxes of files from one department to another while urgent messages shot around the building by a tube system, like those in old-fashioned drapery stores. At set intervals a third secretary carried current files from the Third Room to the assistant, and then to the head of department, and performed the same service in reverse. No one else was allowed to do this, on security grounds. It is hard to imagine anything more anachronistic, but this was before the security shock of 1951, and well before the technological revolution.

Even more anachronistic was the handbook on diplomatic etiquette that appeared about this time. Its author was Marcus

Cheke, the Vice-Marshal of the Diplomatic Corps (he of the quill pen). The Foreign Office had its share of eccentrics, but Marcus Cheke was one of the most egregious. Tall, and of almost military bearing, he would stride through the corridors, flourishing a cigarette in a long holder, and declaiming. 'This way, Excellency', as some hapless foreign dignitary scampered breathlessly along behind, on his way to an audience with the Foreign Secretary. His book was a classic of the genre, already out of date even in the late 1940s. Among other useful hints it gave precise instructions as to what cabbalistic letters you should inscribe on your visiting cards, which corner you should turn down, and when you should deliver one personally; what you should say at funerals; and what you should *not* say at dinnerparties (*never* mention birth control). Despite the Vice-Marshal's encounter with Caroline, the book made no allowance for the existence of women diplomats, and that dress and other protocol would require modification. Copies circulated like wildfire and it was pronounced a comic masterpiece. Someone at a Washington cocktail party left a copy in the ladies' cloakroom, where it was snapped up by a gossip columnist and given wide publicity, spiced with derisive asides.

A few days later Bevin's private secretaries found their master in a towering rage. He shut himself in his office, and shouted at anyone who tried to enter. At last a junior secretary – a woman – managed to penetrate the sanctum. Ernie, as he was affectionately known, glowering balefully, pointed a stubby finger at the diplomatic manual and exclaimed, 'Either 'ee or I must go.' Neither of them went, but the manual was quietly dropped.

There was an amusing sequel. During one of the periodic outbreaks of tension with Guatemala, which claimed sovereignty over what was then British Honduras. HMS *Sheffield* was despatched to cruise off the Guatemala coast (the days of sending Her Majesty's warships to forefend threats to the remnants of the British Empire were not yet over). The Guatemalan Ambassador was General Ydígoras Fuentes, a fiery character, renowned for pugnacious reactions in inverse proportion to his diminutive stature. He, too, was an unpredictable eccentric. Our paragon of diplomatic etiquette and discretion, Marcus Cheke, chatting to another diplomat at a reception, delivered himself, in loud and mordant terms, of an exceedingly uncomplimentary opinion about Guatemala and Guatemalans in general, and General Ydígoras in particular. He had not noticed the tiny figure of the General bobbing up and down in indignation behind him but was not long left in ignorance. Eyes flashing, the doughty Ambassador leapt in front of the Vice-Marshal of the Diplomatic Corps and challenged him to a duel! The Vice-Marshal was for once at a loss for words. The memorandum in which he tried to explain the incident ended, rather lamely: 'I then proceeded to the buffet ...' We third secretaries had a field day. Since Marcus Cheke had been challenged it was his right, we reckoned, to choose the weapon. We knew that he and his wife practised archery and a series of anonymous caricatures made the rounds, depicting this ill-matched pair (the Ambassador barely came up to the Vice-Marshal's top waistcoat button), poised with bows stretched and arrows at the ready. To our disappointment, the matter was settled by a written apology by the Vice-Marshal.

General Ydígoras went on to greater, and sometimes bizarre things, such as instigating the 'shrimp war' between Guatemala and Mexico. Some years later, in Bogotá, I found the good General again in ambassadorial functions. We became friends and he seemed to bear me no grudge for having been the author of the many protest notes lodged with him in London about British Honduras. Shortly afterwards he became President of Guatemala, an office which he exercised with characteristic idiosyncrasy. Later still, in the 1970s, when on an official mission to Guatemala, I visited him, an old man in retirement, and we recalled the occasion on which he had challenged Marcus Cheke.

Ernest Bevin, the other man who had – figuratively – crossed swords with the Vice-Marshal, was a big man, in every sense of the word, and remained disarmingly true to his working-class origins. Self-educated, his life's work had been as a trade union leader until, with the coming of the war and a national coalition government, he had been Winston Churchill's inspired choice as Minister of Labour. Many eyebrows had been raised when Clement Attlee gave him the Foreign Office, but he proved a good, if unconventional, Foreign Secretary.

I had not been long in the Foreign Office when, because I spoke Spanish, I was invited to a dinner given by the Foreign Secretary and Mrs Bevin in honour of Perón's Foreign Minister. This posed a sartorial problem. My white 'parachute' would hardly do. Evening-dresses were still scarce and very expensive even if you had the clothing coupons. I kept up appearances by making most of my clothes, but there was no time to run up a long dress. I bought a pink one, with silver stripes, that cost one month's salary. Most touchingly, my old headmistress, Miss Cadbury, when she heard about this, sent me a cheque for £20, an extraordinarily generous gesture, all the more remarkable given her spartan Quaker disdain for social frivolities.

On the appointed evening I changed in the resident clerk's flat at the top of the Foreign Office, and presented myself at Carlton House Terrace. I was a-titter with nerves as I ascended the staircase, but was immediately put at my ease by Mrs Bevin, a tiny woman, who exuded perfect naturalness as if she had been greeting one to tea in a terrace house in Bristol. There had been concern about her husband's health, and she disarmed me by linking her arm through mine and saying, confidingly, 'I've been told I must get him to stay in bed, but how on earth do you think I can?' – this, gesticulating at the Secretary of State's imposing bulk.

Relaxed, I enjoyed my first official banquet, despite an Argentinian naval officer's determined attempts to play footsie with me under the table. It ended too late to go back to Hampstead and Evelyn Shuckburgh and his wife, Nancy, took me back to their house. In the morning Nancy lent me some clothes – except shoes, which did not fit – so I turned up at the office incongruously shod in silver sandals.

Affectionate stories abounded about Ernest Bevin's unorthodox approach to affairs of state. One recounted a meeting of the Allied powers where a French delegate was holding forth at interminable length. Ernie, receiving this cascade of words at second-hand through an interpreter, was visibly bored. When the orator imprudently paused for breath, he leaned his vast torso across the table and, smiling engagingly at the speaker, entreated him in wheedling tones, 'Feenee?' Punctured, the poor man sat down and no more was heard from him.

The resident clerks had a fund of anecdotes about night-time conversations with the Foreign Secretary. One Sunday evening he rang up in some distress, 'Flo (Mrs Bevin) and me's just got back 'ere and the 'eatings off. Can you get someone to fix it!' On another occasion they were foxed by a further sortie into idiosyncratic French. 'We're going to 'ave a lovely dinner tonight,' confided the Secretary of State. 'Lobster and newts.' Aghast at this unusual culinary combination the clerk on duty, after some delicate probing, ascertained that 'newts' were in fact 'Nuits St Georges'.

The Cold War was just getting into its stride and my responsibilities, in addition to a few countries, included some related subjects: anticolonialism and disputed territories; communist movements in Latin America; arms sales to Latin America (I am ashamed to say); and the Antarctic. These last two subjects involved interesting outside activities. Every year I accompanied South American military officials to the Farnborough Air Show. They were as mystified by the presence of a woman as I was by the technical properties of the aircraft in which I was supposed to be interesting them (fortunately someone from the Ministry of Civil Aviation was always in attendance). For the Antarctic the Foreign Office had a scientific adviser, Dr Brian Roberts, from the Scott Polar Research Institute in Cambridge. He would breeze in, bringing almost visible flurries of snow and ice with him. I was fascinated by Antarctica and longed to go there. Every autumn I saw off the *John Biscoe*, the research ship of the Falkland Islands Dependencies Survey, from the London docks, but it was unheard of for a woman to join such an expedition. Moreover, I had no scientific contribution to offer, although I was a dab hand at drafting the protest notes shoved under the doors of the huts of the Argentinian and Chilean bases, in territory to which Britain laid claim (I was chagrined to learn that, this formality over, the three rivals would join in a friendly game of football).

One day I was appointed liaison officer to a Mexican trade mission. This sent me into a panic as, although I was trying to fill the lacunae in my economic knowledge, I knew next to nothing about trade. My opposite number in the Mexican Embassy came to discuss the arrangements. His name was Fernando Cuén Barragán and, like my erstwhile admirer in Cambridge, he was very Mexican. I did not know whether to be relieved or appalled to find that he was much more interested in persuading me to go out to dinner than debating trade relations. I no longer recall whether these improved as a result of the mission but my dancing certainly did. Fernando disabused me of my illusion that I danced well and gave me a vigorous training in Latin American rhythms. When I visited Mexico in 1956, he showed me the sights, but then I did not see him again until sent to help with the Mexican earthquake in 1985. Then I found a portly gentleman, careworn by responsibility for a large family, in contrast to the carefree bachelor I had known.

I had an active social life for there was no lack of eligible men. I was also attending Russian and Italian classes, and Evelyn Shuckburgh persuaded me to join the Foreign Office Dramatic Club. We performed *Dial M for Murder*. I was also involved in Spanish drama, through the Instituto Español. One of the exiles, Francisco Villegas, a judge under the republic, formed a group to perform classic Spanish plays. We had an ambitious repertoire: I took the female lead in a play by the Quinteros brothers; a dramatised version of Pérez Galdos's novel *Marianela*; and Lorca's *La Casa de Bernarda Alba*. My leading man was usually Mervyn Brown, also of the Foreign Office, and later a distinguished ambassador, and we spent a lot of time gazing lovingly into one another's eyes. Acting with Francisco was always a fraught experience, as he never learned his lines and ad-libbed creatively. This was fine for a native Spanish speaker but hard for me. Moreover, I had somehow to guide the dialogue back on track.

We played to packed houses, in a small theatre in north London, and later in the City Literary Institute, when the Instituto Español closed down, the Franco Government having at last succeeded in cutting off its funds. Most of the audience were nostalgic Spanish exiles, though what they made of our hybrid accents – there were actors from other European countries – I can't imagine. Our last production received a rave review in a Spanish publication produced by the Franco Government. Francisco did not know whether to be gratified or appalled. 'But I am condemned to death by them,' he wailed (a distinction of which he was perversely proud). The irony was that the authors of the piece no longer realised that he was a hunted man and an implacable enemy of the Franco régime. Our success led Francisco to dream, in 1952, of taking wandering troupes through England, in imitation of de Falla's and Lorcas's *Misiones Pedagógicas* in the 1920's. He never quite forgave me for not being able to take part because I went abroad.

The 1951 Spy Scandal

Evelyn Shuckburgh's successor, Stanley Fordham, became ill and for a while Robin Cecil acted as head of department. One day, in late 1950, he told me we were to have a new head of department. Our new boss had had a nervous breakdown he warned, and his marriage had collapsed. We would all have to be sensitive to his state of mind.

Our new boss was none other than Donald Maclean. As we all learned only much later, in May 1950 he had had to leave his post as counsellor at the British Embassy in Cairo, after a series of drunken incidents. In one of these, at a party on a felucca on the Nile, he had tussled with a colleague, Lees Mayall, who ended up with a broken leg, while in another, he had smashed up the flat of two girls working for the US Embassy. A 'nervous breakdown' was diagnosed, and he was sent home for treatment. The more salacious aspects of the affair were hushed up. Still, they were known to George (later Sir George) Middleton, then Head of Personnel Department, and it was extraordinary that Maclean should nonetheless have been appointed Head of the American Department (the South American Department that I originally joined had been merged with North American Department). True, the American Department did not play such an important role in formulating Foreign Office policy as was later made out, but its head had access to important telegrams and Cabinet papers.

Donald took up his post on 1 November 1950. He appeared serene, unfussed and calmly in control of himself and the situation. After a while, news seeped through to the Third Room that his American wife, Melinda, was expecting another child. The marriage, it seemed, had been patched up, another sign that made me conclude, as a junior onlooker, that things were back on an even keel.

But then, I never saw Donald in a social context. As Robin Cecil noted in his book about Donald, *A Divided Life*, 'He never asked any of us out for a meal or even a drink, and consciously evaded any attempts to establish closer relationships.' I perhaps had more personal contact with him than others. Donald and Melinda lived in Sevenoaks, while I now shared a flat outside Croydon, with my Aunt Christina. Donald and I sometimes met on the train and walked together from Victoria Station to the Foreign Office. He never said anything that gave any hint of the personal and ideological turmoil that he must have been undergoing.

The same was true of the conversation at the department's afternoon tea parties, a hallowed Foreign Office tradition, held at four o'clock in the Third Room. We had moved from our privileged position overlooking No. 10 to the old India Office. The Third Room was a cavernous barn, with long draughty windows and ceilings so high they could comfortably have accommodated another storey; a pseudo-minstrel's gallery ran round it from which my former Oxford beau (who, embarrassingly, had joined the Foreign Service and been assigned to the same department) entertained us with violin solos. It had a meagre coal fire at one end to which – an example of positive sexual discrimination – I was allowed to sit nearest.

The tea party was an occasion to discuss not only current issues affecting the department but also wider political topics, at a time when the Cold War was deepening the rift between East and West, and the Korean War had just started. I can still, in my mind's eye, see Donald standing with his back to our cheerless fire, a tall imposing figure, with a shock of hair swept back from an unusually broad brow. I supported the Labour Party, and expressed my views forcibly, especially on issues of social justice. Had I been asked to define Donald's politics, I would have deduced that he was a 'pale pink' Liberal, in keeping with the strong Liberal tradition of his family, and that I was more to the left than he.

One particular event forged a strong bond of allegiance to my boss. I was inordinately proud of the fact that my first Cabinet paper – on Antarctica – had survived, unscathed, the normally unforgiving scrutiny of both Robin and Donald. Thus it was my text that would be seen by the Cabinet which (with a naivety that could not exist at any age in the present era of political disenchantment) I believed to be composed of great and good men, of undeniable intellectual superiority. I suffered a rude awakening when one day I arrived early to find my telephone ringing imperiously. The equally imperious voice at the other end was that of Sir Andrew ('Paddy') Noble, the Assistant Under-Secretary for Latin America, and Donald's boss. Was I, he enquired, the author of the Cabinet paper on Antarctica? Indeed I was, I replied with ill-concealed and, as it turned out, ill-placed pride. Summoned to his office, I bounded up the stairs, to be greeted by a very cold shower. Sir Andrew was well known as a crotchety man who did not mince his words. That day I was put through the meat grinder. The paper was *appalling*, he said, the arguments badly ordered, the syntax faulty and, above all, the sentences too long. Pointing at one of the offending *longueurs*, his voice rising to a crescendo, he almost shouted 'This one should end here ... full BLOODY STOP ... !' With this he banged one fist on the table and with the other made a large hole in the paper with his avenging pen. I stood speechless, tears beginning to flow and, above all, shocked; 'bloody' was not a word in my vocabulary, regarded in my family as swearing of the gravest kind. Deflated, I returned to the department, to find that Donald and Robin wanted to see me on some other matter. I blurted out what had happened to the two of them, tears again streaming. Donald, white with anger, picked up the telephone, and proceeded to give his superior a severe dressing-down. 'If you have fault to find with that Cabinet paper, you should call me, and not pick on one of my junior staff. I cleared that draft and as head of department I take full responsibility.'

Donald's spirited defence won him my unswerving devotion. He had behaved exactly as I thought a boss should. And 'my' paper went to those august gentlemen in the Cabinet with very few amendments.

This incident made me feel more at ease with Donald, and we had little chats when I made the 'paper round'. In early 1951, probably February or March, I had a vivid dream, in which Donald had disappeared. Thus far my dream was prophetic, though I did not discover that until a few months later. The rest was absurd: Donald's wife, (whom I never met) took over the department, and objected to my wearing lipstick! I gaily recounted this dream to Donald, so caught up in the novelty of my tale that I spared no attention to his reaction. Later I could only imagine his feelings. By then, as afterwards transpired, he knew that the trail in search of a Russian agent code-named 'Homer', who had leaked top-secret information from Washington (where Donald had served in the British Embassy several years before) was leading dangerously close to him. He was also back on his binges, causing havoc at various clubs, and frequently missing the last train home. How on earth must he have interpreted my remarks? As a threat? – in which case, was I a member of MI6, placed under cover in his Department? As a warning? – in which case, was I engaged in the same murky business as himself? The imagination boggles. As it was he laughed and said, 'Melinda is not like that. She would never mind your wearing lipstick.'

The dénouement, on Friday 25 May 1951, was another occasion for a curious exchange. The Foreign Office was gradually moving towards a five-day week. Instead of everyone being required to work on Saturday mornings, as had been the case when I joined the office, one senior and one junior officer came in, on a rota basis. Robin Cecil being on leave abroad, that Saturday duty, (26 May) fell to Donald and myself. At 6 o'clock on the Friday afternoon, I took the last round of papers to Donald. His demeanour seemed normal as he casually said, 'Can you manage on your own tomorrow? I can't come in. Something has cropped up.' Flattered by his confidence I replied with alacrity that I could, adding somewhat flippantly that no revolutions loomed in Latin America. The revolution, ironically, was to be much nearer home. That was to be the last time I ever saw Donald Maclean.

What had 'cropped up' was a tip-off, through Guy Burgess, a fellow spy, that Donald's perfidy had been discovered and interrogation by British security was imminent. The two of them slipped over the Channel and made their way across Europe to Moscow. Donald narrowly escaped the net that was closing in on him; that same Friday, 25 May, Herbert Morrison (who had succeeded Bevin as Foreign Secretary) had decided he should be taken in for questioning by MI5 on the following Monday. Burgess was not in the same immediate danger, though he too had been recruited as a Soviet spy at Cambridge in the 1930s. He had just been sent back to London in disgrace, after riotous behaviour in Washington. I had had contact with him, prior to his Washington posting, in the Far Eastern Department, just across the corridor, or lunching at a Whitehall pub that we all frequented, but did not know him well, and had no desire to. He was a disagreeable character. With his early good looks consumed by fast living, he presented an unkempt and often unclean appearance – his fingernails were always black with dirt. His conversation was no less grimy, laced with obscene jokes and profane language.

We did not attach too much importance to Donald's non-appearance on Monday 28 May since Melinda was expecting her baby about then. When Tuesday merged into Wednesday we began to wonder. I kept popping into Donald's office to see if he had turned up. I examined his in- and out-trays, which contained exactly the kind of papers you would expect when someone has left on a Friday evening with the confident expectation of returning; not too much (some business had been dispatched) but not too little either.

Then, on Wednesday 30 May, I found Donald's office swarming with men ransacking every cupboard and drawer under the watchful eye of the head of security. I returned hotfoot to the Third Room with this ominous news, but we still did not rumble the truth. If this seems naive, it must be remembered that at that time it was totally unthinkable that a member of Her Majesty's Foreign Service would ever betray his country, much less defect to another. The Maclean and Burgess episode marked a watershed which was to destroy that happy conception for ever, but then it was still unchallenged. After my discovery we not only said, jokingly, 'Donald is having a baby' but now added 'Donald has done a Pontecorvo' (a scientist who had defected to the Soviet Union) but we did not take it seriously. We had an extraordinary ten days. I remember representing the department at meetings all over Whitehall at levels higher than I had ever experienced before.

The most incomprehensible aspect was that no one in authority spoke to us about the abrupt disappearance of our boss, or even asked us to be discreet. Everything was supposed to go on normally in circumstances clearly far from normal. Even my chums among the resident clerks could throw no light, except to confirm that something distinctly rum was afoot. Privately I wondered whether Donald had had another nervous breakdown, though his calm demeanour on our last encounter made this unlikely.

The revelation, when it came, was devastating. Ten days after Donald's disappearance one of our number in the Third Room came back from lunch with an evening newspaper, blazoning, in huge headlines, the news that Burgess and Maclean had fled. Incredulously we realised that our Pontecorvo joke had been all too near the mark. Even more incredibly none of us was ever questioned. In my case, as the person who last saw Donald before he left the Foreign Office and England for ever, the omission seemed even more inexplicable. My name, however, had registered with the Americans, and the 'Maclean connection' came back to haunt me in 1956.

The only immediate impact was on a holiday I was about to take in Spain, travelling haphazardly by third-class train and bicycle and staying in *pensiones*. Robin Cecil, now acting head of department, told me that I must cancel this holiday, since it was rumoured that the fugitives were in Andorra and it was unthinkable that another member of the department should wander around that same general area, without fixed address or itinerary. In the end, a compromise was reached: I was to check in at the embassy in Madrid, and every consulate along the way. This I meticulously did, though in many places found our representatives surprised by my call. Perhaps things were not as haphazard as they seemed, for I later learned that I had been checked across the Spanish frontier.

Not until five years later, in 1956, did the Soviet Union reveal that Maclean and Burgess were in Moscow. Meanwhile, there had been intense press speculation, rekindled in September 1953 when Melinda disappeared to Moscow with her three children. Prima facie, her decision to join her husband was hard to understand, given the constantly troubled state of their marriage, culminating in his abandonment of her just before the birth of their third child. Moreover, she was probably unaware of her husband's spying activities until after his defection. But she had been left alone to bring up three children, with scant financial support (the Foreign Office had at least been efficient in promptly stopping Donald's pay) and was relentlessly hounded by the press. The deciding factor seems to have been messages that Donald, banished for the first two years to Kuibyshev, a grim town, 500 miles from Moscow, had tried to commit suicide. Their life afterwards was not much happier. Donald's drinking bouts continued and Melinda left him for Kim Philby ('the Third Man'). In 1979 she returned to the USA and their three children also returned to the West. Donald was given privileged status in the Soviet Union but died a lonely death in March 1983.

I remained obsessed for years as to *why* Donald had betrayed his country. I was not surprised about Burgess, whom I could well believe capable of any perfidy. Donald was different. I had recognised him to be a man of principle and an idealist. One could argue that it was precisely because of that that he remained fiercely loyal to the Marxist ideal he had embraced as an undergraduate at Cambridge. But he was a highly intelligent man, an able diplomat and a trained political observer. It could not have escaped his notice that, long before he left in 1951, the Soviet Union had given blatant indications that it was far from being the fair society for which Donald yearned. When he got there he wrote, in a private letter quoted by Robin Cecil in *A Divided Life*, about 'the nightmare of Stalin's and Beria's persecutions' and associated himself with those working for reform, though he did not live to see the Gorbachev era dawn.

Was it the case that, once ensnared by the NKVD, he was trapped for ever? I longed to put these questions to Donald, and an opportunity presented itself in September 1979, when, as Assistant Secretary General of the United Nations, I paid an official visit to Moscow. It was not to be. My Soviet hosts were outwardly all courtesy, but my programme was rigidly controlled. I was not even allowed to see the Russian who had been my deputy in Ethiopia. The word 'No' was never uttered, but a 101 excuses were produced at every turn. When I went later in more propitious circumstances Donald was dead.

Engaged to be Married

The sparse incidence of females meant that there were plenty of eligible suitors but, for a female, diplomat marriage meant the irrevocable renunciation of her chosen career. Once you resigned from the Foreign Service, which you had entered with such difficulty, there was no going back. My colleague, Caroline Petrie, became engaged and I saw her off to Uruguay with her assembled trousseau, but in Montevideo she had second thoughts, and after anguished reflection decided to call it off. Fortunately she was reinstated.

In September 1949 I also became engaged at long distance. My fiancé was Robin (later Sir Robin) Mackworth-Young, who was serving on Malcolm Macdonald's staff in Singapore. Our courtship had been initially whirlwind, and then conducted more sedately through letters. Robin had previously worked in Far Eastern Department, which contained the safe where I nightly deposited our department's keys. One day he asked me out to a meal, and almost immediately afterwards to spend a weekend at his parents' lovely manor house in the Cotswolds. It was an idyllic spring weekend. We went for long walks and Robin, a highly accomplished pianist, played Bach to me. His parents were very kind, but it was an alarming experience: this was a country house in the traditional mould, with a butler and a retinue of servants and croquet on the lawn. Robin's father had been prominent in the Indian Civil Service, his maternal grandfather a colonial governor. His younger brother was engaged to the daughter of a Scottish earl.

Robin was to leave for Singapore in three weeks. A day after our return he walked me round St James's Park at breakneck speed and asked me to marry him. Robin wished the wedding to take place immediately, so that we could leave for Singapore together (the Foreign Office would not pay my fare unless we were well and truly wed beforehand). I said I could not make up my mind so quickly. I saw Robin off at Northolt in a chilly, misty April dawn. There were six months of correspondence, and then our engagement was announced in *The Times* on 6 September 1949. Robin planned a wedding in Singapore Cathedral, but I had no savings with which to pay my fare, much less buy a trousseau. There were also problems at home. My mother, who had successfully established herself as a civil servant, fell seriously ill, and underwent major ear surgery. My father had at last moved from the small printing business where he had worked ever since he was 14, to another printers in Chelmsford but after a year that business went bust. At 56 he found himself out of work. After some months he became a printer's reader with the Sun Press in Watford. This was a blessing in disguise for it involved work more suited to his intellectual capacities, and for the last 12 years of his working life he enjoyed greater job satisfaction – his great pride the production of *Country Life*. At that point, however, he was in lodgings in Watford, coming home only at weekends. My mother could not be left alone and so I moved back to Writtle. That meant four hours' travel a day. There was no way in which I could leave for Singapore.

Meanwhile, Robin had fallen ill and was declared unfit for further service in the tropics. There had been talk of my flying out to bring him back, as he was still convalescent, but that did not materialise. Had that happened, things might have turned out differently. As it was we met in unpropitious circumstances on Marseilles docks, where his boat berthed at an unconscionably early hour on a miserably cold, wet morning in November 1950.

Within a few hours the engagement was at an end. We nonetheless continued the original plan of driving up through France. It was a surprisingly enjoyable journey. We drove along the Côte d'Azur, and to Grasse. We drank Châteauneuf du Pape in Avignon, and traversed the Alps in a snowstorm, to Grenoble, and thence to Paris. We flew to London, and there broke the news to our respective parents. I was touched that Robin's mother seemed genuinely upset. I could not have been the ideal wife she wished for her eldest son, but she was always exceedingly kind. I had been invited several times to Robin's home, including one traumatic Christmas when the butler died of a heart attack on Christmas Eve and, on a happier occasion, when Robin's youngest sister had her coming-out dance. Mrs Mackworth-Young had been equally insistent that I must be presented at court (a prospect that alarmed me greatly) and had even showed me the tiara that I would wear. She and my mother had met for lunch at the Café Royal, and got on unexpectedly well. But I had always been worried that I might be torn between two families with diametrically contrasting backgrounds.

Robin and I remained good friends, though we seldom met. He made a happy marriage, and became the Queen's Librarian at Windsor Castle, where I once visited him and his wife for a Garter Ceremony. On 5 May 1952 I too was married, to another member of the Foreign Service, about to be posted to the British Legation in Manila.

6

Land of the Morning

The Voyage

The wedding passed off in a haze. Besides our families there were Foreign Office colleagues, one of whom was best man, and I distinctly recollect a white rabbit and a sartorially unexceptionable cat, black with a white bib-front, among the guests. When the car to take us away failed to turn up, another colleague sprang to the rescue with his open Alvis, in which we zoomed off with such élan that my going-away hat all but blew off in the path of an oncoming bus.

We flew to Paris next day. On that warm May evening she flaunted all her charms, and we savoured them, knowing it would be long before we came again: tree-lined boulevards, street cafés under bright awnings, unmistakably Gallic klaxons, and that unforgettable Paris smell compounded of garlic, Gauloises, coffee, croissants and a good deal of 'je ne sais quoi'.

Our first-class sleepers were a wonderful contrast to our travel to Spain the previous summer. Then we had spent the night huddled in a third-class corridor, our only comforts a bottle of vin ordinaire and paper pillows that grew as grimy and dispirited as ourselves. We were wedged among several soldiers, a drunk butcher, two or three gaunt old men, and a couple of florid peasant women with baskets of vegetables, eggs and live poultry, including an over-sanguine cockerel, which at frequent intervals vicariously announced the dawn and very nearly failed to live to see it. Every so often an enormously fat man shot out of the nearest compartment, flailed his arms wildly, and cried 'Il faut absolument débarasser la toilette!', although any sensible person could see we were all so inextricably intertwined that, with the best will in the world, it was impossible to get through. When the crush thinned at Carcassonne, a youth was discovered fast asleep in the lavatory. His cries had gone unheard and his efforts to open the door had been thwarted by the mass of bodies shoring it up.

This time we slept in comfort until morning found us in northern Italy, among orchards adrift with spring blossom. In Genoa we wandered sun-soaked streets, talking to stray cats and drinking a lot of red Martini before we boarded our Dutch cargo boat. Of the twelve passengers eight were Roman Catholic priests. On our second night at sea we passed through the Straits of Messina, garlanded in glittering lights, and went up on deck to pay a sentimental farewell to Europe. We were to be away two years, which seemed an eternity. I was haunted by the last sight of my father, looking frail, and wondered if I would see him again. Then the young German priest said, quietly, 'That is the last time I shall see Europe.' Our own qualms dwindled into insignificance.

For the next six weeks we were suspended between two worlds. There is something hallucinatory about the rhythmic rocking of a ship that makes it easy to spend hours in a trance, watching the rise and fall of the sea and the flicker of its reflection on the bulkhead. And there was a fascination about living in close contact with people we would never meet again who acquired the absorbing near-reality of characters from a novel or play.

The voyage was a happy time with a myriad new experiences crowding in on us. In Port Said, first seen at dawn, shimmering in opalescent haze on the horizon, the foredeck was transformed into a miniature Eastern bazaar, and we tried our hands at bartering with clamorous Arab vendors hawking a galaxy of goods. At midnight we moved off into the canal. A streetlight cast ambiguous light on a circle of pavement and stippled the dark water; a dhow paddled quietly past; and the breeze wafted to us an eery wisp of singing, like a shiver through the air. Later the moon rose over the desert, silhouetting a solitary clump of palm trees against the sand. Next day Ismailia was a distant, luminous mirage, glimpsed from the Bitter Lakes. At sunset we lay off Suez, lazily golden in the fading light.

In the Red Sea the ship churned through molten blue glass, past barren islands of burning rock, occasional desolate lighthouses staring white in the pitiless sun-glare. No whisper of breeze tempered the impossible heat or rippled the syrupy surface of the sea. The edge of the sky was rimmed with an angry orange haze, like the reflection of a vast furnace. We were glad to get up at dawn and see the blue rocks of Aden against an aquamarine sky, even at that early hour faintly veiled in heat haze. Hardly had we anchored than the familiar flurry of small boats closed in on us, and the shouted bargaining and banter began over the ship's side.

A chance encounter with a retired English colonel, engaged in locust control, led to an invitation to drive round the town in his Land-Rover. I have a jumbled recollection of the Arab quarter: filthy narrow streets lined with tumbledown wooden stalls, pulsating with humanity like an overripe cheese. A few aimless camels picked their way fastidiously between the beggars, the would-be guides and fortune-tellers, and the vast, obscene hulk of flesh, topped by a fez, of a sufferer from elephantiasis. All the brightest colours of the spectrum were there, and over it all hung a composite smell of human excrement and exotic spices.

Then there were doldrum days in the Indian Ocean while seas rolled endlessly past, and huge cloud castles tumbled across the horizon. Our first distant sight of land for many days was Sumatra, looking like a toy island, with its miniature coves, and rocky islets, tiny huts clustered together, and an occasional plume of smoke spiralling up from palm groves and green hills.

A bevy of outrigger canoes nosed us into Singapore Harbour, like schooner fish round a whale. There was much cargo to be unloaded, and for several days the winches creaked and groaned over the holds. Having little spare cash we explored the town on foot, trudging through the poorer quarters without meeting another European: crowded streets strung with washing like welcoming banners, but the scrutiny to which we were subjected by the jostling crowds, and the penetrating glances from eyes half-glimpsed in dark doorways, seemed far from welcoming. Well-worn clichés about East and West suddenly became troublingly real. The essential otherness of the East was everywhere about us: in the Chinese hieroglyphics scrawled over the grimy arcades; in the foetid staircases and the smells of cooking and spices and other more elemental things that permeated them. At night people slept in the streets, on a bedstead if they were fortunate or curled up on the pavement.

In contrast the wide squares and imposing buildings in the centre of the city seemed unreal; tea in the famed Raffles Hotel, still a bastion of colonial Empire, almost an anticlimax. As the dark came plummeting down, we wandered along the seawall into another world again, drawn by the glow-worm light of a myriad charcoal braziers into a maze of raggle-taggle stalls, selling pungent food of every description. On our return voyage, after over two years in the East, the otherness of Singapore no longer overwhelmed me. Now I mourn its passing, for visiting since I found that all that exotic exuberance that had so affected me has been tamed into a prosperous, disciplined and ultra-modern city that somehow lacks a soul.

For three days we sailed over a halcyon China Sea. Each night the moon scythed a broad swathe of light across the water, and the ship's wake was starred with phosphorescence. Then, one morning early, we found the blue peaks of Hong Kong Island looking in at our porthole, and the sun rising over the mysterious mainland of China proper. It was a case of love at first sight, from the moment when the pilot – a dapper little Chinese, clad in white ducks – scrambled up a madly swinging rope ladder, shoved up by several generations of his family, who were precariously bobbing up and down in a tiny sampan below.

We docked in Kowloon, hemmed into the wharf by an army of square-hulled junks. During five days in Hong Kong we divided our last £20 between kitchen utensils and oriental trinkets. But we fingered jade and ivory, embroidery and rich brocades and swore we would come back. We rode the lumbering ferry to Hong Kong, bathed in a periwinkle sea at Repulse Bay, and from the top of the Peak saw ships sprawled like tiny insects in the straits and, on the other side, a diadem of islands.

Hong Kong and Kowloon were hives of unceasing activity. The veined bare legs of the rickshaw-pullers scurried past in the streets; and in the strait the women, in tight, shiny black dresses, poled their sampans while their babies rocked to sleep in the bottom. In the shops sewing-machines whirred day and night, and radios tinkled out the monotonous half-tones of Chinese music. All of one's senses were assaulted at once. The street was a jangle of motor-horns and cheerful, antiphonic voices and smells of cooking and sandalwood whiffled out of doorways.

Europeans were not allowed to travel on the lower deck of the ferry, but we rubbed shoulders with the ordinary people in the buses and trams, and walked through areas where mud huts clung crumbling to the hillside. At night we watched naked children dive into the dock, and life on the junks where the women cooked and laundered while the men clacked mah-jongg tiles late into the night. There was plenty of poverty, but fewer beggars than anywhere else in the East. Even among the most down-and-out you could sense a will to work. Hong Kong was still far from being the extraordinary centre for finance and trade it later became, but the seeds of that subsequent success were plain to see.

Life in Manila

Before dawn on 9 June 1952 we entered Manila Bay through the narrow gateway formed by the Bataan peninsula and the island of Corregidor and saw the city strung along the curving shore of the bay, with a range of cloud-speckled hills behind, blue and hazy in already unbearable heat. We soon learned that these hills, beckoning with the promise of cool breezes, were the haunt of bandits and communist guerrillas, the Hukbalahaps. Seven years after the war much of the city was still in ruins, laid utterly to waste during the Japanese defence against liberating American forces in 1945. The old Spanish city of Intramuros, which took 200 years to build, had been destroyed in a few days, and now only its gaunt grey walls remained. The new city springing up was brash and featureless, with few vestiges of the Spanish heritage of the country – a Spanish colony for over three centuries until the Americans ousted Spain in the war of 1898.

The chargé d'affaires of the British Legation, who met us, told me that the new United Nations office wanted to employ me. I firmly declined, having decided to research into the life and work of the Filipino national hero and novelist, José Rizal, executed by the Spaniards in 1896.

We spent our first six months in Pasay City in a Quonset, or Nissen hut, left over from the war, that we had rent-free on condition that we paid five servants and looked after a sloppy spaniel called Tiji. A long avenue of palm trees led to a wide lawn planted with bushes of scarlet and yellow hibiscus. The grass was starred with the waxen yellow-tipped petals of a frangipani tree, an orchid dangled nonchalantly out of a fork in the mango tree that overshadowed the house, and in a far corner banana trees and a grove of papayas were laden with fruit. The rest of the five acres was wild pasture, hedged in scarlet hibiscus. The owner had come to the Philippines with the American forces in 1898 and stayed to make his fortune. During the war he and his wife were interned, their house was occupied by Japanese forces and destroyed when the Americans retook the city. The ruins stood in one corner of the grounds, two or three rusty torpedoes lodged ominously beneath the swimming-pool. After the war the owners settled in the Quonset hut built by the American navy, with a bedroom, kitchen, and shower built on. There were ceiling fans and mosquito netting but no air-conditioning (a rare luxury in those days).

Lorenzo, the No. One houseboy, managed everything. Pedro, his brother, was the No. Two houseboy, and Casimiro, a thin, grey-haired old man, the cook. At night, responsibility for our wellbeing was taken over by a shambling figure wearing battle-dress and an over-large topee resting so low on his nose as almost to obscure his sight. He had the reassuring name of Jesús, and the added protection of two shady-looking mongrel dogs but the dogs never attacked anyone but us, and whenever we came home late we were greeted by a trio of snores. The fifth member of our domestic entourage, Bela, Lorenzo's mother-in-law, was the *lavandera*, or washerwoman. She was old and frail, her activities further impeded by the wooden-soled *bakis* in which she shuffled about, and her long, traditional *mestizo* dress, with its enormous, stiffened sleeves, the *pañuelo* framing her crinkled, cinnamon-coloured face. Every day she laundered mounds of washing, crouching over a shallow zinc pan of cold water, skirts tucked up over scrawny brown knees.

On our second evening, Pedro, departing for the night, remarked in bright, conversational tones: 'You sit in the chair in which our master sat when the man came to the door with the gun.' He pointed to the front door, a flimsy affair of mosquito netting, opening straight into the sitting-room. We went to bed reflecting apprehensively on the tales of robbery and violence that filled the local papers and on the 80 tree-shadowed yards that stretched between us and the road. At 2 a.m. we were awakened by a ghoulish, banshee howling. It was only after some moments of terror that we discovered it was Tiji having a nightmare.

My first expedition with Casimiro to Pasay market was a lively and odorous experience. Among other purchases he returned yanking a squawking fowl by the legs, which he despatched outside the kitchen door. Lorenzo and Pedro's cleaning ritual began with a few airy sweeps around the room with a broom of feathery grasses, followed by a virtuoso demonstration of figure-skating, balanced on the outer husk of a coconut, by Pedro, whose pirouettes and glissades had all the elegance of formal ballet. The floor maintained a marvellous sheen from the natural oil of the coconut. Pedro had a gift for arranging flowers: frangipani floating in a glass bowl; a night-blooming ceres, brought in at dusk, its petals closely furled, so that we could watch them unfold into a large starry flower; or an enormous bowl of trailing scarlet hibiscus. He quickly picked up a British accent, drawling a 'Hullo-o' into the telephone that hoodwinked our friends.

Lorenzo, who had a penchant for our gin, kept a running feud with Casimiro. One hot morning I was reading under the mango tree when the air was shattered by the clatter of falling pans, loud yelling in Tagalog and an occasional screech from Bela. Having just read about a squabble between two teenagers over a ping-pong game that ended in 16 deaths and a jeepney accident, I rushed into the kitchen, visualising a horrid scene of bloodshed. Lorenzo brandished a saucepan, Casimiro cowered in a corner, and peering over the top of the washhouse steps was Bela's furrowed face. The peace I negotiated was of short duration. At six o'clock next morning Casimiro pushed a crumpled note under my door. Quaintly penned by one of the scribes in the market, it began formally. 'Dear Madam, Excuse me for giving this concise note to you ...' later getting more lurid. 'Lorenzo and Pedro always hate me. They want to kill me and they have always a sword, or a large knife. We are not talking to each other.' This was alarming but it was not clear what I could do since the note begged me to keep the matter a secret! To my relief the dispute evaporated.

We parted with Bela, who had taken to muttering witch-like imprecations over the ironing and, with an efficiency not displayed in other directions, locked us out on four occasions. Her successor, a blithe young girl called Conchita, I chiefly remember for another graphically worded epistle:

> Man [presumably Ma'am]
> I am sorry enough I was unable to come for bodily incapacity
>   rather because I am sick.
> Very Respectfully Yours
> Conchita

I was not getting very far with Rizal. Spanish was no longer 'alive' (to use J. B.'s expression) in Manila, except among old aristocratic families. I met Senator Claro Recto, a Spanish scholar and authority on Rizal, and the dashingly handsome Secretary-General of the Foreign Ministry, Leoni Guerrero, offered help. When this took the form of dropping in for tea on torrid afternoons I was obliged to discourage him. My progress was slowed by the heat, which sapped my energy and by my diplomatic wifely duties, calling on ladies in other embassies, coffee mornings and mah-jongg parties.

Exploring Manila was more rewarding. Filipinos liked to refer to Manila as 'the Pearl of the Orient Seas', which aptly described my first sight of the city's shimmering white skyline across the blue waters of the bay. A closer look revealed a very variegated pearl.

Along the boulevard that swept around the curve of the bay there were tall hotels and office buildings, nightclubs with chromium-topped bars and suggestive lighting, and stark white mansions, in the old Spanish colonial style, with graceful white arches, pillared balconies and patios trellised with elaborate ironwork *rejas*. But the poor lived at the gates of the rich, in a jumble of tumbledown huts cobbled together from corrugated iron, petrol cans and driftwood. Mongrel dogs with angry yellow eyes rooted dispiritedly among the garbage, and babies, brown buttocks bare, played beside open drains that ran past shack and mansion alike, thick and blackish-green. Filipinos who were neither rich, nor miserably poor, lived in traditional timber-frame houses with wooden balconies, and windows with tiny opaque panes of mother-of-pearl shells. Down-town, where balloons bobbed like garish, giant nosegays against the grey, eroded bulk of Quiapo church, there still existed whole sections of weathered wooden and bamboo buildings, and the big-wheeled *calesas*, with their high-stepping ponies, their burnished brass side-lamps, and straw-hatted drivers, seemed to come straight out of a nineteenth-century print.

For me, Quiapo and the Chinese quarter were the real Manila. I entered a different world whenever I crossed the River Pasig, blotched with islands of bright green weed, moving slow and brackish out to the bay. In the older quarters you could lose yourself in a maze of narrow alleys, where strange, piquant scents floated on the air, the odour of spices mingled with the reek of sewage, and pungent whiffs of garlic, the staple ingredient of Filipino cooking, licked out like flames from dark doorways and stopped the breath in your throat. Quiapo market was the most redolent place of all, the sweltering air ripe with the smell of raw meat, fish and rotting vegetation. It was several miles from Pasay and, as we had no money for a car, I played safe, as I thought, by taking a taxi. Filipinos are a happy, carefree people, never more so, I discovered, than when they have one foot on an accelerator and one not very steady hand on a steering wheel. The other, you could be sure, was gesticulating to emphasise the central point of an argument, or describing cabbalistic signals out of the window, spreading alarm and confusion among those following.

Despite centuries of Spanish occupation, bullfighting never caught on in the Philippines, but there was so much of the same *Death in the Afternoon* atmosphere about Manila traffic that driving seemed the local substitute for the corrida. Taxi-drivers stuck up a dog-eared postcard of Christ or the Virgin on the dashboard, as a matador might hang a crucifix round his neck before entering the arena, draped a miniature wreath of everlasting flowers over the mirror, mercifully obscuring whatever might be going on behind, and then drove like the devil, confident that they had made their peace with the next world. The taxi would swerve in and out of traffic, lurch drunkenly round corners on the wrong side, and squeal to an abrupt and unsignalled halt. In my fevered imagination, I could almost believe the last black object we missed by a hair's breadth had a large pair of horns ... or perhaps it was just the 'moment of truth'?

When you finally arrived at your destination the driver flashed such a triumphant and slightly astonished smile that all the bitter words you had been saving up evaporated. You usually did reach your destination – provided you had given precise instructions. Manila taxi-drivers in 1952 never knew where even the most well-known places were. A studiously blank 'Huh?' was the invariable reaction when you gave the address. Either every other driver had arrived the day before from the provinces – which gave rise to alarming speculation about their life expectation – or else the art of driving exacted so much of their attention that they never had time to memorise the routes. If no further explanations were forthcoming after the initial 'Huh?' the driver simply drove off, giving a misleading impression of a man in a hurry and with a mission. Some time would elapse before the hapless passenger realised that it was all to no purpose but the driver would only be hurt if you berated him, for he had quite genuinely acted for the best, inspired by nothing but a laudable desire not to disappoint you.

I turned to the buses, whose crew were not only quite clear about where they were going, but made sure that no one within a hundred-yard radius was left in any doubt either. As the bus hurtled along the conductor hung out of the doorway, clinging by his little finger and the corresponding digit of one foot, bawling at passers-by a curious, raucous sound resembling the squawk of a startled duck. It was only after diligent application to local phonetics that I realised he was shrieking 'Quia-a-apoquiapoquiapoquiapo'. It would have been less dangerous, less vocally exhausting for the conductor, and more readily informative to would-be passengers, had the bus carried a destination plate, but that would negate the whole purpose – not, as I first thought, a praiseworthy wish to ensure that no one boarded the wrong bus, but rather to obtain as many passengers as possible, whether stunned into submission, mesmerised by abracadabra-like repetition, or simply willing to do anything for a quiet life. The flailing hand and leg of the conductor served as a handy scoop to snatch unwitting passers-by off the sidewalk.

There was no municipal bus service and no bus stops, the Philippines having discovered the joys of privatisation long before the western world. It was quite usual to see a couple of buses from rival firms racing hell for leather, to the acute danger of themselves and everyone else on the road, in order to see which could be the first to pounce upon some unsuspecting citizen who would descend at Quiapo market with a dazed expression as if he knew not where he was, still less how he came to be there.

The most popular passenger vehicle was the jeepney, a converted jeep, a legacy of the American forces and a most uneconomic mode of public transport. The convergence of thousands of these vehicles on the centre of the city had a constipating effect on traffic, lines and lines of them unable to move an inch, gay pennants drooping forlornly, bright paint blistering in the heat. These jaunty little craft had feminine names – Eva, Carmen, Sweet Betsy – and carried on their back steps legends such as 'No kissing please' or 'Don't bother to knock', that bore wry witness to their braking power. They reflected the Filipino's light-hearted attitude not only to driving, but to all things concerned with Life, Death and the flimsy barrier that separates them.

I was usually the only non-Filipino using public transport. Foreign acquaintances were horrified. 'You travel on *buses*?' they cried incredulously, as who might say 'You take *opium*?' or 'You drink *methylated spirits*?' Such remarks angered me because I was always treated with great courtesy. The conductor would stop his frenzied shouting to help me aboard and three or four men would jump up and as like as not wipe the seat before offering it to me. Such attentions were embarrassing; they made me feel conspicuous and 'different', but they were typical of the innate courtesy of the ordinary Filipino.

The pace of social life was frenetic. Many Americans and British were 'old-timers' who survived the Japanese occupation and incarceration in Intramuros, and seemed to be frantically making up for those lost years. Filipino high society and officialdom also attended their parties, but 'ordinary' Filipinos were seldom present. When they were, they huddled in a corner, sipping Coca-Cola, while the rest consumed vast quantities of alcohol. You would be invited for eight, but dinner would not be served until midnight. Curry lunches on Sundays seldom appeared before five or six o'clock, though guests would have been standing around, glass in hand, since midday. When the food came it was well past its best, like most of the guests. If you did not drink, the wait was purgatory. I was no teetotaller, but could not take more than a couple of drinks, while constant late nights, on top of the heat, exhausted me.

My husband took to this style of living like a duck to water – only unfortunately he did not stick to water. When he indulged excessively, this intelligent, considerate and highly amusing man turned into somebody very different. At our very first reception – when we were making our social bow – he publicly insulted me, declaiming to all and sundry that he had 'married beneath him'. In private he became violent.

Barely a month after our arrival I realised that my marriage was heading for the rocks. One night I spent anguished hours walking up and down the beach. My one burning desire was to go back to England. I was also worried about my husband's career because, after the Maclean affair, the Foreign Office dealt summarily with behaviour formerly regarded as of little significance. Suddenly a future I had looked forward to with confidence was collapsing in ruins. Return home was impossible. I had no money, the Foreign Office would not pay the fare, and I could not ask my parents, not only because they had little money, but also because I could not admit that I was making a mess of my life when they had sacrificed so much. My mother had opposed the match, but her objections – which I discounted because I thought no prospective son-in-law would pass muster – had only made me more determined. Now I realised, too late, that perhaps something more intuitive had been at work in her mind.

There was only one thing for it: to accept the job with the United Nations and earn money for my fare home.

My Initiation into the United Nations

So, on 26 July 1952, I joined the Manila office of the United Nations Technical Assistance Board, as a local staff member, at a monthly salary of US$100. It would be over a year before I earned my fare, but working was better than brooding over my troubles at home. Though my title was administrative officer (it was to have been secretary until I pointed out that I could not type), I became a general dog's-body, doing the accounts, writing letters, speeches and reports, and negotiating with the Government.

I had no idea that my decision on the beach that desperate night was to change the whole course of my life, in a classic illustration of one of my mother's favourite sayings: 'When one door closes, another opens!!'

The Philippines office was one of the first to be opened under the 'Expanded Programme of Technical Assistance' (EPTA) set up in 1949 by the UN General Assembly, to assist poorer countries in their development efforts. EPTA was structured on a collegiate basis, under the UN Technical Assistance Board, comprising the heads of the specialised agencies and headed by a gifted Welshman, David Owen, who had the imaginative idea of setting up a network of 'resident representatives' in developing countries.

Our first resident representative was William J. Ellis, formerly director of the UNESCO Regional Scientific Office in Manila. Bill was Australian, tall, handsome and a delightful personality, with a penchant for the ladies. Most ladies returned the compliment and there were a number of broken hearts (mine not among them, I hasten to say). He was a good scientist but management was not his forte.

The Government had given us an office building in the grounds of the Philippine General Hospital. The walls, originally white, were green with mould, the roof leaked, there were no fans and no mosquito netting. The heat, especially in the afternoon, was unbearable. So were the mosquitoes, which, sensing new blood freshly arrived from England, congregated in the kneehole of my desk. My face, legs and arms were swollen and red with bites. The contrast with my husband's air-conditioned office in the British Legation and with UN Development Programme (UNDP) premises today could hardly have been greater. I became very ill, with excruciating pain in all my bones. The doctor diagnosed infantile paralysis, so I was relieved when he revised that to something of which I had never heard – dengue fever. It was a most painful illness and recurred several years later, when I was travelling on a steamboat down the River Magdalena in Colombia, days from medical help.

My constant cajoling of the Foreign Ministry to repair the roof before the rainy season produced no effect. We had buckets everywhere catching drips when emissaries arrived one Saturday and announced that they would start on Monday and begin by removing half the roof ... Frantic efforts to find alternative accommodation failed, so I squeezed everyone into the other half. The Norwegian pulp and paper expert, a charismatic but volcanic character named Per Klem, who usually annoyed me by calling me 'Babyface', on this occasion threw a chair at me.

Every rainy season floods rendered even main streets impassable. Nothing was ever done to prevent this predictable annual disaster. Newspapers blamed the Spaniards for failing to lay a proper drainage system, blithely overlooking the fact that they had been gone more than 50 years. One night, working late, I found myself stranded, the street a roaring river. Attempts to rescue me failed and I had to sleep on my desk until the waters subsided next morning.

The Filipino brand of English bore little relation to the original tongue – it was American, overlaid with a Filipino accent. At first I concluded that the Filipino staff were courteous, but not very bright; whenever I gave an instruction, they did something completely different. Eventually I realised that they did not understand a word I said and, considering it rude to say so, simply did what they thought I meant. Scores of candidates for the post of my secretary failed to qualify. Then one morning a small girl with a long pigtail applied, who took dictation and typed like greased lightning. I hired her on the spot. Her name was Valentina (Nena)

Lim. That day saw the beginning of a lifelong friendship. With my encouragement Nena took a BA in Spanish, made a career with the United Nations, and educated her younger siblings and their offspring.

Our projects were varied and scattered all over the Philippines: furniture manufacture; textile design and weaving; marble quarrying; statistical training; education; community development; pulp and paper manufacture; and health projects targeting smallpox, malaria and bilharziasis (or schistosomiasis), to name only a few. Many broke new ground. The pulp and paper project was originally based on the pine forests in the mountain province of Luzón. The team was headed by the aforementioned Per Klem, singularly under-endowed with Norwegian phlegm. When it transpired that there were insufficient pine trees, research began into the use of bagasse from the sugar industry in Cebu. A huge row broke out, in which Per Klem was accused of falsifying the number of pine trees. Meanwhile Bill Ellis had signed a contract with Scandinavian firms to continue the research, without consulting Headquarters. A senior UN official, Gustavo Martínez Cabañas, a distinguished Mexican, came to unravel the mess. He told me he had read Ibsen on the long flight, to understand Per Klem's complex personality better. Whether or not that helped, I cannot say. Per Klem went. So did Bill Ellis, a very embittered man. Bill had done nothing wrong, but simply been too trusting. He returned to UNESCO in Paris, and died tragically in a plane accident in France, with his last female companion.

Harry Keith, an Englishman turned Canadian, head of the Food and Agriculture Organisation's forestry team, was put in charge but left me to run things. This was a wonderfully maturing experience. Harry and his American wife, Agnes, had spent many years in North Borneo, about which Agnes had written a book, *Land Below the Wind*. They and their young son barely survived the Japanese occupation and Agnes related their ordeal in another book, *Three Came Back*, which was made into a movie. It was a strange experience to go with them to see the film when it was shown in Manila.

After a few months a new resident representative was appointed. J. P. Ross, who was British, had written for *Punch*, and within minutes of the arrival of another directive from New York I would find J. P.'s scathing comment, in verse, in my in-tray. He was a considerate boss and a dynamo of physical energy, diving spectacularly off the high board at the Army and Navy Club. This same dynamism sometimes intimidated Filipino callers, on whom he bore down at speed, beaming, hand outstretched, and was positively dangerous to his colleagues. If a sudden idea struck him when I was bending over his desk, going through a draft, he would thrust back his chair, right into my solar plexus. One day I came back from the Foreign Ministry to witness an extraordinary scene. Profiting by my absence, he had asked Nena Lim to help him remove a large map of the Philippines he coveted from my office to his, not bargaining for the resistance of the concrete walls of our otherwise crumbling building. I beheld my boss perilously perched on one leg on a window ledge, trying to bang in a nail, which repeatedly ricocheted. At every futile attempt his cry rang out, 'Fetch the nail, Nena', and she ran about like a small puppy to retrieve it. Then a stronger hammer blow sent the nail under one of the swinging half-doors into the patio. Nena dashed in pursuit but when she did not immediately reappear, J. P. leapt from his perch, and charged through the half-door, just as Nena was re-entering, and flattened her. At this point I intervened to forestall further physical damage, and suggested we should perhaps call the office handyman.

Even in those early days there were moves to reduce the UN budget. Our office had been open less than two years when James Keen, a senior adviser to David Owen, came to see whether it could be closed. A tall, distinguished Britisher, with a wonderful head of grey-white hair, he liked things short and to the point. 'Hrrmph – not such a dragon after all' were his first disconcerting words to me (a reference to rather acrimonious correspondence with New York about my pay and status). For two days I watched an irrepressible and voluble J. P. drive James into a frenzy of ill-concealed irritation.

I tried to patch things up by inviting them to dinner. Claude, J. P.'s wife, commanded him to prepare a gin and lime and soda for James whom I was attempting to cajole out of the silent gloom in which he sat sunken. The awakening came from an unexpected quarter. There was a loud explosion and icy liquid descended from the ceiling to drench us both. J. P. had mixed the drink in the cocktail shaker, shaken it with his usual vigour, and the top had blown off. The appalled silence that followed as we all drank in this situation – in more senses than one – was broken by a low keening sound from James, rocking back and forth, his usually immaculate locks hanging dank and dishevelled over his eyes. This moan eventually erupted into words enunciated on a rising crescendo, 'I cannot think how anyone could be so STUPID as to shake gin and lime and soda.' He repeated this like an incantation as I tried to mop him up, reminding me of Toad of Toad Hall, sitting in the road after the motor-car destroyed his caravan, chanting, 'Poop-poop, poop-poop.'

All was not lost. The office was not closed. James and J. P. were reconciled and James became a close friend. His opening words to me could more appropriately have been applied to himself.

I was well-known at the airport where I collected our weekly diplomatic pouch from New York. So, when I had to ship Satan – a large King poodle, belonging to an American friend, whose husband, a colleague in the British Legation, had died suddenly – he was allowed to remain free until he pranced jauntily into the cargo hold with me, and was put in his cage, behind webbing guaranteed to resist two tons of pressure. From the airport building I watched, with premonition, as the huge plane aborted its take-off and returned. Horror-struck, I saw Satan descending from the hold, spitting out bits of wood, wagging his tail and looking well pleased with himself. I learned, as I shamefacedly collected him before a large public, that he had not only broken out of the cage and the webbing, but had pushed into the cockpit where the astonished pilot suddenly felt someone licking his ear.

Miraculously, the same crew agreed to take Satan on the following week's flight, this time more securely caged. But when, on a similar mission for another American friend, I took her canary for embarkation to Mexico in a tiny rattan cage, the authorities looked at me warily, and demanded something stronger.

I loved my job and soon realised that I wanted to continue working in poor and deprived areas of the world. This was a volte-face from the ambitions of our group of third secretaries in the

Foreign Office to spend our lives in a charmed circle between London, Paris, Rome and Washington. 'Development' was a new and exciting concept and I believed that the UN was the proper vehicle through which to help developing countries – many of them newly independent – to achieve it.

My work brought me into contact with Filipinos in all walks of life. On visits to community development projects, and to the Secondary and Normal School in Bayambang in Pangasinan Province, I rubbed shoulders with rural folk and saw life in the flooded rice paddies, where ungainly *carabao* (or water buffalo) provided draught power. In villages of nipa palm huts, which were perched on wooden stilts, I experienced the overwhelming hospitality of the really poor. One morning I was expected to consume 22 breakfasts – each abounding in Filipino delicacies with which my stomach never came to terms, washed down with Coca-Cola, for which I never had a taste then or thereafter.

The fact that I had taken a job caused considerable fluttering among the diplomatic ladies. The formidable doyenne, the Australian Ambassador's wife, protested to the British Minister. In the end I was excused coffee mornings, and mah-jongg parties, on condition that I did not flag on other obligations. This was physically taxing, since I had to combine late nights with long office hours and a very early start every morning.

When the Quonset owners returned we moved to a cramped, very hot apartment in Malate, nearer the centre. I spent my first savings, not on a passage home, but on an air-conditioner for the bedroom. If you cricked your neck you could glimpse the blue of Manila Bay between ruined buildings, but I desperately missed the garden. Furniture was provided from a store in the British Residence and I had my first experience of bedbugs, late one night when my husband was out. I was covered with angry red bites, and the mattress had to be burned.

Clemente, our new cook, hailed from the Visayan islands. He was exasperatingly slow, but scrupulously honest and, mercifully, did not drink. Once when I offered him a glass of champagne, he said accusingly, 'Look, mum, it's made my ears stick out and go all hot!' It seemed a malignant fate indeed that afflicted Clemente with fits of the hiccoughs that lasted a week and caused suspicion to dawn in the eyes of many a guest.

Apolonio, who followed Clemente, was very different – nervous, and agile, with a disconcerting habit of turning his eyes heavenward and intoning, 'You want iggs, mum?' When his wife, Aniceta, visited her ailing mother in Iloilo she sent a letter written in an exquisite hand, clearly not hers, and language rich in flowery vocabulary and recondite turns of phrase:

> Hoping you in the midst of excitement upon receiving this missive of mine which is far from your expectation. Hope you are in the midst of good health and happiness upon reaching through the kingdom of your presence.

Any excitement I might have felt was tempered by the next paragraph which told of her mother's death and asked for money for the funeral. The end was another burst of purple prose:

> Hoping to hear your sweet reply. Till we meet again sooner. Best regards to everybody and keep the most of it. Good night and may God bless us all.
>
> With oceans of love and sweet kisses
>
> Aniceta

On nights untrammelled by social obligations we would walk by the sea wall at sunset. In Manila the sun dies with a bang, not a whimper. One evening we would see the mountains of Bataan stark against a scarlet sky, as though reflecting all the blood spilt on those tragic shores, on the next silhouetted against a backcloth of palest lemon. The skyward-gazing maiden whose contours, according to local lore, form the rounded hills behind Cavite, would trail her long tresses in waters that were one evening lilac, and the next turquoise. As the sun plummeted into the rainbow sea, a sudden ocean breeze rustled the dry leaves of the stunted palm trees, bringing with it the foetid smell of Manila Bay, redolent of rotting weed and the dead animals whose corpses so often bobbed along the shore where even the sand was black, a river smell having nothing to do with the saline, antiseptic tang of open sea.

Every night the ordinary people of Manila came to watch the spectacle, perched on the outriggers of *bancas* drawn up on the sea wall, dark figures gazing seaward over the fretted skeletons of unsalvaged warships, in a brief escape from the squalor of their working lives. The spell lasted only a moment. Then the old lady who had been shading her eyes with a worn hand would gather up the skirt of her *bahulawak* and move on; the fisherman begin again to chip the barnacles off his upturned *banca*; and the diminutive shoeshine boy take up his melancholy cry, 'Shi-I-ne, sh-I-I-ne', a forlorn cadence at odds with the cheeky grin with which he confronted a life that could never have been kind. A cloud of balloons would bob towards us, and carts of ice cream, Coca-Cola and Filipino specialities, like *pancit molo*, trundle past.

A patter of bare feet along the stone wall would herald another hopeful vendor, twin cans swinging from yokes on his shoulders, hissing invitingly, 'Balut, balu-u-t!' but our squeamish occidental stomachs turned at the thought of consuming a rotten duck's egg, feathers and half-formed bones swimming in greenish-black juice – an exquisite flavour, according to Filipino friends: 'Once you have tasted it, you will never forget it', they would say, with unconscious irony.

Whole families, trousers and skirts tucked above their knees, would be searching for mussels, plunged in black ooze up to their elbows, delving round the spars of ancient wrecks and a rusted ship's boiler, said to be a relic of the Spanish American war, now petrified in mud. In the shallows a fisherman would make a graceful movement, his cast net would billow like a chequered mushroom against the fading horizon and fall into the sea. Quite suddenly dark would fall, Cavite a glittering necklace of lights across the bay. Voices floated strangely disembodied around us. Bats skimmed the surface of the sea, and the cicadas began to rasp their nightly chorus. Later, when we leant out of the window to get some fresh air before going to bed, the *bancas* would be out fishing with paraffin lamps, a glow-worm fleet floating on the dark bay.

Liberty and democracy were the great gifts that the United States had bestowed on the Philippines by ousting the Spaniards at the end of the nineteenth century, and had restored by ejecting the Japanese in 1945. Yet high political office remained the pre-rogative of old, wealthy families, essential to consolidate their inherited privileges. President Quirino was cast in that mould,

and tenaciously clung to power. His electoral campaign compounded all the excesses and razzamataz of American models and
adopted a jingly theme song that made one cringe. The first line,
and the tune, still ring in my ears, 'Quirino is the father of the
nation ... ' Magsaysay, who succeeded him, represented a break
with that tradition. Here was a man truly of the people. He came to
our office, shook hands with everyone, and demonstrated an
impressive degree of knowledge about the United Nations. He
exuded charisma, but I sensed a naivety that I feared would inhibit
his navigation of the sinuous currents of Filipino politics, and his
presidency did not fulfil the bright hopes it had inspired, before it
was cut short by his death in an air crash.

Another exception to the rule, in a different way, was the
Foreign Minister, Joaquín Miguel Elizalde. He was the scion of a
wealthy Spanish family that had lived for generations in the
Philippines, their fortune deriving from hemp and sugar estates.
'Mike' as he was known, led a cosmopolitan life. He had a ranch in
Virginia, and in his younger days he had played international
polo. Politics was by no means the be-all and end-all of his life and
he handled the country's foreign affairs in a relaxed manner.
He was a great Anglophile and often invited us on weekend
excursions on his yacht. But Mike also felt himself to be very
Spanish, as he invariably spoke Spanish with me, and asked me to
call him Joaquín. He was not a great foreign minister, but he was a
generous host and a good friend. The only embarrassment was that
we saw rather more of him than the British Minister did.

Exploring the Philippines

The relentless social whirl continued to distort our lives. I lived on
a knife's edge. Sometimes my husband would not come home until
morning, sometimes not for two or three days. I dared not confide
in anyone and had neither the temperament nor the experience to
deal with the situation. I retreated into my work, and whenever
possible left Manila. The Hukbalahap insurrection was at its height
and travel dangerous, even around the capital. Tagaytay, a ridge
2000 feet above Manila Bay, was reached by a road winding up from

the rice plains, through groves of papaya, coconuts and bananas, and barrios filled with excited Sunday cockfight crowds and their panniered horses. The other side dropped sheer into a volcanic lake at sea level. The air was refreshingly cool, but there were shootings and ambushes, and armoured tanks were stationed along the road to guard the rice harvest.

You could travel safely by day to Baguio, a hill town hidden in pine forest, some 200 miles north. We ventured further northwards to Bontoc, and to the Banawe rice terraces, which encircle the hillsides like the frilled skirts of a flamenco dancer. This was mountainous country, inhabited by Igorot tribes whose tradition of headhunting had enjoyed a revival during the Japanese occupation. Despite the chilly climate the men wore only a G-string, supplemented in the rain by a cloak of palm leaves. Because of their war-like character Northern Luzon had remained largely uncharted during Spanish times. At the turn of the century it had gradually been opened up by American missionaries, becoming a Protestant stronghold in an otherwise Catholic country.

Northwards from Baguio a narrow dirt track wound serpent-like round a mountainside luxuriant with pines, subtropical vegetation, and magnificent tree-ferns. Below yawned a sheer abyss, mercifully obscured by swirling clouds of mist. We travelled by local bus, rickety affairs, with long bench-seats, and open sides affording an all too clear view of potential perils. The conductor collected fares swinging along outside the precipice side of the bus. Survival depended on the driver's skill but confidence was hardly boosted by a list of injunctions placing responsibility unequivocally on the passengers: 'Passengers ride at their own risk', 'Stop driver when driving fast' (some hope; they all belted along at terrifying speed) and – the most alarming caveat of all – 'DO NOT RIDE WHEN DRIVER IS DRUNK.' Not 'if' but 'when', warning that this was a likely hazard.

In the Bontoc Hotel, a decaying wooden structure infested with mosquitoes, the 'bedrooms' were cubicles with partial wooden walls. Sleep was a communal affair, punctuated by the chatter and loud snoring of fellow-guests and dogs baying to the moon. Yet another hazard were the frequent landslides, making the road impassable until the bus passengers' concerted shovelling cleared the obstacle. Even that was not always successful and we were unable to reach a village called Tinglayen, on a first attempted sortie into Kalinga country, north of Bontoc.

The director of fisheries, who rejoiced in the name of Dr Deogracias ('Thanks be to God') Valladolid, invited us to the Hundred Islands, off the eastern coast of Luzón, in the Gulf of Lingayen. The St Andrew's Night Ball fell on the eve of the journey, and a 5 a.m. return home left us ill-prepared for the rigours of a very rough road. Deogracias' driver drove at breakneck speed, hustling coveys of chickens, pigs, dogs and brown-bottomed children in terrified flight as we sped through barrios of nipa huts. Every time we flashed past one of the old, moss-covered stone churches he took both hands off the wheel to cross himself. Confident he had made his peace with his Maker, he resumed his mad career, with no thought for the readiness, or otherwise, of his passengers' souls. When the heat became too much, lithe young boys shinned up palm trees, and showered us with green coconuts, hacking them open with axes, so that we could drink their cool milk.

The Hundred Islands, partly coral, partly volcanic, actually number over 400, some mere knobs of rock. Some had miniature black cliffs dropping sheer into turquoise water, others minute beaches of whitest sand. None were inhabited. We sailed round this enchanted fairyland in a *banca* bearing the dispiriting device, 'O God help me.' The Almighty had much to answer for in these parts.

One would not have been surprised to meet Prospero and Caliban, so that we were at first unfazed to round a promontory and find a dwarf paddling in the shallows, three shipwrecked sailors playing poker on the beach and, sitting on the steps of a leafy hut, an exotic young woman, who compensated for the scantiness of her attire by draping herself in the folds of an enormous boa constrictor. At the appearance of a fat man in a blinding Hawaiian shirt and a large straw hat, puffing at a cigar, we understood that a film was in the making – 'an adventure story, in Tagalog,' he said, waving a pudgy hand, 'all about jungles and caves and a queen of the Amazons.' The lady, who was excessively anxious that I try on her boa constrictor, was not she, but an even more glamorous creature, her careful make-up and hair-do much at variance with the animal skin in which she was clad. We later saw the film, which was predictably hilarious.

In February 1954 I visited the long chain of islands to the south of Luzon. An ancient ship called *The Turk's Head* carried cargo and deck-passengers down to Sulu near Borneo, another area seething with guerrilla activity. I was the only non-Filipino on board. The British community were horrified. Even my husband was perturbed when he saw me off at midnight in the murky port of Manila, and gave me a rusty Boy Scout knife for protection. My shabby cabin was already occupied by a host of large cockroaches and I was an object of cynosure for the milling crowd of Filipinos who slept on deck, and stared for hours through my porthole. Other deck-passengers included sheep, cattle, *carabao*, poultry and tanks of fish.

At dawn next morning I went up on deck as we passed the island of Mindoro, the 'Island of Gold', its topmost peak fittingly draped in a scarf of golden cloud. All around were little green islands, with palm trees and untrodden white beaches, the sparkling sea dotted with the brightly coloured sails of outrigger canoes. My enjoyment was rudely interrupted by a stentorian voice bellowing, 'Señora!' I jumped round to find a huge white-haired man in blue pyjamas bearing purposefully down on me and hurriedly clutched my little knife. I felt exceedingly foolish when my accoster introduced himself as our doughty captain come to offer me the freedom of the flying bridge. He wore pyjamas all the time – blue in the daytime, red in the evening, when the mah-jongg session began. So did all the passengers, and I began to feel quite overdressed. My cabin boy, Ernesto, reverently hung mine, which I wore only at night and in private, on a coat hanger. I was unfamiliar with Filipino pyjama etiquette, and only later saw the Foreign Ministry pamphlet warning Filipino diplomats that Westerners were inclined to look askance at such attire paraded on public occasions.

When we sailed into port our captain appeared on the bridge resplendent in uniform lavishly adorned with gold braid. He was a colourful character, a Spanish mestizo, whose burly build dwarfed the other officers. When they confided to me that the captain had his mistress on board, locked in his cabin, the voyage took on distinctly Somerset Maugham characteristics. During our long days drifting southwards, the captain regaled me with bombastic stories about his exploits against the Japanese. They had hoodwinked him by running up English flags on their vessels, ordering him to stop and then torpedoing his boat. He ran it onto the rocks and fought as a guerrilla in the mountains of Cebu for the rest of the war. I felt so much a part of his entourage that, when we docked in Cebu and a sugar planter commented – as an elegant, high-stepping *calesa* trotted towards us along the quay – 'Here comes the captain's wife', I dashed off to warn the First Officer. 'Don't worry,' he assured me. The lady on board, whom I never actually saw, had been transferred to another cabin.

Conditions were primitive – toilets did not work, their doors would not lock, washing facilities were limited to the stopperless basin in my cabin, and food was basic. But everyone was anxious to please, and every day I awoke to a new vista of blue-green seas sprinkled with enchanted islands. My ears were constantly assaulted by the ship's loudspeaker system blaring 'Stranger in Paradise', but that well described my situation. Daily we docked at some new port, sometimes on larger islands, sometimes in remote bays where we anchored offshore. In Cebu (site of Magellan's first landing in the Philippines), I was met by Mrs Mary Osmeña, daughter-in-law of a previous vice-president, whose husband had been executed by the Japanese when he refused to become their puppet governor. I was taken over cement and paper factories and wined and dined in a house that had been a Japanese brothel, where stones in the garden were still red with their victims' blood. In Dumaguete the Spanish company of Tabaclera showed me sugar cane being processed in their sophisticated mill, and by the age-old native methods where *carabao* strained to turn the wheels. I caught up with *The Turk's Head* near the tiny town of Bais, rushed down the wharf on a handcart propelled furiously by two men along the railway line used to load sugar.

When we entered Moro country, where Moslems predominated, the men were turbaned, both they and the women wore sarongs, and all had teeth stained red from chewing betel-nut. The coloured sails of their *vintas* (small boats) speckled the sea and in one, with tattered pink flags atop its roof, I glimpsed the passage of a Moro wedding, accompanied by much banging of gongs. After Zamboanga, where gleaming dolphins piloted us into port, we meandered along the sinuous southern coast of Mindanao and the Moro Gulf, loading logs. In Cotobato, hidden behind mangrove swamps in the Mindanao River, I was regaled with the story of a man who was swallowed whole by a crocodile, but rescued three hours later, after war gongs had been beaten and his tribe had slain the predator. Silvery flying fish escorted us into Lebak and Buli-Buli, in the south of Basilan, tiny bays where loading went on all night by the light of a full moon – floating islands of logs hemming the boat in; lumberjacks astride the giant trunks, connecting them to the winches, then jumping into the water. Scenes of great confusion, shouting, and whistle-blowing abounded as *bancas* and outrigger canoes struggled through the swaying logs to deliver passengers. I went ashore, swam in a rocky pool full of naked brown children, and met Yacau people, down from the hills to sell smuggled cigarettes. The men were resplendent in scarlet turbans, huge scarlet sashes, and tight black breeches with gaiters of coloured stripes. The women, too, wore breeches and gaiters, with checked overskirts.

In Jolo, capital of Sulu archipelago, a Moro insurrection had rumbled on for years, led by a notorious outlaw called Kamlon. Despite the recent truce of Tawi-Tawi there had just been an incident, and armed jeeps patrolled the town. I strolled through markets and mosques, and the sea villages of the Samals, whose wooden houses were built on rickety stilts over the water. Smuggling and piracy, as much as armed revolt, were major sources of livelihood for these tiny palm-fronded islands, their white beaches strung like pearls across the Sulu Sea almost to the shores of North Borneo. Nearly 50 years on, unrest lingers on in that beautiful but troubled paradise, an object lesson for would-be peacemakers on the intractability of conflicts deeply rooted in cultural, ethnic and religious differences.

With our last cargo – several tons of abaca – safely on board we slipped out of harbour at midnight, the moon stippling the water with mother-of-pearl. At first we had strong winds and choppy seas, then torrid heat. Water had to be thrown over the pigs, sheep, cattle and *carabao*. Fish died in the tanks. A pig and several hens jumped overboard. Others continued to lay eggs, fighting cocks crowed, and a mix of farmyard smells assaulted our senses. One torrid afternoon somewhere between Negros and Cebu the sultry air was riven by the shout, 'Man overboard!' The engines stopped, the captain danced and gesticulated on the bridge in his bright pyjamas, and a boat was lowered. As it circled round and round, passengers pointed excitedly, but choppy waves defeated the search. After several hours we sailed on. The victim had been on his way to Manila, to collect his veteran's pension. Two passengers saw him jump, apparently frightened by a quarrel.

Just before we left the Philippines I escaped from Manila and walked across the central mountain chain of northern Luzon, from west to east, and fulfilled my earlier thwarted wish to visit the Kalingas, one of the seven main Igorot tribes.

The overnight bus to Bangued, supposed to take seven hours, turned into a 14-hour nightmare, in a ramshackle vehicle packed with seething humanity, baskets, sacks and squawking livestock. The seats were of hard slatted wood, Filipino size, so my knees were jammed against the seat in front. The only light was a candle end stuck to a seat, a thunderstorm erupted and the roof leaked. In the middle of the night, uncomfortably close to Mount Ararat, the headquarters of the Hukbalahap guerrillas, the bus broke down. Uproarious laughter greeted this happy occurrence from all except me, and it was only after my stern insistence and the provision of my torch that conductor and driver were shamed into venturing out into the cloudburst to make repairs. The engine somehow strung together by wire and string, we limped wet and exhausted into Bangued, further delayed because the conductor and driver stopped for two suppers and a bout of gambling.

Marian Davis, an Anglican missionary was waiting for me, but the 'bus' into the mountains (an ancient US weapon-carrier) was stuck on the other side of the River Abra, some bright spark having destroyed the bamboo raft, on which it was daily poled across the fast-flowing torrent, before a new one had been completed. We caught up with it by hiring a jeep and a smaller raft, and spent the rest of the day in more bumpy travel, made bearable by sun, beautiful scenery and the lilting folksongs of the Tinggian passengers. Dusk brought us to a tumbledown hut deep in the forest, at Maceneogeog, where we slept on the floor, along with a gang of road workers and a colony of rats. Next day, with *cargadores* and a pack-horse we trekked for hours through dank rain forest where an army of leeches fastened ravenously on our legs. The *cargadores* tramped stolidly on, while I squirmed, wresting the obscene parasites from my skin with a spurt of blood, only to find them stuck fast to my fingers. We emerged from this living horror on the banks of the Sultan River, a torrent of clear water bubbling over grey and white pebbles, and saw before us the green rice terraces and serene valley of Balbalasang ('the Beautiful Place'), the most northerly Anglican mission, thronged with grass-thatched huts.

The mission had a kindergarten and a clinic to which patients were carried from surrounding villages in blankets strung between two poles. They paid for treatment, sometimes small sums of money, but more usually the accounts book read 'one eggplant', 'two tomatoes and an egg' or 'six camotes'. The Anglican priests were native Igorots, as was the teacher. They gave a party for me, with Tinggian folk songs – the haunting *sali domai* – and dancing, with musical accompaniment by *balingbings*, a primitive instrument of split bamboo that the Tinggians play as they walk along trails. I bathed in a pool between two waterfalls where vivid dragonflies, petrol-blue and garnet red, skimmed the golden water, and two enormous turquoise butterflies, wings frilled in black lace, sunned themselves on the encircling grey boulders.

I set off for the eastern side of the Cordillera at 4.30 a.m. accompanied by the *cargadores*, a Tinggian girl, Eleanor, who carried our provisions on her head, and two Igorot Anglican priests. This was a pleasanter walk, through open valleys watered by rushing mountain streams, tributaries of the Sultan, which we crossed innumerable times on stepping-stones or swaying bamboo bridges. Rain and bad news awaited us in Salegseg: the truck to Bontoc was two days late, and the store where we were to sleep was locked, the owner away ... We spent two nights in a derelict hut on a muddy hillside, sleeping huddled on the floor. The Tinggians are naturally resilient and although wet, cold and tired, the *cargadores* turned their rice cans upside down and used them as improvised gongs, Eleanor twanged her *balingbing* and sang, and everyone wound up dancing.

We were in Kalinga country. Kalingas, a warlike people, unlike the Tinggians, are famed for their skill in negotiating peace pacts. As good chance would have it, a pact was to be celebrated between Salegseg and Limus, another Kalinga village. The pounding of rice and preparations for a banquet of roast pig in the house of the Salegseg pact-holder went on all day. Warned that if anyone sneezed during the feast, there would be brawling and even loss of life, I, an inveterate and unregenerate sneezer, deemed it prudent to attend only the postprandial ceremonies. We sat on a beaten earth floor, round a tall jar of *basi*, the potent rice wine of the region, served in a dirty bamboo bowl passed from mouth to mouth. There was a brilliant display of oratory from the two pact-holders, then dancing to strangely compelling gong music. My efforts to imitate the Kalinga peace dance were the comic turn of the evening. As the *basi* circulated faster, so the speeches multiplied, mostly from gnarled old men, clad only in G-strings, toothlessly munching betel-nuts and spouting great jets of juice to splash scarlet on the ground. Then, to my amazement, in these mountains cut off from the world, I heard the phrase 'United Nations'. One of the priests explained that the Salegseg pact-holder was appointing mo as chief diplomatic adviser, in view of my 'long experience of peace-keeping with the United Nations'.

Prudence dictated that I disavow any such connections and I made a lame speech explaining that I worked on the economic and social problems that often caused conflict. My priest friend translated this at considerably greater length, with many embellishments, to judge by the admiring, if inebriated, glances in my direction.

Despite the appearance of an ugly-looking centipede eight inches long ('a bad omen' – the old men shook their heads) and ceaseless imbibing of *basi*, which is like liquid fire, we learned next morning that the main grievances between the two communities had been resolved. And although I recognised the driver of our lorry as one of the most enthusiastic topers of *basi* at the ceremony and caught sight of injunction No. three hanging above his head ('Do not ride when driver is drunk'), we reached Bontoc safely.

Farewell to the Philippines

I lived a double life in the Philippines: one as a diplomatic wife; another, far happier, enjoyed in my daily work, and my escapes, alone, to far-off corners of the islands. The same duality informed my feelings about the country, not only because my personal life was unhappy, but also because of the general tawdriness. In half a century the most superficial trappings of the American way of life seemed to have swamped the earlier cultural heritage. True, that heritage was mixed – a medley of Spanish and indigenous influences. True, the Spanish had also been interlopers. And yet I sensed that that earlier blend of intermingled cultures had more closely reflected the innate grace, courtesy and elegance of the Filipino race. It was these qualities, as well as a simpler and more wholesome approach to life, that I found outside the capital. I genuinely loved the Philippines in contrast to my strong antipathy to Manila.

When the time came to leave in July 1954, my emotions were equally mixed. I was sad to leave Filipino friends and resign from my job, which had given me solace from private pain as well as opening up fascinating new horizons. But I knew that our marriage could not withstand a second tour. I had hung on for over two years, because I still hoped that if we could get away from Manila and its temptations, then the relationship and my husband's career might be saved. Not long before he had disregarded a warning by the minister that the next transgression would mean instant banishment home.

Unhappy as the personal memories were, the Philippines had been an important experience for me. I had always regretted leaving the Foreign Office, but now I had learned that work other than diplomacy could enthral me. I had become alive to the plight of the peoples of the developing world, and committed to trying to help them, though my chances of doing so were diminished by the need to resign from my job. And I had tasted the pleasures of travelling in wild places, an addiction that endures to this day.

7

English Interlude

We travelled home as the sole passengers of a cargo ship, joining the *Benavon* in Hong Kong, on 13 July 1954 after a few days in our beloved Repulse Bay Hotel. We had taken a train to the frontier and tried to cross into China proper, but were stopped at the border by distinctly displeased and heavily armed guards.

Our first port of call was Keelung, in Formosa (now Taiwan), then fearing imminent invasion by China. We were escorted there by flying fish and dolphins and, less agreeably, by an American Navy plane flying low overhead to ensure the ship maintained its course.

We were to stay with the British consul at Tamsui, 30 miles away, but the authorities would not allow us ashore, because Britain had recognised mainland China. This was ironic, since China had not allowed us in either. Eventually we were permitted ashore at 1 p.m. next day, on strict condition that we were back on board by 11 p.m. The consulate was housed in a sixteenth-century Spanish fort leased to Her Majesty's Government in the 1860s, on condition that the ancient cannons were kept ready for war and available to the military in time of need. They hardly seemed appropriate weaponry for the current crisis. After tea we went to a cocktail party from which we left late. The car suffered a burst tyre, and it was already 11 p.m. when we reached the port. The *Benavon* was moored offshore, entailing a good 30 minutes' walk along a dark, sinister wharf, through groups of curious Chinese coolies, stevedores and policemen who spoke no English. I fell over a hawser and hurt my ankle and, as my husband strode ahead, I found myself alone and without money. I was acutely frightened, but finally managed, through sign language, to get myself rowed out to the boat. Hardly had we left the wharf when a hail from my husband made us return to collect him. He had stumbled on a military area with gun emplacements, but fortunately none of the sentries, leaning on their rifle butts and smoking, had challenged him. We scrambled aboard after midnight, and were severely taken to task by the 'Foreign Affairs Police' next day. Our every step had been followed.

Two days at sea brought us back to Manila, where our heavy luggage was loaded, along with tons of evil-smelling copra. There was a whirlwind round of farewell parties and a large crowd came on board to see us off.

Our voyage took six weeks: long leisurely days at sea interspersed with lengthy stays in port, loading exotic cargo. We spent several days in the Rejang River in Sarawak, its shores walled in jungle, where we loaded huge logs and I had a sliver of glass removed from my foot by the Malay dresser in a makeshift clinic, in the presence of a large audience of Dayak tribesmen, who found the experience considerably more mirthful than I.

After Singapore we sailed up the Malayan coast to what was then Port Swettenham, and had an adventurous trip by local bus to Kuala Lumpur. The Malayan emergency was at its height and in the middle of the rubber plantations our bus was searched by British military in armed Land-Rovers. We fell in love with Kuala Lumpur, then still a small town, its wide streets bordered with flowering acacias, its colonial government buildings a fantastical architecture of domes, towers and slender minarets, winding staircases and narrow windows fretted with delicate lattice-work carvings. Today they are dwarfed by huge, characterless skyscrapers.

But it was Penang that wove the greatest web of enchantment. Its narrow, crooked streets were bordered by shopfronts washed all the colours of the rainbow, with louvred shutters at their upper windows, and tumbling rooves of weather-faded, curly red tiles. Through secretive doors we glimpsed hidden courtyards, rooms hung with tapestries, carved screens of dragons and peacocks and pagodas. We visited the Buddhist temple and rode on the tiny railway that climbed over 2000 feet above the town to the top of Penang Hill, raised on tall piles above the surrounding jungle. There one could see as far as the shadowy landscape of the mainland, shimmering in heat haze. As the train hurtled downwards, death-defying monkeys chattered and played on the track, leaping off at the last moment, in a dizzying display of aerobatics, onto swaying branches in the forest many feet below, some clutching a banana, some with babies clinging to their backs. Just before sailing we swam in aquamarine waters from a beach of perfect white sand, without another human being in sight.

Tossed by the south-west monsoon, the *Benavon* rode a stormy sea to Colombo, in what was still Ceylon. My diary, remarking how friendly and cheerful we found the Singhalese, and on the tranquil atmosphere of Colombo, makes sad reading now, after so many years of bloody turmoil. We walked at sunset on the Galle Face, in a rainbow mist of spindrift from the crashing sea, reflected in the jewel-coloured saris of beautiful Singhalese women enjoying their evening promenade along the shore.

As we voyaged westwards, the force of the south-west monsoon increased, and the ship pitched violently, though the days were fine and sunny. I was exhilarated by the wild motion of the sea, and won a bet from the captain by walking the deserted foredeck, where it was difficult to stand upright. Nonetheless, it was a relief to reach the calmer waters of the Red Sea and then the Suez Canal. At Port Said we loaded British Army lorries and sailed into a deliciously cool Mediterranean, past Malta and Sicily. The coast of North Africa was a blue ridge on the southern horizon followed, later, by the sere landscape of Spain to the north, and the looming hulk of Gibraltar.

Return to Cambridge

At Tilbury docks there was a joyous reunion with my parents. We rented a thatched cottage in the New Forest, where we planned to spend our three months' leave, while awaiting another posting abroad. My fear that news of my husband's behaviour in Manila might have reached London proved unfounded for we had barely settled into the cottage when my husband was told to report for duty as one of the private secretaries to Anthony Nutting, then Parliamentary Under-Secretary of State, an important and sensitive post.

This set all our plans awry. We had no home in England, London rents were exorbitant, and it would be hard to live on the basic Foreign Office salary. Clearly I had to find a job, but where? As if by magic, a letter arrived asking if I could assume the supervisory functions of Inez Macdonald, who was ill, both at Newnham and other Cambridge colleges. The job was part-time, and payment, none too lavish, was by the hour. It also meant enormously hard work, as I had not touched my academic books for six years.

To reduce travel and lodging expenses, I crammed all my supervisions into two consecutive days each week, leaving my parents' home (where we stayed, while looking for something else) before 6 a.m. one day and returning at midnight the next. In between I squeezed in 16 hours of teaching, dashing between the colleges. I found an excellent pied-à-terre with Mrs Peryt who, with her Polish husband, ran a lodging house for undergraduates. One night a week they gave up their bed-sitting-room, where I would sit before a blazing fire, marking essays while Mrs Peryt served me my evening meal. Another who was very kind was Dr Freddy Brittain, a loveably eccentric don at Jesus College, mad about rowing, and famed for a collection of hundreds of cockerels – the Jesus mascot – in every conceivable shape, form and material. He insisted that I take the Jesus undergraduates at noon, and stay for lunch in his rooms.

During the rest of the week I had essays to mark, and reams of reading to get through, as well as domestic chores and house-hunting. Living at my parents' house was a strain all round. My husband was often late home, and we gravitated from an excessive social life in Manila to practically none at all.

In the spring of 1955 the attic flat in my sister and brother-in-law's Victorian villa in Roehampton became vacant. We planned to redecorate it during the Easter break but on the eve of our move my husband collapsed on the escalator at Edgeware tube station and was rushed to hospital for an emergency appendectomy. The

Foreign Office sent him to convalesce on the Isle of Wight, while I spent my Easter vacation painting every room in bright colours, getting a cricked neck whitewashing ceilings, and sewing and hanging curtains. Everything was ready when my husband came back.

By then, life should have been on an even keel, but incidents still occurred. On one occasion, to my alarm, my husband did not return from a cocktail party at the Soviet Embassy until next day – he had gone on to nightclubs with some of the Russians. I found I could take it no longer. I saw my life collapsing in ruins. I had given up two careers and had no proper job. I had lost confidence in myself, personally and professionally. One August day in 1955, I packed my bags and left while my husband was at work. I fled first to friends in Norfolk and then went to ground in Mrs Peryt's shabbily comfortable front room in Cambridge. Had my husband come to look for me immediately I would almost certainly have gone back.

When term restarted Mrs Peryt found me a bed-sitting-room elsewhere, a bleak place, where I cooked on a gas ring and daily hauled coal for the fire up from the cellar. Being permanently in Cambridge I could take on more supervisions, but my earnings did not make a living wage. This hand-to-mouth existence was salutary, for I came to realise that even living in these depressed and depressing circumstances was better than the ostensibly more comfortable life I had left behind. So when, three months after my departure, my husband appeared unannounced one Sunday morning and begged me to return, there was no hesitation in my refusal.

I had to remake my life somehow. One possibility was to return to an academic career. Poor Inez Macdonald did not recover from her cancer and her death left vacant a lectureship in the Cambridge Spanish Faculty. I threw my hat into the ring, but without great hope, for there were other more highly qualified contenders. Accordingly, when Denis Healey won a seat in the House of Commons, I applied for his former post of head of the International Relations Department of the Labour Party. To my amazement I was short-listed and underwent an intimidating interview by a group of Labour politicians, chaired by Herbert

Morrison. I was told that the decision lay between me and one other candidate, a man. I was deeply interested in politics and the idea of getting on the springboard for a political career held considerable attractions.

Fate stepped in. Out of the blue I received a telephone message from James Keen (he of the cocktail-shaker fiasco), who was passing through London. He had heard from Malcolm Adiseshiah, a mercurial and highly intelligent Indian, who as Assistant Director-General of UNESCO had visited us in the Philippines and later in London, that my husband and I had separated. Both of them, as well as Gustavo Martínez Cabañas, had reported favourably on my work to David Owen, who wanted me to rejoin the UN immediately, this time as deputy resident representative in Mexico, an international professional post. I had to take a decision before learning the outcome on my other two irons in the fire – academic and political.

Return to the United Nations

Christina drove my parents up to Cambridge and we spent one whole Sunday agonising over what I should do. In the end the UN option won. My parents thought it helpful for some distance to be put between me and the traumatic events of my personal life. I had always longed to go to Latin America and I kidded myself that, during my two-year contract, I could do research on Latin American literature that would heighten my chances of a university post. I accepted the offer, and agreed to leave on 5 December, only a week or so later. I began furiously making preparations, but then, in typical UN fashion, a pall of silence fell. The proposed date of my departure for New York slipped past without any message. Christmas, with my parents, came and went. I began to think that it had all fallen through and no one dared tell me.

Then, just after New Year, I received an urgent summons to fly to New York on 8 January for two weeks' briefing, and then proceed to ... Colombia! Mystified, I later learned that the resident representative in Mexico, Raymond Etchats, had refused to accept me. A woman, he objected, could not possibly work in a senior role in the 'macho' environment of Mexico. Shades of the Foreign Office, I thought, as I swallowed my disappointment.

The Colombia appointment was for three months only. The deputy there had been transferred to New York, and the resident representative had suddenly resigned. Hence, the Bogotá office was rudderless. One of the technical assistance experts was appointed in an acting capacity but as he was unfamiliar with the workings of the UN my presence was needed to support him.

In New York I discovered a sinister reason for the silence and delay. Mervyn Brown, my erstwhile leading man in Spanish plays in London, was serving in the UK Permanent Mission to the United Nations. To my naive surprise, I learned that, in the aftermath of McCarthyism and the witch hunt against supposed communists, the United States Government was still vetting staff appointments to the United Nations, in contravention of the statutes and international character of the organization and its supposedly independent civil service. The Americans had noted – how? one wonders – that I had worked closely with Donald Maclean and demanded clarification from their British colleagues. The UK Mission, Mervyn told me in confidence, had cabled London, and the Foreign Office had sent assurances that I was 'clean'. Reassuring as this was, it left a nasty taste. It was also ironic that the Americans were the only ones ever to query my association with Maclean.

There was much to do before my departure. I wanted a divorce but then only three grounds were possible: adultery, cruelty or desertion. I knew that the first had taken place but could not prove it. I could prove the second, but to do so would wreck my husband's career and I wanted to avoid that at all costs. Through solicitors, I proposed that he should divorce me for desertion, a lengthy process, but the least of all the evils. True, I would appear as the 'guilty' party, but this would not harm my career prospects and would safeguard his. My husband flatly refused. He did not want a divorce, though he must have known that reconciliation was impossible.

It was highly unsatisfactory to fly off to the other side of the world for two years with all of this in limbo. A married woman of uncertain status, or a divorcée, would have a difficult row to hoe in Latin America. Such considerations seem quaint today, but were all too real in 1956. I decided to change back to my maiden name, and revert to single status to all intents and purposes. This was done through a statutory declaration and a new passport.

Jet aircraft were not yet roaring across the commercial skies, and transatlantic flights required refuelling stops at Shannon in Ireland, and Gander in Newfoundland. You left London at 8 o'clock at night and arrived in New York about 7 a.m., 16 hours later.

At Northolt Airport, on 8 January 1956, I bade a tearful farewell to my parents for another two years, on a wintry night, a blustering wind blowing the first snowflakes across the runway. We had a bumpy descent into Shannon, where we learned that dangerous weather conditions over the Atlantic would not allow us to proceed. We were given dinner, and put in cell-like rooms with bunks in a wooden building on the airfield. At dawn we struggled across the tarmac in the half-light and the teeth of a gale to reboard our plane. I still recall the smell of peat bog, wafting in on the salty wind.

Over Newfoundland a raging snowstorm prevented our landing in Gander. After circling for what seemed like hours, the plane, buffeted by ferocious winds, finally landed in a blizzard at the military airfield of Stanleyville on the other side of the island. The base was buzzing with US troops en route to Europe. There was not a seat to be had and food had run out, the troops being given priority.

Tired, cold and hungry we waited for several hours before the weather in New York improved. Even so, our descent into that city was one of the worst I have experienced, and many passengers were sick. I had other things to worry about: I had no money. Foreign exchange restrictions were still tight in England and I had not had time to complete the lengthy process of obtaining dollars. Naively I had thought that I would be met, as in Manila we had always met visitors from New York, but instead of arriving in daylight we landed the following midnight, over 17 hours late. Luckily, a fellow passenger lent me five dollars for my taxi into the city.

I had been put in the Beekman Tower Hotel, on First Avenue, an ultra-respectable establishment, considered suitable for single ladies travelling alone. From my window, at about 2 a.m. that wintry night, I gasped at my first close sight of the towering Manhattan skyscrapers of central New York sparkling with a million points of light that dimmed the stars in the frosty sky above. Exhausted as I was, I felt exhilarated by the magnificent skyline, an omen of an exciting new life. I was less enchanted next morning, when the first words I heard at breakfast came from a waiter shouting raucously, 'One toasted English!' Unversed as I was in the so-called English muffin or the New Yorker's clipped economy of speech, it sounded positively threatening.

My digestion of the facts and figures I was supposed to assimilate during the next two weeks was severely hindered by the ministrations of the UN Medical Service. They decreed that I had so much wax in my ears that I could not possibly be hearing properly and syringed my ears so vigorously that they deafened me completely – a frightening experience in a huge, strange city.

Everyone emphasised that I was the first international woman field officer being sent in a representational position by the UN and it was crucial that my mission should be a success, as it would serve as a precedent for other women. This placed an alarming burden of responsibility on my shoulders. Moreover, what I was told about the problems confronting the office and some of the representatives of the specialised agencies, not to mention the fact that Colombian women still did not have the vote, made the chances of failure seem dismayingly high. No one could tell me what would happen after this three-month assignment, other than that they would try to 'sell' me to a resident representative less sensitive about the impact of a female on the government than the man in Mexico. More encouraging was the warm reception given me by the Colombian Ambassador to the UN who plied me with advice and useful introductions.

American friends showed me the sights of New York and the contrast with my cloistered life of the previous six months could hardly have been greater. But though I was bowled over by Manhattan, I knew that I did not want to stay. My over-powering desire was to return to development work in the field.

PART THREE

Field Missions in the New World and Africa

8

The Athens of the Americas

The Avianca flight to Colombia left New York at 10 a.m. but did not reach Bogotá until midnight, stopping at the Caribbean port of Baranquilla. There I realised my dream to set foot on the continent of Latin America. I floated down the steps of the aircraft on a wave of euphoria, even imagining my emotions to be similar of those of 'stout Cortés, silent, upon a peak in Darien', though goodness knows what I thought I had come to conquer. I knew I would always recall that moment.

And so I have, for more mundane reasons. My romantic reverie was interrupted by an Avianca stewardess, demanding briskly: '*Qué le provoca*?' (literally 'What is provoking you?'). I was struck speechless. *Nothing* was provoking me; I was living a great and unforgettable moment. I was still searching for a reply when she repeated the offending phase, adding for clarification, but only to my confusion, '*Un tintico*?' What on earth was a *tintico*? I came down to earth with a crash, and was beset with panic that my Spanish had not survived even the first hurdle.

Later I learned that '*Qué le provoca*?' is the polite Colombian way of asking you what you would like to have, and a *tintico* is a very small cup of very black coffee. I felt vindicated later when a Latin American visitor from the World Health Organisation (WHO), asked by the Minister of Health whether he would like a *tintico*, and thinking it meant a small glass of red wine (*vino* tinto) expressed preference for cognac, which had to be hastily fetched from the corner café.

As the plane doors opened in Santa Fé de Bogotá, 2600 metres above sea level, a most agreeable scent assailed me, a mixture of eucalyptus, wood smoke and some indefinable high-mountain aroma that I was ever after to associate nostalgically with the savannah of Bogotá and its surrounding hills.

I was whisked away to a modest *pensión* in the centre of the city and spent Sunday exploring. I immediately fell in love with Bogotá, then a comparatively small city of less than a million inhabitants, its fringes lapped by the surrounding savannah. Every morning early you would see *campesinos* (country-folk) walking into market huddled in their *ruanas* (the Colombian poncho) against the dawn chill, and leading donkeys laden with produce for urban dwellers who had not yet discovered the blessings (or otherwise) of supermarkets. Town and countryside merged into one another. The old part, near the Presidential Palace, remained quintessentially colonial in its architecture and in the maze of narrow, cobbled streets, lined with shuttered stone houses whose secretive façades and ancient, iron-studded doors sheltered flowering patios clustered round a central fountain.

The rainy climate was not unlike that of England, but without snow or harsh winters, and there was the same store of jokes about the weather. One of my favourite related to Jiménez de Quesada, the Spanish conquistador who led his men up from the Caribbean coast through the torrid jungle of the River Magdalena, until at last they reached the airy uplands of the savannah. There Jiménez de Quesada ordered the survivors to pitch their tents, adding 'When it stops raining, we will move on.' That, the story went, was how Bogotá was founded ... Another joke concerned Montserrat, the hill that towers over Bogotá, crowned by a church which is a place of pilgrimage for sinners who are sturdy as well as repentant. 'When you can see the top of Montserrat,' the story goes, 'it is about to rain.' Pause: 'When you can't, it's raining already.'

I was quickly made to feel at home. Marcel Croisier (the French expert temporarily in charge of the UN office) and his wife had daughters of my age and treated me as a member of the family. On my first day I met Elfriede Sollmann, a WHO maternal and child care expert. She was older than I was, but we discovered that we had both been taught Spanish literature by Helen Grant, my old Cambridge supervisor. Our friendship lasted until Elfriede's death in 1997. Since I was to stay only three months, I lived in a series of temporary homes. In the end I stayed 15, and so lived like a gypsy. The reaction of my Colombian friends was noteworthy, especially when I moved into a delightful little mews house. It was, they intimated tactfully, unseemly that I, a single woman, should live alone; and entreated me to share a home with Elfriede – something that neither of us had the slightest desire to do.

Marcel Croisier was only too glad to devote himself to his technical mission and leave the running of the office to me, putting in an appearance for important visitors, or high-level meetings with the Government. Since Marcel spoke scant English, and far from fluent Spanish, I acted as interpreter from French into Spanish and vice versa, a salutary experience that at last disentangled the two languages in my mind. There being no other international officer, I again found myself doing everything from signing cheques and trying (usually ineffectually) to make the accounts balance, to calling on government ministers. We had a large mission, in areas ranging from industry, vocational training, agriculture and employment to educational reform and public administration.

Soon after my arrival I was bidden to a regional meeting of resident representatives in Mexico in February 1956. James Keen wanted to present me there in the hope that one of them would accept me as his deputy. Raymond Etchats, the host, greeted me with some embarrassment. Another initial encounter was not encouraging: Miguel Albornoz, the resident representative in Argentina, Paraguay and Uruguay (whom I succeeded in Uruguay the following year) demanded peremptorily that I take dictation. I was glad to be able to reply that I had never learned to type, much less take shorthand. There was also some function where my presence, as the only woman, was considered unsuitable. I was given the role of rapporteur, so my evenings were taken up writing notes while the men were out enjoying themselves. Towards the end Julia Henderson, then head of social development at UN Headquarters and a good few years my senior, came to brief us on her recent tour in Latin America. She did so brilliantly, with a wealth of cogent analysis that shamed the men and rejoiced my heart. Quite unfairly Julia never became the first woman Assistant Secretary-General. She was more qualified than most men who scaled those heights, but her American nationality, and the practice of filling such posts by outside political appointments, told against her.

I was dazzled by Mexico, and could not quell some regrets that I had not been assigned there. Here indeed was a great city, designed with a sense of grandeur and beauty, like some New World Paris. Its grand boulevards, sweeping the length and breadth of the city, interspersed with immense fountains, flowering gardens and over-life-size statues, exuded confidence and national pride. Yet this was no pale reflection of a European city. Wherever you went you were left in no doubt that you were in Mexico – the vibrant colours, the markets, the thrilling music of the *Mariachis* (traditional Mexican musicians) and the sheer abundance of Mexican creativity, reflected in everything from crafted silver to the architecture itself, in which so much of Mexican culture was intertwined. The Zócalo, the rose-red square around whose vast open space are clustered the ancient cathedral, lopsided from many earthquakes, and the main government buildings, encapsulated the rich tapestry of Mexican history, most of all the Aztec heritage, still vivid through layers of superimposed civilisations.

I visited Aztec ruins, the ancient floating gardens of Xochitl, the archaeological museums, and thrilled to the rhythms and sheer *joie de vivre* of the Mexican Folklore Ballet. Fernando Cuén Barragán, my friend from Foreign Office days in London, whisked me round all the sights and took me to a steer-lassoing event that I found exciting but cruel – though less so than a bullfight.

I returned to Bogotá slightly drunk with the sheer beauty and vitality of Mexico. I could see why J. B. loved it so – it more than met his criteria of being 'alive'. That was before smog began to obscure the splendours of the capital or the earthquake destroyed much of its treasures.

Head of Mission in Colombia

I returned without any inkling of a new destination; James Keen had not managed to sell 'the slave girl'. Moreover, the eventual incumbent of the Bogotá post was not immediately available. So the three-month mission became extended, month by month. In August 1956

Marcel Croisier left and New York appointed me Officer-in-Charge. I trembled all the way back from the airport after seeing the Croisiers off. Our programme was large, and the international personnel included a few prima donnas, all men considerably older than myself, while the inter-agency rivalries that bedevilled the UN system from the start were alive and well. The government, a military dictatorship, presided over by General Rojas Pinilla, could hardly have been more *machista*. As the only female UN international field officer and now the first woman placed in charge of a country programme, I felt the responsibility to be overwhelming.

In fact it was one of the great formative experiences of my life. Thrown in at the deep end I found that I could swim; there is nothing like having major responsibility thrust upon one when young to bolster one's confidence and capacity. It is a challenge that should happen to more women, and that more women, often excessively diffident, should be prepared to accept. The team of experts that I was to coordinate were as apprehensive as I at the outset, but we were soon working harmoniously together. The same was true of the government which, when the time came for me to leave nine months later, requested that I stay on as the titular resident representative.

The political situation was complicated. The country had not recovered from the so-called *Bogotazo* in 1948, when the popular leader, Gaitán, was assassinated, and the capital erupted in a frenzy of rioting, killing and looting. The star of Rojas Pinilla's government, in power since 1952, was waning, amid rumours of corruption, and because freedom-loving Colombians chafed under military rule. Violence was endemic in parts of the countryside, most notoriously in the Department of Tolima, home of beautiful music and dances but also of gruesome acts of barbarism. This was the fruit of age-old rivalries between the two main political parties, the Conservatives and the Liberals, though it was hard to tell their policies apart, as noted in a satirical song by two popular folk-singers, Garzón and Collazos, themselves natives of Tolima. This compared them to two local flowers – 'cambulos' and 'gualandayas', the ones blue and the others red, but otherwise indistinguishable. Those highly nuanced allusions were as close as anyone dared get to a song of protest.

One weekend Elfriede and I visited Tolima, riding in on horseback to an isolated coffee farm, belonging to a friend. The place was half-abandoned and we slept in hammocks on the verandah, at times disturbed by sinister rustlings and flickering lights in the undergrowth encircling the hacienda. Riding farther afield on Sunday morning we came upon a village of thatched huts, totally abandoned, with only a few hens and pigs scavenging in the dust, the embers in the cooking fires still glowing red. The people must have fled a few hours earlier. It was an eerie experience. Looking back, the whole expedition was rash, and we were lucky to return unscathed.

Our mission was providing assistance to important development projects, as well as some much needed reforms. A major endeavour was the multipurpose river development project in the Cauca Valley, near Cali. The big mover was the World Bank, but my FAO team was advising on agricultural aspects. The reform of the education system and of the public administration were both the brainchildren of the brilliant and dynamic young Minister of Education, Gabriel Betancur Mejia, who also chaired the Commission on Public Administration. Gabriel had made his name earlier by setting up ICETEX, which gave state loans to enable outstanding students to study abroad, in return for a pledge to return and repay the loan. It provided access to university education to thousands of Colombians and profoundly affected the country's development through the influx of highly qualified graduates. It still exists, and has parented a network of similar institutions in other Latin American countries.

Gabriel's thesis was that education is the key to development, and that money spent on it should not be considered as social expenditure but *investment*, a novel idea at the time. After a long struggle, he managed to convince the World Bank (which previously refused to finance educational projects because they were not deemed to produce returns on capital in the accepted manner), as well as the Inter-American Development Bank. In Colombia the main effort centred on preparing a five-year educational plan, the first such in Colombia, and I believe in the world, assembled by a team of experts provided bilaterally by Spain under the leadership of Ricardo Díez Hochleitner, who was to do great things later, both at UNESCO and in his own country. Some UNESCO experts were also assisting, and I became personally involved. That work transformed the Colombian education system.

The work in public administration was not so successful, mainly because of deeply rooted traditions. It was not for lack of good advice. The UN team was excellent, led by a brilliant Frenchman, Maurice Chailloux-Dantel, who sadly died prematurely. Gabriel's idea was to transform the Colombian administrative system by putting in place a career civil service, discouraging nepotism, and overhauling government organisation and procedures. Perhaps the endeavour might have been more successful had he stayed longer in government (he resigned early in 1957). But he probably put his finger on a basic problem when, gazing over the ancient ramparts of the lovely old colonial port of Cartagena de las Indias, he remarked to me: 'Had the British fleet defeated the Spanish here' (which they came within a whisker of doing) 'then Colombia and the rest of Latin America would have had a British administrative system, rather than the Spanish one that still gives us so much trouble.'

Some other projects betrayed typically Colombian characteristics. Elfriede had a moral dilemma in her maternal and child care course, when the authorities decreed that a student could not attend because she was a *Protestant*! Herself a Quaker, Elfriede said that in that case she could not teach the course and the matter was resolved, after much anguish. In the intensely Catholic Bogotá of those years it would simply not occur to anyone that you could be anything but a Catholic if you washed behind your ears and were socially acceptable. People were quite stunned when they found that I was not, as on one regrettable occasion when I inadvertently served meat on a Friday to important officials.

Colombia was the site of another pioneering endeavour: Radio Sutatenza, the first radio programme in Latin America (and I believe in all the developing world) aimed at educating rural folk. It was started by a Catholic priest, Father, later Monseñor, Salcedo. Programmes giving advice on agriculture and health as well as literacy classes were beamed out from a small village in the mountains and UNESCO experts provided technical assistance.

Monseñor Salcedo's initiative was remarkable in a church still embedded in the conservatism of the nineteenth century, and more concerned with maintaining a hierarchical society in which the peasants would retain their traditional place at the bottom of the pile.

I went several times to Sutatenza, a typical highland village huddled round a large cobbled square, where folk from the surrounding countryside brought their produce to market. One Sunday morning I was persuaded to visit some outlying parts of the community on horseback. The horse would not go despite urgings and, after a few miles in a stop-go fashion, one of the Colombians said to me, 'You've got to thwack it hard.' I did so, and hey presto, my sluggish steed was galvanised into action and took off at the speed of light. Once in full flight, there was no stopping him. Clearly he was thinking, 'I've had enough of this tomfoolery for one day', for he ran in a circle, heading back for the village. Try as I might, I could not rein him in, and concentrated my energies on staying on his back. I was clinging to his mane when we surged into the square at full gallop, scattering market women, chickens, pigs and donkeys in all directions and narrowly missing baskets of vegetables, fruits and eggs. Reaching our starting point, the horse stopped dead in his tracks, and I all but shot over his head. *Campesinos* came clustering round, not clamouring, as I feared, for compensation for their scattered wares, but chorusing praise for my riding prowess. Too embarrassed – or perhaps too vain – to put them straight, I simply smiled modestly.

Life in Bogotá

Bogotanos proudly called their city 'the Athens of the Americas'. I went to many lectures and immersed myself in Colombian authors, still hoping to return to the academic stage in Cambridge. The place abounded with poets. A favourite joke was of two poets meeting and simultaneously putting their hands to their breast pockets, saying threateningly, 'If you read me yours I'll read you mine', just as in bygone times their hands might have gone to their swords, in readiness for a duel.

The *bogotanos* speak Spanish with a formal precision and sonority that set them apart from the rest of Latin America. Some phrases that initially stumped me came from the seventeenth century, carefully preserved, long after they had been lost in Spain. The office driver, José, never used the formal Spanish address *Usted* (which derives from *Vuestra Merced* or 'Your Grace,') but addressed me as *'su persona'* ('your person'), prefacing his remarks to me, with unconscious condescension, with the phrase, *'Pero señorita, pónga su persona a pensar'* ('But, Señorita, just set your person to think.' I was left with the sense of some alter ego out there who could do the thinking of which José was clearly convinced that I was incapable. Soon I was speaking with a near approximation of the Bogotá accent, and had dropped the *ceceo*, the Spanish lisping pronunciation of the letter 'c' as 'th', so painstakingly drilled into me at Cambridge. It sounded affected to Colombian ears, and was about as popular as someone not English insisting on speaking with an Oxford accent in the USA.

Formality was the very essence of social life. Bogotá was then a sober, almost frugal city, partly as a result of the climate, partly because of the innate temperament of its denizens. It might as aptly have been called 'the London of the Americas'. There was something irrepressibly familiar in the sobriety of dress, the men's Homburg hats and dark overcoats, the women's trimly tailored suits. It seemed no wonder that several Colombians I had met in London had settled so easily into that northern environment, indistinguishable from their English counterparts.

One must not push the analogy too far. I soon found in the office that an English sense of humour not only fell flat but risked causing offence. It was not that Colombians lacked humour, it was just different. Nor were their ideas of time and punctuality exactly British. They were best summed up in the story of the radio announcer who declared, 'I shall now tell you the exact time' – pause – *'Son las seis pasaditas'* – 'It's just a tiny bit after six o'clock.'

Despite long hours there was time for enjoyment. A favourite Sunday outing was to the picturesque village of Tabio on the savannah to eat the local delicacy of *sobrebarriga y papas churreadas* – a special cut of beef, with spicy potatoes. For a while Elfriede and I took lessons from a fierce Portuguese riding-master, who had us galloping around, bareback, in the circle described by his lethally cracking whip, but enthusiasm waned when I fell on my head and was nearly knocked unconscious. There was also much music and occasional dancing.

Within an hour or so of Bogotá lay a warmer, subtropical world on the eastern side of the Andes. On Sundays we would descend into the steep valley where the falls of Tequendama, (favourite launching site, the legend went, of star-crossed lovers who had decided to precipitate themselves into the next world), crashed in a crystalline spiral into a deep gorge. Below there were bananas, bougainvillea, hibiscus and many other tropical delights, as well as rustic hotels with cloudy swimming-pools, leaving much to be desired in sanitary conditions but welcome respite to the cold austerity of cloud-enshrouded Bogotá.

For Easter 1956 we flew to Popayán, the southern colonial city near the Ecuadorian border. We stayed in a white-walled *pensión*, and followed the colourful, passionate ceremonies of Holy Week – the procession of the Virgin Mary borne high upon the shoulders of the faithful, through cobbled streets, fringed by convents, richly ornate churches and arcades wreathed in bougainvillea – in a ritual unchanged in almost 500 years.

Nor were my journeys confined to Colombia. I was bidden to Jamaica, to meet David Owen, the head of the UN Technical Assistance Board, for the first time. The meeting took place in the office of the British colonial governor, Sir Hugh Foot, later Lord Caradon. Having sized up the only female field officer on his staff, David was whisked away to official appointments. I was to spend the day with Lady Foot, at a cricket match between Jamaica and the Duke of Norfolk's touring eleven, where David and the governor joined us for lunch and the afternoon's play. David confided that he felt less than an overwhelming passion for cricket, and requested George Cadbury, the senior UN expert, to extricate us at six o'clock sharp.

When six o'clock came the match was working up to a dramatic finale, rare in cricket, and the excitement was frenetic. The trees were full of gesticulating Jamaicans, swaying and chanting with no regard for life and limb. George Cadbury came, as instructed, but found us ungratefully hissing, 'Go away ... !' Jamaica won, on the last ball, when all its supporters fell out of the trees and surged on to the pitch.

Journeys in Colombia

In Colombia I was able to indulge my taste for travel in remote parts acquired in the Philippines. After a train journey to the head of the River Magdalena, Elfriede and I embarked in an antique paddle-steamer, reminiscent of those seen on vintage films of the Mississippi, only here there were no gambling casinos, elegant ladies, swaggering beaux nor even gangsters. The journey down to the Caribbean coast took four days of sailing between jungle-clad shores, tying up at night in mangrove swamps, or in primitive ports of wooden jetties and tumbledown shanties, in riverside townships reached by neither road nor rail, where the steamboat was the only contact with the outside world. My enjoyment of this incursion into an anachronistic enclave that had hardly changed for a century was marred by a recurrence of dengue fever from the Philippines. It was alarming as well as excruciating and I was glad to arrive in the sordidly dispiriting port of Baranquilla to obtain treatment.

Another journey took me, this time alone, to a rural education project in the Guajira, the semi-desert peninsula shared with Venezuela. I flew to Santa Marta, a picturesque town to the east of Baranquilla, white houses strung like pearls around an iridescent Caribbean bay, slumbering between a glistening white strand and the snow-clad Sierra Santa Marta. A small plane took me to an airstrip near the project, where I spent two days marvelling at the abnegation of teachers who strive to educate the young in God-forsaken places in the developing world, despite abysmal living conditions and minimal facilities, forgotten by the distant government. I nearly had to stay with them indefinitely, as there was no transport out. Eventually I got a lift on top of a lorry, full of young people. We drove all night, a warm tropical night of full moon, bouncing through endless miles of scrub and sand, the moonlight casting strange, dancing shadows over the stark land-scape, the sky ablaze with stars and the air full of mingled fragrances wafted on the night breeze. It was an exhausting but exhilarating experience.

In 1956 I spent the most unusual Christmas of my life. The remoteness and inhospitable geography of the Colombian part of the Amazon basin made it impossible for the ministry of education to provide normal services to Indian tribes still living very primitive lives and the responsibility had been delegated to Catholic missions. Their headquarters, or *Prefectura Apostólica*, was located in the small town of Leticia at the precise point in the so-called *Trapecio* where the frontiers of Colombia, Peru and Brazil meet on the banks of the Amazon. The Apostolic Prefect, Monseñor Marceliano Cañyes, an impressive, bearded Catalan in his early forties, had spent many years in the jungle. His otherwise handsome face was pock-marked by smallpox and burnt dark by the tropical sun. When he embarked on the river and removed his cumbersome soutane, to travel in slacks and singlet, with a pith helmet on his head, he looked more like a genial river pirate than a priest.

I flew down on 21 December with Monseñor Marceliano and Monseñor Nyisztn, a Hungarian refugee who had worked with Cardinal Mindszenty until the latter had been imprisoned by the Communist regime. He was a cantankerous old gentleman who loved his creature comforts and would have tried the patience of a saint. In an unpressurised military plane, the cargo baled and roped in front of us, we flew over the cordillera through torrential rain, which dripped through the roof, and landed at Apiay, a military airport in the plains of the Llanos. There followed three hours of flying over jungle, broken only by brown ribbons of rivers – Vaupés, Caquetá and Putumayo. The Amazon, from the air, looked narrow and a dirty mud colour, but in my journeyings on it I was to find it immensely imposing, over one-and-a-half miles wide, though still thousands of miles from the ocean, with jungle-covered shores so distant that one had the impression of floating on a vast lagoon.

Leticia was a pretty town, pleasantly shaded with trees, the houses of white painted boards with palm roofs but the streets were a quagmire of mud, almost impassable even for the mission's lorry. I stayed at the sisters' convent but had all my meals in Monseñor's house. I joined in the activities of the mission, visiting the hospital and the health centre, attending church services, travelling up and down the river between schools sparsely scattered in clearings in the jungle. In the evening we would go down to the banks of the Amazon to watch the sun set red behind the jungle on the other side of the river, in Peru – a truly majestic sight. Our evenings were spent in discussion of many topics, from the Spanish Civil War to religion, on which Monseñor Marceliano held unexpectedly liberal views.

Monseñor Marceliano was the prototype of the best type of sixteenth-century missionary – a mind alight with adventure and humanitarian ideals, as well as religious zeal. Sor Vicenta, the mother superior, a jolly *antioqueña* (from the Department of Antioquia) exuded much the same spirit. Once when our boat came adrift and was being carried downstream she calmly picked up her long white skirts, started the outboard motor, and got us back to our moorings in a jiffy. A young priest, Padre Ignacio, had been a professional footballer, and now tore around Leticia on a motorcycle, his surplice tucked up round his waist, the ends flying in the breeze. The remoteness of their lives, and the vast, largely uncharted region that they covered, beggared belief. One afternoon a French Canadian priest arrived by river after a journey of eight days – all to get a visa.

Every day at 5 a.m. a brass band banged in the dawn, accompanied by rockets and clanging church bells. On Christmas Eve a ferocious tropical storm broke and midnight Mass had to be cancelled. After supper Padre Romualdo arrived with his flute, we had wine and cheese, and sang Christmas carols and Spanish folk-songs. Three Masses were celebrated on Christmas Day in a full church. There was a choir of young men, slightly discordant; and the parish band, complete with guitars and maracas as well as wind instruments, blew its way laboriously through various numbers, including several *villancicos* (carols) that had the lilt of dance tunes. At each devotion the national anthem was played.

The Mass was a mixture of pagan ritualism and an ingenuous faith that was quite moving: the rich robes, the swinging censer pouring forth clouds of incense; the tawdry artificial flowers; the bald electric light bulbs round the image of the Virgin; the ragged trouser legs and mud-caked boots visible below the creased red robes of the acolytes. At the end of the first Mass the congregation filed up to kiss a doll dressed in blue, representing the infant Christ, Padre Ignacio solicitously wiping off the traces of each kiss with a scrap of rag. During the third Mass Padre Romualdo played the Coventry carol, obviously for me, for I had sung it the previous evening.

In the mission's *deslizador*, or motorboat, we criss-crossed the Amazon to Brazil and Peru in search of supplies, unhindered by customs or immigration. The nearest Brazilian village, Benjamin Constant, was an insalubrious collection of rough wooden houses on stilts over pools of stagnant water, ideal mosquito breeding-grounds, where pigs and vultures picked their way among the refuse. It was hard to imagine anything further from the idyll of Paul and Virginie created by the French author.

Pleasanter excursions took us to necklaces of lagoons, hidden by the jungle wall marking the main river, and reached by narrow creeks overarched by tall trees looped with creepers and orchids, and fringed with bright green mangrove swamps. These waters were alive with brightly coloured birds, trees laced with egrets, brilliantly blue kingfishers, parrots and even gulls and ducks. Giant butterflies in dazzling colours floated by, and the jet-black water was constantly rippled by shoals of fish or broken by the bouncing snouts of *bufeos*. The Indian families fished with harpoons, we with a cast net that quickly caught our lunch, including the tiny, red-bellied pirañas that would as readily have eaten us alive had we ventured into those waters. Along the slimy mud shore crocodiles basked and slithered, lying in wait for a meal.

Our longest trip took us 50 miles up river to Puerto Nariño. We passed several canoes, one with a rounded roof of dried leaves, while in another the doubtless aristocratic passengers held a black umbrella against the sun in one hand, while paddling madly with the other. At the water's edge women knelt in canoes, washing clothes, and naked Indian children waved excitedly. Our engine broke down several times. Then, when Monseñor Nyisztn was proclaiming at ever briefer intervals that he had no spinal column left, we came into sight of Puerto Nariño. It consisted of the priest's house, the chapel, and two *internados*, one for boys and one for girls, lying on low green hillocks above a beautiful lake off the main stream.

In the afternoon Padre Casimiro, a gaunt bearded man straight out of an El Greco painting, took me into the jungle. With machetes we hacked through thick undergrowth and trailing lianas and slashed trees to mark our way out. There was something frightening about the pulsating growth all around us stretching untracked for thousands of miles; the giant ants swarming along the rotting tree trunks; the pale green light and foetid atmosphere; the one solitary bird call leading one on like Circe herself; and the clouds of whining mosquitoes. My mood was scarcely cheered when we sat on a putrescent log and Padre Casimiro solemnly warned that this was a presage of the grave, when worms would consume us also. In the distance thunder rumbled and the jungle shuddered around us.

Don Casimiro confided that he had left Spain because he could not stand the régime, but could not discuss politics with the two lay teachers, Teresa and Jesús, who supported Franco. That night at supper, however, a fiery conversation, Catalan v. Basque, erupted between Monseñor Marceliano and Padre Casimiro about the Civil War.

This verbal battle ended abruptly, when Monseñor Nyisztin, whose cantankerousness was surpassed only by his gluttony, made a gurgling noise and passed out. His face was bright puce, and we feared a stroke or heart attack. The arrangement had been for me to sleep in the empty *internado*, while the two bishops would stay with Father Casimiro. The buildings were connected by a long narrow path, immured on either side by impenetrable jungle. I had been given a small torch in case anything went wrong during the night, and I had to make this hazardous journey. When we restored Monseñor Nyisztin to consciousness, it was clear that he must also stay in the *internado*. I had not much fancied spending the night alone, far from everyone else, but this prospect was no more enticing. I got hardly a wink of sleep on account of Monseñor Nyisztin's snores loudly audible through a thin partition. One part of me longed for the noise to subside, while the other realised that, if it did, I would have to brave the dark walk through the jungle to get help. As it was, his stertorous breathing continued unabated, and in the morning he was restored to his old petulant self. It was just a case of excessive overindulgence and my night alone with a monseñor in the Amazon jungle made a memorable anecdote.

I flew back to Bogotá with Monseñor Nyisztin in the plane of a certain 'Mr Mike' which carried exotic species to Miami zoos and should have arrived a week earlier, thus prolonging my stay. It was supposed to leave at 5 a.m. but luckily did not as, the only sign of Monseñor Nyisztin was flickering candlelight and the sound of muffled curses. At the airstrip in the jungle there was no activity, apart from the mosquitoes who made a hearty breakfast. About 6.10 a.m. a dilapidated lorry, known as the Phantom, limped into sight with some 50 prospective passengers clinging to every foot and handhold. After disgorging them the lorry careered along the airstrip to clear away the animals, and everyone surged towards the plane, clutching paper bags, bulging cartons, squawking parrots tied to their owner's wrist and jam jars of tropical fish. One of the sisters carried a turtle, which bore a smug expression, undoubtedly savouring all the fish it had devoured in the convent. No one weighed or labelled the baggage, no tickets were requested, no questions asked, and it was every man for himself. Three of the less fortunate didn't get seats, and had to hang from non-existent straps.

Just after 6.30 a.m., we took off, barely missing the trees at the end of the runway, the passengers hemmed in by an assorted cargo of monkeys, tropical birds and fish. I had my feet on a flimsy plywood case, marked 'Fragile', which I afterwards discovered contained two boa constrictors, each 14 feet long and thicker than a man's thigh. It didn't need a major process of thought to realise that the 'Fragile' referred to the case rather than the contents. On arrival in Bogotá we were subjected to rigid customs examination. As I watched these very poor people being made to untie their bundles I couldn't help thinking of the three million pesos lost daily through coffee smuggling, without anything being done.

During the long evenings in Leticia, Monseñor Marceliano taught me to play chess. An insufficiently sensitive pupil, I had eventually beaten him, horrifying the other fathers: clearly it was more than their lives, or even their vocations, were worth to win, which was why they no longer played with him. Being of a forgiving nature, Monseñor always had a game with me whenever he came to Bogotá. I formed a warm friendship with this remarkable man, whom I greatly admired. Born into a poor family, he was the son who, in time-honoured Spanish tradition, had been offered to the church, which would provide education and a living for life, albeit a harsh one. Living in those inaccessible regions of limitless horizons, remote from outside contact, and in a church still circumscribed, especially in Colombia, by narrow intellectual horizons, he was the most tolerant and open-minded Catholic priest I had met. I could not help wondering what feats he might have achieved in some other walk of life. As it was, he unselfishly dedicated his life to peoples forgotten by the world.

Revolution and Departure

I was told that when the new resident representative came in May 1957, I would be transferred to Uruguay, as full resident representative. It was a small programme, but a feather in my cap. I wanted none of it. I loved Colombia, and felt that I could do many more useful things now that I had come to know the country and its people. I had made friends whom I was loathe to leave, and had lost my heart to one Colombian in particular.

New York was adamant, under pressure from the UN Commission on the Status of Women, to appoint at least one woman to join the solid male phalanx of resident representatives. Only I had the right experience and they promised it would mean promotion (I was still only a P.2, the second lowest rung of the professional ladder). The only alternative was to get a job in Bogotá. Some interesting overtures were made to me, but common sense told me they were likely to be precarious. In the event it was lucky for me that my pleas to remain in the deputy post went unheard.

I left with a bang, rather than a whimper. Colombia staged my first, but by no means last, experience of a revolution. The political situation had been deteriorating rapidly and in early May

1957 simmering popular discontent erupted into outright revolt. We all held our breath as thousands of school children marched along Carrera Séptima below our office, shouting for Rojas Pinilla and his government to go. I had my first experience of tear gas, as the military blanketed the centre of the city with foul, choking fumes. But we had expected something worse.

Loud explosions punctuated my efforts to pack, it became difficult to move about in the city, and I told Headquarters that it might be impossible to leave on the appointed date of 10 May. At the eleventh hour Headquarters informed me 'regretfully' that the promotions committee had decided that I was 'too young and inexperienced' to merit promotion. I retorted that in that case I was too young and inexperienced to take command as resident representative in Uruguay and hadn't I better remain in Bogotá in a post more commensurate with my age and perceived capacities?

This feud by cable ran parallel with the escalating revolt against the Government. After some very near squeaks, popular will reigned triumphant, without major military confrontation or bloodshed. An ingenious weapon devised by the Colombians was the massive use of car-horns, relentlessly pounding out the victory sound – the rhythm of the first bar of Beethoven's Fifth Symphony, used in British broadcasts to occupied Europe during the Second World War. Day and night the implacable message was pumped out by individual citizens all over Bogotá, reverberating from the surrounding hills.

Why did the Government not use military action to put down the revolt? Perhaps Rojas Pinilla thought the movement was too unanimous, across all classes, to be resisted; perhaps, therefore, that the cost in blood would be astronomically high; perhaps the memory of the *Bogotazo* was too fresh; or perhaps he was just tired of it all?

At any rate, on Sunday evening, 5 May, it was announced that Rojas Pinilla would go into exile. The chorus of klaxons grew to astronomic proportions, celebrating victory within grasp. I went with Gabriel to a packed Mass, where joy and relief shone on every face. Afterwards we stood at the door of the last of my many residences in Bogotá, listening in the darkness to the cacophony of horns, and other sounds of wild celebration.

It was an intoxicating moment. I found myself torn between joy that the people had triumphed, and sadness that I could not work with them to build the new future that beckoned.

Rojas Pinilla left Colombia on 10 May 1957. So did I – pure coincidence but one that enabled my Colombian friends to make pointed political and even more personal jokes. Nor was my departure easy. The remnants of 'peaceful' conflict were still around, the streets littered with tintacks to which the UN car fell victim. Gabriel came to the rescue, and drove me to the airport. There was hardly anyone else to see me off, travel around town being still restricted and the airport virtually closed for the general's departure.

As we taxied out to the runway I could hardly see the airport building recede into the distance for the tears coursing down my face. I doubt if even Rojas Pinilla could feel as sad and emotional as I did, as he took off from another part of the airport.

It was small consolation that I would not have had a happy time had I stayed. Months later David Owen confided to me that the new incumbent in Bogotá had launched a scurrilous campaign against me, claiming that my popularity with the Colombian authorities was due to my liberal dispensation of sexual favours to most of the Cabinet. Had that calumny been believed it would have been the kiss of death to my budding career. That it was not was a miracle, for David had met me only once, and none of the other senior officials (all men) knew me well. David said they ascribed the attack to the man's insecurity, and professional jealousy, because the Government had insisted that they would have preferred me to him. I thought it stemmed from something else. During a visit to Bogotá some months before the gentleman in question made strenuous but unsuccessful efforts to stay the night after a dinner I gave for him. This was his revenge for that rebuff.

It was a sobering illustration of the perils and pitfalls confronting a lone woman professional in Latin America in the 1950s, especially if you were young. But the term 'sexual harassment' had not yet been invented, and there was no redress. You just had to stick it out as best you could and hope that Providence was on your side.

9

The Purple Land

First Sight of La Paz

I hedge-hopped across the continent, stopping in Ecuador, where I briefly tasted the wonders of Quito, the most exquisitely preserved colonial heritage of all the Americas. In Lima, I enjoyed the old-fashioned luxury of that most British of hostelries, the Hotel Bolivar, and savoured the *pisco sours* for which it is justly famous. I visited museums and steeped myself in Inca arts and archaeology.

La Paz came next. From our DC-4 the coastal strip of the Peruvian desert seemed to mark the frontier of an uncharted world towards which the aircraft strained, its engines climbing at full throttle. We seemed barely to clear the jagged summits, which barred the horizon in an apparently impenetrable phalanx. It was the season of dry, cold, sunny weather in the Andean highlands and its bare, lunar landscape was limned with crystalline clarity against a cobalt sky. Lake Titicaca appeared below, penetrated by long fingers of land and ruffled by the wind into a myriad shades of blue. Harvest time was approaching and the subdued hues of the *altiplano* were mottled with warmer patches of yellow and bronze. In contrast the drab, adobe homesteads seemed to blend into the earth from which they had been built.

Then came the first breathtaking sight of the Cordillera Real (the Royal Cordillera) which borders the eastern edge of the Bolivian *altiplano*, and outvies the majesty of its name. From the grandiose, tumbled peaks of the Illampu at the northern end a fretwork of silvery pinnacles stretches for over 100 miles and guards the approach to La Paz, where the Illimani stands sentinel over the city.

The sense of unreality heightened as we landed. There was no sign of town or airport, only the flat expanse of the *altiplano*, stretching as far as the eye could see and broken only by a few small huts. These were the airport for, in keeping with the sturdy sense of individualism that infuses all aspects of Bolivian life, each company had its own miniature terminal. In a small room, seething with customs and immigration officials and boys throwing luggage around, the sparse oxygen available was diminished still further. The newcomer was left in no doubt that the dominating life principle was the survival of the fittest against tremendous odds.

After a short drive we came upon the missing city. The earth fell away abruptly, careening down into a deep ravine where, hundreds of feet below, the blue and red roofs of La Paz shone in crisp sunlight. The town straggled down this narrow defile cleft between the mountains, untidy lines of adobe huts, roofed with corrugated iron, pushing encroaching tentacles into the folds of the steep escarpment marking the end of the *altiplano*. This imposing panorama was given depth and magnificence by the Illimani, brooding with folded wings on the skyline like the legendary white condor of the Andes.

There was a vertiginous quality about the descent into La Paz, the narrow road twisting tortuously back on itself as it edged its way down the mountainside. The almost hallucinatory effect of the rare mountain air stretched the nerves in taut expectancy, heightened perceptions and gave a new dimension to vision. Along the way donkeys and sheep were being hustled along; lorries, piled improbably high with *campesinos* and produce, rocked perilously down the road. Lower down passers-by picked their way between the *cholitas* who squatted in long lines, clinging to the steep streets, their bowlers tilted at equally impossible angles as if in counter-equilibrium, as they offered their wares of vegetables and fruits, meat, trinkets and protective charms, tumbled together on the ground. It was a kaleidoscope of colour, synthesised in the swirling bell skirts of the women, brilliant reds and blues, oranges, pinks and mauves flaunting, as in some exotic ballet, against the background of sombre earth-coloured buildings and the unclouded winter sky.

The classic advice to the new arrival was to take a *maté de coca* – an infusion of the coca leaf supposed to relieve the effects of altitude – and to rest for 24 hours. I drank the bitter-tasting *maté* but rest proved impossible and I went out for a stroll. Soon I came to the Calle Zagárnaga, a narrow cobbled street climbing steeply alongside the San Francisco church, and proffering every conceivable kind of local merchandise: bright skirts and *aguayos* (the women's shawls) swinging like banners on poles in doorways; bowler hats nodding in serried ranks above; inside, counters piled with silverware, old and new, walls hung with the brightly beaded blouses and hats worn by Indian women on ceremonial occasions, and flamboyant devil costumes and masks in the tradition of the Oruro carnival. There is nothing one cannot buy in the Calle Zagárnaga, down to magic potions and the dried llama foetus which local superstition maintains must be buried in the foundations of every dwelling.

It was the scene outside the San Francisco church that most enthralled me. Its mellow walls glowed against the deepening blue of a sky shading into evening, and the magnificently carved façade, with its Spanish baroque pattern translated into Indian motifs by local craftsmen, portrayed the intertwining of the two cultures that formed this nation. In the foreground an aged merry-go-round creaked and groaned, bearing on each of its battered steeds, a *chola* (as women of mixed blood are called), or an Indian woman. Round and round they gyrated, with immense dignity and solemnity, their russet faces impassive as the horses rose and fell, their bowler hats tipped at the accepted, provocative angle, their babies trussed in shawls on their backs, sleeping or gazing out at bystanders with the same unwinking stare. It was at that moment that I resolved to come back to work in Bolivia, though how on earth I would manage this I could not imagine.

Début in Montevideo

Miguel Albornoz, whom I was replacing in Montevideo, was no ardent feminist: it was he who, in Mexico, had been as much astonished as affronted to learn that I could not type. But he was a stickler for protocol and had arranged my ceremonial reception at the airport by government dignitaries. His dismay was palpable when I telephoned to inform him that fog had caused my flight to be diverted from Buenos Aires, where I was to have spent the night. The airline was flying to Buenos Aires next day, but there seemed no point in my going since I had been bound for Montevideo anyway. Miguel was aghast. '*De ninguna manera!*' he cried. 'No way! You must go to Buenos Aires and come back in the *proper* manner. And tonight you remain incognito.' I skulked furtively into the Victoria Plaza Hotel, left before dawn, explored downtown Buenos Aires, and was received with due pomp and circumstance on my second landing in Montevideo.

My advent caused a more serious diplomatic contretemps. Uruguay prided itself on a democratic tradition and advanced social legislation unsurpassed on the continent, and was a welfare state long before the term was coined in postwar Britain. Women had the right to vote, could petition for divorce and were given considerable advantages in any settlement. Liberal doctrines in favour of the female sex did not extend to acceptance of a woman as head of the United Nations mission. The authorities greeted the proposal with consternation, and it was only after David Owen's personal intervention that my agrément was forthcoming. When I assumed my functions, one of the main concerns was that the Inter-Ministerial Commission of Technical Assistance met only after 9 p.m. at night and sat until the early hours because civil servants were employed only half-time. They had several other jobs and late evening was the only time the commission could meet.

The atmosphere at my first meeting was frosty. I was the only woman and they reacted with disbelief to my assurances that gender would in no way impair my willingness to meet with them at any hour. Their major preoccupation was how a lone female was to get home in the middle of the night. This problem was solved by appointing a subcommittee whose members took it in turn to escort me. Not long ago, at a reception in London, the Vice-President of Uruguay reminded me that he had been one of those late-night escorts, forty years before.

The early months were gruelling, as I had to convince this sceptical audience that I knew my stuff. Language was another pitfall. My Spanish was fluent, but in the vernacular spoken in the River Plate many words in common usage in Colombia and Spain had different, obscene meanings. I lived in terror of reducing all these men to ribald laughter by some slip of the tongue. After a while I was able, discreetly, to nudge some of the decisions on development priorities into more rational directions. A first tenet of the Uruguayan concept of democracy seemed to be, 'Never agree with anyone else.' Our midnight sessions were frustrating as well as exhausting.

Government structures reflected the same 'free-for-all' policy. There were two main political parties, the *Colorados* (reds) and the *Blancos* (whites). The former, mainly urban-based, were the more powerful, led by a remarkable political dynasty founded by José Batlle y Ordoñez, thrice President, and the architect of the political, economic and social reforms that had given this small country one of the highest living standards on the continent. His son was now leader of the party. The *Blancos* represented rural interests, especially those of the large *estancieros* (sheep and cattle ranchers). Their leader was a patriarchal figure, Luis Alberto Herrera.

Uruguay was governed by a national council of nine members, drawn from both parties, and with a rotating chairmanship. Admirable as this was in providing checks and balances to guard against dictatorship it was also extraordinarily effective in preventing clear decisions. I called on all the members of the council. My attempts to engage Batlle (then President of the Council) in a discussion of Uruguay's economic prospects and needs produced only a well-rehearsed disquisition on the virtues of *hierba maté*, the pungent infusion beloved of the *gauchos* (cowboys) and partaken of by every Uruguayan worthy of the name, sucked through silver straws from a silver-embossed gourd. 'This,' declaimed the President, 'is why Uruguay has a wonderful health record. The *gauchos* had to *boil* the water, and so did not acquire intestinal infections.' A reasonable enough thesis, it seemed hardly sufficient to revolutionise a nation's health.

My encounter with Herrera, the 'grand old man' of Uruguayan politics, was almost comic. He was then over 80, deaf as the proverbial post, and his glory was more past than present. After ten minutes of shouting into the ear he proffered at close range, I retired defeated. He concluded I was a Colombian living in Italy, just arrived from the United States, and leaving the following week. As we said goodbye he kindly wished me a *muy feliz viaje!* ('a very happy trip'). Nearly two years later it was my turn to wish him the same as he embarked on his final journey, on the occasion of his funeral, a huge event that brought Montevideo to a standstill.

The Foreign Minister did know who I was, but was at pains to stress that I could not hope to equal my predecessor. More encouragingly, the Chief of Protocol, who had an un-Uruguayan predilection for exquisite formalities, greeted me on that occasion, and all subsequent ones, as 'Your Excellency', in a manner reminiscent of Marcus Cheke. One day he was not available and a disgruntled porter received me gruffly, in the most contemptuous terms imaginable, '*Y usted qué quiere, jóven?*' ('And what do you want, young 'un?').

I was the only international officer in the office and all the local staff were female. It was my only experience of working in an all-female office and, contrary to traditional prejudices, we made a harmonious team. Our programme was not large but owing to the bizarre bargaining in the Inter-Ministerial Commission it encompassed a wide array of subjects — agriculture, fisheries, education, vocational training, textiles, public health, social welfare, cartographic training, deep sea diving and salvage work, meteorology, civil aviation, public administration (including reform of the postal services) and even some mining prospection.

Apart from an active cultural life, Montevideo bore the air of a cosy provincial town, slumbering in the lee of the hill (the Cerro) that had inspired Magellan to name it, 'I see a mountain.' There were few architectural gems: the town was a network of streets of grey stone buildings and terraced houses. There was a distinctly bourgeois, almost Victorian atmosphere about the place, tinged with a self-satisfaction, born of the awareness that theirs was a stable society, democratic, well provided for, and immune to the revolutions that beset its Latin American neighbours. The countryside, celebrated in W. H. Hudson's book *The Purple Land*, was similarly featureless – rolling pasture lands with scarcely a low hill to be seen from the River Plate to the Brazilian frontier, and hardly a human being either; of a population of two and a half million, 40 per cent lived in Montevideo. As in Wales, there were more sheep than people. The country's greatest asset was the string of bays and golden beaches along the north shore of the River Plate estuary, studded with modest resorts. Punta del Este, where the muddy brown waters of the River Plate met the white-crested Atlantic breakers, was more glamorous with its opulent villas and exotic nightlife, and was mainly favoured by Argentinians from Buenos Aires.

I arrived in winter, a dank and dismal season, which took toll on my health. While decorating the flat in Roehampton, I had fallen downstairs and bent my tailbone. Now I had excruciating back pain, and could barely walk. The specialist wanted to operate, but I refused. He told me that I could lead a 'normal life' for 'a few years yet' but must not walk far, dance, travel in jeeps or ride a horse. I asked him what he meant by 'normal'. In despair and total scepticism I went to see a Frenchman, who was not only a *chiropracteur* but also practised *kinésologie*. When he massaged my back I felt great warmth and the sensation of electric currents passing through my spine. I had gone into his office almost on all fours, and emerged walking upright. Despite intermittent problems with my back, I have continued to do all the things the Montevideo doctor advised against 40 years ago.

I rented an apartment in Pocitos, with a balcony overlooking the water, but was able to enjoy only the first weeks of summer, as my home leave was due on completion of my two-year contract. The United Nations offered me a permanent appointment and I abandoned my plans to return to an academic career. There were developments on the personal side also. My husband had lifted his opposition to divorce and admitted adultery. His circumstances had changed drastically; he had had to resign from the Foreign Service after leaving a despatch case containing confidential papers on top of a bus and his career could no longer be harmed by divorce.

The divorce case, heard in London on 14 January 1958, was a painful experience. Despite the admission of adultery, my barrister insisted that I recount some of the happenings in Manila. Almost worse was the knowledge that, as a result of other unfortunate incidents, my husband had lost another job after leaving the Foreign Service. The divorce proceedings had been put in train long before these calamitous events but it was nonetheless harrowing to confront him when I was well established professionally, and he unemployed and penniless. I was granted the decree nisi, with costs awarded against him, a mere technicality, since I was the only one able to pay. We did not meet again for 40 years during which he conquered his alcohol problem, found new employment and remarried.

The possibility of remarriage arose briefly in my own life, from an unexpected quarter. On my first day in Montevideo, when I was bent on creating an image of seriousness and efficiency, my secretary came in, bearing a long cable. 'This came from New York,' she said, looking rather pink, 'but I think it must be personal.' It was my turn to blush. The cable was from Joaquín Elizalde, former Foreign Minister of the Philippines, now their Permanent Representative to the United Nations. It contained an eloquent proposal of marriage. This was truly a bolt from the blue. My husband and I had seen him in London in 1955, but I had never heard from him in the intervening two years. The cable was followed by a gold cocktail watch (an 'advance engagement ring'). I penned a careful letter saying I felt deeply honoured *but* etc., etc. Joaquín was not to be put off. Another kilometric telegram arrived, begging me to stay a decision until we could meet. That did not happen until I passed through New York in December 1957.

Joaquín and his chauffeured Cadillac met me at the airport and in between my official meetings whisked me round the most glamorous places in New York: dinner on the evening of my arrival at the Four Seasons (where Barbara Hutton, the Woolworth heiress, sat at the next table, clearly bored by her latest young man), and on to see *My Fair Lady* (he must have paid a fortune for the tickets, then virtually unobtainable but I regret to say I fell asleep, worn out by the 24 hour flight from Uruguay); dancing at El Morocco; daily bouquets of flowers. I refused, however, a pressing invitation to enter Cartiers, as we strolled along Fifth Avenue, or to visit his ranch in Maryland, where, he assured me, a new leather saddle and a special horse awaited me. Given the paucity of my equine experience this latter prospect held more alarm than allure. Nevertheless this ardent wooing could not fail to flatter and appeal. Joaquín was 30 years older, but he was a kind man, a considerate and generous companion, whom I had always held in affectionate regard. But I was still romantic enough to think that only passionate love should be the basis for marriage, and sensible enough to realise that the kind of life we would have together, while offering companionship, luxury and financial security, could never fully satisfy me. During my stay in England I was besieged with flowers, photographs and telephone calls, but when I returned to New York in March 1958 Joaquín realised that my mind was made up. A year or two later he married a young Filipino film star, and they had a son. It was the only time in my life when someone seriously rich became interested in me.

Expanding Responsibilities

While in Europe I visited the UN specialised agencies in Paris, Geneva and Rome. The rivalries fragmenting the UN system were increasing, each organisation vying for a larger share of the technical assistance cake, because projects boosted their image and brought juicy overhead funding. Some, notably WHO and FAO, instructed their field chiefs to guard the autonomy of their organisations and undermined the resident representative's authority. The intensity with which these aims were pursued varied according to the policies and character of the the Director-General and the personalities on the ground. I had a good relationship with the WHO Chief of Mission, but difficulties with FAO. There was, moreover, dissension *within* the FAO team, with the Australian deputy doing his best to unseat the Chief of Mission, a worthy but pedestrian Texan. This unseemly squabble became known to the Government and in Rome Ad Boerma, the Dutchman then Director of Economics (later Director-General) of FAO, poured his heart out to me about his difficulties with Dr B. R. Sen, the autocratic Director-General. I was astonished that he should confide his problems to a junior official whom he had only just met, and even more so by his conclusion that the only solution in Uruguay was to make me FAO's Chief of Mission, something that ran counter to Dr Sen's fiercely independent stance. But so it was agreed, the first time that such an arrangement was made.

When I returned to Montevideo in April 1958, having stopped over in my beloved Colombia, a new request came: would I become acting resident representative in Argentina as well? This was a result of a chain of circumstances. Pérez Jiménez, the Venezuelan dictator, had been overthrown, and the exiles returning to form a democratic government had requested that Raymond Etchats (then resident representative in Buenos Aires), be sent to Caracas to help restore their shattered country. There was no question of refusing the Venezuelan request but no replacement for Argentina could be found at the drop of a hat. To my amazement I learned that Raymond himself had suggested my name, presumably smitten with remorse at having rejected me as his deputy in Mexico.

FAO also asked me to head their mission in Argentina, so I had four offices to run in two countries. They were separated by a one-hour plane hop across the River Plate but Argentina was in a completely different league, both as regards the size of the programme and the complexity of its politics and government structures. Each week I spent several days in Buenos Aires, travelling on the overnight ferry or the decrepit seaplanes that went from the port area, until one of them sank on take-off, the passengers, of whom I was happily not one, being rescued from the wings. (On another occasion the pilot, being unable to get his craft airborne, simply drove it across the surface of the water!) In Buenos Aires my vast office, in a government building on the Avenida 22 de Julio, had been Eva Perón's in her heyday, when she was dispensing social largesse in her role as Lady Bountiful.

It was a punishing schedule but it helped to offset my growing frustration with my work in Uruguay. That stemmed partly from my desire to work with the really poor, and Uruguay was hardly poor. There were pockets of underdevelopment, especially in organisation and administration. Getting a government decision was like squeezing blood from a stone, and the red tape was horrendous. Ministers would give you an appointment, often at an ungodly time, and keep you waiting two hours. The country was clearly heading for a fall. Cracks were appearing in its hitherto blessed economy, favoured by nature and the homogeneity of its population (the indigenous inhabitants had been eliminated). The palmy days, during the Second World War and the Korean War, when Uruguay's prime products of meat and wool had commanded high prices, were now over.

The warning signs had not sunk into the minds of the powers-that-be. I vainly strove to interest them in administrative reform, and in an economic study by the UN and the Economic Commission for Latin America (ECLA). I began to see a green light only in 1959, at the end of my mission.

Agriculture was another priority. For six years the World Bank had been negotiating a loan to fund intensive programmes of improved pastures, animal breeding and irrigation, drawing on the experience and similar conditions of Australia and New Zealand. As FAO was to provide the technical assistance, I was involved in difficult and lengthy negotiations. This was the first agricultural loan the bank ever made. They had been reluctant to enter this field at all, so their tenacity in pushing the deal through was as remarkable as the Government's obstinacy and procrastination. The programme became one of the most successful in Uruguay, but was not enough, on its own, to check the country's slow but inexorable decline.

In my efforts to expand the programme's horizons I came upon a remarkable experiment in rural education, started by Miguel Soler and his wife Nelly. Miguel had studied at UNESCO's Regional Centre for Fundamental Education in Patzcuaro, Mexico. The project, La Mina, was in the northern Department of Cerro Largo. My office being still without a vehicle, I travelled by bus to Melo, the provincial capital, accompanied by a UNESCO expert, Maria Teresa Femenias, a Chilean lady of uncertain years, very plump and very flirtatious, as suited her name. She whiled away the long hours as we bounced along the potholed road exerting her somewhat overwhelming charms on the bus driver. Whether as a result of her attentions or the appalling weather the bus broke down and we spent hours marooned in pouring rain in a bleak wayside store, where the main commodity on sale was rows of metal chamberpots stacked to the ceiling. It was midnight when the bus limped into Melo where the local education supervisor and Miguel Soler awaited, at pains to explain that special arrangements had been made for our comfort in Melo's main hotel. There the landlord proudly escorted us to the best room at the head of a considerable retinue. Moments of pure bathos followed as he tried to fling the door ceremoniously open. It was locked. Various keys were tried, then the awful truth dawned: the door was bolted on the inside, a supposition confirmed by the sound of heavy snoring. Much bellowing and banging on the door at length aroused the slumberer within. The door flew open so suddenly that the distraught landlord and his cohorts nearly fell into the room, and a short, fat man, half-clothed and very drunk, stumbled out, flailing his arms and mumbling incoherently. A stunned silence ensued, our hosts crestfallen and embarrassed. It was Maria Teresa who sprang to the rescue. 'Ay!' she lamented, rolling liquid black eyes and wiggling ample hips. '*What* a pity he wasn't young, tall and handsome!' The tension exploded in general laughter.

In La Mina the Solers had created a nucleus of rural development based on the school, assembling a team of enthusiastic young teachers, including some trained in agronomy and public health. Their work covered scattered communities of poor *gauchos* (cowboys) and their families, scraping a living from smallholdings. This glimpse into rural poverty was an eye-opener compared to the solid bourgeois comforts enjoyed by the inhabitants of Montevideo, and cast a sobering light on the acclaimed 'welfare society'. I learned a lot about the problems of land-ownership and the sociological impact of the introduction of barbed wire in the nineteenth century, which enabled the large *estancieros* to enclose large ranches and marginalised other rural folk. There was scant support from the national authorities. There was no central Ministry of Education; primary and secondary education were run by separate councils, composed of representatives of both parties, neither efficiently administered. There was little or no contact between the two levels of education, and none whatsoever with ministries involved in rural welfare. No one in Montevideo wanted to admit that rural poverty existed.

I tried to get support for La Mina from the government and UNESCO, so that it could become a pilot experiment for the rest of the country. When my old friend, Malcolm Adiseshiah, Assistant Director-General of UNESCO, paid an official visit in October 1957 I whisked him off to La Mina, thereby obliging government officials to go too. Time was short, and it was impossible to refuse the offer of a military plane, although the third Minister of Defence in two months was even then resigning, for the same reason as his predecessors – unexplained crashes of military aircraft! Confidence was not boosted by the requirement to sign a waiver exonerating everyone of responsibility if anything went wrong. It fell to a new low when we arrived over the landing-place, a field well populated with cattle, sheep, horses and even ostriches. Our pilot's tactics were even more alarming: he simply swooped down until we seemed to graze the ground, and then zoomed up and around again before diving once more to scatter livestock in all directions. By the third time the passengers were distinctly green. Malcolm, a great believer in Indian soothsayers, tried to console me by saying it was not in his stars to die that day. I was not so sure about my own but we landed safely.

My efforts to help La Mina were unsuccessful, even my modest aim of providing them with a vehicle. I had travelled with Miguel in the horse-drawn cart in which he visited far-flung communities in all weathers, returning late at night, drenched to the skin. The preferred vehicle was a German UNIMOG, a four-wheel-drive truck that could travel on the roughest terrain and draw a plough. It cost US$3000 but since the Inter-Ministerial Commission of Technical Assistance refused to include La Mina among priority projects UNESCO could not supply it. Through friends and lectures and broadcasts during my home leave, I scraped together the required US$3000. Success seemed in my grasp but the Uruguayan government insisted on charging 100 per cent customs duties – another US$3000 I had no hope of raising. Normally, UN-donated equipment entered free of all import dues. The Uruguayans claimed an exception in this case because the vehicle was donated by individuals. I argued the absurdity of this position to the highest levels of government, but La Mina never got its UNIMOG.

Worse, a whispering campaign began against La Mina, portraying it as a dangerous leftist undertaking, as if community development was synonymous with communism. The President of the Council for Primary Education even attempted to denigrate me, hinting darkly that I 'drank whisky for breakfast'. At that time I loathed whisky, and in dismissing these allegations I pointed out that, *were* I to drink at breakfast, which was not the case, then my tipple would be gin.

Adiseshiah was so impressed with La Mina that UNESCO made several offers of employment to Miguel. He stalwartly refused, believing it his duty to work in his own country. When the attacks continued, I persuaded him that nothing could be gained by staying and he accepted a posting in Bolivia, where he did outstanding work. He went on to become head of the Patzcuaro Fundamental Education Centre in Mexico where, sadly, Nelly died. Later Miguel worked in UNESCO in Paris and in my view is the best Latin American expert on rural education. We have remained friends for over 40 years.

My Parents' Visit

I saved enough money for my parents to visit me for Christmas 1958. My mother was enthusiastic but my father hung back, fearing that if he sought leave from his job as printer's reader, they might ask him to retire (he was 64). An angry letter came from my mother — written on a train bound for Hereford and my grandmother — saying that she had told my father that *she* was determined to come, whatever he did. It was as if, after 36 years of marriage, she had 'gone home to mother'. The ultimatum worked. They sailed to Montevideo in a passenger-cargo ship, sat at the captain's table and my father, under duress, invested in his first (and only) dinner jacket.

My mother had never set foot abroad and my father had done so only as a soldier. The holiday was an enormous success. I had never seen my father so happy and carefree. We travelled the length and breadth of the beaches of Uruguay, visited *estancias*, and were royally entertained by my Uruguayan friends. I took them to Chile, stopping in Buenos Aires where I was still running the UN office. In Chile I had good friends, Valentina and José Luis Ugarte. Valentina had been a UN expert in social welfare in Uruguay and she and her husband had become almost my second parents. With them we toured the environs of Santiago, and spent a weekend at Viña Del Mar. My plan was to return on the train that threaded its way through the Andes to Mendoza, in the hilly, wine-growing district of Argentina, and thence across the rolling plains of the pampa to Buenos Aires, but at the last moment the service was suspended. The Ugartes arranged for a car and driver to take us to Mendoza where we could catch a plane. A reliable driver and vehicle had been promised.

At 5.30 a.m. a sober-looking little chap in a black suit and trilby hat appeared in an equally sober black car and we bowled through the outskirts of Santiago in a sparkling summer dawn. Once we began to ascend the foothills the road became more rugged. We happily greeted a *huaso* (a Chilean cowboy), resplendent in his brightly coloured poncho, silvery spurs gleaming as he too rode into the mountains, his dog scampering along behind, and he gravely and courteously lifted his flat black hat in reply. Euphoria did not last long. A few bends and several hundred feet higher, the radiator started to boil and a hasty pit stop was made by a mountain stream. The stops became more frequent and the car laboured more and more as we climbed higher. Our resourceful driver met the challenge by running backwards at every curve to the edge of the precipice, to get a jump start. My mother, seated in the back, had all too good a view of the scenic panorama that would engulf us if the driver erred by so much as an inch, and was not amused. The driver had lost his spruce appearance, hat pushed to the back of his head, face rubicund and streaming with sweat which I felt, unkindly, must help fill the radiator as he bent over to replenish it.

Periodically the *huaso* whom we had passed caught up with us. Each time he gravely raised his hat – I could not help detecting an ironic flourish – the dog wagged his tail, and even the horse gave signs of recognition. It was ignominiously clear that he had the most effective means of transport (no motor vehicle passed in either direction).

When, by some miracle, we reached the top, we heaved a misplaced sigh of relief. At the border we handed over our passports and were requested to provide our maternal surnames, according to Hispanic practice. My father demurred. Whether he could not remember (it was a complicated name) or was being obtuse I do not know. The immigration man became officious, even threatening 'without a maternal surname it is impossible to cross the border' – as who might say 'without a valid health certificate' or 'a clean police record'.

It never occurred to us to say 'Smith', knowing he could never be the wiser. After a brief family conclave, we came up with the answer: 'Collicott'.

'How?'

'Có-lli-cót'. (I pronounced it very slowly, giving it a Latin American twang ...)

'How do you spell it?'

'C-o ...'

After several repeats the immigration man threw up his eyes, his pen and the sponge and, calling on the Almighty for patience, said wearily, 'It doesn't matter. You may pass.'

The road lay downward but I was horrified to see that our redoubtable driver was freewheeling in neutral. It took much argument to persuade him to use the gears. When, after more heart-stopping experiences, we arrived in Mendoza, we discovered that the brakes had been jammed all the way up to the crest of the Cordillera, and had failed completely as we arrived at our destination.

I had long wanted to see the Iguazu Falls. Pluna, the Uruguayan airline, having invested in Vickers Viscounts, the flight to Paraguay now took two hours instead of four. That was the theory. It took four *days*. First, departure from Montevideo was delayed by 24 hours of horrendous weather. Then we were marooned for two days in Salto, in north-east Uruguay, on an airfield more like a muddy marsh, from which we could not take off. There is nothing like misfortune to bring people together. When we finally resumed our journey, the crew and the few remaining passengers were on close friendly terms. I played the role of stewardess and served the canapés; also having embarked in Montevideo three days earlier, the crew were as tired and bedraggled as ourselves.

My troubles were not over, for the same storms had hit Paraguay. I left my room in the 'best' hotel in Asunción (I don't know how many stars it boasted, but it had huge cockroaches) at midnight in the pouring rain, and took the bus to Iguazu. We ploughed along a track hewn out of the jungle, almost axle-deep in thick red mud. The only other passenger was a buxom lady clutching a live hen and a basket of eggs. The driver was as persistent as myself in trying to reach Iguazu, but we became completely bogged down, and had to dig ourselves out. By 8 a.m. I was back at the hotel, muddy and wet, having spent all night in the bus. I took a plane to San Paulo and did not see the Iguazu Falls until 20 years later.

Dag Hammarskjöld's Visit

A notable official visitor was Raúl Prebisch, the renowned Argentinean economist, then Executive Secretary of ECLA. Prebisch was a formidable man, physically as well as intellec-tually, who did not suffer fools gladly. Fortunately we got on well and the foundations were laid for a friendship that lasted until his death. He came to Montevideo for negotiations preparing the Latin American Free Trade Association (ALALC). A main bone of contention, uncannily similar to those besetting the European Union today, concerned the monetary arrangements between the signatory countries. Prebisch had pronounced views on this, contrary to those of the International Monetary Fund (IMF). He bore me off to the office of the IMF representative and in a masterly combination of histrionics and intellectual brilliance withered that poor gentleman into stunned silence. I was torn between admiration for Prebisch's eloquence and pity for his victim.

The most nerve-racking visit was that of the UN Secretary-General, Dag Hammarskjöld, in August 1959. David Owen warned me that there would be difficulties, citing a disastrous visit to India a few months earlier as a cautionary tale. The resident representative in New Delhi, James Keen, had done what we all would have done: he gave a reception in honour of the Secretary-General. Hammarskjöld was furious, complaining that James was stealing his thunder. Not long after poor James, who loved India, was replaced by someone of Hammarskjöld's confidence.

The message I received was unequivocal. 'Whatever you do, be *inconspicuous*! Take *no* initiatives and leave everything to the Uruguayan Government. The Secretary-General's Office will liaise directly with their Permanent Representative in New York.'

All very straightforward, were it not for the fact that organisation was hardly the Uruguayan Government's forte. Moreover, their UN Ambassador was a vague, elderly professor, notable more for his cultivated background than any penchant for action. I was called in by the Foreign Minister, who begged me to organise the visit and was visibly irritated when I said I was under instructions to leave everything to the Government. 'Besides,' he went on plaintively, 'the Secretary-General has put us in a very difficult position by arriving on a *Saturday*. Don't they realise that Uruguay, a civilized country, observes *el sábado ingles* (the English Saturday) and works a five-day week? Neither the President or I can meet him, nor can there be a guard of honour, for we've no budget to pay the soldiers' overtime. We cannot consider the Secretary-General an official government guest during the weekend.'

I telegraphed this singular message to Andrew Cordier, the head of Hammarskjöld's office, taking care to stress, tongue in cheek, that I continued to abide by my instructions to play no role. A very prompt reply came back. New York, said an indignant Mr Cordier, could not understand Uruguay's extraordinary interpretation of the working week, and could I please tell the minister so, and generally take matters in hand? This was just as well, for through my personal contacts I learned that two *estancieros*, with ranches at opposite ends of the country, happened to meet at the opera and, almost as in an old-fashioned farce, turned simultaneously to one another, saying with ill-concealed pride '*Oye, che*, you'll *never* guess who's coming to my *estancia* next Sunday ...' None other than the Secretary-General of course, several people in the Foreign Ministry having shown initiative.

The question of Hammarskjöld's status was solved in a typically Uruguayan manner, once again raising eyebrows in New York: he would be 'semi-incognito' during Saturday and Sunday and become an official government guest on Monday morning. The Director of Protocol would receive him at Carrasco Airport, and an 'informal programme' would be arranged for Sunday (the *estancia* visit now reduced to one).

I had taken precautions to ensure that I would be inconspicuous at the airport, standing discreetly in the background with my small band of UN experts. My departure to Carrasco was delayed by a panic request from the Foreign Ministry for a UN flag – they had lost theirs – but I arrived in time, or so I thought, until greeted by the Director-General of the airport, Victor Garin, uncharacteristically agitated. Victor was an extraordinarily dedicated public servant; though paid on a half-time basis, he worked long hours and bought items such as runway lights from his own scant money to keep the airport going. We went on fishing and bird-watching excursions together, and he had honed my driving skills; he had even offered to teach me to fly, an opportunity that, to my later regret, I declined. On this occasion he probably ensured my survival in the United Nations.

'The plane from Asunción arrived early,' he gasped, 'and there is no one to greet the Secretary-General except a crowd of Hungarian exiles protesting about UN inaction during the 1956 uprising. I've kept the plane in the air, circling, until you arrived, but the pilot is becoming angry and I'm running out of excuses.'

Since it was a bright sunny afternoon and Carrasco a singularly unbusy airport, the pilot's perplexity was understandable. I explained that I could not possibly receive Hammarskjöld alone, and together we chased over the airport, running the missing Uruguayan officials to earth in the bar. The Director of Protocol (an eccentric character who favoured long dark overcoats with velvet collars, and a black Homburg hat pulled low over his eyes, attire that gave him a sinister appearance, lending credence to the rumour that he dabbled in black magic and had written a thesis on the devil) was already a little unsteady. I chivvied him out on to the tarmac, while Victor dashed up the control tower to give the green light for the plane to land.

With difficulty I persuaded our over-eager hosts that Raúl Prebisch, who was accompanying the Secretary-General, should sit with him in the official car, rather than myself. Surprisingly, given overtime constraints, an escort of police motorcycles materialised but due to their inexperience and the appalling state of the road several of them came a cropper, and we left behind us mounds of twisted wheels and flailing limbs.

Our destination on Sunday was supposedly secret but a long procession of press cars pursued us. At the *estancia* we were driven around in two jeeps. The ground was sodden, and my jeep became firmly stuck. The *estanciero*, Gallinal, a delightfully forthright man, and no respecter of persons, was driving the other vehicle and, oblivious of Hammarskjöld at his side, he rammed us but the jeep remained stuck. Since the mud was knee-deep I had to manoeuvre myself out on to the bonnet, and leap on to another vehicle. This had to be accomplished in a not very ample skirt (in those days trousers were unacceptable, even on a semi-official visit), making it impossible to avoid exposing a fair amount of leg and underwear, to cheers from the attendant journalists whose cameras snapped merrily away. For one trying to be inconspicuous it was hardly a star performance.

Next day the Secretary-General visited my office, and expressed genuine interest in the briefings given him by my team. There was trouble, however, at his press conference. He had been incorrectly briefed on an important matter, but his aides were too scared to give him the corrections that I conveyed to them, as he was already irritated by things that had gone wrong on the trip. I thus had to listen to the Secretary-General saying in public something I knew to be untrue. After his departure the Foreign Minister came to my office, demanding to see the relevant files, something that could only happen in Uruguay. I had to admit that the Secretary-General's statements had inadvertently been wrong.

On the last evening the Foreign Minister gave a 'stag' dinner for Hammarskjöld. I was the only woman and, to my acute embarrassment, as we filed past the reception line, a parliamentarian, whom I had not previously met, proclaimed in stentorian tones, '*Mrs* Hammarskjöld, I presume?'

Things did not get better. Seeing Hammarskjöld looking bored as he talked to the Minister of Health, I tried to enliven the interchange by reminding him that he had been interested in the rural public health projects described by the WHO representative. Hammarskjöld obligingly warmed to the theme but I had forgotten that the Minister of Health, a charming elderly doctor, was extremely deaf. He wore a hearing aid but it seemed to be defective. 'I beg your pardon?' said the minister politely.

When this little *pas de deux* had been repeated a couple of times, the minister took out his hearing aid, peered at it closely, shook it and replaced it. Hammarskjöld rather wearily again started to talk about public health. This time the minister not only removed his hearing aid but extracted a small screwdriver from his pocket and started to tinker with it. Hammarskjöld retreated, doubled up with mirth. It was the first time that I saw him unbend.

That night I gloomily concluded that, after this chapter of accidents and my singularly ineffectual attempts to melt into the background, my chances of advancement looked slim. Next morning, however, the great man himself invited me to ride beside him to the airport.

'That gentleman last night,' he said. 'Did you say he is the Minister of Health?'

'Yes, Secretary-General.'

'H'm, he seemed to be in dire need of medical attention himself, wouldn't you say?' And there was the faintest glimmer of a twinkle in the Secretary-General's eye.

Even more amazing was to learn from David Owen that Hammarskjöld had formed a good opinion of me and our programme.

Pitfalls of Protocol

The Uruguayans considered protocol anti-democratic, preferring ceremonial occasions to evolve spontaneously. One year, the Uruguayan authorities cooked up a splendid ceremony for UN Day, 24th October, in the main plaza, in the shadow of the statue of Artigas, the national hero and architect of their independence. Organised with more flair and enthusiasm than attention to detail, it was a less than unqualified success. It was to culminate in the release of 1000 white doves as a symbol of peace. Unfortunately there were not more than a couple of hundred. Second they were neither doves, nor white, but ordinary grey-blue city pigeons that the municipality had hastily collected from the streets. Third, they were not homing pigeons and, released with a flourish from their crates, merely fluttered around despondently, finally settling on my hat and the head of the long-suffering Artigas, where they vented their spleen by liberally spattering the poor man with droppings. The assembled diplomats hastily hoisted umbrellas.

The Pope's decision to bestow a cardinal's hat on the Archbishop of Montevideo caused public euphoria and a political crisis. The ruling *Colorado* party was dogmatically secular, and one of its strictest credos was the absolute separation of church and state, carried to the extreme of depriving God of a capital letter in their official newspaper. So the news that the newly blessed cardinal was arriving by sea from Rome, to be greeted by cheering crowds and an open-air Mass, caused a constitutional tizzy. Should the Foreign Minister attend or not? The Cabinet discussed the issue for hours, deciding in the end to subordinate its principles to national pride and a healthy political desire not to offend the general populace, most of whom remained staunchly Catholic.

The Foreign Minister arrived only minutes before the triumphal cortège bearing the cardinal from the port. A platform had been erected outside the cathedral, with an altar and chairs for ambassadors and national and church authorities. The plaza in front of the cathedral was jam-packed with thousands of people. A prescient municipality had foreseen the need to restrain their ardour but had quixotically opted to do so with a chain of Cub Scouts, stationed so far apart that their hands barely touched.

When the triumphal cortège arrived cheering crowds surged onto the road and the Cubs went down like ninepins. Such was the press of bodies that the Cardinal's car remained firmly stuck, unable to go forwards or backwards. Nor could he alight and ascend the steps to the impromptu dais where the priests and the rest of us awaited. The general frustration found its most vigorous expression among ordinary folk unable to catch a glimpse of their hero. Someone had the bright idea of jumping on to the dais and the example was seized upon by others. Uruguayans do not suffer from any lack of avoirdupois. I can still see in my mind's eye the enormous market woman who, not content with the vantage point of the dais, climbed on to one of the rickety chairs provided for diplomats by the simple expedient of placing a pudgy hand on the head of the German Ambassador, who had the misfortune to be sitting on the next chair, to heave herself up. By now the dais was a surging mass of people, cheering so loudly that the din masked the sound of an ominous cracking noise. When the dais began to wobble and tilt there was a concerted rush for the safety of the cathedral, as the whole contraption came tumbling down. Miraculously, no one was hurt, but the celebratory Mass was abandoned.

Similar chaos surrounded the change of government in March 1959. The *Blancos* wanted to celebrate their electoral victory over the *Colorados*, the first time for many years. It was a day of sweltering heat and high humidity. The Diplomatic Corps were bidden to arrive at 1 p.m. at the Congress where the President, Martín Echegoyen, was sworn in and embarked on a long speech. The place was packed to the rafters, seating arrangements were inadequate, and oxygen in short supply. The President passed out in the middle of his speech but revived, and plodded on to the end, while one ambassador had a seizure and was carried out. Afterwards we made our way to the Casa de Gobierno where, if you were lucky, you got a glass of champagne and a sponge biscuit.

Soon we were hustled out on a minuscule dais erected on Plaza Artigas to view the victory parade. There being no room for chairs, protocol had marked out each place with a chalked cross. There we had to stand, under a broiling sun, for the next four to five hours while Uruguay's armed forces marched interminably past. I had always imagined them to be exiguous, and several of us concluded that the same contingents went round several times. If this was meant to boost the country's image it did little for the morale of the rapidly wilting captive audience. Several people fainted and their inert bodies were hoisted out over our heads. At least the dais did not collapse. The protocol placement of the United Nations coming after the ambassadors had advantages, as I was able to prop myself up against the back railing. When I got home, after seven gruelling hours, I found that the back of my new suit was streaked with red stripes. The paint on the railings had been wet ...!

Posting to La Paz

In 1959 Uruguay suffered calamitous gales and floods. Even my flat on the eighth floor, facing the estuary, was awash. The Department of Paysandu was particularly affected. The River Uruguay burst its banks, roads and railways were blocked, and thousands of poor rural people rendered homeless. This was before the era of mass international humanitarian relief. Disaster relief was a national affair, with the local UN office helping as best it could.

An Air Force General, Oscar Gestido, was put in charge of the operation. General Gestido was a remarkable character. Even the armed forces were not particularly efficient in Uruguay – General Gestido was an exception. His reputation as an outstanding administrator led to his being appointed, on retirement, to head the notoriously incompetent state railways. Like Mussolini, he was famous for making the trains run on time, the difference being that General Gestido was a convinced democrat.

The General and I toured the disaster areas in buses that invariably left at 3 a.m. and sometimes in rickety planes, landing on bumpy airstrips mired in mud, to bring such succour as we could. I remember one poor woman – my own age, but looking decades older – who had six children and showed us the sodden ruins of what could only have been a miserable hovel. The more I saw of General Gestido, the more I admired and liked him. In my last months in Uruguay we became good friends.

My restlessness with the Montevideo posting had long been known in New York and there had been rumours of a transfer, even back to Bogotá, as resident representative. In early 1959 during a regional resident representatives meeting in Venezuela, in a military aircraft flying over the oilfields of Maracaibo, David Owen offered me two options: to stay in Uruguay for another two years or to go to another, larger country, as deputy; I was too young, he explained, to take charge of a large programme. I replied that I longed to work in a really poor country, and did not mind being No. Two, provided my boss was someone from whom I could learn and not just a figurehead for whom I would do all the work. David raised a quizzical eyebrow: and asked jokingly, 'Bolivia?'

'Done', I said, with alacrity and to his astonishment. For me, it was a dream come true.

Months passed without news. I was concerned about my lack of academic qualifications in economics and decided to take a year's study leave without pay. My first choice was the course for government officials from developing countries at the World Bank's Economic Development Institute, but the fees were too high and the Technical Assistance Board (TAB) had no money for staff training. I had savings to cover modest living expenses, but not high fees. I came to an arrangement with Queen Elizabeth House in Oxford, whereby I would follow a tailor-made course, emphasising development questions not yet covered by traditional economics curricula.

In September David Owen asked me to postpone these plans, and my home leave, due in December 1959, as TAB still wanted me to go as No. Two to Bolivia, where an important ECLA mission on development planning was to start. I agreed, but still the call did not come. No one would accept the No. One post in Bolivia, which many regarded as a hardship post, at an altitude dangerous to health. Eventually Anthony Balinski agreed to do so, part-time, concurrently with his post as resident representative in Ecuador. He would visit La Paz every two months. Otherwise I would be in charge. In the middle of 1960 Balinski would move to La Paz and I would be released, without pay, to pursue my studies.

In December 1959 I flew to La Paz to meet the government authorities, returning to Montevideo for Christmas and a round of farewell parties. On my transfer from Bogotá my luggage was nine months in transit and arrived in a sorry state, an experience I was determined not to repeat so I decided to travel by boat to Buenos Aires, and then up to Bolivia by train. I had 14 crates, and 17 pieces of hand luggage, including a nutria fur coat and a guitar. Montserrat, my Spanish maid, would accompany me.

A large crowd came to the port to see us off. I was touched to receive a farewell telephone call from General Gestido. We had often discussed the ominous, but still generally unperceived, decline in Uruguay's fortunes, and the dangerous ineffectualness of the collegiate system. My parting words were: 'General, my wish for Uruguay is that the National Council is replaced by a single President, and that that man will be you. That is the only salvation I see for this country'.

This was positively prescient: General Gestido was not in politics and the collegiate system seemed entrenched. Yet in 1966, all that came to pass and Gestido became President. I sent him a cable recalling our farewell conversation. He was sworn in in March 1967 but in December 1967, after barely nine months in office, General Gestido suffered a fatal heart attack. I have often thought that, had he lived longer, Uruguay might have been spared the Tupamaro guerillas, and the horrors of military dictatorship, all phenomena totally at odds with the fiercely democratic country that I had known.

Goodbye to Uruguay

The original title of W. H. Hudson's book about Uruguay, when published in 1885, was *The Purple Land that England Lost*. Initially his autographical hero deplored the fact that the British, who briefly occupied Montevideo in 1806, had then abandoned it, arguing that, had they stayed, Uruguay would have been well administered, instead of the tumultuous country over which Hudson roamed in the nineteenth century. At the end he changed his tune: 'After my rambles in the interior ... I cannot believe that if this country had been conquered and recolonised by England ... my intercourse with the people would have had the wild, delightful flavour I have found in it.'

Nearly a century later, I too found a charm and warmth among the Uruguayan people that outweighed the frustrations caused by general insouciance and anathema to organisation. As I discovered on a brief visit in 1995, nearly 35 years later, those qualities survived 12 years of harsh dictatorship, from 1973 to 1985, and were perhaps strengthened by that experience. I was greeted as if I had never been away.

─── 10 ───

On Top of the World

My journey from Montevideo to La Paz took two weeks instead of the scheduled four days, during most of which time I was cut off from the rest of the world. Montserrat and I, with our mountains of luggage, boarded the train to La Paz in Buenos Aires, in a dilapidated carriage bearing the legend 'Made in England, 1904'. The train diminished in size and elegance as we travelled northwards and at La Quiaca, on the frontier, we were unceremoniously evicted because the line in Bolivia had been washed out by torrential rain, and there were rumours of a miners' revolt in Huanuni.

My crates were abandoned on La Quiaca's bleak station and we pushed the rest of our luggage on handcarts across the border into Villazón, a dusty *altiplano* village, bisected by the railway line. We spent several days in the 'Gran Hotel Panamericano', the grandest thing about which was its name, daily interrogating the increasingly inebriated station-master. When, in a rare moment of lucidity, he prognosticated that the next train would leave in a month, it was time to move on. My money was running out and I could not communicate with La Paz.

We travelled on top of a lorry across the mountains to Tarija, where there was an airport, a journey of four hours that lasted nearly 24. Just after midnight, in a torrential thunderstorm and at an altitude of about 4000 metres, the lorry burst a tyre and the lorry driver sheepishly announced that he did not have a jack. It was dawn before help came and by then the track was reduced to a quagmire. We shoved it out but it was with a mud-spattered face and filthy clothes that I presented myself at the airline office as the new Head of the United Nations in Bolivia. I could forgive the clerk for not believing a word of it, but not his advice that flights were booked for the next 15 days, and that we should take a lorry to Villazón and catch a train ...

My office in La Paz, contacted by radio, told me that New York was bombarding them with cables about my whereabouts. They sent money and arranged passages on a military transport plane to Cochabamba. Two days later we reached Cochabamba, and completed our odyssey in some style, as the only passengers on a DC-4 plane sent there on government business, with stewards and air hostesses dancing attendance. Two days later the same DC-4 crashed on a regular flight from Cochabamba. There were no survivors.

One month later the first train steamed into La Paz from the Argentinian frontier and vindicated the Villazón station-master. It contained my 14 crates, all intact.

An Idiosyncratic Revolution

Bolivia in the late 1950s and early 1960s was a heady place to be, and not simply because of the altitude. I felt, literally and figuratively, on top of the world and 'love at first sight' blossomed into lasting passion.

In 1952 the country had undergone a profound political and social revolution. Since independence from Spain in 1825, Bolivian politics had followed a chequered path of coups and attempted revolutions. The one constant factor was the downtrodden state of the indigenous masses. The First Constitution, drawn up by Bolivar for the country that bore his name, conferred sovereignty on the people and abolished slavery, but the enlightened ideals that inspired the first stirring calls for independence held little appeal for *criollos*, the American-born Spaniards. Jealous of the trade monopoly that favoured merchants who stayed safely at home in Spain, and of the superior privileges accorded to the *peninsulares*, born in metropolitan Spain, their aim was not to transform the fabric of society but to adapt it to their own advantage. It was a situation not dissimilar to that of the Universal Declaration of

Independence (UDI) in Rhodesia in 1965: colonial settlers rebelling against centralised colonial power for their own ends, and not those of the indigenous population.

In the nineteenth century, Bolivia lost its Pacific coast and valuable nitrate deposits to Chile, and rich rubber-growing areas of the Amazon basin to Brazil. The crowning blow to national confidence came in the 1930s with the disastrous Chaco war against Paraguay, which had far-reaching political and economic consequences. People of all social strata had fought and died together, and it was mainly the Indians, ill-clothed and under-nourished, who perished on those cruel sands, chewing stoically on their wads of coca.

The Nationalist Revolutionary Movement (the MNR) grew out of this tragedy. A brief spell in government culminated in a bloody revolution in 1946, when President Villaroel was hung from one of the lampposts in front of the palace. Later its electoral victory in 1951, initially foiled by a military junta, was restored by a successful revolution in April 1952. Under President Víctor Paz Estenssoro sweeping reforms were introduced: the liberation of the Indians, until then feudal serfs on the landowners' estates; agrarian reform; universal education; universal suffrage; and the nationalisation of the mines.

After new elections in 1956, Hernán Siles Zuazo, the hero of the April 1952 revolution and a man of great physical and moral courage, succeeded Víctor Paz. Bolivia was still struggling to make its revolution work. The miners and *campesinos* were better off than before 1952, but expectations were excessive and for the first time both sectors had political power and arms, albeit obsolete. The Government had a tiger by the tail, and its survival depended on being able to demonstrate economic progress benefiting all levels of society.

External assistance was direly needed but there were only two main sources – the United States and the United Nations. The former was larger but was regarded with some reticence by the national authorities, who feared excessive American influence. The United States was itself ambiguous towards the MNR, tainted first with suggestions of Nazism during the Second World War and then, paradoxically, of communism, because of the 1952 reforms.

The UN in Bolivia

The responsibility falling on the United Nations was thus considerable, but resources under the Expanded Programme of Technical Assistance were exiguous, though later supplemented by pre-investment funds from the UN Special Fund, created in 1959. The Special Fund was part of the compromise reached when developing countries campaigned during the 1950s for a Special United Nations Fund for Economic Development (SUNFED), to provide low-interest capital instead of the market rates charged by the World Bank. The other part of the compromise was the Bank's creation of the International Development Association (IDA) to provide concessional capital to poorer countries. The Bank refused to lend Bolivia any capital on whatever terms, however, because the country was defaulting on its external debt.

The United Nations was popular because it had helped the fledgling revolutionary Government from the start. Following a mission led by a distinguished Canadian, Hugh Keenleyside, UN experts were appointed to senior positions in key ministries, not as advisers, but with line functions. Such a system would today be considered an affront to sovereignty. For Bolivia in the 1950s the contribution of these men (no women!) was a godsend to a government struggling with huge problems, among them the traditionally poor quality of Bolivian public service, and this experience spawned a programme later offered to other countries, known as OPEX (operational and executive), under which international officials filled key gaps, the UN topping up the national salary. Bolivia came to be the crucible for innovative approaches.

Bolivia had the largest UN programme in Latin America. Since Anthony Balinski visited infrequently and confined himself to high-level liaison with the Government, my responsibilities were heavy – another maturing experience. My major task was to support another experiment for which Bolivia was the guinea-pig, the brain-child of Raúl Prebisch, the Executive Secretary of ECLA. We aimed to help the Government design a development plan that would facilitate rational use of all its resources, benefit the population as a whole and attract external support. Our team of experts from the UN, the Food and Agricultural Organisation (FAO) and ECLA was led by Pedro Vuskovic, who 12 years later became Minister of Economy in Salvador Allende's ill-fated government in Chile. This was the first mission of its kind, but similar groups followed elsewhere and led to the establishment of the Latin American Economic and Social Planning Institute (ILPES). But in 1960 development planning was a novelty in developing countries, not looked on with favour by the United States.

Another innovative enterprise, the Andean Indian Programme, inspired by Jef Rens, the Belgian Assistant Director-General of the International Labour Office (ILO), covered Peru and Ecuador as well, and aimed to incorporate Andean Indians into the mainstream of development, through integrated rural programmes. In each country pilot centres were established but Bolivia was the only one where the political and legal structures were conducive to such an experiment.

Once the Special Fund began we launched several pre-investment studies, the most notable being the Airborne Geophysical Mineral Survey of the Cordillera and Altiplano. There were many agricultural projects, and others in education, statistics, meteorology, public administration and public health. My job was to plan this programme with the Government and administer it effectively. I was also responsible for the security of all UN personnel, no mean task in those troubled times. My work could not have been more varied and I drove to the office each day reflecting pleasurably that I had no idea what it might bring.

In 1960 there were elections and Paz Estenssoro again became President. I took my delayed home leave but the study leave that was to follow was cancelled because of the Congo crisis.

I went on briefing visits to all the specialised agencies, driving to Paris, Geneva and Rome in my new Volkswagon Beetle, the first car I ever owned, and taking my mother with me. My father joined us for his one week's holiday and it was a happy interlude. The VW beetle went by sea to Mollendo, in Peru, whence I drove it up over the Andes. Three years later I did the same with its successor, this time from the Chilean port of Arica, ignoring the pleas of the

Bolivian Consul that there was no road. He was almost right, for it was only after numerous adventures that I arrived in La Paz.

Balinski went to the Congo and a new resident representative had to be appointed. The UN never promoted a Deputy in the same country, and so I was told I was not eligible. There was, however, the usual difficulty of finding someone to work in Bolivia. Living conditions were difficult and home comforts few. To take a bath you had to plunge an electric element in the tub, either before you filled it with water or after – I forget which, but if you did it the wrong way round you got electrocuted. Many basic foodstuffs and commodities were unavailable. Notwithstanding, while embassies gave their staff 25 per cent incentive and hardship allowances, the UN applied a *minus* cost of living allowance, *deducting* 10 per cent of everyone's salary because living was supposed to be cheap. In vain I argued that this was because many staples on the UN cost-of-living index were unobtainable, and so no one could spend money on them.

The Government insisted that they wanted me, and no one else, as resident representative and David Owen finally acquiesced. My promotion, however, lagged well behind my responsibilities. I was still only a P.4 (level 4 in the professional scale), several steps below the norm for someone heading a large programme. Youth and gender came into the equation; I was still the only woman resident representative in the world, as well as the youngest.

I never did get that study leave. Instead, I enrolled for an external Bachelor of Science in Economics, at London University. I sat the Part One examination in the British Embassy in La Paz in 1963 (how many other candidates, I wondered, spent the first evening not swotting for the morrow's exams, but at an official presidential banquet?) and Part Two in England a year later.

Víctor Paz Estenssoro was an outstanding politician and statesman. A single glance from his magnetic dark eyes transfixed you completely. Another unusual characteristic was his strict punctuality. Many attributed this to his having been Ambassador to the Court of St James, but one day he confided to me that he owed his life to being punctual. During the ill-fated Villaroel presidency, when he was Finance Minister, he arrived early at a reception given by the Paraguayan Ambassador, who filled the time by showing him around the grounds. Thus it was that Víctor Paz spied an easily scaleable wall; during the 1946 coup he climbed his way into asylum and avoided being murdered as was his unfortunate President. Once, unaware he was to be present, I arrived at a ceremony *en hora boliviana*, and had the embarrassing experience not only of having to tiptoe across a vast expanse of highly polished parquet, but also of receiving a presidential reprimand, expressing surprise that a British person could be late ...

Don Víctor's poker face concealed a tremendous sense of humour. Years later, when he was again President and I was Assistant Secretary-General in New York, a gringo setting up a wildlife trust in Bolivia asked me to intercede with him to stop the export of rare squirrel monkeys to the United States for experimental purposes. He did not know what a great favour he was asking: because of certain facial characteristics the President was secretly nicknamed *El Mono* (the monkey). Greatly daring, I called Víctor Paz. There was a disconcerting silence.

Then the President said, 'But, of course, my dear Margarita. Who could be better qualified than I to rescue monkeys?'

To which I had the presence of mind to quip in return, 'And who more than you knows the pains of involuntary exile?' There was a chuckle at the other end.

Víctor Paz was a superb manager, delegating to the full, but implacable with any minister who failed to produce effective results. I worked closely with him and he would invite me to cabinet meetings if development issues were discussed. This could not have happened anywhere else and was testimony to the uniquely symbiotic relationship between Bolivia and the United Nations. The same mutual confidence existed with the Minister of Economy, Alfonso Gumucio, known as *Flaco* (the thin man) because of his rail-like figure, a visionary who had linked Santa Cruz and the eastern lowlands to the *altiplano* through the construction of the Cochabamba–Santa Cruz highway, and with Roberto Jordán Pando, the brilliant young Minister of Rural Affairs, who became the first Planning Minister.

La Paz in those days bore the air of a once-thriving town that had met with some cataclysmic disaster, its skyline littered with the bleak skeletons of unfinished buildings. Their windowless, roofless silhouettes stood like tombstones commemorating the building boom that accompanied the galloping inflation of the 1950s and as swiftly petered out when stabilisation measures were introduced in 1956. Ministries were housed in decrepit buildings; the crumbling wooden staircases of the Ministries of Labour and of Rural Affairs, crammed with supplicants, made one fear for one's life as one clawed one's way to the minister's office. The dirt and smell were indescribable. The Planning Board worked from a small house and my office was a modest affair on the twelfth floor in Calle Colón. The lift was erratic as was the one in the Ministry of Agriculture, where I had my FAO office, for I was again FAO's country representative. I was also in charge of the UN Information Centre and, for a while, of the Andean Indian Programme. My figure and my adaptation to altitude benefited greatly from constantly running up and down stairs.

It is hard to convey the enormous euphoria that swept us all up in its grip. We worked together enthusiastically with no difference between Bolivian and international personnel. We were young and idealistic, full of energy, and inebriated by the unique opportunity that this special juncture of Bolivian history opened up. Our illusions did not go so far as to make us think we could change the world, but we believed we might play a modest part in making a difference in Bolivia, especially the lot of the poor. My first five and a half years in Bolivia were the happiest and most satisfying of my working life. There was a tragic denouement but I see today the fruition of many seeds sown then.

We worked hard but we also enjoyed ourselves. For carnival we went to Oruro to watch the magnificent *Diablada* (devil dance) from the vantage point of the Hotel Eden, another hostelry whose idyllic name belied the facts (the landlady, on being shown a pool of water that had dripped through the roof into a sagging bed, merely lifted her eyes to heaven, as if demanding divine intervention, and exclaimed: 'Aa-y-y-y, *Dios*! The rain does this every year'!) All discomfort was forgotten when the first *comparsa* of devils came caracoling round the corner, 100 pairs of feet dancing as one with marvellously formal precision, and the workaday street exploded in a blinding galaxy of light and colour, transforming the normally down-at-heel air of Oruro, that most frugal town.

There was no TV, no theatre, only rarely concerts (visiting orchestras were deterred by the lethal effect of the altitude on their wind sections), and films were invariably ancient, cinemas frequently flea-ridden. So we made our own entertainment at parties, usually in my home. I had been able to rent President Siles' house, an adobe structure opposite the military garrison in San Jorge, only because an American couple had been refused permission to do so by the US Embassy, on the grounds that 'Bolivian shooting was notoriously inaccurate' (a prescient statement). Those nights were lively with Bolivian folk music and dancing. Several people played the guitar; we hired the best charango[1] player in Bolivia who also, improbably, worked in the barber's shop opposite the Ministry of Finance; we performed songs and skits satirising our everyday work, and danced until dawn.

The development plan was no dry and formalistic document. A decade before the International Labour Office launched an international conference on 'basic needs', Bolivia tried to apply that very concept. The matrix was based on the assumption that each inhabitant must have access to a minimum amount of calories per day, so many yards of cloth, so many pairs of shoes, etc. Likewise the number of school places and hospital beds was woven into the equation. Nor did the plan await completion before producing results. The newly-created Inter-American Development Bank was casting about for programmes and projects and, thanks to the plan, Bolivia received the Bank's first line of credit anywhere.

The Cold War was intensifying amid fears that communism might spread through Latin America as a result of Soviet support for Fidel Castro's revolution in Cuba. In 1961, the Kennedy administration launched the Alliance for Progress, promising significant financing for Latin America countries fulfilling certain conditions, and convened a conference in Punta del Este in August 1961. A main criterion was the presentation of a national

---

1. The *charango* is a small, stringed instrument, traditionally made from the carapace of an armadillo.

development plan, something the United States had previously opposed as a sinister Soviet invention. Bolivia was the only country that could comply.

On the eve of the conference we spent most of the night stapling the document together. I was one of the bleary-eyed group that boarded the plane next day, for *Flaco* Gumucio, who was heading the delegation, had insisted that I go along as adviser. New York had objected, and refused to pay. *Flaco* had flown into a rage and scraped the bottom of Bolivia's scant finances to pay my fare. There was no money for per diem, and I spent several nights sleeping on a table in the delegation's office until Victor Garin rescued me, lending me his apartment in Punta del Este.

Uruguay had the presidency of a conference that required the most delicate of diplomatic handling in the person of a senator who had never managed such a meeting before and invariably put his foot into it. The Cuban delegation was headed by the fiery Che Guevara, and use of the Spanish alphabet meant that he was sitting cheek-by-jowl with the US Secretary of the Treasury, Dillon. A primitive system of earphones had been installed. The President constantly forgot to switch off his microphone when consulting the official next to him and the assembled delegates were treated to such gems as 'Oh, my God! I *told* you that if I gave the floor to that *idiot*, he would mess it all up ...'

Che was the star. He made a brilliant, very long speech in Cuban revolutionary style, laced with malicious humour and delivered with perfect timing and dramatic effect. After a lengthy dissertation on American aid to Cuba in pre-Castro days, and a plea for a new approach to development cooperation, he ended his peroration by declaring, 'And what did Cuba become, as a result of all that aid ... *El paraiso de las letrinas* (A paradise of latrines)!'

Bilateral discussions with the Americans were difficult and hampered by a language problem so I acted as interpreter. At one tense moment when I intervened as adviser, one of the Americans snapped: 'You shut up; you're just the interpreter' – a point on which I swiftly disabused him. There were no women on any of the delegations.

On some matters Cuba and Bolivia made common cause. In 1964, three years later, Che Guevara and Roberto Jordán Pando headed their respective delegations in Geneva at the meeting that created the UN Conference on Trade and Development, another brain-child of Raúl Prebisch. This double propinquity, combined with the unforgiving memory of computers, has continued to haunt Jordán Pando. I happened to be on the same plane in November 1996 when the immigration officials in Miami detained him for five hours until a phone call to Washington secured his release. He later became Bolivia's Ambassador to the United Nations in New York!

Our aim now was to implement the plan. Funding was provided not for the overall plan, but for individual programmes – the Trilateral Plan for the mining industry was one outstanding outcome. The plan also incorporated existing activities such as the Andean Indian Programme which had four pilot bases, three of them on the *altiplano*. The fourth was Cotoca, 25 kilometres from Santa Cruz, the first colonisation experiment in Bolivia. Colonisation flourished subsequently, but not always with beneficial effect; many fleeing the extreme poverty of the *altiplano* now cultivate coca in the Chapare. Our experts worked closely with local communities to develop programmes tailored to their wishes. Schools were the first priority of the *campesinos*, who helped to build them and contributed to teachers' salaries. Agriculture and health projects built on local tradition; thus, the *Yatiri* (the Andean witch doctor) was incorporated into modern practices of prenatal care. Vocational training centres trained the young in carpentry, simple mechanics, cooking and nutrition.

The story of Acción Andina has never been told with the wealth of romantic detail it deserves. Jef Rens, its founder, was idiosyncratic and sometimes irascible. On one visit an experiment in improved pasture impressed him greatly. He clutched a bouquet of these grasses as the jeep bumped over the *altiplano*. Suddenly he barked, '*Arrêtez!*' (stop). Alighting, this tall, incongruous figure advanced towards an unsuspecting cow munching the sparse *altiplano* grass. Arm outstretched with the succulent posy, Jef commanded sternly, '*Mange!*' (eat!). Jef always spoke French and made no accommodation for the cow's limited linguistic knowledge. The cow gazed at him uncomprehendingly. 'Mange!' said Jef again, thrusting the grasses under the cow's nose, but the cow remained impervious to the attractions of improved pasture, and flicked her tail insolently before bowing her head again. Jef bellowed, '*MANGE!*', but the cow stalked off in disdain. '*Merde!*' swore Jef, flinging down the disdained feed. He did not speak for the rest of the journey.

My visits to field projects were veritable expeditions. There were only 500 kilometres of paved road in Bolivia and they did not lead out of La Paz but linked Cochabamba with Santa Cruz. There were no bridges over rivers that swelled into impassable floods during the rainy season. I was once stranded for a weekend trying to reach Cochabamba, and convoys sometimes waited three weeks for waters to subside. My jeep was always well-loaded with emergency rations, a bedroll and a bottle of whisky, for *altiplano* nights are perishingly cold. Even if you reached your destination, home comforts were singularly lacking in wayside hostelries. As many beds as possible were crammed into a room – once I shared a wayside dormitory not only with my male colleagues, but with *campesinos* who arrived throughout the night – and washing facilities often comprised a communal tin basin in a courtyard. I sometimes did not undress fully for a whole week.

The unexpected was the norm. One Saturday I returned from home leave to be handed a telegram from Potosí saying simply, '*Estoy en el calabozo. Sácame rápido*' (I'm in the dungeon. Get me out quick!). It came from Henri Gumbau, an idiosyncratic Frenchman who ran the Otavi base, two and a half days' journey from La Paz. He had been thrown into jail on a trumped-up charge, to do with a typewriter he had loaned to a local staff member, but before I could get the authorities on the job on Monday he had negotiated his release and treated the local police chief to a slap-up dinner.

Gumbau performed miracles at Otavi, among them building the first rural hospital in Bolivia, of which I laid the first stone in March 1960. The villagers provided labour and local materials while equipment was donated from abroad. The result was a modest adobe building with 14 beds, a public health clinic, and a small operating theatre. Local people were happy to have pills prescribed, but baulked when it came to operations. One day there was a fair to which community leaders came from far and near, among them a man with a sick donkey. A gelding operation had gone septic and the owner sought the doctor's help. Fortunately the doctor, who was a Bolivian born in Potosí and familiar with *campesino* mentality, agreed to perform this unorthodox operation. The donkey was anaesthetised and, under the intent gaze of the community leaders, the wound was lanced and stitched. Shortly afterwards, the donkey shambled to his feet and began to graze, publicly vindicating the doctor's skill. From that day on, people no longer hesitated to use all the hospital's facilities – another useful object lesson in how to make technical cooperation work.

When I left Bolivia in 1965, the Government wished to give me the country's highest decoration, the Condor of the Andes, but this was forbidden by the UN. Instead they gave my name to the Otavi hospital. Despite many setbacks it still functions and still bears my name.

Gifts to Acción Andina were sometimes mixed blessings. A consignment of ambulances from the Czechoslovakian Government raised the hackles of the US Ambassador and concerns about our political affiliations, although Czechoslovakia was a bona fide UN member – another example of Cold War susceptibilities affecting technical cooperation. Then there were the Citroën '*deux chevaux*' cars provided by France, singularly unsuited to Bolivia's rugged terrain. I helped drive one vehicle to Cotoca. The little car struggled gallantly over the backbone of the Andes but subsided in the sandy streets of Santa Cruz, then more like a wild west outpost than the booming oil town today. We loaded the car onto a lorry for the last 25 kilometres and for eight hours lurched through the night, from one pothole to another, arriving as dawn was breaking.

In 1963 I had a dramatic experience in Cotoca while supervising the transfer of vocational training equipment to a rural polytechnic in the Cochabamba valley. This had been agreed with the Government but the locals had a different view. Loading was proceeding apace when a cloud of dust appeared on the horizon, resolving itself into a company of 100 men, flourishing a motley collection of ancient rifles, machetes, axes and sticks. They had been drinking all night, and began hurling the machinery down from the lorries. Our little band was lined up against the machine shop that began to look alarmingly like an execution wall and the French project director, who had been in the Maquis, implanted a kiss on my left cheek with an air of 'those-who-are-about-to-die'. It was a tense moment, but I managed to persuade one leader, less inebriated than the rest, to restrain the others while we made our getaway. Our troubles were not over. Trees had been felled to block our escape, and the jeep had to bump along the single-track railway. Luckily we did not meet a train.

When we reached Santa Cruz I had a radio conference with the President. Víctor Paz's reaction was a masterpiece of under-statement. It began: 'But you, Margarita, understand the *idiosyn-crasies* of this country, better than anyone ...' and advocated patience. I was still at the radio station a few minutes later when a peremptory presidential message instructed the local authorities to retrieve the equipment and transport it to Cochabamba.

Another colonisation project – just over the Peruvian frontier, at San Juan del Oro, in the Tambopata Valley draining into the Madre de Dios – became a subject of controversy, and my colleague in Peru, René Gachot, and I were asked to investigate. For three days we walked some 100 kilometres in awful conditions; unseasonable rain soaked us as we toiled along a narrow track that swooped down into deep valleys, only to climb steeply up again on the other side, and crossed swamps, where we sank knee-deep in mud. Every night we slept rough, amid alarming stories of rattlesnakes. The path was as congested as Piccadilly Circus, with trains of 20 or 30 loaded mules careering along, bells ringing to warn of their approach, and men scampering past us at a shaming pace, bowed under planks and corrugated iron roofs on the way in, and tropical produce on the way out. It was an extraordinary demonstration of people performing daily miracles of endurance and courage in their search for a new life only a little less unbearable than on the *altiplano*.

Spontaneous colonisation was also taking root in Bolivia. I visited the rich area between the Chapare and Chimoré rivers to see FAO experiments in tropical agriculture. The precipitous track that provided the only access stopped on the banks of the Chapare, and at Villa Tunari vehicles had to be slung over a deep gorge, on a platform swinging high above the water, manipulated by pulleys slung between towers on either bank. Villa Tunari was the prototype of a frontier settlement, bustling with life, its muddy street clogged with lorries under which people slept. I dossed down on the dining-table of the overcrowded one-horse hotel, and my colleague in a hammock strung from the rafters, both of us kept awake by the relentless snoring of other inhabitants. When a proper road was built, access for colonists became easier. But so did the massive production of coca, a social and international problem with which Bolivia still struggles today. What I saw in Villa Tunari in 1962 belonged to a more innocent era.

I visited all the regions of Bolivia, from steamy, tropical Riberalta in the north, where the streets were paved with grass, to the icy uplands of the *altiplano* and the Cordillera. On one hike along the snowline of the Cordillera Real, from Chacaltaya to the Cumbre de Yungas we found ourselves stuck on a snow slope and had to slide on our backs down a steep ice-covered scree, narrowly missing a cluster of spiky rocks. On another occasion we climbed to the peak at 17 000 feet above the Yungas Pass, arriving soon after dawn to see almost the whole of Bolivia spread before us, from the snow-capped pinnacles all around, to the subtropical valleys below and then, beyond the blue glimmer of the forests, 100 miles away or more and two or three miles below, to the broad plains and lazy rivers of eastern Bolivia, the Oriente, that drain into the Amazon.

One did not need to go out of La Paz for unusual experiences. On one occasion the Interior Minister gave a farewell party for the French Ambassador, and applied the old Bolivian tradition of locking all doors to prevent anyone leaving. Determined to escape I climbed out of a bathroom window and crawled to the front drive. An irate shout from within warned that my departure had been noticed. My driver, Victor Vera, was never surprised by anything, but even his jaw dropped as he saw me running hell for leather towards him, at two o'clock in the morning, evening shoes in hand, with the minister in hot pursuit. I flung myself in the car just in time and off we sped, leaving an angrily gesticulating figure in the moonlight. The rest of the Diplomatic Corps remained hostage until eight o'clock next morning.

When Sargent Shriver, President Kennedy's brother-in-law, came to launch the American Peace Corps his visit coincided with that of my boss, David Owen. The Foreign Minister gave one official lunch for both, and it was Shriver who thanked our host, launching into an eloquent peroration about the landscape, the people, Bolivia's culture and unparalleled charms. His voice rose to a crescendo as he declaimed. 'Please raise your glasses and drink with me to this unique and unforgettable country ... "*Viva el* Perú!"' There was a stunned silence, until Nuño Chávez, the witty Minister of Mines, saved the situation with a winning smile, 'You mean of course, *Alto* Perú' (Alto – or Upper – Perú was the colonial name for Bolivia).

New aid organisations began to appear. The World Food Programme assigned its first project in Latin America to Bolivia, involving tons of cheese from Canada, which arrived by train through Peru and across Lake Titicaca. The consignment got stuck in a rail wagon at Guaquai and was soon giving off most noxious smells. Acrimonious correspondence sprang up between WFP Headquarters, the Government and myself as to who was responsible for disposing of the offending cheese. While the bureaucratic wrangle raged on, the cheese became more rancid and the stench more noisome. In the end the station master took matters in his own hands and pitched the lot into the lake.

With the advent of the Labour Government in the UK in 1964, and the creation of the Ministry of Overseas Development, the British bilateral programme began. The British Ambassador appealed to me for advice. I consulted *Flaco* Gumucio, and we concluded that tropical agriculture was an area in which Britain had outstanding expertise, because of its colonial past, and Bolivia great needs. Together we designed a project that led to successful cooperation between the UK and Bolivia that still continues.

Towards the end of 1961 my father was suddenly told that he must retire, and he became depressed. He was 67, but in good fettle, and only in the last ten years had been able to fulfil his talents. Some immediate distraction was called for and I booked a passage for my parents on the next boat bound for South America. They stayed seven months and we travelled back to England together in July 1962, on the *Reina del Mar*. My mother again successfully tested her theory that if you speak English loudly and slowly enough, you cannot fail to make yourself understood; she regularly marched off to the markets, armed with a bilingual list and accompanied by my driver, who did the haggling with bowler-hatted *cholitas*, perched on top of their wares, their voluminous skirts and petticoats tucked up around them.

I took my parents on several field trips, including a circuit of the Acción Andina bases and down to Cochabamba. I can still conjure up the image of my mother, then 64, carting large stones to shore up the wheels of our vehicle when we got stuck in a river at 14 000 feet. We slept in primitive places and often started before dawn. My parents rarely, if ever, drank alcohol, but I discovered that at that hour, with temperatures well below freezing, they did not say no to a warming tot. I took a Primus stove to ensure that they always had their 'early morning tea'. After visiting many communities on the *altiplano* my mother said, 'I thought I knew what it was to be poor, from my own youth, but I have never seen poverty like this.'

When we boarded the *Reina del Mar* the passenger list read: 'Mr and Mrs Anstee and daughter'. My mother was delighted: 'Frankly, dear, I was getting tired of being introduced everywhere as "Miss Anstee's parents".' I spent the rest of my leave hunting for a retirement home for my parents. On my last day I signed a contract for a small house, with the delightful name of Pippins, in the village of Wedmore in Somerset, together with part of a cider orchard, which they turned into a garden. Their visit to Bolivia and our sea trip home was the longest time we had had together for many years. It was our last family expedition.

Shades of the Cold War

Professionally, 1962 threw up several challenges. Paz Estenssoro, a wily political bird, constantly played off the United Nations against the United States. Being the only other major actors we acquired a political significance far beyond our monetary importance, and I constantly found myself balancing on a slender tightrope.

We were starting a programme of geological exploration for natural gas and oil, with Yacimientos Petrolíferos Bolivians (YPFB), the state oil company, headed by the President's brother, José Paz Estenssoro. As usual the UN presented qualified candidates for each expert post, from which the Government made its choice. They included a Russian candidate. I was on a field trip and my deputy was in the act of signing the form letter to the Foreign Minister when he received a telephone call from the US embassy requesting omission of the Russian's name. How the Embassy became aware of internal correspondence that had arrived by diplomatic pouch remains a mystery; this was par for the course during the Cold War. My deputy told the caller that it was out of the question to remove any candidate, and despatched the letter unamended. 'You did quite right,' I said, and put the matter out of my mind.

A few nights later I was at a dinner that the Minister of Defence was giving for the President. Most of the Cabinet was there, but only three foreigners: the United States and German Ambassadors and myself. The American, Ben Stephansky, was a political nominee of the Kennedy administration, with whom I had established a good rapport, despite the spat over Czech ambulances.

After dinner Ben bore down on me, demanding to know why we had included the Russian's name. We were the cynosure of all eyes and I caught sight of the President enjoying himself hugely. I spoke quietly but Ben showed no such scruples. In vain I tried to make him understand that the Soviet Union was a member of the United Nations and that I was an international civil servant, on oath to take instructions only from the Secretary-General, and not from any member state, including my country of birth. I could not help adding, 'Not that Her Majesty's Government would dream of such a thing.' Stephansky was too irate to notice the irony. There were innuendos that if I did not watch my step, my career prospects could be affected. I brought the conversation to an end saying I would be very surprised if the Bolivian Government selected the Russian, as there were other excellent candidates.

Next day I was horrified to find in the Communist weekly, *El Pueblo*, a large headline '*Deshojando La Margarita ...*' (Taking the petals off Margarita = the daisy, a play on my name), followed by an eerily accurate account of our argument. Worst of all, the article praised me for having maintained the international ideal. With friends like these, I needed no enemies. It seemed likely that the US Embassy would attribute the leak to me and to pre-empt this I sought Ben out. He amazed me by responding: 'We never take *El Pueblo.*' I could not help feeling that the embassy was short-sighted in not reading *El Pueblo*, whatever one thought of its politics. A few days later, contrary to my predictions, the YPFB Head accepted the Russian candidate – I am sure, deliberately. Stephansky was obliged to ask Víctor Paz to rescind his brother's decision, which he did.

At about that time I invited the new head of the United States Agency for International Development (USAID) for drinks to discuss cooperation between our programmes. I was dumbfounded when he suggested that many problems would be avoided if I went to bed with him. 'We know a lot about you,' he said darkly, 'and about your son in boarding-school in England.' This did arouse my interest as I was unaware of his existence.

The plot thickened when my deputy reported that a young man in the US Embassy – clearly a CIA operative – had got drunk at a party and said, 'Your boss ought to be careful. We know who visits her, and we have her telephone tapped.' Almost simultaneously the Swedish head of our mineral survey told me that, at another social event, the No. Two at the US Embassy had made allegations about my political affiliations and private life, again implying that the embassy had special sources of information. In the village-like atmosphere of La Paz I had always realised that there was intense speculation about the only woman head of mission, but discretion had not paid off. When my former secretary in Montevideo stayed in my house until she found other accommodation, I was stupefied to learn that, no evidence of other relations being detected, it was rumoured that I was a lesbian …

I took the bull by the horns and went to see Stephansky. I asked him how there could be genuine cooperation between us if I was being spied upon and my telephone tapped. Ben seemed shocked. If he knew what was going on, he put on an excellent show of ignorance and indignation.

'Tell me the names of the people who said this,' he demanded, 'and they will be out of the country within 24 hours.'

I refused to comply, pointing out that to do so would be to stoop to the same level of gossip and slander. The identities of the informers were irrelevant. I wanted the fire put out, not just the smoke; that is, an immediate stop to telephone-tapping and surveillance.

There was an interesting sequel. The ambassador convened the embassy staff and demanded to know who had given the information. The junior man kept quiet but the Minister Counsellor admitted his part and was sent packing to Washington in a matter of days. That gave me no satisfaction and seemed unfair; he was merely one of the bearers of the smoke. I never did know whether the fire was put out – indeed, wondered whether it was within the ambassador's power to do so. I simply took more care when making telephone calls.

Perils of Air Travel

In 1963 I had to deal with four fatal events: a road accident, two air crashes and the suicide of one of our geologists. The most dramatic of these were the air crashes.

The national airline, Lloyd Aéreo Boliviano (LAB), had an excellent record but, in March 1963, its DC-6 crashed at 16 000 feet on Mount Tacora in the western limb of the Cordillera. I had the grim task of identifying and collecting the body of a UN expert, Stephen Leigh. It took two days to reach the site, in a C-47 that flew first to Tacna in Peru and then to Charaña, a desolate *altiplano* village. Seats had hastily been installed in the plane but no one had thought to screw them to the floor, so that at take-off we all slid inexorably backwards. Simultaneously the door flew open, as we hung grimly to the side of the plane. A crew member was sent to the back, with another man to hang on to *him* while he leaned over the widening gulf between us and the *altiplano*, and dragged the door shut, securing it with a rope. This performance was repeated on every flight until the pilot accepted my suggestion that the door be secured *before* the plane took off. He insisted on flying several times over the site of the crash, swooping low over the wreckage and then banking steeply to avoid the crown of another hill.

Helicopters ferried the pathetic sacks of human remains to Charaña, where they were placed in rough wooden coffins and flown to La Paz. Having identified Leigh I spent a bitterly cold night clanking back to La Paz in a dilapidated *auto carril* – an old car, fitted with grooved wheels and given a new lease of life on the railway. Next day I was at the airport with a hearse to collect Stephen's coffin, only to discover that an American consul had decided the body belonged to an American and had taken it to Arica for shipment to the United States. I flew to Arica, sweltering in late summer heat in another dilapidated C-47, and came back with Leigh's coffin and two others lashed to the floor beside me. A week had gone by since the accident, the stench was overwhelming, and a storm tossed our plane mercilessly across the cordillera as night was falling and a strange yellowish light flickered over the *altiplano*. It was an apocalyptic experience.

So was the second accident, when one of two UN planes undertaking the airborne geophysical survey, with three Swedish experts aboard, crashed in the mountains south of Uncia. The mines were undergoing one of their periodic bouts of unrest. A sentry shot at us as we left La Paz at midnight and at Catavi, the centre of the trouble, rifle butts were thrust through the window but they let us proceed. At midday we reached a desolate spot where we descried 30 or 40 Quechua Indians descending the hill ahead at a jog trot, carrying improvised stretchers and running in relays like the *chasquis* of Inca times. They had found the wreck before the search party. Not a thing had been stolen.

The ordeal was not over. The plane that should have collected us failed to arrive and we had to transport the bodies back to La Paz on a decrepit lorry borrowed from the mine. At around three o'clock in the morning a tyre burst and the coffins had to be lifted out onto the road. A full moon cast a leprous light over this ghoulish scene and the long mournful plain.

Flaco, who came to pay his respects when at last the coffins lay under the United Nations flag in La Paz, said to me, 'You see? The mountains were angry at the intrusion; they have claimed their own.' The *supay*[2] had the last word.

Precarious as it was, air was often the only viable form of travel, roads being largely non-existent. In the tropical lowlands the DC-3 was the country bus. The people who clambered aboard, clutching squawking hens and other loudly protesting livestock, had never travelled in a car or lorry.

In 1964 I designed a project to benefit the small mining cooperatives which extracted gold from the Tipuani River, north of La Paz. There was no road, and the journey by foot or muleback took five days. By air it lasted 33 heart-stopping minutes, passing from 14 000 to 20 000 feet, without oxygen, and then as swiftly down to 1500 feet. We flew in the inevitable C-47, with a cargo of beer on the way in and gold on the way out.

The weather was bad but at mid-morning the pilots announced that it was safe to take off, since they could see the football pitch at the Milluni mines, just under the pass over the cordillera. As we passed through the snowbound defile between Huayna Potosi and Chacaltaya an impenetrable featherbed of cloud billowed ahead. The pilots, who had invited me into the cockpit, said reassuringly that they were flying on instruments but reassurance was short-lived when I saw that they consisted merely of a stopwatch, a compass and an altimeter. The co-pilot called out the minutes from the stopwatch while the pilot steered his course, dropping at nearly 1000 feet a minute as green hummocks of hilltops popped up through the clouds like floating ant-hills.

Tipuani airstrip was guarded by a pair of hills, between which the plane had to squeeze, swerving full-tilt to the left at mid-point to avoid another hill before hitting the ground, and bucketing madly over the grass. Then the plane had to swing back to the right to avoid hurtling into the river. Split-second timing and consummate skill were necessary to avoid disaster.

Six months later the same pilots and plane crashed on the snowy slopes of Huayna Potosi. Visibility had been poor, and the

2. *supay*: evil spirits living in the earth, who have to be appeased.

pilots had been warned not to fly. Yet they had gone, perhaps because they could descry the football pitch at Milluni, or because they placed too much faith in their 'instrumental' approach.

Collapse of a Dream

Although things did not go seriously wrong until 1964 there were frequent alarms and excursions, often coinciding with United Nations Day. On the eve of one anniversary when armed miners and *campesinos* were entrenched in the surrounding hills, I emerged late from my office to find a solitary gunman firing up and down the street, and ran half a mile to the car. Next day, though the town was dead, the Government insisted that I held the UN Day reception, 'to show that everything was normal' and sent three ministers to prove it while the rest of the Cabinet sat in emergency session.

Another year we set up an exhibition in the Prado, the main thoroughfare, in a tent loaned to us by the Bolivian Air Force. A loudspeaker nearby blared forth the militant views of housewives from the Catavi mine, whose aptitude for strident oratory seemed unimpaired by their hunger strike. On the eve of the anniversary, by an unfortunate confusion of identity, angry crowds set fire to the Air Force tent and with it the UN exhibition. Another year the UN Day material – which a frugal Headquarters had insisted on sending by surface means, a contorted sequence of boat, train and bus – sank on the primitive ferry across Lake Titicaca.

When Adlai Stevenson visited Bolivia I was surprised to find the chief of the secret police imperiously waving my car to the head of the cavalcade leaving the airport. The chilling reason for according this unwonted pre-eminence to the UN soon became clear. The Government, warned of a bomb attempt, had set up a dummy cavalcade to divert the attackers, while the distinguished visitor was smuggled down by a back road. Fortunately for me there was no bomb attempt and the only calamity that befell Adlai Stevenson was to get stuck in the lift in the Hotel Crillon.

In 1964, when elections were due, our ten-year plan was starting to produce results: 1963 saw the economy grow nearly 7 per cent.

And yet on 4 November 1964 the Government was overthrown. Víctor Paz Estenssoro's political acumen had for once deserted him and he acceded to American persuasion to run again for the presidency, although immediate succession was forbidden. Curiously, the State Department, which had previously regarded him with suspicion, now thought he was the only guarantee of continuing stability, when it would have been far better had he remained as an *éminence grise*. Paz Estenssoro took office on 6 August 1964 but three months later was overthrown by his vice-president, René Barrientos, an Air Force General, with the support of the armed forces.

Barrientos was a brave and skilled airman but cast in the mould of Bolivia's eccentric *caudillos* of the nineteenth century, such as Melgarejo, renowned for sending the British Ambassador packing, tied facing backwards on a donkey, because he would not drink beer from the same bowl as Melgarejo's horse Holofernes. (This led to the apocryphal story that an indignant Queen Victoria, foiled in her intent to send a gunship because Bolivia had no sea coast – though that loss came later – decreed that the country should be expunged from the maps in school books throughout her realms.) Barrientos had two wives, one in La Paz and one in Cochabamba, which caused protocol complications on the occasion of De Gaulle's state visit to Cochabamba. Barrientos' relations with the fair sex did not end there. There was ribald wordplay on *Cuerpo de Paz* (literally 'peace body') when rumours spread of an infatuation with an American Peace Corps girl. On another occasion an irate Bolivian father despatched a well-aimed bullet, as a result of which Barrientos, by then President, could not sit down for several weeks.

At the end of October 1964 Jef Rens and I were to visit all the Andean Indian bases, then being expanded into a national rural development programme. Three weeks earlier, returning from a prospective oil strike at Bulo-Bulo in the eastern jungle with our geologists, we arrived after nightfall at a crossing on the Yapacani and had to doss down on the riverbank. On the day of the new trip I awoke with a huge swelling on my leg: a *borro* (a singularly unpleasant butterfly-like insect) had laid its eggs there, but the larvae, instead of emerging after weeks of snug incubation, had died inside. They had to be excised immediately to prevent septicaemia. Had my leg blown up a day later, I would have been far from medical facilities.

Our trip was cancelled except for the last event, the inauguration of a UN vocational training project in Cochabamba. We were to fly down with President Paz on Saturday 31 October. Hours before, his ADC telephoned to say that this too must be cancelled, because of the deteriorating situation. Four days later the Government fell and the President fled into exile. Only then did we learn that the plotters had planned to dispose of him with a burst of machinegun fire at the inauguration of the UN project. I preferred not to reflect how the rest of us would have fared, or how fast I could have run with my bandaged leg.

Despite warning signs the outbreak of the revolution on 4 November took everyone by surprise. At eleven o'clock I was in the Sucre Hotel, trying to persuade a recalcitrant Rens to take the first plane and desist from his ambition to act as mediator. Suddenly firing erupted in the upper reaches of the town and panic-stricken people began pouring down the Prado. Víctor, my driver, did not demur when I told him to drive me back to the office to collect our staff. He crashed straight through the municipal flowerbeds and fought his way against a tide of cars streaming down both sides of the avenue. We got everyone out, but some took refuge in my house, a far-from-safe place. Nearby the small hill of Laikakota, defended by militiamen, was being ruthlessly bombed. Armed units siding with the coup were firing from Miraflores, on the other side of the valley, on to the still loyal San Jorge garrison opposite my home. As the American Embassy had predicted, the aim was bad and soon my roof was riddled with holes.

Miraculously, the telephone was working. Early that day the Minister of Mines, René Zavaleta, had called to tell me that the Cabinet had sat all night and to warn me that the end was near, only to find that the Chief of the Secret Police was bugging our conversations. René had sworn at him, enquiring acidly why he was interfering now when all his wiles had not prevented the debacle.

Now, as bullets and shells burst overhead, I tried to telephone Western Union to send a telegram to Headquarters (this was before the days of telex). We had elaborate instructions on procedures in case of a revolution, which all proved totally unworkable in Bolivia. I thought I might fulfil one of the requirements – inform New York – but even this intent was foiled when the Western Union man told me he was hiding under a table, avoiding a blaze of machine gun fire outside, and that their main transmitter had been blown up. Retrospectively this communications breakdown was a blessing in disguise. Some years later I happened to be present when a dozen people in New York were shouting conflicting advice down the telephone to a hapless resident representative facing an emergency. In 1964 I was alone and had to rely on my own judgement, but at least that ensured singleness of purpose and action.

At about two o'clock the shattering commotion ceased and I went cautiously out on the terrace. It was a brilliantly sunny day, the sky an unflecked blue, the air like ice-cold wine. A few soldiers were straggling up the other side of the ravine. All was eerily silent. Then came the sound of an engine chugging laboriously up from the valley. Some political or military leader, perhaps, driving up to take control? Not at all. A broken-down lorry hove into sight, full of crates of soft drinks, on which sat three small boys, presumably ready to disperse refreshments to the contending sides. Behind trudged a solitary soldier, in full battle kit, munching a banana.

The phone rang. It was the Peruvian Ambassador to tell me that ministers had sought asylum in his and other diplomatic missions. Their houses were being looted and they were concerned for their families' safety. There was a general appeal that I, as the UN Representative, should go to the presidential palace and request protection of human rights. I thought quickly and said that I should be accompanied by the Dean of the Diplomatic Corps. The Papal Nuncio being away in Rome, the mantle had fallen on the Yugoslav Ambassador. He had served with the partisans but was not at all keen on my proposition, reluctantly acquiescing when I promised the protection of the UN flag.

I collected the ambassador from his residence and we drove up towards the Plaza Murillo, as through a city of the dead, save for intermittent bursts of gunfire. Suddenly Víctor said, 'Look, there is a UN Land-Rover full of armed men.' I dashed across the street and embarked on an indignant harangue, tailing away lamely as I became aware of serried ranks of rifles levelled at me. The vehicle had been commandeered by university students but to my surprise they obeyed and returned the Land-Rover.

The Plaza Murillo was deserted, a man's shoe abandoned before the palace door. Later we learned that the miners' leader, Juan Lechín Oquendo, who had supported the rebels, had been carried in triumph to the palace a few minutes earlier on the shoulders of his supporters, only to be met by gunfire. In the ensuing mêlée he lost his shoe and some of his comrades their lives.

We were ushered in immediately. A few unshaven civilians lounged on their rifles on the staircase, many the worse for drink. The most senior person was an army Colonel, who had also been imbibing not wisely but too well. General Ovando, he explained, had taken control of the country until General Barrientos could arrive from Cochabamba. But there was conflicting information about Ovando's whereabouts. It subsequently transpired that he had disguised himself in the bloodstained shirt of a wounded civilian and escaped in an ambulance via the back door. The colonel invited us to wait in the presidential office. There we found the Catholic bishop, Monseñor Kennedy, bound on a similar mercy mission, and prudently standing between two of the long windows, for bullets frequently whizzed past outside. The Colonel was loquacious though hardly diplomatic. 'The Communists,' he declaimed, blissfully oblivious of the fact that one of his public hailed from a Communist country, 'are massing at the top of the city and must be stopped.' The palace was alive with rumours: the President of the new military junta, General Barrientos, was at that moment landing at the airport, would come early tomorrow morning, or the next day ... who knew?

Meanwhile, enquired the Colonel, would I like to sit in the President's chair? I dismissed this bizarre suggestion, but could not help reflecting that if I picked up the telephone and snapped out a few orders with sufficient authority people would jump gratefully to attention. There was total political vacuum, a gaping pause in history that anyone with decision might fill.

General Ovando never turned up, and after an hour or two the ambassador and I left, requesting the tipsy Colonel, without much confidence, to pass on our appeal for the observance of human rights. Someone was delegated to 'protect' us but was too far gone in his cups to be coherent so that, when the rector and students of the university tried to wrest my car from us, it was we who had to do the talking.

The political hiatus lasted 24 hours. Next day saw General Barrientos in La Paz, and a military junta installed.

It was the end of many dreams. I went to see the American Ambassador, Douglas Henderson, a likeable career diplomat who had succeeded Ben Stephansky. I found him nearly in tears. He seemed quite unaware that, as everyone suspected and was later proved, the rebels had had ample help from the American military and the CIA. The State Department and the Pentagon had been working in contrary directions. The great irony was that in August 1963 Víctor Paz had been officially invited to Washington by President Kennedy, a signal honour for a small remote country that nonetheless found itself at the heart of the Cold War. At a critical moment following the Cuban missile crisis, Kennedy wanted to adopt the Bolivian revolution as a democratic counterweight to the Soviet-supported Cuban revolution. Had he not been assassinated soon afterwards Bolivian history might have been very different.

I went to visit the ministers who had escaped into embassies and were soon to go into exile. One asked me to take care of a cherished packet of love-letters, the only thing he had salvaged in his flight. On my next visit to Lima I took an anonymous taxi to visit Víctor Paz and his wife. It was a sad reunion: they were beginning a long exile, and our conversation was full of nostalgia about what-might-have-been.

Our ten-year plan fell into desuetude. Paradoxically, the economic upturn that the plan helped to produce was one of the factors causing the revolution. Earlier no one had wanted to assume government because the situation was so bad. Now the coincidence of renewed growth and the resurgence of the armed forces had produced an irresistible temptation. The rural development plan became distorted, with emphasis on investment on infrastructure at the expense of the integrated approach that had been the core of Acción Andina's philosophy. Now USAID, rather than UN, took the lead role.

Rumour was rife in La Paz that, because I had worked closely with the previous Government, I was to be declared *persona non grata*. I had no great desire to stay, but neither did I want to be banished when I had done nothing contrary to my duty as an international official.

The oil and gas exploration on which we were advising YPFB had found an important strike of natural gas – the first in Bolivia – at Naranjillos near Santa Cruz. The new President decided to attend the inauguration of the well and I was invited. We left in two aircraft, I the only woman and only foreigner in the first, which carried Ministers, military people and high officials and was piloted by Barrientos. I had been piloted by him before when Paz Estenssoro was President ... The second plane was crammed with journalists and cameramen. When we slipped over the last escarpment of the mountains to fly into Santa Cruz, we hit turbulence. I was horrified to see that two single-engined Air Force planes had positioned themselves at our wing-points. The pilots, delirious with joy at the triumph of their General, were throwing their caps in the air and waving both arms, in an alarming display of 'Look, no hands!' Luckily the air currents bounced all the aircraft at the same time and in the same direction but it was still a relief to land, the small planes sheering off at the last moment.

My UN geologist awaited me with a jeep but as we passed the President's station wagon I saw that he was beckoning me to sit beside him. In front were the driver, an Air Force General, and another officer, while the back was packed with ADCs. There was no way I could refuse. We drove to an open-air restaurant for lunch, with lashings of beer, of which he partook generously.

Afterwards I was again bidden to the President's side. Now jungle proper, thick vegetation and creeping lianas closed in on us, and the track became rougher. I tried to engage the President in discussion of the importance of the gas find for Bolivia but to no avail. He took my arm and said dreamily, 'Look, señorita, how beautifully green it is here, so warm and inviting' and, suiting the action to the word, snuggled closer. While I desperately rattled on about investment prospects, gas pipe lines to Brazil and, who knew, perhaps to Argentina and even Chile ...? Barrientos' eyes glazed over and his head fell on my shoulder. Soon it descended to my bosom, a location clearly much to his liking, though not to mine. The senior Air Force officers looked back with odiously conspiratorial glances, plainly thinking, 'So this is number X?' Gingerly I lifted the lolling Presidential head and held it in a more decorous position.

A spurt of vivid, leaping flames ahead revealed a clearing with the well in the middle and the perennial brass band, which promptly struck up the national anthem. The Air Force officers jumped smartly out, stood to attention, and saluted. The ADCs followed suit. The President went on snoring gently. I shook him hard. 'Señor Presidente, we have arrived.'

He came to with a start and demanded, almost accusingly, 'Where the devil is my cap?'

I felt like replying, 'How the devil should I know?'

We both dived about the vehicle, and found his cap under the seat. I placed it on his head, brushed the dust off his uniform, and pushed him out just in time to salute the last strains of the anthem (fortunately very long).

From being a potential *persona non grata*, I had suddenly become altogether *too 'grata'*. I did not know which was worse. Fortunately there was no sequel. The gas discovery, however, was to have a major impact on Bolivia's economic prospects. The military junta, in this as in other spheres, savoured the benefits of the MNR government's efforts.

Early in 1965 Headquarters proposed my transfer to Chile, a plum posting. Everyone was surprised when I turned it down but the only posting I would consider was another poor Andean country, and Ecuador was not open. I did not like the tendency to keep resident representatives in the same regional compartments and wanted to widen my experience. I had worked in Asia and three Latin American countries, and now wanted to go to Africa. Ethiopia was suggested and I agreed, liking the thought of that very special kingdom and of still living at high altitude in a mountainous country.

There were many *despedidas* (farewell parties), official and unofficial. The Foreign Minister, General Joaquin Zenteno, presented me with a Bolivian necklace on the back of which the date, the occasion and his name are engraved. A few years later Zenteno played a key role in capturing Che Guevara when the latter came secretly to Bolivia to foment revolution. Subsequently Zenteno was gunned down in Paris, almost certainly in retribution.

At my *despedidas* I missed many people with whom I had worked, now in exile. The Sunday before my departure I went incognito to the prison to see those who remained there. I was searched for arms but then wandered at will. I had never expected to enter a prison and hear my name called loudly from all sides. The political prisoners were allowed individual cells and to furnish them. One of them loudly described his escape plans but, notwithstanding this indiscretion, did later escape. The former Finance Minister, Augusto Cuadro Sánchez, barely looked up from his typewriter to explain that he was being paid by the military junta to prepare tax reform proposals – 'Something your people never managed to do' he added and that the money came in very handy to pay his legal fees. He was under contract to the same authorities who were pressing charges against him!

My official farewell of the Head of State was unusual for by then there were two: General Ovando was now co-president with Barrientos. A protocol problem arose – with whom to shake hands first? On the day before my departure I flew with Ovando to Oruro, to sign an agreement for a mineralogical research institute, and we drove through the streets in an open car under cascades of confetti, for all the world like a bridal pair.

I left on 18 June 1965, not to return for seven years. In 1966 Barrientos was elected President. On 27 April 1969, he was killed in suspicious circumstances when his plane flew into overhead wires. His vice-president assumed the presidency but on 26 September 1969 was deposed by another military junta, headed by Ovando.

After the 1964 revolution, Bolivia suffered 17 years of military dictatorship, and a return to the old curse of coups and counter-coups.

11

At the Court of the Lion of Judah

When Headquarters consulted the Ethiopian Permanent Representative to the United Nations, a fiery gentleman called Ato Tesfaye, he flung my curriculum vitae down and shouted, 'A *woman*! What on earth is *she* going to do in Ethiopia?' – a strange reaction, given a long line of Ethiopian empresses, going back to the Queen of Sheba. When I reached New York from La Paz I had to wait ten days before being granted a perfunctory interview with Ato Tesfaye, which he was clearly in a hurry to leave for lunch.

Fortunately the Government proved less averse to the notion of a woman heading the UN Mission than their New York representative On Sunday 15 August 1965, I had my first sight of Addis Ababa, surrounded by its blue-green hills, and groves of gum trees where smoke from early morning fires hung in the air, pungent with the all-pervading smell of eucalyptus. I had with me my Bolivian cat, Ananay. In La Paz I had also a dog, Hualaycho, but the cat was most attached to me, and I left the dog with my cook. Ananay had spent an unhappy two months in quarantine. An impasse had ensued; the Ethiopian authorities would not allow in an animal not vaccinated against rabies, while the British Government would not allow the vaccine to enter the UK. My parents had volunteered to take Ananay but at the last moment my predecessor obtained agreement for him to enter without being vaccinated. Ananay was rushed to London, and put on the same flight as myself. His coming was a decision I was later bitterly to regret.

Ananay and I were installed in a bungalow at the Ghion Hotel, a traditional Ethiopian establishment. My office was in Africa Hall, an imposing building housing the UN Economic Commission for Africa (ECA). I was also the UNDP Liaison Officer with ECA and soon became fast friends with the Executive Secretary, Robert Gardiner, a redoubtable Ghanaian.

Once again I had to prove to a sceptical government that I knew what I was about. Ethiopia being a very poor country our programme was large, and covered virtually all sectors. Agriculture loomed large, with projects ranging from veterinary training to forestry and agricultural research and extension. An ambitious multi-purpose project in the Awash Valley, linked to dams financed by the World Bank, aimed to develop irrigation and settle nomadic populations.

On my first Sunday the volatile Minister of Agriculture, Ato Akaleworq Habtewold, declared David White, the Project Manager of the Animal Health Training College in Debre Zeit *persona non grata*. White was under medical orders to avoid standing but the minister flew into a rage when he arrived unannounced on a Sunday morning, and he did not immediately rise to his feet. I persuaded the minister to change his mind but it was a salutary insight into the prickliness of some Ethiopian dignitaries.

I was to have a deputy and an assistant resident representative. New York wished to promote Subbaraman, the Indian Assistant Resident Representative, to be deputy but warned me that the Russians had designs on the post. I was asked to try to resolve the matter in favour of Subbaraman. I was thus astounded to learn from a minister at the first official dinner I attended that the Government 'accepted Mr Georgy Kozhevnikov as Deputy Resident Representative.'

'Who,' I enquired, 'presented the candidature?'

'Oh, the Soviet Embassy,' came the reply.

I left the Soviet chargé d'affaires in no doubt of the irregularity of his action, reflecting that this was the counterpart of similar misunderstandings about the United Nations that I had experienced in Bolivia from the other superpower, and par for the course in the Cold War. My remonstrations had the same effect as water off a duck's back. So did my recommendation to New York that

Subbaraman be appointed deputy. Neither the United Nations nor the Ethiopian Government wanted to tangle with the Soviet Union.

Rather naively, I expected Georgy Kozhevnikov to be bright but not nice. He turned out to be the reverse – not an unqualified advantage, as I was to find out. All initiative had been squeezed out of him. He incessantly made notes, even recording the opening greetings at meetings, but usually missed the point. Georgy lived in the Soviet compound, and I was aware that these 'records' found their way into embassy hands. On balance I decided that it was no bad thing they were inaccurate ...

Rents in Addis Ababa being astronomical, I was a long time in finding a modest two-bedroom bungalow on the outskirts of the city. It had a large garden with a view across the valley to blue eucalyptus-clad hills, and was reached by a cart-track, more often used by cattle than wheeled vehicles. This was part of the delights of a city where the rural mixed indistinguishably with the urban, where cattle, goats and sheep – and even affronted-looking camels – roamed the main thoroughfares. On one occasion when Prince Sadruddin Aga Khan, then UN High Commissioner for Refugees, was visiting, we drove to the palace in one of the Emperor's limousines, escorted by motorcycle outriders whose chief function was to act as shepherds, scattering flocks of sheep from our path.

My neighbours were indigent families, living in tumbledown shanties, who, my landlord was at pains to assure me, he would immediately have moved, to which I retorted, 'If you do that, I shan't take the house.' I was nonetheless uneasy about my neighbours. On my first night I went to a dinner in the Volkswagen Beetle, which, over two strenuous days, I had driven up from the Red Sea port of Assab, across the burning inferno of the Danakil Desert. I returned to find my gates hermetically bolted, and no amount of bell-ringing, banging or shouting could rouse my night *zabanha* (guard) or his dog. Suddenly a torrent of scantily clad men, shouting incomprehensibly in Amharic, burst out of the shacks. For a petrified moment I feared the worst – alone, late at night, in a place where no screams would be heard. But the crowd was venting its wrath not on me but on the sleeping *zabanha*. They hammered on the gates, yelling abuse, until the sheepish boy appeared.

After that we became fast friends. Whenever they celebrated a wedding or christening, they connected a cable to tap electricity from my bungalow. When I left they gave me their own farewell.

Making friends with Ethiopians in the circles in which I worked proved more difficult. Personal invitations were formal, to restaurants, not private homes. I desperately missed the homely gatherings that had cemented friendships in Bolivia, and danced alone to Bolivian music in my isolated bungalow, to the mystification of my night *zabanha* patrolling the garden, as the rain clattered down on the corrugated iron roof and hyenas howled eerily outside. Each dawn I got up to write my book on Bolivia, a work of nostalgic recollection in a distant continent that seemed very alien.

For some months I survived with a camp bed and plastic garden furniture. The United Nations still refusing to allow airfreight, my personal effects travelled by train to Lake Titicaca, by boat across the lake, by train to a Peruvian port, and by boat to Marseilles, where they were transhipped to Djibouti, for another train journey up into Ethiopia. There they disappeared. A visit to that steamy port unearthed my crate abandoned at the back of a warehouse and no longer intact.

Meanwhile, I acquired domestic staff. Ali, a Muslim, was a brilliant cook, who, though illiterate, spoke French. I, in shameful contrast, mastered the hieroglyphics of the Amharic alphabet, but could not sustain a conversation or understand texts that I could read phonetically! Like many illiterates, Ali had a prodigious memory. Each Sunday he rattled off every item he had bought during the week, to the last birr. Ali went through wives as a knife goes through butter and, as he grew older (he was in his mid-sixties) so the ladies he brought to live in the small house in the corner of the compound grew younger and more nubile. There was only one at a time, but progeny multiplied, and the garden resounded to the scampering of all too many tiny feet. I tried to interest him in family planning, pointing out the economic burden of so many children (though I suspected that I bore most of it). Ali listened politely but continued his merry philandering course.

Mammo, the houseboy, was very different – tall, handsome, with a dashing moustache, he was the epitome of elegance when serving in formal Ethiopian dress – white jodhpurs, white tunic cinched with a broad red cummerbund. Mammo was a Christian, spoke English and had only one wife. He did, however, drink, a failing that decimated my bar, and caused ructions with Ali, a good teetotal Muslim. Mammo, in turn, objected to Ali buying meat from a Muslim butcher friend. Tender meat was hard to come by and the *filets mignons* Ali served up were impeccable. Matters came to an ugly head when Princess Aida, the Emperor's granddaughter, came to lunch. Mammo expostulated that I could not give meat killed by Muslim custom to a member of the imperial family and the Ethiopian Orthodox Church. I found him and Ali settling the argument with kitchen knives, and had to interpose myself between the blades. Torn between domestic peace and edible meat, I opted pragmatically for the latter.

His Imperial Majesty

The formality of Ethiopian social life stemmed from its ancient imperial court. The Emperor, cloistered in sumptuous marbled palaces guarded by lions that wandered unfettered, where cheetahs stood like living statues on grand entrance steps, ruled as an omnipotent feudal monarch of old. He claimed descent from King Solomon and the Queen of Sheba, whose amorous encounter was immortalised in innumerable Ethiopian paintings that looked like strip cartoons. When he drove by, everyone had to alight from their cars and Ethiopians prostrated themselves. When he opened Parliament ladies had to wear hats and long dresses.

It was unprecedented for the Emperor to receive a lady head of mission – I was the only one – and hat and gloves were de rigueur for my first audience on 10 September 1965. Male colleagues had to wear full morning dress, including top hat. On entering the throne room I had to make three low curtseys, one at the door, a second half-way and the third on arriving before the throne where the Emperor took my hand. The same procedure was repeated backwards at the end. This daunting manoeuvre over highly polished parquet was made more difficult by the perverse positioning of the doorway, diagonally placed in relation to the throne so that, not having eyes in the back of my head, I rarely ended up at the right place. The greatest hazard came from the Emperor's pet chihuahua, which pranced about, yapping menacingly at my heels.

Since nothing of significance could happen without the Emperor's say-so I saw him frequently. He was such a diminutive little man that it was hard to imagine him as a not always benevolent despot, despite his grand gold-decked uniform. I was fascinated by his hands: tiny, almost feminine, with long, finely tapered fingers. Despite wartime exile in Bath, the Emperor spoke only French or Amharic. To ensure a direct exchange I always used French, though I found constant use of *Votre Majesté Impériale* quite a tongue-twister. Our meetings remained rigidly formal but we came to know each other well. There was often a shrewd twinkle in the imperial eye.

The Emperor's granddaughter, Princess Aida Desta, and I had been at Newnham College together but she was living in Tigre Province, where her husband Ras Mengesha Seyoum, was governor. At a lunch soon after my arrival my hosts' children exclaimed excitedly, 'A princess is coming.' When a slim young woman arrived, with her husband, the Deputy Prime Minister, I delicately ascertained her relationship with Aida. I discovered only that she was born in England, and had spent most of her life in Herefordshire. My driver, Tafessa, told me that she was the daughter of Ato Abebe Retta, the Minister of Health. Of humble origins, Ato Abebe was educated by priests in Gondar. He graduated to the court and when the Emperor fled into exile, after the Italian invasion in 1935, became his chauffeur in Bath. A love affair developed with Aida's mother, Princess Tenagne Work, the Emperor's daughter and eldest child, by then a widow (her husband, Ras Desta, was killed in battle with the Italians), and Mary was born. The baby was sent to Herefordshire and brought up by a beloved nanny. After years of virtual oblivion the Emperor sent for her and told her she must learn Amharic and marry an up and coming politician. Mary talked incessantly of England like any homesick expatriate. That sense of alienation was to culminate in tragedy. After the Emperor's overthrow, her mother, her sisters, and her husband were imprisoned for years. Mary, left outside with her two children, was unable to bear the isolation and committed suicide.

Years earlier Aida had also been recalled from England to make an arranged marriage to Ras Mengesha Seyoum, great-grandson of the Emperor Yohannes. She, too, had to learn Amharic and, having attended school and university in England, was more English than Ethiopian. By the time I arrived she had had six children and a serious illness that entailed her being rushed to the Unites States for a rare, life-saving operation.

Travels to the North

Project visits took me far afield – to the Animal Health School in Debre Zeit; to Jimma, the coffee-producing area, and to the Awash Valley. In November 1965 I travelled north, by the main highway to Gondar, one of the few benefits bestowed by Italian occupation along with a common language in a country where Amharic was little used outside Addis Ababa. With the WHO Mission Chief and another English doctor I visited rural health centres, headed by Ethiopian public health assistants, who had trained for two years at a school in Gondar which we assisted. Those that showed promise were admitted for training as doctors. Ethiopia could not afford to educate all the doctors required and in remote areas needs could best be served by people with good basic training, while doctors who had undergone a rural apprenticeship were more likely to benefit the general population. At one centre a procession of men clad in the classic Ethiopian garb of white *shammas* (a muslin-like tunic) and jodhpurs rushed in, carrying a man on a makeshift stretcher from a village far away across the mountains. The man was suffering from severe headaches, to cure which the local medicine man had hammered nails into his head. The doctor just arrived from England said, 'I've heard of many remedies for a headache, but never this!' The fact that the patient was taken to the centre showed growing confidence in the new approach. The public health assistants became agents of change in areas where traditions stretched back hundreds of years.

Gondar was a city of fabled but now crumbling castles, towers and turrets. In the seventeenth century it was the capital of the Ethiopian Empire, the seat of a court of many splendours but also of Machiavellian intrigue, a combination that led to its ultimate decadence and decline. Ethiopia, the only African country that had not come under colonial domination apart from the brief Italian episode, had nonetheless been affected by European influences going back to the twelfth century, when the legend of a powerful Christian emperor, Prester John, ruling in these parts, had raised hopes that he might help the Crusaders against Islam. Others had followed: the Venetians and the Portuguese, who, from the time of Prince Henry the Navigator, left their imprint on the architecture and the language. Then came the Jesuits until their expulsion in the mid-1600s. Nearby Lake Tana, which we visited, is dotted with island monasteries.

I continued northwards, alone, to Aksum, according to Ethiopian lore the realm of the Queen of Sheba, whence she set out for her fateful encounter with King Solomon. Ethiopia claimed to have the oldest surviving monarchy in the world and until the end of the nineteenth century the emperors were crowned in Aksum. The astonishing stelae, needle-like monuments of granite, probably date from the third or fourth centuries and, with their carvings of doors and windows, resembling ancient skyscrapers, testify to the accomplished remarkable heights of civilisation attained by the kingdom of Aksum.

I travelled on to Asmara, the capital of Eritrea. In 1950, the United Nations determined that Eritrea, a former Italian colony, should be federated with Ethiopia, while retaining considerable autonomy, but in 1962 the Emperor had annexed the country and curtailed its powers of self-government, fuelling a strong separatist movement. Asmara reminded me of a sleepy Italian town but beneath the calm exterior I detected ominous rumblings. I knew several Eritreans holding government positions who made no secret of their concerns about the future of their homeland.

My journey southward to Mekele, where Princess Aida lived, involved rough cross-country travel and I arrived tired and travel-stained. There I dazedly walked into the exact replica of an English country hotel, far different from the basic hostelries of previous nights, complete with chintz-covered armchairs, fitted carpets and an en suite bathroom with a geyser producing blissful hot water. Aida had created this gem from the bombed ruins of a castle belonging to Dejasmatch Abraha, an arch-rival of her husband's forebears. It was a living reflection of her deep nostalgia for England. Before that two castles – the other belonging to the descendants of the Emperor Yohannes – had glared at one another from opposing crags, symbols of the feudal rivalries with which Ethiopian politics were still riven.

Washed and brushed, I dined at the second castle with Aida, whom I had not met for nearly two decades. Her husband was opening a road to the Danakil Desert, previously only a camel trail bringing vital supplies of salt into the highlands. Next day we set off to find him. Mekele was not a prepossessing place. Most streets were unpaved but passers-by prostrated themselves face down in the dust when they saw the princess approaching, a deference I sensed she did not like. Outside the town the limp body of a man swung from a lofty gibbet, while vultures floated above.

We eventually sighted Ras Mengesha Seyoum atop a bulldozer, spearheading the onward thrust into distinctly inhospitable terrain. It was typical of Mengesha that he was driving the bulldozer just as, on a later visit, he insisted to my alarm in taking over the controls of the small plane in which we flew from Addis Ababa. In Mekele, Mengesha had launched projects to generate employment and raise abysmally low living standards, to which I was able to loan some short-term experts. Mengesha epitomised a new kind of Ethiopian noble, bent on alleviating the plight of the people, while Aida was working with hospitals and orphanages. I came away impressed by their dedication and the enormity of the challenge.

The Sandfords

My understanding of the complexity of Ethiopian culture, history and politics was greatly enhanced by two remarkable Britishers, Daniel and Christine Sandford. He was already in his eighties, she a year or two younger, but both were full of vigour and enthusiasm. Brigadier Sandford fell in love with Ethiopia in 1907, when he rode from Aden to visit his brother in Khartoum, an extraordinary journey at any time. In 1923 he resigned from the army and acquired Mulu Farm, settling there with Christine, who had read classics at Cambridge, one of the early graduates of Girton College. Mulu was then a long day's ride on horseback from Addis Ababa. In this remote outback Christine bore and raised six children.

Driven out by the Italian occupation, the Sandfords returned penniless to England. The Brigadier became Treasurer of Lincoln Cathedral, where he was run to earth when the British, planning to reinstate the Emperor, were seeking someone with intimate knowledge of Ethiopia. In 1940 Sandford returned at the head of Mission 101, to organise patriot resistance to Italian occupation, six months before General Orde Wingate's army began its victorious campaign. On 6 May 1941 he accompanied the Emperor on his triumphal re-entry into Addis Ababa and always remained close to him. The Emperor returned full of zeal for education. He asked Christine to educate the children of the court nobility and this led to the establishment of the Sandford school, later known as the British School.

Every Sunday the Sandfords held open house in their mud-walled farmhouse, idyllically wreathed in bougainvillea, but blessed with the most minimal facilities. Innovative farmers, they exported strawberries to Europe, and carried out their own rural development programme to help local villagers. No other foreign-born person could match their understanding of Ethiopia and its many peoples, from the Emperor down, to whom they referred affectionately as 'the little man'. I took every new expert to Mulu, as an essential part of their briefing. Despite the difference in age Christine and Dan became my dearest friends.

I sought Christine's assistance in developing my garden. She would arrive driving a vehicle packed with plants, wearing a long cotton dress, a battered straw hat, and ancient plimsolls. One counsel she gave me had almost catastrophic results: 'Bought grass seed won't withstand the drought. Just send your *zabanha* out to cut squares of local grass.' One night an irate farmer came to call, clad in white *shamma*, waving his tall stick about alarmingly, and accusing me of stealing his pasture. After that Christine brought me turf from Mulu.

My great companion was Ananay, who loved chasing lizards that were always too fast for him. And then tragedy struck: rabies was endemic and since my veterinary team had no vaccine I took Ananay to an Ethiopian clinic. The building was being redecorated and the vaccination took place outside. Terrified by the car journey and cage, associated with hated air travel, Ananay suddenly lashed out, lacerating my arm and, escaping my grasp, bolted into the undergrowth. I searched for hours, went back every night to call him, and offered a reward but never found him. I was all too aware that cats were considered a delicacy. I could not bear to think what had happened to the poor, terrified animal, that would have been safely with my parents had I left him in England. It took me a long time to recover, which must seem absurdly sentimental to anyone who has not experienced loneliness in a distant country.

In June 1966 I was smitten with agonising stomach pains. Subbaraman drove me to the Seventh Day Adventist hospital, reputedly the best in Addis Ababa, where an American missionary doctor plied me with questions. In my pain-dazed state I did not grasp where these were leading until a particularly intimate enquiry jolted me into the realisation that he thought that I was about to miscarry and that Subba was the progenitor. Mortified with embarrassment I sent my subordinate from the room and told the doctor that, short of immaculate conception, there was no way in which I could be pregnant. Appendicitis was more plausibly offered next but my faith in Seventh Day Adventists was further punctured when only my scanty Amharic saved me from having an injection administered intravenously instead of in my posterior. The doctor's parting words were, 'If the pain doesn't go in 24 hours, we must operate.' It didn't but one constant refrain rang through my head: 'I will *not* be operated on in Ethiopia.'

A Defining Encounter

Shortly afterwards the first global meeting of UNDP resident representatives was held in Turin, Italy. On 1 January 1966, EPTA and the Special Fund had merged into the UN Development

Programme (UNDP). Paul Hoffman, now in his eighties, became UNDP Administrator while David Owen, previously on a sup- posedly equal basis, had to play second fiddle, a poor reward for having created the network of resident representatives and built the programme from scratch.

The Special Fund's more centralised approach than the collegiate system of the Technical Assistance Board made it more difficult for specialised agencies to promote their 'pet projects'. Nonetheless, unseemly competition continued rife and there was a confusing proliferation of representatives and UN flags in the field. A few years earlier the Administrative Committee on Co- ordination (ACC) (the highest coordinating body of the UN system, chaired by the Secretary-General) had decreed that the resident representative was the *primus inter pares* but there was no lack of mavericks and prima donnas who defied the ACC decision. I had made proposals to New York for an integrated team approach and was working on a monograph on the administration of interna- tional aid eventually published by Syracuse University in 1969.

These ideas were ventilated at the Turin meeting. Among those present was Sir Robert Jackson, an Australian who had made a brilliant name for himself during the war, first as the young naval officer who persuaded the powers-that-be that, contrary to the prevailing wisdom, Malta could be defended, and then as the Director of the Middle East Supply Centre in Cairo. Subsequently, as Deputy Director-General of the first and largest UN organisa- tion, the UN Relief and Rehabilitation Administration (UNRRA), he had masterminded vast operations to succour millions of refugees and other victims of the Second World War. A brilliant United Nations career came to an abrupt end when, appointed as Senior Assistant Secretary-General (then the highest rank after the Secretary-General), he had fallen out with Trygve Lie over Middle Eastern policies. During the 1950s he headed the massive operation to build the Volta River dam in Ghana, and advised Kwame Nkrumah, Ghana's first President. Now he was Senior Consultant to Paul Hoffman and general troubleshooter.

When I had first met 'Jacko', as he was universally known, in New York in June 1962, I had declined his invitation to dine as I was accompanying a delegation of Bolivian Ministers. We had both attended a regional meeting of resident representatives in Mexico in 1965 but contact had been purely formal. In Turin we did dine together, on a beautiful summer evening, and found a meeting of minds about the UN system. That evening was to affect my life profoundly, professionally and personally.

From Turin I went on home leave and in August drove my parents to Scotland. We spent a week exploring the west coast area around Ballachulish, marred only by my mother suffering bouts of vertigo that we attributed to ear operations 20 years earlier. On the morning of our return it was I who fell ill, wracked by intense stomach pains. Neither of my parents could drive and I somehow managed the lengthy journey fortified, I am ashamed to remember, by sips of brandy (that was before the breathalyser), and stopping only to buy a bowl to be sick in and consult a doctor. He diagnosed appendicitis and recommended immediate operation, but I was determined to reach home. The next day my appendix was removed in Weston-super-Mare. The surgeon told me that the infection verged on peritonitis and that, had it erupted in Ethiopia, the consequences could have been fatal.

I convalesced at Pippins during some glorious September days, nursed by my mother, though she could not have felt well herself. My dramatic collapse diverted attention from her symptoms that were not merely a recurrence of former complaints.

The Awash Valley – Melka Warar

In October 1966 I experienced a *coup de foudre*. The impact was mutual: the other person, unconnected with the United Nations, briefly passing through Addis Ababa. So began a passion likely to last to the end of my days, giving a few heady interludes of happiness, and rather more of pain and loss – an *amour impossible*. The day after this encounter, I left at dawn on a field trip with the Minister of Agriculture that I could not cancel. By the time I returned he would be gone. We had two projects in the Awash Valley: one dealing with the institutional strengthening of the Awash Valley Authority (AVA) and its integrated programme of river basin development; the other a research station at Melka

Warar, experimenting with irrigated crops. I spent a gruelling Saturday bucketing along rutted tracks beside the winding river, visiting various works. It was fiendishly hot, I was emotionally exhausted and my mind was elsewhere.

In the evening we arrived at the research station's bungalow and I sank gratefully into a chair, a gin and tonic and pleasant lethargy. The British project manager and his wife were preparing dinner for the Minister of Agriculture and a small group, while others were to have a barbecue outside. Mouth-watering smells emanated from the kitchen, and a cool breeze wafted in from the bush where the cicadas chirped their nightly chorus. Suddenly I was jolted out of my reverie by a stream of foul language, shouted at full volume.

I rushed into the kitchen to find my project manager hurling insults against all Ethiopians and throwing the dinner down the sink. His outburst had been caused by one of the Ethiopians insisting that everyone should eat together, thus upsetting the elegantly laid table. I steered the irate man into the bedroom that his wife and I were to share and where the minister might be less able to hear. I pointed out that his outburst would make his position intolerable and damage a successful project but he continued to rail in a loud voice, deaf to my demands that he apologise to the minister. Instead he started undressing while his wife, clearly in awe of him, sat disconsolately by. Keeping my gaze fixed on a far corner of the ceiling I continued to harangue him but he announced that he was going to bed and did so.

I was left with an insulted minister, dinnerless guests and no bed for myself. I rustled up some roast goat from the barbecue, but it was very late before a subdued group sat down to a less than festive meal. It was a beautiful moonlit night and we all strolled out in the bush. The minister was a gentle man, unlike his fiery predecessor, but his hurt and indignation were evident and, as we walked under the sparse acacia trees he did not hide the serious consequences of such blatant discourtesy. Touchingly, however, he was concerned that I no longer had anywhere to sleep. 'You must have my bed,' he cried. 'I am a poet' (which he was) 'and can sleep out here under the stars.' Implicit in this was the sentiment that he did not feel welcome in the bungalow, and I had to work hard to persuade him to occupy the bedroom assigned to him.

Next day we inspected the experimental plots in a decidedly strained atmosphere and the ludicrous events of the weekend brought me abruptly down to earth. There could hardly have been a more effective antidote for romantic thoughts.

Later the FAO Chief of Mission, an elderly Scotsman, who had declined to accompany us, had the gall to say to me patronisingly, 'Well, you needed a man there. A woman can't deal with that kind of thing.' I thought I had managed rather well, considering it was the first (and, thankfully, the only) time that a member of my mission did 'the full Monty' in my presence. I had avoided the project manager being declared *persona non grata* but he left soon afterwards. It was a classic case of a brilliant scientist temperamentally unfitted to adapt to a developing country.

My next visit to Melka Warar in December 1966 saw another example of autocratic behaviour from a less unexpected source, the Emperor, or HIM (short for 'His Imperial Majesty') as he was generally known. He wanted to see the experimental station and wished me to be there – a command performance. For security reasons, his movements were kept secret. Late one night I was told to be at the airport at 6.00 a.m. There a small plane awaited with a newly-arrived Belgian pilot who cheerfully announced that he had no idea where Melka Warar was, and had been provided only with a road map. Could I show him the way? I ascertained that he at least knew where Awash Station was, after which we followed the river. The Awash meanders widely so it was after a circuitous flight that we spied the station where the Emperor's helicopter was already parked. Alas, a camel train had kicked sand over the white stones that marked the airstrip. Back we went to swoop low over the research station until a jeep was despatched to show us where to land.

After inspecting the experimental plots we were bundled into jeeps and took off into the surrounding bush. The Emperor was in the first, I in the second, wedged alongside the portly figure of Crown Prince Asfa Wossen. We wove along sandy tracks, between acacias, low scrub, and euphorbia cacti and whenever we came upon a group of nomads, their camels piled with chattels, the Emperor threw out handfuls of lucre. The nomads looked completely mystified. They had probably never seen birr notes before, since they traded by barter, and I do not believe they had the slightest idea that the small man in the front jeep was the Negus, King of Kings, Lion of Judah. It was a revealing illustration of the patriarchal and feudal concepts by which Haile Selassie still reigned, for all his modernising initiatives.

When we returned to the bungalow for lunch I badly needed to retire to a private place of which there was only one. Naturally, I gave HIM precedence but when I made tracks towards the same place, the Chief of Protocol courteously explained that this was not allowed, since the Emperor had just used that facility. The euphemism 'throne' took on a whole new meaning. I was the only woman; the men had wandered off into the bush and, backs turned, were contemplating the landscape. I nearly asked the protocol chap which was worse: to use the lavatory after the Emperor or have an accident in the imperial presence? Afterwards I hardly waited for HIM's helicopter to cover us all with dust, before dashing back to the bungalow. I did not detect any imperial aura gracing the austere confines of the toilet and felt relief rather than reverence.

The Emperor's favourite UN project was the umbrella factory, the brain-child of a British expert from the International Labour Office (ILO). He had decided to produce umbrellas, because Ethiopia has a long rainy season and ceremonial umbrellas play a central part in religious and cultural life. Once, going to Mulu, I glimpsed a cavalcade of horses and ponies, splendidly caparisoned, bearing grandly robed dignitaries under a panoply of colourful umbrellas processing across a distant plain. All the factory's employees were disabled, their tasks devised according to their disability. Handicapped people were considered shameful in Ethiopia and hidden away or reduced to begging. At the factory it was touching to see beggars pouring in to seek work and dignity.

The project was a commercial success, even exporting umbrellas to India, and became the only state enterprise in Ethiopia to make a profit. When I returned after the revolution the factory was still functioning, an outstanding example of a successful technical cooperation project.

The Awash Valley – Assayita

In 1966 Christina, my aunt came for Christmas. I whisked her away on a field trip to Assayita in the far reaches of the Awash Valley where an FAO expert was advising local farmers on cotton production. We spent the first night in Kombolcha but had hardly begun the descent from the highlands when our driver slumped over the wheel, muttering what Christina interpreted as 'tired'. 'Have some water,' she said helpfully, getting out the flask. What he had actually said was 'tyre'. Luckily the Mitchell Cott's cotton plantation at Tendaho had a repair shop and we left the tyre to be mended but made the lonely crossing of the Assayita desert without a spare wheel. There was barely a track, and we saw no living soul until we reached the dusty little town of Assayita where the Awash disappears into the sand.

This was Danakil country, home of fearsome warriors and wandering nomads, followers of Islam who had for centuries resisted the incursions of Ethiopians from the central highlands. I had an audience with the Sultan of Aussa, an appointee of the Emperor but a far from docile collaborator. We met by moonlight outside his modest abode, and I had only the impression of a dark face and massive frame cloaked in billowing white robes. We discussed the development of the area, now that irrigation was possible, politics, and the Sultan's relationship with court and government. I had been warned that it would be a heinous insult to refuse rancid camel's milk, a special honour and delicacy, and gulped it down, thankful that the dim light made it impossible for me to see it properly or the Sultan to see my expression. He presented me with a carved scimitar, a lethally sharp instrument used by the Danakil to cut off the genitalia of vanquished enemies. Seven years later it was too rusted to extract from its scabbard, but Chilean secret police confiscated it as 'a dangerous weapon' after the Pinochet coup.

The Sultan asked me to take one of his advisers to Addis Ababa, a burly black giant, white-robed and turbaned, hailing from the Sudan. We were glad to have him with us as we retraced our way across the desert, devoid of life save for a glimpse of a rare Simean ass.

We spent the night in the Mitchell Cott's plantation and collected our mended tyre. This was just as well, for next day we suffered yet another burst. The Sultan's henchman, so silent that Christina forgot he was there and threw her mackintosh over him, proved an unexpectedly dab hand at changing a wheel. Thereafter I instructed that all field vehicles should have *two* spare wheels.

The Sandfords gave a large Christmas party at Mulu. A strong taste of paraffin permeated the food and Christina was violently ill. After Christmas we travelled in Kenya and Uganda. I had been several times to Nairobi, where Tom Mboya, the brilliant Minister of Development, and Philip Ndegwa, his Permanent Secretary, who often visited Addis Ababa, had become close friends. A few years later Tom was assassinated, a tragic loss for Kenya.

We travelled to Kampala on an anachronistically English train and a sizzlingly hot night. Even hotter suet pudding sent the temperature in the dining-car several degrees higher. We had the privilege of knowing Uganda before Idi Amin ravaged it, of seeing the Murchison Falls unspoilt, travelling by boat up the river teeming with wild life, and sleeping in a bungalow where there were, not fairies, but hippos at the bottom of our garden. Kenya also seemed an untroubled country then. We savoured the delights of the reserve just outside Nairobi and of Amboseli, where an inquisitive zebra poked his head through the flap of our tent during the night and at dawn we saw lions contentedly snoozing on banks of wild thyme, and cheetah chasing their prey across wind-silvered grasslands.

My Mother's Illness

In February 1967, while accompanying Robert Gardiner to an ECA ministerial meeting in Lagos, Nigeria, I received a telegram to say that my mother was seriously ill. I managed to telephone her doctor and he advised that I should come immediately. A British Airways Britannia was leaving for London on Friday allowing me to spend two days in England, and return in time for our return charter flight to Ethiopia. In Kano in northern Nigeria the engines were revving up for the last lap to London when I saw a luggage train weaving wildly about and the driver leap to safety. There was a sickening thud, fire engines rushed out and we had to disembark. The luggage train had crashed into the plane's underbelly. I was appalled to learn that no London plane would call at Kano until Monday, for I knew a direct Nigerian Airways flight would be leaving Lagos that night. Why could it not pick us up? For hours I argued vainly with the airline representatives before calling Robert Gardiner to get the government to intervene. But while I had easily called a Somerset village, it was almost impossible to telephone within Nigeria – a heritage from colonial times. By dint of perseverance I got through, and the plane was diverted to Kano.

My mother was a shadow of the person I had left four months before. She had been ill since October but had forbidden my father to tell me. There was no clear diagnosis. The doctor suggested a nervous breakdown, because she was worried about me, an unlikely supposition, given her resilient temperament and that in Ethiopia I was in far less danger than in Bolivia. The doctor thought, and I desperately hoped, that she would recover from this mysterious decline, if I were nearer home. Over the next few months I sought to bring this about.

The Awash Valley – Crisis

Meanwhile our largest project, the Awash Valley, was in crisis. The Managing Director of the Awash Valley Authority, Ato Seyoum, was a pleasant but ineffectual political appointee. Only the Emperor could change him but how could this be brought about? I hit on the idea of presenting to HIM a report on the project, bound in red leather and gilt, using the occasion to convey our worries in veiled language (the direct approach did not work in Ethiopia and the Emperor was adept at grasping subtleties).

On the appointed day, the FAO representative, the project manager and I presented ourselves at the palace, in full fig. I had rehearsed a delicately nuanced speech in French. On the way I asked for the report, the peg on which my speech was hung. My heart sank with premonition on learning that Ato Seyoum would bring it. I told the Minister of Court that we could not go in until he arrived. The minutes ticked by. The Minister of Agriculture arrived, but Ato Seyoum did not. The excited yapping of the chihuahua heralded the Emperor's entry into the throne room and both ministers insisted that His Imperial Majesty could not be kept waiting.

Inside we sat in two half-circles before the throne, we three to his right, and Ethiopian dignitaries to his left. HIM looked expectantly at me. I felt desperate. My carefully planned scenario was unravelling. The only solution was to filibuster but French is an unforgivably logical language that does not suffer procrastination gladly. I abandoned my rehearsed script and plunged into a long dissertation, dredging up every abstruse detail I could recall about the Awash Valley, with one eye alert and one ear cocked for the door behind me to admit the miscreant. The Emperor's eyes became glazed and my tedious discourse ran out of steam. The dread moment loomed when I would have to end lamely, 'And so, *Votre Majesté Impériale*, I have come here today to present a report that I don't happen to have with me ...'

Then I noticed a barely discernible undulating motion that resolved itself into the figure of Ato Seyoum, advancing flat on his stomach to the far end of the circle. Glimpsing a flash of red and gold in his hands, I hastily brought my peroration to a climax and, jumping to my feet, swooped backwards until I reached Ato Seyoum, scooped the report from his trembling hands and then advanced again to present it, with a triumphant curtsey, to the Emperor. Although I say it myself, it was a tour de force (or, more properly, farce, if the pun may be excused) but we had signally failed to get our message across.

By coincidence Princess Aida was dining with me that evening. 'His Majesty,' she said (she never called him 'my grandfather'), 'was perplexed by this morning's audience.' I refrained from commenting that he had every reason and, without revealing our underlying purpose, explained my embarrassment at not having the report to hand. Next morning I was transfixed to see a curt announcement in the newspaper that Ato Seyoum was no longer head of AVA ... because he had arrived late at an imperial audience! We had achieved our objective for completely extraneous reasons, but the shortest distance between two points in Ethiopia was never a straight line.

In June 1967 Paul Hoffman asked me to describe the work of a resident representative to the UNDP Governing Council in Geneva. The summons seemed heaven-sent, coming just after a message from my *grande passion* expressing the vain hope that we might meet in Geneva around the same dates. My joy was short-lived: my reply crossed with a letter from him saying it would be best if we never met again ... I arrived in Geneva in no state to give a coherent public speech. It was Jacko who picked up the pieces over dinner, followed by brandy in the austere surroundings of the Cornavin station, and I gave a reasonable performance, despite what felt uncommonly like a breaking heart.

During the council I agreed with senior UNDP and FAO officials that we needed a policy review meeting about the AVA with the Government, and must find a project manager with broader experience. Then a bombshell dropped. In Geneva I received a copy of a personal and confidential letter from FAO (the original had gone to Addis Ababa), requesting my opinion on a proposed candidate, a Trinidadian, working in ECA, a competent agronomist, but with no experience of multipurpose projects. The senior FAO man attending the council instructed Rome to drop the name, and I thought the matter closed. I went on to England, where Georgy telephoned me. He mentioned the FAO letter and I expressed surprise that he should have opened an envelope marked for my personal and confidential attention. 'Never mind,' I went on. 'It's water under the bridge, because we've agreed that this man isn't qualified.'

There was a long silence. Then Georgy said, 'But I offered him the job, and he accepted.'

In vain, for the damage was done, I pointed out that it was not for our office, but FAO Headquarters, to offer the job, that the letter hadn't asked me to approach him but simply give an opinion ...

When, in agreement with FAO, the news was broken to the man that his name could not go forward and why, he wrote to the FAO Director-General, all local ambassadors, the President of Trinidad, and sundry other world statesmen, including the British Prime

Minister, with accusations of racism. The Trinidadian community split down the middle when the Trinidadian Ambassador counselled moderation and there were even calls for the ambassador's dismissal. The subject became the talk of Addis Ababa's endless cocktail parties and at one almost led to fisticuffs.

Had Georgy acted with malice aforethought he could not have created more havoc. Being nice and not very bright can be just as dangerous as the other way round. Notwithstanding the unpleasantness, FAO and UNDP refused to bow to pressure to appoint someone inadequately qualified and the furore abated.

UNDP agreed to give me a year's leave without pay, but I needed a job to support my parents and myself. A post materialised in the Ministry of Overseas Development but then something unforeseen happened. In May Dudley Seers, Director of the Institute of Development Studies at Sussex University, whom I had known in Latin America, came to Ethiopia with Thomas Balogh. I had met Thomas at a meeting in the Houses of Parliament in 1964, where I had spoken on Bolivia, followed by a party in Hampstead given by Helen Grant, my Cambridge supervisor. From there he, David Owen and I had been erratically driven by Sir Andrew Cohen, then Permanent Secretary in the Ministry of Overseas Development to a party in his own house. Andrew's wife arrived with Larry Adler, there were showbiz people, economists, international officials all milling around together and David Owen emerged confused from an encounter (luckily only verbal) with a heavyweight boxer he met on the stairs. Andrew gave up playing host, and a small group of us ended up on the terrace, eating strawberries and drinking vin rosé, on a balmy summer evening.

Shortly afterwards Harold Wilson, the Labour Prime Minister, appointed Thomas to head his 'think-tank' – the first of its kind. Given our short acquaintance I was amazed when, during lunch at my house, Thomas invited me to become his deputy. After the Governing Council I flew to London to be interviewed by Harold Wilson and, more dauntingly, by his powerful private secretary Marcia (later Baroness) Falkender. To my surprise, and some alarm, I was asked to start on 1 November 1967.

Farewell to Ethiopia

My last months passed in a haze. There was a flurry of diplomatic activity when Hernán Santa Cruz of Chile and Ad Boerma of FAO arrived in July, both candidates for the post of Director-General of FAO, vying for Ethiopia's support. Knowing both well, I found myself in an awkward position. I gave a lunch for Boerma, and it was he who won Ethiopian support and the election. With the Vice-Minister of Mines, Ato Teshome Gebre Mariam, I travelled to Kebre Mengist, 300 miles south in Sidamo Province, and launched a gold-mining project, part of the economic diversification programme to reduce the country's reliance on coffee exports. The policy review meeting on the Awash Valley project took place in early October and Jacko, who attended as UNDP's trouble-shooter on multipurpose river development projects, helped me with my packing.

I had at last made Ethiopian friends and did not want to leave. They invited me to their homes to partake of *injera* and *wat*, the traditional Ethiopian fare, eaten out of a communal basket where *injera* – a pancake made of *tef*, a grain resembling millet – serves as table cloth and cutlery. I was even forgiven for using my left hand (left-handedness was frowned upon) to peal off strips of *injera* and wrap them round the spicy stew. There had been weekend camping trips to Lake Langino, in the Rift Valley; to Lake Abbaye, stained pink with the reflection of thousands of flamingos; and once to Lake Margarita where our camp was invaded by vicious mosquitos and marauding hippos lumbering on shore for a midnight snack. I had travelled the length and breadth of the country, even beyond Harar and Dire Dawa to Jijiga, the furthermost outpost of the Ethiopian Army, marooned in the searing desert of Ogaden, in the frontier area disputed with Somalia. I had made progress with Amharic and learned enough about the country's history and culture to whet my appetite for more.

The Emperor bestowed on me a beautiful gold bracelet, interwoven with lion and giraffe hair, bearing his symbol of the Lion of Judah. There were farewell visits and goodbye parties. On 24 October, I hosted the UN Day reception and next morning left for Europe.

Princess Aida saw me off with Teshome, who had commissioned a street artist to paint the saga of my time in Ethiopia, along the lines of the Solomon and Sheba paintings. I was a large, goggle-eyed blonde, wielding a film camera (which I never did), towering over diminutive, equally goggle-eyed Ethiopians, gazing up at me with exaggerated respect (my larger size indicated my supposed importance). The last vignette was of Kebre Mengist, where my protruding gaze was fixed avariciously on a pile of gold, as if I was about to nick it. There were tears in my eyes as I boarded the plane.

Return to Ethiopia

Later there was greater cause for grief. On 11 September 1974, one year to the day after the horrendous coup I lived through in Santiago, Ethiopia also fell prey to bloody revolution. Young government officials had long spoken to me of the need for change and for a while a gradual evolution seemed possible. Endelkatchew Makonnen, who (then an undergraduate at Oxford) had partnered Princess Aida to the Newnham Ball in 1947, and for whom I had given a farewell dinner when he became Ethiopia's Permanent Representative to the United Nations, was appointed Prime Minister. But soon a darker revolutionary tide surged up, mainly from the non-commissioned ranks in the armed forces, sweeping Endelkatchew into prison and premature death. The Emperor, also imprisoned, died on 27 August 1975, almost certainly murdered. In May 1966, I had witnessed adoring crowds celebrating the twenty-fifth anniversary of HIM's triumphal return in 1941. There had been a huge parade of an apparently loyal army, and grizzled old warriors, clad in traditional *shammas*, brandishing pikes and staves. Even the lion dozing on top of an armoured car had bestirred himself and stood to attention, seeming to acknowledge allegiance to the slight, uniformed figure on the saluting dais. Now the Lion of Judah had fallen for ever.

Aida's husband, Mengesha Seyoum, and their sons escaped from Mekele into Sudan. Aida went to Addis Ababa to be with her only daughter and was imprisoned by the new Government, the dreaded Derg, with her mother and sisters. They slept on the floor of one room, with one rudimentary toilet, and were forbidden any contact with the outside world – not even radio or newspapers. Despite strenuous efforts by the UK Government, Newnham College and others, the royal women remained imprisoned for 14 years. When I visited the country on official missions my pleas to see Aida were ignored.

Ministers and high officials with whom I had worked were thrown into the cellars under the imperial palace where the Emperor had kept his champagne. One black dawn 64 of them were summarily executed. I knew almost everyone on the list. Among them was Prince Iskander, Aida's only brother, ministers and many young technocrats, bright hopes for the country's future development. Teshome was luckier, but he endured eight years in those dungeons not knowing whether he too would be taken out to die.

Brigadier Sandford died in 1972 and was spared the tragedy of seeing Mulu Farm seized for a second time, this time by the revolutionary Government. Christine's letters to me showed remarkable tolerance, despite the destruction of their life work. Her main concern was for 'the little man', whom she described as bewildered by what had happened.

Many blamed the Emperor. His court and style of government were an anachronism in the 1960s. I believe his main crime was to live too long and fail to ensure a smooth transition to the Crown Prince, who might have become a constitutional monarch. That should not detract from Haile Selassie's achievements. He came to the throne in a country on the point of anarchy, gave it unity and stability, and catapulted a society, still steeped in the Middle Ages, into the twentieth century, opening it up to modern education. The cruellest irony was that it was the young men whom the Emperor had sent abroad, and who had experienced democracy elsewhere, who first began to kick against the trammels of despotism. Then they, in turn, were ruthlessly overthrown by tidal forces of change surging up from the undertow of society.

I did not return to Ethiopia until May 1981, through a strange mix-up the only passenger on a British Airways flight. The captain had never been to Addis Ababa, air-traffic control was deaf to our dawn approach, and I had to help the pilot find the airstrip. It was the only light moment. All my surviving Ethiopian friends were still in prison. I visited my old house, and found that my servants were dead, except my day *zabanha*, who now headed the local *kebede* (local commune). Outside, despite seven years of a government that had seized power in the name of social justice, stood the same decaying hovels, festering in open sewage. My same dear neighbours poured out, embracing me and praising Heaven that I was still alive. I reciprocated the sentiments, but grieved that they had not achieved the better lot they deserved. My 1984 visit was happier. Teshome had been released, and I took him to a geothermal project we had started together in the Rift Valley. I was amazed to find him unchanged – full of humour, and without recrimination.

Best of all was to return in June 1989 and find Aida enjoying relative freedom. I had not seen her for 20 years, of which she had spent 14 cruelly imprisoned. We had tea in the modest villa where the royal ladies were living, and I was astonished by the dispassionate way in which they talked of the lost years. Reunion with their children was still a dream, since Mengistu would not let them go abroad.

In 1991 the monstrous Mengistu regime was overthrown and Aida rejoined her family abroad. When the victors at last swept into Addis Ababa, President Meles Zenawi showed political maturity surprising in a young man who had known only guerrilla fighting. I met him in 1993, when I was leading negotiations between the Angolan Government and UNITA in Addis Ababa and was impressed. But the subsequent upsurge of fighting with Eritrea aroused new fears.

PART FOUR

Interlude in Europe

12

10 Downing Street 1967 – 68

W hen I started work at No. Ten on 1 November 1967, I was catapulted from the problems of a poor developing country to those of a developed country in deep economic trouble; from handling practical, operational programmes to attending endless Whitehall meetings and writing innumerable memoranda on economic and financial matters. Now it is accepted practice for the Prime Minister to have a 'think-tank' with a considerable staff. Ours was the first, and very tiny, set up by a Labour Government chronically suspicious of the 'Whitehall mandarins', regarded as traditionally anti-Labour members of the old 'Establishment'. The aim was to ensure that the Prime Minister had access to independent advice before taking major economic decisions. This innovation was not welcomed by the higher echelons of the Civil Service, later dramatised in the TV series *Yes, Minister* in the person of Sir Humphrey. Tommy Balogh's irrepressible personality, abrasiveness and refusal to accept fools (i.e. those not in agreement with himself) gladly, did not smooth distinctly troubled waters.

The inevitable conflicts of wills was a contest between David and Goliath. The think-tank consisted only of Tommy, his deputy (myself) and a brilliant young macroeconomist, Andrew Graham, with another Oxford economist, Theo Cooper, working part-time. My predecessor, Michael Stewart, had left to work in Kenya. An article in *The Times* of 3 July 1967 gives some idea of the precarious standing of our unit:

Whitehall observers, who have come to recognize Mr Stewart's ... skill at piloting both his own and Dr Balogh's more erratic ideas through the rat-infested water of inter-departmental committees, are wondering if this is the end of Mr Wilson's private economic brains trust. Despite occasional victories, for example over aid to Zambia and India, and pioneer work on the North Atlantic Free Trade Area idea, it is pretty clear that the Balogh shock troops lost the major battles on economic policy: the Plan, the Common Market and others too secret to mention, though too easy to guess.

This mantle that had now fallen on me, and it was made clear to me, by everyone from Harold Wilson down, that my major responsibility would be to improve Tommy's image, and that of the unit in Whitehall's 'rat-infested waters'.

On my first day Tommy announced, 'I want you to represent me this morning at the Committee for the Security of Oil Supplies' (known as 'SOS' for short). He added kindly, 'I will introduce you.' This was all the brief I had on a subject about which I knew little. We arrived at the Ministry of Fuel and Power a few minutes late. Tommy did not know where our meeting was and he charged into one room after another, with me in embarrassed tow, his tonsure of long white hair flying in the breeze, loudly declaiming, 'SOS? SOS?'. Heads turned and mouths dropped at the sight of this extraordinary apparition as bewildered committee members struggled to comprehend whether this really was an SOS, and the building was on fire, or simply the visitation of a madman.

That baptism of fire was repeated many times. Tommy would instruct me to uphold a particular line at a Cabinet committee, usually running counter to mainstream Civil Service thought. I would feel I was making some headway by leavening the intellectual argument with some diplomatic ploys and a modicum of charm, when in would burst Tommy, looking as if he had been catapulted from outer space, all guns blazing, and the fragile house of cards I had built up would collapse.

Tommy's thinking was usually light miles ahead of everyone else's. His extraordinarily brilliant mind would reach a conclusion while the rest of us were still struggling with the premises. The drawback of this almost instinctive process was that, while he was often blindingly right, he could sometimes be blindingly wrong.

His friendship with the Prime Minister was of long standing and Harold Wilson consulted him frequently, especially during those first weeks of November 1967. Sterling, then still a reserve currency, had come under such heavy pressure that the crisis culminated in the devaluation of the pound on 17 November 1967 (the occasion of Wilson's famous 'pound in your pocket' speech). Tommy had urged the Prime Minister to take this difficult step when Labour came into power, but his advice had not been heeded. My friends had a field day, joking that less than three weeks after I had joined this inner economic team, sterling had come a cropper.

Dreaded scourge of bureaucrats as he was, Tommy proved a most congenial boss. He expected us to perform almost impossible feats with the scantiest of weapons, but he never blamed us if we failed to bring them off.

Our success depended on having access to all secret papers, as well as to the Prime Minister. This was anathema to Sir Burke (later Lord) Trend, Secretary to the Cabinet and Head of the Cabinet Office. Proximity to the Prime Minister was ensured by our being on the No. Ten side of the green baize door with the Cabinet Office, and by our submitting advice directly and not through Sir Burke. Access to top secret papers was easier to withhold, though it was usually achieved, after some acrimonious exchanges. Jacko knew Trend well, and invited me to lunch with him and Sir Denis (later Lord) Greenhill, the Permanent Secretary at the Foreign Office, before I assumed my functions. But Trend, though affable, never forgave me for being on the other side of that green baize door, an arrangement not of my making.

Since we dealt with the highest affairs of State, top security clearance was required. I had provided four British referees. David Owen and Jacko vouched for my activities abroad and both were interviewed before I set foot in No. Ten. My own security vetting was set for 30 October, but was postponed for several weeks. Goodness knows what secrets I might have revealed in the interim, but as the interview turned out it was unlikely to add to HMG's knowledge about me.

The man from MI5 was small, nondescript and charmless. We were in Tommy's office on the third floor, overlooking Downing

Street and the Foreign Office (later we moved to the ground floor, nearer the Prime Minister's Office).

After some unexceptionable opening gambits my inquisitor interrogated me about the reputedly left-wing associations of my 'brother'. I was open-mouthed with astonishment until I recovered sufficiently to reply that I did not have a brother. This in no way placated my interlocutor, who was obviously convinced that I was lying. He pressed me so strongly that I began to wonder whether my parents had been keeping some dark secret. It was only when he released further details that I realised that he was talking about my ex-brother-*in-law*. It was the turn for his jaw to drop when I pointed this out, adding, as tartly as I dared, that the man in question was a member of the Labour Party, which, if I was not mistaken, was the elected Government and therefore presumably not a security risk?

Unabashed, my tormentor fired off a host of intimate questions. The climax came with the following exchange:

Security chap: 'Have you any children?'

Me: 'No.'

Security chap (keen not to miss a trick): 'Have you *ever* had any children?'

Me: 'No.'

Security chap: 'Are you *sure*?'

Me (torn between intense irritation and an irrepressible desire to laugh): 'Well, I think I would have noticed, don't you?'

The most charitable conclusion was that the man had never vetted a woman before. I was reminded of the USAID assertions in Bolivia about 'my son at public school'! It seemed that everyone wanted to wish a secret child on me.

The most glaring omission in the Downing Street interrogation was the lack of any reference to my acquaintance with the two spies Donald Maclean and Guy Burgess. My interlocutor was clearly unaware that I had been the last person to see Donald on the night he defected, that my movements in Spain had been followed by the security service, or that the Americans had questioned my UN appointment in Colombia. I kindly passed the information on to him, remarking that I would not like it to come up later and give the impression that I had not been frank.

The man must have departed in great confusion for Tommy came to see me in some agitation. 'He's left all his notes on you on my desk!'

I laughed and said, 'Well, shouldn't you send them to wherever?'

But Tommy, despite his outward self-assurance, retained the sensitivities of a middle-European Jew. 'I think it's a trap,' he muttered darkly. A little later he reappeared, looking more cheerful. 'I've found a solution,' he said gleefully, 'I've pushed them under my blotter.' No one ever asked for them.

We worked long hours, on a wide spectrum of economic subjects. Every day brought new challenges. The Labour Government was beleaguered by the financial markets, which lacked confidence in its ability to maintain a stable economic policy because of trade union demands. The situation was not long eased by the November 1967 devaluation: sterling was still a reserve currency and this, combined with the responsibility for sterling balances of countries in the sterling area, rendered UK finances vulnerable to the slightest external shock.

Our work being secret I have no papers of that era, and my engagement diary simply records the innumerable committees I attended by acronyms I can no longer decipher. Economic forecasting as a tool of economic policy was the subject of many meetings with the Treasury, and notes to the Prime Minister. Not being an econometrician I was never quite convinced of the usefulness of the process. Discussions and papers on prices and incomes policies and employment issues also occupied a great part of our time. An innovation of that era was the National Economy Development Council (NEDC – more familiarly known as 'Neddy'), a tripartite body that met monthly under the Prime Minister's chairmanship. It brought together the Government, the Confederation of British Industries (CBI), and the Trades Union Council (TUC). At that stage Neddy made an important contribution towards reconciling the opinions of government employees and workers and formulating a coherent economic policy.

We also served as the Prime Minister's eyes and ears in the inner sanctums of Whitehall. Some senior civil servants looked on us as spies, but it was surely not unreasonable for the Prime Minister to have access to an independent view, presented in a more digestible form than Cabinet documents. That view would seem to be vindicated by the subsequent flourishing of the think-tank, on a much grander scale, in succeeding governments. Ours was a pioneer unit, bound to encounter vigorous opposition.

Oiling the cumbersome machinery of government was another priority, and it was on our advice that a senior executive of Marks and Spencer's was brought into Whitehall to adapt successful procedures in the marketplace to lessen bureaucratic trammels in the public sector. A parallel initiative was the temporary exchange of senior civil servants and business executives, so that each could get a better idea of the other's world. Those were the first beginnings of a new approach to government that continues to the present day.

Perhaps the unit's most important contribution was to the negotiations over North Sea gas, the great potential of which had just been discovered. Numerous private oil companies, including some from the United States, swarmed in to take advantage of this major bonanza. Tommy was convinced that the Labour Government was being taken for a ride. Our arguments for a tougher stance boiled down to the slogan, 'A penny off North Sea gas', a reference to the clauses in the contracts stipulating the prices that could be charged by companies winning concessions. The Government, economically weak, was easily swayed by arguments from Whitehall mandarins that the deal was in grave danger of falling through if they attempted to strike a harder bargain. Tommy stuck obdurately to his guns and we, his acolytes, were sent hither and yon to carry the gospel. We won through, but our ranking in the popularity stakes sank even further. Subsequent events proved that this was a case in which Tommy was blindingly right. The Treasury and the taxpayers were saved a great deal of money. Recognition came late, but I was glad to see that a few years later, Tommy, by then a controversial Minister of Energy, was accorded credit for this remarkable achievement in the face of formidable Whitehall opposition.

We were not alone in our struggles. Each of the key ministries had its posse of economic advisers. Professor (later Lord) Nicky Kaldor, another former Hungarian exile, was at the Treasury, engaged in usually friendly rivalry with Tommy. They were known by their numerous detractors as 'Buddha' and 'Pest'. Once a week we all got together for a working lunch and to exchange experiences. It was a very stimulating environment.

Within No. Ten the atmosphere was cordial. I had had qualms about working for Harold Wilson on account of his earlier manoeuvrings in the Labour Party, during Hugh Gaitskell's time, from which I had deduced that he trimmed his sails to suit the prevailing wind. My impression from working with him was different. He was a considerate and courteous boss – when we went to Neddy meetings he always insisted that I sit beside him in the car – and by no means projected the image of the domineering personality I had envisaged. Perhaps that was his undoing.

Marcia Falkender, the *éminence grise* in his office, was publicly portrayed as an ogress but I had good relations with her, as I did with Michael Halls, the Prime Minister's Private Secretary, and Michael Palliser, who dealt with foreign affairs, was an old friend from the Foreign Office.

Personal Crossroads

Although intellectually invigorating, this was not a happy period. I went home every night loaded with papers and there was no opportunity to develop a normal social life in London. Encounters with UN visitors passing through were more a manifestation of a previous life, with the exception of Jacko, who came frequently to see his son Robin. We developed the habit of dining together and going to films and plays.

Jacko's marriage to the well-known economist Barbara Ward, was to all intents and purposes long over. In the spring of 1968, however, both of them were in London for Robin's school holidays and gave a dinner party to which I was invited, together with David Owen, who also happened to be in London. I had long admired Barbara Ward since I had listened to her, as a schoolgirl, when she was a member of *The Brains Trust* on BBC radio. During dinner in the Hyde Park Hotel Barbara talked brilliantly and incessantly, waving her hands about a great deal. The rest of the company was mesmerised into almost complete silence. Even the usually loquacious Jacko could hardly get a word in edgeways. It was a star performance, but one that did not allow any other actors on the stage. I also had my first encounter with Robin, who received us graciously, sitting up in bed in his pyjamas. He was 12 years old.

Other friends who came to visit me in London were Prince Sadruddin Aga Khan, then UN High Commissioner for Refugees and Raúl Prebisch who was then heading the UN Conference on Trade and Development (UNCTAD). Knowing Raúl's gourmet tastes, I assumed that he would like to eat in a first-class restaurant, rather than in the trendy restaurant opposite my flat where one could also dance. Raúl took umbrage, indignant that I assumed that he was past dancing the night away. We had a rollicking evening and spent another in the way I had planned, dining at Rules.

My most unusual visitor was Georgy Kozhevnikov, my deputy in Addis Ababa, on his way back to Moscow. He and his wife, Valentina, were very chuffed to pick me up at 10 Downing Street for lunch at the Oxford and Cambridge Club, another new experience. They insisted on lunching early, to be in time for the afternoon showing of the film *Dr Zhivago*. 'We must see it,' confided Georgy, 'as we won't be able to in Moscow.' Coming from such an arch-conformist this was startling, as were their enthusiastic ravings over Buckingham Palace, Windsor Castle, the changing of the guard and all the trappings of monarchy. They sounded like royalty-struck American tourists.

Through Tommy's hospitality, and in No. Ten, I rubbed shoulders with many of the stars of the Labour Party – Barbara Castle (whom I came greatly to admire and thought had a raw deal – she should have been our first woman Prime Minister), Richard Crossman, Anthony Crosland, Tony Wedgwood Benn, Roy Jenkins and the irascible and unpredictable George Brown. It was a privileged experience. Nevertheless, I missed my operational work in developing countries and found it limiting to work in a purely national context.

Over it all hung the pall of my mother's illness. Every Friday night I took a late train to Bath, motored to Pippins, and returned to London late on Sunday. During the weekends I tried to alleviate my father's intolerable load, and had more papers to read. My mother's mind was as keen as ever, but her physical capacities were failing visibly, and the diagnosis of a nervous breakdown was becoming ever more unconvincing. Through Jacko I was able to have her seen by Sir Ronald Bodley Scott (then the Queen's Physician, and an old friend of Jacko's from wartime Cairo). Despite many tests, the diagnosis was still unclear. She was put on high doses of cortisone, which relieved some symptoms but caused dreadful side effects.

The summer of 1968 brought some pleasures – among them a grandstand view of the Trooping of the Colour on the Queen's official birthday, and a garden party at Buckingham Palace – but a plethora of problems, too. Tommy was awarded a life peerage in the Queen's Birthday Honours and relinquished his post. I was left in charge of the think-tank, but with Tommy's departure the feud with Burke Trend resurfaced. He insisted that I should channel advice to the Prime Minister through him. I consulted Harold Wilson who insisted that I should report directly to him. I was caught in a vice between the two.

My career was at a crossroads. Now, if ever, was my opportunity to re-enter the UK, either in the political sphere or in the Civil Service. Politics appealed to me more: there had been that earlier turning point in 1955 when I had had to choose between the Labour Party and the United Nations. Now, in 1968, I was well placed to seek selection as a Labour candidate with the Prime Minister's personal support. At the same time UNDP was gratifyingly anxious for me to accept another resident representative posting. Paul Marc Henry, one of Paul Hoffman's two deputies, came through London and urged me to go to Morocco, which was nearer Europe and my parents than any of my previous postings.

In the spring of 1968 Jacko confided to me that the UNDP Administrator had asked him to undertake a major study on the overhaul of the UN Development System. I was thrilled at the news. From the field I had been one of the system's most vociferous critics, and had once sarcastically remarked, 'Any relationship between the programme and the priority needs of a developing country is purely coincidental.' That was an exaggeration, but I despaired at the constant competition between agencies, and the pressures their visiting firemen put on recipient governments. I had written various papers proposing a more integrated approach, putting the country's interests first. I knew that Jacko shared my views. With his operational experience, unmatched by any of the top men in UNDP, he was just the man for the job.

I was surprised to find Jacko reluctant to accept Hoffman's proposal. Only later did I come to appreciate his concerns about the political infighting and personal rivalries at the highest level of governments and of the United Nations that would bedevil any attempt at a logical solution and make the position of its architect invidious. My 15 years in the field had largely shielded me from such machinations.

A few weeks later Jacko told me that he was prepared to do the study, but only if I accepted to be his 'Chief of Staff'. This put me in a dilemma. It was a unique opportunity to try to bring about long overdue reforms, but I did not want to lose the opportunity of returning to field work, my first love. From a personal viewpoint Geneva had the advantages of being even more accessible to London, in a family emergency, than Rabat. There was a more delicate problem: while I felt great affection for Jacko he harboured warmer sentiments towards me, according to him ever since he first met me in 1962. My heart was elsewhere. I felt that this could place an intolerable strain on our relationship if we worked closely together. When I mentioned this, Jacko wrote me a letter reassuring me that he accepted the situation and still hoped I would agree to go to Geneva.

During that summer, I came to realise that my experiences in Whitehall had laid to rest the desire I had half-cherished since 1955 of returning to the UK to enter politics or government service. The decision thus narrowed down to a choice between Morocco and Geneva. When UNDP agreed to hold the Morocco position until the Capacity Study was finished, I accepted the Geneva appointment. The UK Government released me to accompany Jacko to the June session of the UNDP Governing Council in Vienna, which authorised the study, and later to attend preparatory meetings in Geneva in July and September.

The Mandarins' Victory

Any regrets I felt at relinquishing a plum job as head of the Prime Minister's think-tank were dissipated by the events of that summer. Sterling came under intense pressure again and the problem of the sterling balances once more raised its ugly head. An atmosphere of crisis pervaded Whitehall. The Prime Minister daily requested the advice of our unit. Then the mandarins played their trump card. They refused to release vital papers on the grounds that they were 'Top Secret'. Denied that access, there was no way in which we could provide sound counsel.

Another element, almost banal in its stupidity, emerged. In order to meet Tommy's urgent demands for my services in 1967, UNDP had agreed to pay me for the six weeks' leave due to me. Now, with its usual exquisite sense of timing and inflexibility, the UNDP administration had second thoughts. They confronted me with an ultimatum: if I did not take the leave before going to Geneva I must reimburse US$2000. My year in the UK was already costing me dear; my UK salary was lower, I had to make up the totality of my UN pension contributions on the whole of the international salary I was foregoing, and because of UNDP's intransigence in refusing a perfectly reasonable arrangement proposed by the UK Treasury, I was even having to pay income tax on those additional contributions. An additional US$2000 would be crippling. Since New York insisted that I must report in Geneva on 1 November, the only way of avoiding yet another financial penalty was to leave No. Ten six weeks early.

But paramount in my mind was the need to put the think-tank on a proper footing. On 5 August 1968 I wrote a personal letter to Harold Wilson, of which these are key extracts:

> May I stress that in reaching a decision, the material considerations are not the over-riding ones? I had long wanted to serve in my own country and it has been a special honour and pleasure to work for you. I would be happy to stay on to the end of my term if I felt I could perform a real service ...
>
> But it is here that my principal doubts arise. The other day you made some kind remarks about the briefing you are

receiving from this office and I am grateful for this expression of confidence. However, I must in all frankness say that I do not think we are providing the level of briefing we could, and *should*, be doing because (despite the excellent collaboration of your own Private Office and DEA) I have found it impossible to obtain access to certain high-level meetings and highly classified documents on economic policy.

I should be most grateful for your advice as to what you would wish me to do. In asking this, may I reiterate that I would have no hesitation in accepting the personal disadvantages of continuing until October 31, provided facilities were assured for giving adequate service.

While awaiting a reply I took a week's leave – my first for two years – to visit Bolivian friends in Malaga. It was interrupted by the Czechoslovak crisis, when Soviet tanks destroyed the brief Prague spring, war again seemed possible in Europe, with implications for the financial markets, and I had to hurry back to London.

A month after its despatch there was still no decision on the matters raised in my letter. On 3 September I wrote to Michael Halls, the Prime Minister's Principal Private Secretary, pointing out that, if I was to accede to UNDP's demand, my last working day would be 17 September. I do not know what went on behind closed doors but the delay indicated that, when the chips were down, the Prime Minister was reluctant to take on the mandarins that the think-tank had been set up to circumvent. Perhaps my initial appraisal of him had been at least partly right. On 8 September I received a reply that completely skirted the main issues I had raised: the Prime Minister was very sorry to see me go, but understood the reasons.

At our farewell meeting Harold Wilson graciously thanked me for my services, and he and his wife came to my farewell party. Later he sent me an affectionately inscribed photograph bearing the message, 'With very warm thanks and every good wish for your future work in the fight for world development'.

The episode demonstrated the weakness of elected government ministers, including the Prime Minister, in the face of the collective might of the 'Sir Humphreys'. In my view, Harold Wilson could – and should – have made a stand. His failure to do so spelt the death knell for that first think-tank. Andrew Graham gallantly carried on until elected to a fellowship at Balliol College in early 1969. In my letter of congratulation, I could not help adding: 'The only thing which makes me a little sad about your appointment is that I assume that this will mean the demise of our unit, swallowed up at last by the mandarins'.

One of my last submissions, on 11 September, urged a stronger UK policy towards international organisations. I argued that this was an area where the UK could still wield beneficial influence on world affairs, despite loss of empire and continuing economic difficulties. While other countries scrambled to obtain top posts for their nationals (often not well qualified), the UK stood back. This admirable detachment, in the true sense in which the international civil service had been created, had led to a situation in which the only top post held by a UK national was the secretary-generalship of the World Meteorological Organisation. I urged that the UK should take a more active role in high-level appointments, not necessarily proposing British nationals, but pushing for the most qualified person, including candidates already within the system, in preference to the prevailing procedure, where the choice usually favoured outside political appointees.

I cited the current leadership crisis in UNDP, where Paul Hoffman had been appointed Administrator, with Owen relegated to a secondary position, although they had previously held equal status. It had been assumed that Owen would take over when Hoffman, then nearly 80, retired but the US Government continued to insist that the post should be occupied by an American, although their nationals also headed the World Bank, the IMF, ILO and UNICEF. HMG – then the second largest contributor to UNDP – had accepted this reasoning and not supported Owen. Consequently UNDP was limping from year to year under the shadow of a leadership crisis. I emphasised that I was in no way criticising Mr Hoffman, who had done a splendid job in launching the Special Fund. Nor was I suggesting that HMG should, tardily, support David Owen. What I did argue was that HMG ought to press for new and dynamic leadership for UNDP. Among existing officials I said that Paul Marc Henry – a Frenchman – was probably the best.

With unwitting prescience I added, 'I am conscious that the far-reaching reorganisation study on which I am soon to start work will be useless unless this crisis at the top is resolved'. Another sentence read, 'From a totally internationalist position one could argue that to insist that a US national should be Administrator of UNDP in perpetuity would amount to a kiss of death for the concept of multilateral aid.'

In the event, Paul Hoffman stayed on several more years as Administrator, retiring aged well over 80. He was succeeded by a US banker with no experience in development or of UNDP. For 30 years more, the post was occupied by a US national, although the US had long ago ceased to be the major contributor.

For the next six weeks I divided my time between Pippins and my Chelsea flat, where I finished my book on Bolivia. Thanks to the help of Mary Gibson, who worked there before her marriage, Longmans agreed to publish it, a rare moment of delight in a difficult year. It came out in 1970 under the title *Gate of the Sun, a Prospect of Bolivia* and an American edition was published a year later.

My parents came to stay so that more extensive tests could be done on my mother. Bodley Scott finally diagnosed systemic lupus erythematosis, a disease that normally afflicted young women. In the relief of at last knowing what was wrong, I did not realise what a cruel disease it was, or how black the prognosis.

Late on 29 October I drove Jacko to Dover in my VW. Next day we took the first car ferry and drove across France on a perfect autumn day. We spent the night in Reims, and toasted our new high-risk endeavour in champagne. On 31 October we reached Geneva.

13

UN Reform: The Study of the Capacity of the UN Development System, Geneva and New York 1968–70

The Vision

Next day our small team assembled in Geneva. There were only three of us besides Jacko, although others came to help from time to time.

The scope of our mission had widened enormously since Jacko and I discussed it over dinner in London a few months earlier. Originally the Capacity Study was limited to UNDP and measures to render it capable of handling a doubling of its resources, hoped for over the next five years. At its June session in Vienna, however, UNDP's Governing Council decided that our work should encompass the entire UN Development System. This was logical, since UNDP operated through many specialised agencies, but it presented a huge challenge. We were expected to recommend measures that would transform a system that had grown up piecemeal into an effective vehicle for providing technical cooperation that was truly responsive to the needs and priorities of developing countries and that also reflected the policies of the international organisations. These two objectives were almost impossible to reconcile since the specialised agencies clung to their autonomy and 'agency shares' that would ensure them their slice of the cake.

The ultimate aim was more vividly described in Jacko's 'letter to a head of state' that prefaced our final report than by the turgid language of the Governing Council. It was to enable 'governments and UN organisations' to

> look forward with vision and determination toward the end of the century and map out a strategy for development that will seize people's imaginations and give hope to those who are in need and inspiration to those who have the power to make great changes.

The underlying premise was that technical cooperation through the United Nations would play an increasing role in promoting world development, and that UNDP would be the main channel for providing it. We were conscious that this was a historic opportunity at a critical point in North–South relations. A parallel and complementary study was being carried out by the Commission on International Development led by Lester Pearson, the former Canadian Prime Minister, and was also due to report in the autumn of 1969. Their task was to survey the problems of development cooperation worldwide, particularly the overall financing needs (i.e. not only through the United Nations); ours to examine the role of the United Nations development system within that process. Their report dealt with the philosophy, policy and substance of development cooperation; ours with the operational and practical implications for the UN system of increasing needs and the demand for a more effective response.

The Governing Council insisted that our report should be totally independent, submitted directly to it, unexpurgated, with the comments of UNDP and the agencies to follow afterwards. Some council members urged the Commissioner (the title given to Jacko) to pull no punches, be bold and imaginative, and that his report should be written in 'non-UN language'. We responded accordingly and in some quarters were never forgiven.

After a brief stay in the Cornavin Hotel, I moved first into an apartment and then found a bungalow perched in the foothills of the Jura, above the ancient city of Nyon. It lay between the villages of Trélex half a mile below, and St Cergue high above on the escarpment, and had a breathtaking view across Lake Léman, extending, on a clear day, to the glistening snow peaks of the Alps, and the dominating mass of Mont Blanc. I knew I would be able to work well in this beautiful and peaceful spot. At night the bells of the cows pastured in the flower-strewn meadow in front of the house lulled me to sleep. Now that lovely hillside is blemished by ugly houses ...

Jacko, who for years had lived in hotels, took over my apartment.

The Work

Within the overall vision we had to undertake detailed work on every aspect of UN development work: general policies; pro-gramme development; the formulation, approval, execution and evaluation of individual projects; as well as the administrative, staffing and financial implications of our proposals. We reviewed masses of information and opinions provided by resident representatives, specialised agencies and over 100 member states. These were remarkably frank and strikingly consistent on key issues. We held meetings in New York and Europe with two bodies set up to assist us, an inter-agency advisory group and a panel of consultants comprising eight independent persons, drawn from all regions of the world; attended the Governing Council sessions; and travelled to Montreal, Washington, Paris, Rome, Brussels, The Hague, London and Vienna for talks with governments and organisations. In Washington we had the first of several meetings with the Pearson Commission, who were much more richly endowed and had a large staff. When we met them, our tiny group appeared puny in comparison. But Lester Pearson and Jacko had been friends since the early days of the United Nations and we worked well together.

In between these journeys, we were hard at work on the substance of the report. Jacko had a great gift for bringing a team together. I had the task of writing the final report. Each person's analysis was exhaustively discussed by the whole team, to ensure the consistency of the final proposals, and there were hours and even days of sometimes heated exchanges.

I spent Christmas with my parents but our only other break was a weekend at the San Domenico Hotel, a former monastery in Taormina, Sicily. Glorious spring sunshine and the idyllic terraced gardens tumbling down to the Mediterranean were a welcome respite from our exhausting schedule.

Easter came, and with it sun and the welcome visit of Mary and James Gibson. We walked in the woods picking primroses, built a primitive barbecue in my garden, drove to Lake Annecy over the French border for a prohibitively expensive gourmet lunch, and round the shores of Lake Geneva for a picnic. Jacko applied the same logistical planning to a picnic as he had to the wartime supply of the besieged island of Malta. As we drove into Nyon, he recited a long list of things to buy ending with 'oranges'. After a pause he specified '*Blood* oranges'. A quiet voice came from the back – from James, who had never met Jacko before and who had a delicious sense of irony – 'Any particular blood group?' That silenced even Jacko.

Then the talking had to stop, and the serious business of writing began. I spent the next five months cloistered in my little house, except for the first half of June, spent in London, the Governing Council's summer session in Geneva, and a visit to New York and Ottawa in July. My stay in London was necessary because my mother's condition had worsened and she was in St Bartholomew's Hospital. The Gibsons kindly gave me a quiet room, where I spent the days writing, and in the evening visited my mother. The disease was attacking her hearing, her sight, her senses of touch and taste, and her mobility. Only her lively brain and wit remained unimpaired, together with her indomitable will to recover.

In Trélex I started at 5.30 a.m. and wrote all day in my study, overlooking a pleasant prospect of fields and mountains, until 11 p.m., save for an afternoon break. I had missed fresh milk during my years in developing countries, and expected to find it in Switzerland, only to discover that it was *pasteurisé*, *désodorisé*, *decrémé* and systematically robbed of all taste. But in Trélex I could buy milk before it went into the collective churn. So every afternoon I walked down the hill, swinging my little milk can, past the wooden-fronted houses, with their balconies hung with geraniums, cheek-by-jowl with the cattle byres, to the centre of the village, where the milk was collected in a huge steel pan. It was warm from the cows, unpasteurised but delicious, and never did me any harm. The village shopkeepers were more welcoming than the xenophobic citizens of Geneva. Trélex was another world, rural, peaceful and without complexes or stress. Or so I thought, until a year or two later, I learned that one of my friends had committed suicide ...

Every day our driver collected what I had written, in exchange for an earlier batch corrected for revision, and food. Jacko ensured that I had no distractions! He was a hard taskmaster, but we were both perfectionists, resolved to make the Capacity Study an outstanding report with as few loopholes as possible for opponents to pick at. It went through eight versions and Jacko calculated that I wrote over two million words by hand.

At weekends we worked together at Trélex, but with pleasant distractions. On Saturday mornings we shopped in Nyon and drank capuccino in a café overlooking the lake. When the weather permitted, we had barbecues in the garden and on Sunday evenings took long walks through the woods that clothed the Jura, stopping for a drink at the café in Givrins, the neighbouring village. Those woods boasted every variety of wild flower and each Sunday I filled a large vase that lasted all week. Occasionally we drove up to St Georges – where, in the earlier weeks, snow still lingered – and walked on the barren, tundra-like slopes of the Jura. As the weather grew warmer, I took to writing on my terrace. One day a sleek tabby cat appeared from nowhere and sat firmly on my papers. I made enquiries but no one claimed him, and Thomas, as we christened him, settled in happily, and gave me company during many lonely days.

During the Governing Council's June session in Geneva Jacko invited Paul Hoffman to Trélex one evening so that we could explain our thinking about country programming, and the mechanism of Indicative Planning Figures (IPFs) designed to secure its smooth financing. Hoping to accompany intellectual indoctrination with blandishments of agreeable food and drink, I prepared the ingredients for a daiquiri, which I knew to be Paul's favourite drink from the occasions when he had taken me out for dinner in New York, and Jacko planned a masterly barbecue. Alas, the heavens opened. Poor Jacko dashed in and out, a mac draped over his head, to stoke his drenched charcoal, and bring in a sodden collation. Despite these unpropitious circumstances Hoffman appeared amenable to our arguments, but I doubt if they sank in. I often wondered whether the Capacity Study would have met a kinder fate had the weather been better on that critical evening.

We went to New York at the end of July to give advance warning of our views to UNDP senior staff and were given dinner by Myer Cohen (one of Paul's two deputies) and his wife in an apparently amicable atmosphere. Appearances were to prove deceiving.

On the last day of September 1969 the Capacity Study was completed. Publication had to take place simultaneously in all six official UN languages, and would take six weeks. Jacko and I were exhausted, physically and mentally. After months of grinding work October stretched ahead of us, free of commitments other than proofreading and supervising the technical production.

It was a superb autumn. Day after warm day the sun shone from a cloudless blue sky as the woods around Trélex gradually changed to a spectrum of gloriously burnished hues. We went to Zermatt, so punch-drunk that we nearly took the wrong train and arrived in a zombie-like state. A few days of sparkling mountain air restored us. We walked long miles across those sunny uplands, among the alpine flowers and trees donning their autumn colours. Once we went above the snow level and admired, from a respectable distance, the beetling crags of the Eiger. We ate too much, and slept the sleep of the just – or so we liked to think. Back in Geneva, we spent a day on the lake steamer that daily plies to the head of Lake Léman.

On my last day we hiked up to St Cergue, where we lunched in the sunshine, gazing out on the panorama of alpine meadows and woods careening down to the lake shore, with the crenellated peaks of the Alps glistening on the far horizon. Coming back we took the little train that puffs up and down the Jura, and whose horn, daily sending a happy carillon pealing across the valleys, had often cheered my solitary hours of writing.

It was a day charged with emotions that mirrored the fading beauties of summer. As we climbed through the woods, a sere yellow leaf drifted slowly downwards, turning and swaying in the dappled, hazy sunshine. It seemed to symbolise the end of a very special time. We had lived through an extraordinarily intense period that had brought us much closer together. My feelings for the other person in my life had not changed, nor his for me. We had met briefly and there had been letters, but the obstacles to our ever being together seemed insurmountable. My affection and admiration for Jacko had deepened and we shared much in common: both wedded to the international ideal; both obsessive workaholics; both deeply interested in the natural world; both rather lone souls. Amidst the crushing hard work there had been many happy hours and almost daily companionship. Jacko had revelled in a more domestic existence that had earlier been denied him. I was tiring of confronting the world on my own in far-off places and it seemed we had all the elements for a fulfilling relationship.

Jacko had, de facto, been separated for several years. On that walk in the Jura he spoke of asking Barbara for a divorce, although the prospects did not look promising, since she was an internationally renowned pillar of the Catholic Church. All we could do was follow our appointed ways and hope that something would work out.

Packing up the house seemed a very final act. Taking leave of Thomas was worse, although I found a good home for him. On Saturday 1 November, I flew to Rabat.

The Aspirations

I had only two weeks there, paying official calls and visiting projects, before returning to Geneva. There the Capacity Study was before us, neatly bound in UN blue, and in all the languages. Elaborate arrangements had been made to ensure that the report landed on the desks of the recipients simultaneously all over the world, to prevent bowdlerised interpretations gaining ground before everyone could judge for themselves.

The report comprised two volumes. The first summarised the main themes, and was preceded by letters to Paul Hoffman and to the President of the Governing Council, Aga Shahi, the Foreign Minister of Pakistan. A passage from the second of these epitomises the aspirations of Jacko and our team:

> It is imperative that international organisations should function effectively for the sake of all mankind. It is imperative that they should do so in meeting the commitments that they have now undertaken in cooperating with the less privileged parts of the world. My only reason for accepting this task was the hope that the study might ultimately help people in the developing countries. I believe that this work transcends any other human endeavour. If official reports were ever dedicated, this one would be dedicated to the peoples of the developing countries.

This theme was spelt out in the unusual document that followed – a letter from Jacko to the head of state of a fictitious developing country, in which he put the report in its political context. It exuded an Australian forthrightness that charmed many but alienated others, such as the oft-quoted observation that the UN system was 'becoming slower and more unwieldy, like some prehistoric monster.'

There were other departures from UN practice. Every chapter was headed by a quotation taken from different languages and cultures. I had specially selected the one for the first chapter from Cervantes: '*Dos linajes hay en el mundo, como decía una abuela mía, que son el tener y el no tener*' ('There are but two families in the world, as my grandmother used to say, the Haves and the Have-nots'). Sadly that was true in the sixteenth century, was true 40 years ago and, more unforgivably, is still true today.

I had made a special effort to write in a clear, direct style, avoiding the circumambulation so beloved of UN documents. It was possibly this unaccustomed readability that heightened the report's impact: negatively on those predisposed to disagree with its findings, since there was no fudging of arguments; positively on those favourably inclined.

The Capacity Study is also the only UN document to make acknowledgement to a cat:

> Last but not least my gratitude is expressed to a feline friend, Thomas, who arrived unannounced from the Jura, settled down happily amongst the papers and did his best to prevent this Report from being written by firmly sitting upon it. I can only hope this is not a precedent for governments.

The Russian translators had difficulty with the phrase 'by firmly sitting upon it'. They finally opted for 'by swishing the papers off with his tail'. Either way, the comment was all too apt.

The Capacity Study is still the most comprehensive report ever written on the UN Development System. It embraced the wider spectrum of development cooperation needs and the system's role and responsibility in meeting them, but also presented an integrated plan of action, with a phased timeframe.

Contrary to the belief of those who did not like it, because it threatened cosy empires, the study was not pessimistic or negative. It stressed the importance of technical cooperation and pre-investment as keys to economic and social progress in developing countries and reaffirmed that the United Nations was the ideal instrument, *provided* it was made more efficient and effective. The study emphasised that UNDP must be the hub for these activities: it sought to strengthen UNDP's leadership through the 'power of the purse' and greater control over the agencies, as well as through improved organisation and procedures. If these measures were taken, we concluded, there were good prospects for substantially increased resources from the over 100 member states we had consulted. If not, we warned that the gap would be filled from elsewhere, probably by the World Bank, which had learned from experience that capital loans needed the support of technical assistance and adequate pre-investment.

The Recommendations

A major conclusion was that the UN 'machine' was unmanageable and must be brought under control. Our plan of action embraced every aspect: institutional structures; management practices; programming; project formulation, implementation, evaluation and follow-up; information systems; organisation and administration; human resources; financial resources; and contracts and procurement. One critic described it as a 'package deal' but this was its strength, because it combined carefully articulated and mutually reinforcing actions.

The study argued that the UN system had been flawed from the start by its piecemeal creation. In an 'ideal model', all operational activities would be undertaken by an 'international development authority', with the specialised agencies confined to their original roles of research and standard-setting institutions, 'centres of excellence' and storehouses of information. Instead, agencies had become increasingly involved in operations, to the detriment of their main function. Moreover, the allocation of UNDP's resources according to agency shares meant that the cooperation provided did not respond to the priorities of developing countries but to the agencies' vested interests. They had come to rely on UNDP overhead payments to maintain their staffs and funding, and so indulged in self-interested 'salesmanship' with developing countries. One of Jacko's characteristically mischievous suggestions was that we should illustrate this with a cartoon, showing each agency as a different breed of pedigree dog, all with huge 'operational' tails that made them topple over.

It being no longer realistic to overturn existing institutional arrangements and substitute them with the 'ideal model', the study opted for a compromise. This 'recommended model' sought to strengthen UNDP's central responsibility for all operational development activities, reinforced by the 'power of the purse'. The agencies' role as centres of excellence would be enhanced and their contribution to the UNDP's substantive thinking facilitated by a Technical Advisory Panel (TAP), attached to UNDP Headquarters. The agencies could still be executing agents but UNDP could also contract outside the system.

UNDP Headquarters was to be reorganised into four regional bureaux. These were to work closely with the regional economic commissions and it was suggested that one of them might be outposted experimentally to the site of its corresponding commission, with a view to further decentralisation. A unit of programme policy staff would work directly with the administrator and become the 'brain'.

Based on the principle that 'development is home-made', the UNDP programming process was turned on its head: in future developing countries would decide their own priorities, through a country programme coinciding with their development planning cycle, within a financial framework denominated 'Indicative Planning Figures' (IPFs). These were to be projected ahead, on a rolling basis, for five-year periods and would serve as a pointer to contributing governments as to the scale of resources required. There was to be maximum delegation and decentralisation, with the UNDP Resident Representative assuming full responsibility for managing the programme. The UN system should 'speak with one voice', in order to curb the unseemly competition between agencies for projects. Individual agency representation was to be restricted to cases where it was indispensable for dealing with non-operational, substantive matters of its exclusive competence.

In a nutshell, the Capacity Study was predicated on maximum concentration of responsibility for operational development activities at the Headquarters level (vested in UNDP), combined with maximum decentralisation to the UNDP Resident Representative, who would play the same central role as the UNDP Administrator at Headquarters.

In order to ensure that the UN gave prominence to economic and social issues, as well as political concerns, we proposed the creation of a post of Director-General (a 'second Pope' in Jacko's colourful language) second only to the Secretary-General. We also suggested that various governing bodies should be amalgamated, and that the secretariats of the regional economic commissions might eventually be merged with of the UNDP Regional Bureaux. In short, the study's recommendations should lead, over time, to something very near the 'ideal model'. Our plan was supremely logical. Unfortunately, the United Nations does not operate logically but through political compromises that usually conspire against rational and effective solutions.

On one key aspect, Jacko was pessimistic. In his letter to an imaginary head of state he expressed doubts about the political will of governments to bring about radical change:

> There is no doubt that this opportunity [to revitalise the UN
> System] exists – but can the governments of the world grasp
> it? ... I am compelled to say 'On the record of the last twenty
> years, probably not'.

In that he was tragically prescient.

Reactions

We flew to New York and on Friday 21 November 1969 gave an advance copy to Paul Hoffman, so that he could consider it before the official presentation on 24 November. Hoffman reacted positively but during the weekend was persuaded (probably by C. V. Narasimhan, then Deputy Administrator of UNDP as well as Chef de Cabinet to the Secretary-General) that, rather than a bold design for the future, with which he could bow out on a constructive note (which was the intention), the report was destructive of his name and stewardship. Our reception on the Monday, when he was surrounded by his praetorian guard, was frosty.

In Washington we presented the report to Pierre Paul Schweitzer, Managing Director of the International Monetary Fund, who was sympathetic to our proposals, and to Robert McNamara, President of the World Bank, who was not. Jacko gave a press conference on 1 December and in London we had discussions with the British Government, including a lunch with Sir Burke Trend, and Geoffrey Wilson, Permanent Secretary of the Ministry of Overseas Development. The former was now more amicably disposed towards me, and both were gratifyingly favourable to our report.

I needed to drive my car to England, where I was to spend Christmas with my parents, before embarking for Casablanca. On impulse Jacko and I went first to Provence and spent a day in the enchanting surroundings of Les Baux. Then a freak snowstorm hit

France, even the Midi, and we struggled for two days through the blizzard to Dieppe, several times landing in the ditch. On 4 January 1970 I returned to Morocco after a horrendously rough four-day voyage from Southampton, in a cross-channel ferry that had no stabilisers to offset the fury of the Bay of Biscay.

The Capacity Study created a stir. Predictably most specialised agencies reacted adversely to proposals that subordinated their operational choices to UNDP and the preferences of developing countries. Governments were more supportive but the proof of the pudding lay in decisions to be taken by the UNDP Governing Council. Our proposals were debated in the council's regular session in January 1970 in New York; in a special session in March 1970, also in New York; and in its second regular session in Geneva, in June. I accompanied Jacko to all these sessions.

After the January session we worked with Hoffman and his senior staff on the implementation of the report, and were consulted by various permanent missions to the United Nations. I left Rabat on 17 January and did not return until 26 February. I very nearly did not return at all. From New York we went to Ottawa for meetings with the Canadian Government, an enthusiastic supporter of our proposals. Our plane to London lost an engine in mid-Atlantic, and we had a few scary hours as we limped back to Kennedy airport. We did not arrive until next afternoon at Heathrow where Robin, newly at Eton, was anxiously waiting.

Given the country thrust and strong emphasis on decentralisation, one would have expected developing countries to be solidly in favour of the report, but it was not always the case. Some of their representatives had occupied, or aspired to occupy, senior posts in UNDP and the agencies and, seeing the way the wind blew in the upper reaches of those organisations, were quick to criticise the proposals. Agencies also exerted pressure through their natural allies in governments – FAO to Ministers of Agriculture, UNESCO to Ministers of Education, ILO to Ministers of Labour, WHO to Ministers of Health, etc. – a cosy relationship for which the study concocted the term 'administrative incest'. Representatives of some smaller developing countries received no instructions from their capitals, and acted on rumours picked up in the corridors and the Secretariat that raised imaginary bogeys. However, the majority of developing countries favoured our proposals.

So did the developed countries, who liked the prospect of increased efficiency, better use of resources and greater account-ability. The Nordic countries and the Netherlands were the most enthusiastic. Some donors were concerned about the financial implications of annually projecting contributions five years ahead under the rolling system of Indicative Planning Figures and doubtful about the wisdom of giving a free hand to recipient governments to determine their own priorities. At the January 1970 session, US Ambassador Arthur ('Tex') Goldsmith burst out, 'Does this mean that Lola gets what Lola wants?' (hardly a flattering reference to developing countries). Nonetheless, the United States became a strong supporter.

There were some strange bedfellows. The March 1970 session was the first occasion on which a Cuban delegation attended the Governing Council. It was headed by Carlos Rafael Rodriguez, then Minister of Economy, who later rose to be second to Fidel Castro. To the acute embarrassment of the United States, the two countries found themselves on the same side, both enthusiastic proponents of our proposed reforms.

Cuba had done its homework better than anyone else. The delegation distributed a book in Spanish and English, analysing our proposals. Their chapters were also headed by quotations, but theirs were all from Lewis Carroll. We had had two quotations from him, the one for the last chapter being the familiar:

'The time has come,' the Walrus said,
'To talk of many things;
Of shoes – and ships – and sealing wax –
Of cabbages – and kings.'

The Cuban quotations were much more recondite. The minister gave a rhetorical address, vintage Cuban style, ending with a rousing peroration. Sir Robert, he declaimed, should have continued to the following line:

'And why the sea is boiling hot'
'*PORQUE, SEÑORES, EL MAR ESTA HIRVIENDO!*'

'Because, gentlemen the sea *is* boiling ... '. Thus the minister dramatically ended his appeal for greater international cooperation to alleviate the plight of developing countries.

When I asked Dr Rodriguez who was the Cuban expert on Lewis Carroll he said simply: '*Yo*' (*I* am). I was left wondering whether Cuban support had been inspired by the minister's passion for Lewis Carroll! Stranger things have happened in international relations.

We met seldom but Carlos Rafael always called me *La Pequeña Alicia* after *Alice in Wonderland* and various Cuban Embassies around the world were bemused by messages to and from *La Pequeña Alicia*. Once, in 1973, at an ECLA regional meeting in Quito, he deftly switched placement cards at the Ecuadorian President's official banquet so that we could discuss the problems of developing countries. The conference was debating a proposed 'Quito Declaration', supported by all delegations except the United States. Next day Carlos Rafael defended the text in a brilliant speech that, to my embarrassment, went something like this:

> The United States wants to teach us a lesson. I have been reminded by a veteran [sic] of international cooperation, whom I shall call *La Pequeña Alicia*, of a passage from Lewis Carroll. When the question was asked, 'Why are lessons called lessons?' the reply was 'Because they lessen!'

> The untranslatable pun was given in English.

I saw Carlos Rafael twice in Cuba. On the first occasion he remarked jocularly, 'Well, you've travelled a great deal, while I stayed here and got married too many times!' In 1990 when I spent three weeks in Havana as Secretary-General of the Eighth UN Crime Congress he was frail and ill. He was also, uncharacteristically, deeply dejected. Cuba was introducing some flexibility into its economic regime. He said sadly, 'I am seeing the collapse of everything I have worked for, and believed in.' I never saw him again.

Carlos Rafael Rodriguez was a Marxist idealogue of the old school, and a highly cultivated intellectual. He was a man of unswerving principles and, however much one disagreed with his beliefs, no one could question his integrity.

The Governing Council's discussion in June 1970 lasted longer than anticipated. Jacko had to travel to Ghana, and I was left to handle an often fraught debate. He had hardly gone when the meeting was interrupted by news that David Owen had suffered a fatal heart attack. Only a year before the Council had paid tribute to him on his departure from UNDP to become Secretary-General of International Planned Parenthood Federation (IPPF).

It was a sad end for the modest Welshman who launched the field network that still functions today, and it seemed symbolic that his final exit should coincide with a new era in UNDP's evolution. There were many tributes in the council and I was asked to speak on behalf of the resident representatives. With only a few moments to collect my thoughts, and in emotional shock at losing a friend, to whom I owed so much, it was one of the hardest things I ever had to do.

The council's resolution on the Capacity Study, immortalised as 'The 1970 Consensus', is regarded as a watershed in UNDP history. It was also an inherently defective compromise in the age-old UN tradition. Jacko had appealed to governments to take decisive action, and not merely 'tinker' with 'the machine'. The consensus went beyond 'tinkering' but fell far short of the Capacity Study's vision of a reformed, strengthened and integrated UN System of Development.

The consensus endorsed the country-centred approach and the concept of country programming central to the study's thesis, but undermined it in practice by discarding rolling IPFs and the approval of programmes to synchronise with each country's planning cycle. It substituted a five-year closed system, whereby *all* country programmes, whatever the timing of the national plan, would be approved for that set period. The global IPF, from which national IPFs were drawn every year, remained static for these five years instead of being projected forward annually.

This inflexibility was a fatal flaw. The country programme no longer interlocked with national plans. Furthermore, instead of a few programmes coming for approval at each council session, they were all presented simultaneously at five-year intervals, placing an intolerable workload on both council and secretariat, and reducing attention to each programme. The inflexibility over IPFs gave no room for adjustment to changing circumstances and was a root cause of UNDP's financial crisis in 1975. All the chickens came home to roost at once.

The council supported the creation of regional bureaux, though not their gradual decentralisation to the regional economic commissions. More serious was the decision of the top men in UNDP to fill each regional director post with a political appointee from the region, supported by his government. This cardinal error led to politicisation of the bureaux and fomented autonomous tendencies. UNDP fell prey to centrifugal forces and Headquarters became more disarticulated, rather than the integrated entity envisaged by the study. Other proposals not implemented included the establishment of a staff college and the development of a career service.

Governments – even the Study's strongest advocates – compounded the problem by failing to take consistent positions in other UN forums. Even some that supported the basic tenet that UNDP must be the sole central fund for financing technical cooperation and pre-investment nonetheless approved and funded sectoral programmes established by specialised agencies determined to become more independent of UNDP. Thus the twin principles of UNDP's 'power of the purse' and the pre-eminence of developing countries' priorities were invalidated.

Nevertheless, the study did transform UNDP's modus operandi. In contrast to high-ranking officials, who feared curtailment of their power, UNDP's rank and file and even agency field staff enthusiastically received it. It became a seminal study for innumerable subsequent attempts to improve UN efficiency. Many still quote it today as the 'Bible' of UN reform – perhaps because, like the Bible, its precepts were never fully put into practice. Lester Pearson's report was less controversial, but his main recommendation, that developed countries should spend 0.07 per cent of their GNP on development cooperation by 1975, has still not been implemented either, 30 years later.

Many considered the study a masterly work. Jacko's prestige soared in many quarters, but sank to rock bottom with Paul Hoffman, hitherto his staunchest admirer, who had even considered him his heir apparent as administrator. Whether that would have happened is doubtful, since the US Government clung to the post. It is nonetheless tantalising to reflect that, had Jacko not carried out the Capacity Study, then he might have become administrator. In that event no study would have been necessary, as he would have carried out its tenets in practice. Instead Jacko was once more relegated to the wilderness and my promotion was deliberately delayed.

The Capacity Study was the big opportunity to right the mess caused by the piecemeal development of UN. Failure to seize it fully was a tragedy for the whole System and for the developing world. The same issues come up time and again: the centrifugal disarticulation and failure to speak with one voice or to use scarce resources effectively in an integrated way. One sees it now not only in development cooperation but in peace-building and humanitarian operations. This is why member states continue to clamour for reform and the US Congress has found a pretext to withhold contributions, though it is governments who are chiefly responsible, through lack of political will and vested interest in the status quo.

One sobering lesson of the Capacity Study is that logical, across-the-board reform cannot work because, by the time all member states have agreed a compromise reflecting the least common denominator of their respective interests, the end result is – to use Jacko's favourite phrase – 'a dog's breakfast'. The only way forward is through specific, major changes that will have a multiplier effect.

The major tragedy 30 years ago was Paul Hoffman's failure to understand that the Capacity Study was not intended to undermine him or UNDP but to *strengthen* both. A heaven-sent opportunity was blocked because it threatened the ambitions of senior officials who had previously operated like demigods. Had Hoffman accepted the study, the outcome would have been very different for him, the UNDP and above all for the Third World. Our warning that the UNDP was at a crossroads was all too prescient. Is it coincidence that the World Bank now has a much larger programme of technical assistance and pre-investment – supposedly UNDP's domain? That the great increase in UNDP's resources never materialised? That

UNDP has spent years, desperately seeking a role by jumping on every fashionable development or humanitarian bandwagon? The sad fact is that UNDP lost its way in 1969–70. And the agencies remain as competitive and conflictive as ever.

The point was poignantly brought home on 29 January 1997 when Kofi Annan, who had just assumed leadership of a United Nations in deep crisis, besieged by demands for major reform, unveiled a commemorative portrait of Jacko in the Palais des Nations in Geneva, and, in front of the television cameras, implored: 'Jacko, where are you now, when I need you?'

One lasting thing came out of the Capacity Study – the relationship between Jacko and myself. We were to work together again later, and our companionship lasted until his death in January 1991.

PART FIVE

Return to the Field: Morocco and Chile

In the Shadow of the Atlas

An Uncertain Welcome

On my arrival in Rabat my deputy, Jean-Pierre Schellenberg, took me to lunch. We had hardly sat down when he burst out: 'Headquarters are out of their minds to send a woman to an Arab country. It simply cannot work.'

Scarcely charmed by this welcome I replied that I hoped to prove him wrong, and Jean-Pierre promised support, despite his reservations, and gave it unstintingly. When I left I was touched when he referred to our first talk in his farewell speech, adding gallantly that the intervening two years had proved him wrong. Few men would have made that admission publicly and with such grace.

Jean-Pierre had reason for his initial reaction. Paul Marc Henry, the Deputy Administrator, had to travel personally to Morocco to intercede with the Prime Minister, Dr Mohammed Benhima, who had objected that a female head of mission would 'embarrass the king'. When I arrived Benhima had been transferred to the ministry of Agriculture and was one of the first ministers I called on, as I was once more the FAO Country Representative.

Swiftly dispensing with all niceties, Minister Benhima launched into virulent criticism of FAO, and the deficiencies of UN development cooperation. When he paused for breath, I said: 'Your Excellency, I agree but we are trying to do something about it.' And I embarked on a synthesis of the Capacity Study, adding, 'Now it is up to governments to see that our recommendations are implemented, if you really want change.'

Benhima's demeanour changed instantly. He bombarded me with questions and next day visited my office to see the report. Two important consequences followed: Morocco became a firm supporter of the Capacity Study; and Benhima and his wife became my closest friends in Morocco. He afterwards told me that my vigorous reaction at our first meeting, when he had deliberately sought to test me, had changed his opinion about my suitability.

Meetings with other ministers went more easily on my first visit, before I returned to Geneva and New York for the presentation of the Capacity Study. In retrospect, I wonder I was as well received as I was, for my diary shows that between November 1969 and March 1970 I spent only six weeks in Morocco. After that, apart from attending the June 1970 Governing Council in Geneva, I became once more a full-time resident representative.

It was several months before I found a suitable home. Villa Rachid, in the residential quarter of Souissi, was a low, white stucco house, blinkered to the street, with all the rooms facing on to a garden of lawns and orange and lemon trees. The front wall was a mass of pink and white oleanders and purple bougainvillea. The dining-room was small but the living-room immense, opening on to a large covered patio where I ate all my meals in the warmer weather.

I found myself once more living a frugal existence until furniture could arrive but I found an excellent cook, Abdul-Khedir, trained in French cuisine and fluent in French as well as Moroccan dialectal Arabic. Maids came and went, notably one, recommended by my predecessor, who, during one of my absences, gave a party with my food and drink. A more disagreeable problem was the prevalence of the largest cock-roaches I have ever seen, and I have experienced a fair selection. I watched in horror from my bed as they paraded across ceiling and walls, and one night woke up in terror when one fell on my face. All efforts to eradicate them failed, until at last we discovered, and sealed, a hole in the floor. Once a long snake appeared on the wall of the garage, causing panic among the servants.

Our Programme

Our large programme was scattered all over Morocco, mainly in agriculture, since most of the population eked out a subsistence living from the land. There were two large multipurpose irrigation projects in the Rharb and the Souss Valley, and an ambitious integrated rural development programme, known by its acronym of DERRO, in the Rif, east of Tangier, an arid, rocky, and wildly beautiful country, bordering the Mediterranean, where Spanish was spoken and a major product was the drug kef. We were also active in education and public administration, and supported a statistical training centre, INSEA, serving the Maghreb as a whole. Another project in the Rharb mined for potash to diversify Morocco's exports but months of drilling failed to find economic deposits. My project manager discovered good prospects for mining rock salt near Casablanca, and asked for my authorisation to drill there. With government agreement I gave him the green light. Headquarters' initial reprobation was assuaged when economic deposits of rock salt were found that led to a thriving export business with the United States and a petrochemical industry in Morocco. It became my favourite example of a project that failed to meet its original objectives but proved successful in developing a different product in a different region. I promoted another geological project of mineral exploration in the Atlas mountains and to my delight, Henry Meyer, with whom I had survived many misadventures in Bolivia, was appointed as project manager.

Relations with the government were excellent. Most ministers were young, French-educated technocrats. Our focal point was the ministry of the Plan where I worked with two outstanding Ministers; first Mustapha Faris, and then Dr Imani who met an untimely and senseless death a few years later, when terrorists blew up a Pan American aircraft at Rome Airport. Mohammed Faris fared little better; he was seriously injured in the 1972 coup attempt against King Hassan II.

Our day-to-day contact was Mohammed Echiguer, a charming and able young man. He, like Benhima, was a Berber, and became a close friend as well as my Arabic teacher. I had opted to learn Moroccan dialectal Arabic rather than classical Arabic, but Abdul

Khedir's excellent French impeded my progress. Moreover, French was then the official language, and the one in which ministers felt most comfortable. If, during a meeting, someone telephoned a minister on a sensitive subject, he would begin speaking in Arabic, but soon lapse into French. Mohammed Echiguer was not very fortunate either. A year or so after I left Morocco, he died of a terrible cancer, still in his thirties.

The exception to this otherwise congenial company was the head of the DERRO project, Dr Chbicheb, an arrogant man, with an explosive temper. In May 1970 FAO sent a remarkable Frenchman, Raymond Aubrac, a hero of the French resistance during the Second World War, to review our agricultural projects. Together with the dreaded Monsieur Chbicheb we made a memorable trip to the Rif. During long bumpy jeep rides Raymond Aubrac recounted his capture by the Gestapo, along with Jean Moulin, who was brutally murdered by the Germans, and of his own miraculous escape from prison in Lyons, in October 1943, through the quick-wittedness and bravery of his wife, Lucie. Lucie, heavily pregnant, charmed an SS officer into believing that Raymond had wronged her, and demanded to be married to him before his execution. That involved a transfer across Lyons, during which the vehicle carrying Raymond and other prisoners was ambushed by Lucie and her resistance group, who shot the driver. After months of anxious hiding, they were flown to safety in London in a small RAF plane, from a muddy field at dead of night.

In Rabat I discovered the wartime hero's Achilles' heel. One morning, my driver, Driss, found a kitten precariously balanced on the back axle of the car. I took it to my office and plied it with warm milk. My first meeting was with Raymond, and I was puzzled to see him cringing further and further back into his chair. At length the man who had faced torture and death confessed: 'I am terrified of cats!'

His Majesty, King Hassan II

After the former Prime Minister's concerns about my effect on the King, I was intrigued to meet His Majesty Hassan II. He held enormous levees that were all male, with the exception of myself. They involved ambassadors, ministers and other dignitaries and hordes of 'Blue Men' from the desert massed in the background, as in an exotic filmset, in flowing azure robes. In such a throng it seemed more likely that I would be the one to be embarrassed, rather than the King, who always greeted me cordially.

Food, both Moroccan and international style, was always abundant. The drinks in evidence were non-alcoholic, in accordance with Muslim precepts, but there was always a discreet table laden with stronger brew, and Dom Pérignon champagne. The King was known to be a bon viveur, and there was a notable ambivalence about alcohol in Rabat. For my first reception, I bought a lot of Coca-Cola but found that many cases of whisky were also consumed – Coca-Cola was used to disguise the colour.

One evening the King held a party for ambassadors' wives at his palace in Skhirat, along the coast eastwards from Rabat. In vain I pleaded with the Protocol Department that I was nobody's wife, and had done my stint in the men's gathering: it was a command performance. This time the King was the only man present (his turn to be embarrassed? I mused). No other man was allowed because of the presence of 'the mother of his children' (who was not deigned the honour of being called 'Queen', or even 'wife') and several of his concubines. The food could not compare with that at the male festivities and there was no hidden table. At 10 o'clock we were bidden to an open amphitheatre, perched on rocks that tumbled down to the shore. The night was inclement, and a chilly white mist rolled in from the sea. To the consternation of my diplomatic sisters, I purloined some monogrammed royal napkins to mop up the pools of water in the seats.

The King sat in a massive chair, like a throne, numerous minions having first draped it in burnouses so that the royal posterior would not get as wet as ours. As darkness and fog surged about us, hours and hours of Arabic music droned out from the spot-lit stage. The King, sporting a shiny white dinner jacket, looked more like a trendy bandmaster than a powerful monarch. The highlight was a famous Lebanese singer. On and on she sang, to the rapturous applause of the King, and the distinctly more modified rapture of his bedraggled, shivering guests. It was not until 1 a.m. that we were released for the long drive back to Rabat in our sodden dresses.

This was not the only occasion on which royal hospitality posed a positive threat to health. On 10 March 1971, Hassan II departed from precedent and threw a mixed party in his magical palace at Fez to celebrate the circumcision of the Crown Prince, then six years old. A sumptuous feast of French haute cuisine and Arab delicacies was laid before us. The King remained remote on a balcony, speaking to no one. The tour de force was the smoked salmon, some portions of which were rolled around English gold sovereigns. I am not sure how many guests sustained broken teeth, but one ambassador at least developed a great predilection for smoked salmon! As we enjoyed this gargantuan feast, reminiscent of the Arabian nights, we were entertained by White Russian musicians, flown in from Paris, like the food.

Our sybaritic pleasure was abruptly curtailed when the King clapped his hands, and court retainers unceremoniously herded us out onto the battlements. March nights in Fez are not noted for their clemency: spring had not yet sprung, and an icy wind whistled down from the Atlas mountains. In vain we pleaded for coats taken from us on our arrival, with no forewarning of outdoor sports: an extraordinary display of fireworks by skilled French artificers, also flown from Paris. Great bursts of coloured showers and streamers spangled the romantic towers and turrets of the palace with rainbow hues and briefly lit the dark labyrinth of the mediaeval Medina all around us, while rockets streaked across the dark sky like shooting stars. Our enjoyment was severely muted by the perishing cold. The men had dinner jackets but most of the women, myself included, were bare-shouldered. After some difficult negotiation the British Ambassador, his wife and I managed to prise a heavy red burnous off one of the palace guards, and the three of us huddled under it, closely embraced to keep warm.

I kept wondering how the little prince was feeling, cooped up elsewhere in the palace, a notably absent guest of honour. Nor could I help speculating how much all this was costing. As I later learned, the fireworks alone cost US$2 million dollars, rather more than UNDP's annual budget for Morocco.

I suspect that the Crown Prince recovered sooner than I did. I caught a monumental cold, complicated by sinusitis, and was sick for weeks. I was infinitely more fortunate than the Belgian Ambassador: he never returned alive from the King's birthday party at Skhirat a few months later.

By a strange quirk of fate it was Benhima, not I, who embarrassed his royal master (if 'embarrassed' is the proper term), by incautiously drawing the King's attention to growing government corruption. The reaction was fierce and immediate: Benhima was fired as Minister of Agriculture. Since he was a doctor, trained in France, the WHO representative and I arranged a WHO consultancy for him. Benhima was delighted but the King was not; the message came down from on high that he was forbidden to leave the country. Benhima applied to be reinstated in the Ministry of Health but that too was refused.

The vendetta against him was unrelenting and so Benhima, probably the ablest man in the Government, was banished into virtually internal exile. It was a delicate situation, but I had long ago decided in Latin America that I could not abandon friends who fell on hard times. I visited the Benhimas whenever I could, discreetly driving my faithful little Volkswagon Beetle, though I was not naive enough to think my visits went unobserved. I became close to Benhima's wife, Marie-Thérèse, a delightful and intelligent Frenchwoman, and was treated as a member of the family; they dubbed me *Numéro Deux* (No. Two), a joking reference to the Islamic custom of men having more than one wife, and I was invited to call him by his family nickname of Taibi. Benhima gave me fascinating insights into Moroccan history and politics, and court intrigues, as well as into the background of his family, Berbers traditionally loyal to the Alaouite dynasty from the time of King Mohammed V, Hassan II's father.

Benhima remained staunchly loyal to his sovereign, whom he admired as an astute political leader and the lynchpin of a country prey to centrifugal forces. Privately he did not conceal his distaste for certain aspects of the King's personal life. It was common knowledge that numerous concubines rode in and out of the palace in discreetly curtained station wagons. As Prime Minister,

Taibi had sometimes found the King almost too exhausted to deal with state business. I was pleased when Hassan II came out boldly in favour of family planning, a programme supported by my office, through the UN Fund for Population Activities, since Islamic and Catholic countries were reluctant to declare such unequivocal support. Then Taibi told me something I found truly hypocritical: I knew that only one woman was allowed to bear the King's offspring, but not that the concubines were forbidden to use contraception, and that the palace contained an abortion clinic.

That, and Taibi's banishment, were characteristic of the strange mixture of ancient and modern practices at the Moroccan Court, as was the manner of his rehabilitation. No words were spoken nor was he summoned to the royal presence. Instead, on the feast of Aid-el-Fitr in 1971 the King sent him a sacrificial lamb, as he did to all his ministers. He had evidently decided that Benhima was too valuable and loyal to be cast aside for ever and circumstances later proved him right. The second portent of reinstatement was less propitious. Taibi, included in the guest-list for the ill-fated birthday party at Skhirat in July 1971, ended up running for his life along the beach. A year later he was mainly instrumental in saving Hassan II from a second assassination attempt.

Family Matters

Jacko, still a roving troubleshooter for UNDP, fitted Morocco into his itinerary whenever possible and we wrote to one another every day. I had stumbled upon two wild kittens in the garden, one snow-white, the other grey tabby, and during one of Jacko's visits we suddenly noticed that the mother cat was carrying them out into the street. 'It's now or never,' cried Jacko and out we dashed to effect the capture. Once incorporated into my household the white kitten became biddable and so was called 'Now', while the tabby would never let anyone touch it and was dubbed 'Never'. Both developed into randy young ladies, attracting many highly articulate admirers. My garden wall, which screened a convent, was a favourite place for their amorous antics, at times resembling an erotic frieze in a feline Kama Sutra, to the delight of guests lunching on my terrace. What the nuns thought I never dared to ascertain.

Travels to Geneva and New York enabled me to visit my parents. My mother was getting progressively worse. She could walk only a few halting steps with help, and her hands, which had scrubbed floors to keep me at school and performed the finest needlework and embroidery, no longer functioned. Despite the strain, my father appeared in good health, and only once broke down in my presence. He was absolutely devoted and I more than once saw him tenderly comforting my mother. A home help came for a few hours every week, but he did all the laundry and cooking, in addition to tending the large garden that was their pride and joy. I found somebody who would come in daily but my mother would have none of it, appearing unaware of the enormous load on my father, already 76. Afterwards I felt guilty that I had not insisted.

In August 1970 I took home leave. Jacko and I had planned a quiet week's holiday, walking in the Swiss Alps near Sion, before I went to help my father. We met in Geneva and hired a car, forgetting that 1 August was the day on which all French people go on holiday. Part of this general exodus flowed over the border into Switzerland and after Lausanne the road along Lake Léman was totally blocked. It was a scorching day and by the time we reached the hotel we were exhausted. Hardly had we changed for dinner than the telephone rang. It was my father, usually a very calm man, but now distraught. My mother had returned to Bart's Hospital for routine treatment but had gone into shock when the doctors drastically reduced her cortisone dose. She was very seriously ill and I should return to London at once.

Next day we made the wearisome journey back to Geneva, this time along the French shore, stopping for a lakeside lunch in the beautiful little town of Yvoire. We stayed at a London hotel and I visited my mother daily. She survived the incident but it deprived her of more faculties. After her release from hospital I remained at Pippins to help my father. Jacko came for part of the time; he got on well with my parents, and shared a love of cricket with my father whom he sometimes took out to lunch, to relieve the sad monotony of his life. We recouped our lost week's holiday with a few enchanting days in Taormina but I felt guilty at snatching even that respite, instead of staying with my father.

Jacko's position in UNDP was increasingly precarious and he was casting about for alternatives. Our future was also in the air, and he had instituted proceedings to obtain a legal separation as a first step towards divorce. He expressed interest in finding somewhere to live in Tangiers, which would be near me, near Europe and international connections, providing tranquillity for writing. I heard of a small house, and when Jacko visited in October 1970, arranged to see it. The house was delightful, wreathed in plumbago, bougainvillea and oleanders, and perched on a steeply terraced hillside with magnificent views of a rocky bay and the blue Mediterranean below. Afterwards we motored to the Rif to the charming hotel – Le Petit Mérou – that I had discovered there. A series of low white buildings in Moroccan style cascaded down to a bleached sand beach, encircled by tumbled boulders. Beyond stretched a wild and rugged coastline, indented with inlets and rocky caves. We fell in love with the place and the following year came back. By then, alas, Club Mediterrané was established nearby, though we were glad to find our old friends, James (he of the explosive cocktail incident in Manila) and Barbara Keen in residence with their children. Not long afterwards James died as suddenly as his long-time colleague, David Owen.

After several months of vacillation Jacko decided against the Tangiers house. It was a recurring pattern: Jacko would yearn for a settled home, renew the search, but in the end make no decision. For a man renowned for decisiveness it was a strange dichotomy in his personality.

The World Bank in Morocco

In Morocco I again developed close working relations with the World Bank. For years their disdain for UNDP and technical assistance had been ill-concealed and Bank missions tended to bypass the resident representative. They learned the hard way that injections of capital without training in the use of its product

– for instance, irrigated agriculture in a multipurpose river development project – was throwing money away. As the Capacity Study anticipated, they developed their own technical assistance capacity instead of relying on UNDP but their funding was through loans whereas UNDP gave grants. In Morocco we worked together on education and agriculture. The Bank asked me to be their representative in Morocco, an unheard-of arrangement, since both the Bank and the International Monetary Fund considered themselves a cut above the rest of the UN system.

In November 1970 the Bank invited me to their Consultative Group on Morocco, in Paris – the first time a UNDP representative had attended such an event, a practice now routine. Afterwards I snatched a couple of days at Pippins and was there again for Christmas, which was to be our last together.

The World Bank had recently signed agreements with FAO and UNESCO, whereby they would provide technical back-up for the Bank's agricultural and educational missions, thus establishing a direct link to two of UNDP's executing agencies and bypassing UNDP. Their missions imposed a strain on fragile administrative structures. In preparation for an educational loan a UNESCO mission about 20-strong came first. They stayed a month, met educational authorities in Rabat, and travelled throughout the country, taking a large part of the Ministry of Education with them. Shortly afterwards a joint Bank–UNESCO team turned up. The specialities were the same, only the names and faces different. They, too, stayed a month, saw the same people, and visited the same places. I could not believe my eyes when, a month or two later, another large body of men (no women) trooped into my office, and recited the same litany of educational specialities, with yet another set of names attached. They came only from the Bank, which seemed to lack faith in their UNESCO partners, and repeated the circus of visits for the third time. It was a shocking waste of money, as I pointed out to the Bank, which had the grace to agree. Even worse, the Moroccan educational system had seized up entirely during the year that this pantomime occupied, because key officials were left no time for their normal work.

UNDP's Global Meeting in New Delhi

In February 1971 Paul Hoffman convened a global meeting of resident representatives in New Delhi to discuss the implementation of the Governing Council's consensus, especially country programming. It was a fraught affair, at which deep divisions emerged between Headquarters and field staff over the Capacity Study. Considering UNDP's new measures to be inadequate and tired of being lectured to by Headquarters officials without field experience, the resident representatives revolted, setting up their own working group. I declined to be a member, lest my role in writing the study gave Headquarters a pretext for dismissing the resident representatives' paper, but I worked closely with the group's secretary, Garth Ap Rees. The chairman was Anthony Balinski, with whom I had worked in Bolivia.

The activities of the dissident resident representatives led Vaidyanathan, (an Indian close to C. V. Narasimhan, known generally as Vaid, then Head of Administration), to ask Garth to include two pages he had written defending the Headquarter's position. Garth refused because Vaid, never having worked in the field, had misconstrued the resident representatives' concerns. He later burned Vaid's contribution in a meeting of the working group.

Their paper was to be discussed in the final plenary session. When the resident representatives met the day before to finalise the text, John McDiarmid, the resident representative in India, who hoped that Paul Hoffman would extend him for two years beyond retirement, insisted that key paragraphs of the draft be excised, saying, 'We don't have to preach the Capacity Study again to Paul Hoffman.' Balinski, who perhaps suffered the insecurity of the permanent exile, caved in immediately. Against the protests of many, a truncated document was presented, and Vaid insisted on reading his two pages. Nevertheless the 'res reps' revolt' was not without effect. Shortly afterwards a two-man commission was established to make recommendations on improving relations between Headquarters and the field. Nine years elapsed before another global meeting was held in 1980. No one in New York wanted to face another 'frank exchange of views'.

Jacko was at the Delhi meeting, an uncomfortable position given his strained relations with Paul Hoffman, though he was chuffed by the resident representatives' support. Hoffman was now showing his age, repeating old stories and quips and seemed to understand little of the fray erupting all around him. Nevertheless, it must have been a shock to someone accustomed to adulation. He used his last months in office to ease Jacko out of his long-standing role as Senior Consultant, causing outrage among some resident representatives. David Blickenstaff, then serving in Tunisia, wrote to several of us urging joint action to avert the loss of someone so valuable to the programme, while William Harding, in the Philippines, suggested to his government – Canada – that they propose him as Hoffman's successor.

There were pleasanter moments. Jacko took me to see his friend San Carla and the white tigers he had bred, one of Jacko's passions, and on a weekend visit to Agra and its Red Fort we saw the Taj Mahal shimmering in moonlight. On the way back we spent three days at Les Baux, in the lovely surroundings of the Baumanière Hotel we had discovered in 1969. In early spring sunshine we scrambled over the boulder-strewn hills of Provence, and unwound from the tensions of Delhi, where we had once more found ourselves in the eye of the storm.

Among the new faces in Delhi was that of Gabriel Valdés, head of the newly created UNDP Regional Bureau for Latin America. Gabriel had been Chilean Foreign Minister, in the Christian Democrat administration of Eduardo Frei. Now he was looking for someone to fill the resident representative post in Chile, where Salvador Allende's Socialist Government had been voted into office in 1970. I was surprised when, at our very first meeting, he asked me to go there. I had refused that posting six years before, but now the situation was different. I knew a great deal about President Allende from the Chileans who had worked with me in Bolivia. After years of waiting in the political wings, Pedro Vuskovic, who had headed our planning team, was Minister of Economy and Gonzalo Martner, Minister of Planning. The thought of working again with these former colleagues, at a dramatic juncture in Chilean history, was enticing. So it was with a heavy heart that I told him I could not consider it, partly because I had been only just over a year in Morocco, but mainly because I could not live so far from Europe and my parents.

Travels in Morocco

A week after I returned to Rabat, Jacko arrived, together with the Gibsons. I had to visit various projects, and took my guests on a whirlwind tour through the Atlas mountains. It was a hugely enjoyable expedition, despite my worsening cold and sinusitis, the legacy of the arctic firework display in Fez. There were countless hilarious arguments and subterfuges over bills aimed at outwitting Jacko, who always tried to pay. Mary Gibson's diary gives an example:

> 13.3.71 ... Eventually to Zagora, where the Grand Hotel du Sud had thoroughly mixed up our rooms; having sorted this out, we and Aga's young staff [Aga = myself; Jacko's many nicknames for me included 'Agapanthus'] had dinner together, James [Mary's husband] elated to think he had for once succeeded in paying for the dinner, till he discovered next morning that the young had paid for the wine and SIR (Jacko) had been charged 48 dirhams for Mrs G's bed. Altogether a bad night for Jackson, owing to unfortunate conjunction of lighted candle and glass which resulted in unlighted candle and a lot of broken glass ...

There was much ribbing about the hotel thinking that Mary was Jacko's wife, and ever after she was known as '48 dirhams', shortened to 'Dirhams'. Driss, my wonderful Berber driver, entered into the fun, making picnics on barren hillsides and when we had mint tea at the Source Bleue du Meski it was he who said proudly, '*Cette fois c'est moi qui paie*' (This time *I'm* paying).

Zagora lay at the end of the road, where it expired abruptly into the wastes of the Sahara. Before that we had walked in the Mamounia Gardens in Marrakech and witnessed many marvels in the great plaza of D'Jmaa el F'naa. Acrobats and a snake-charmer later entertained us at dinner and a belly-dancer took a shine to

Jimmy, waggling her hips seductively close but he, most ungallantly, fell asleep, swaying gently to the rhythm of the snake. Driving south towards Ouarzazate we took a detour across a stony plateau to the Kasbah at Telouet, the mountain fortress where the Glaoui, the Lords of the Atlas, lived in panoplied splendour until the last great ruler of the mountain passes, T'Hami El Glaoui, betrayed by the French, had to pay homage to the Sultan, Mohammed V, in 1955. The battlemented palace, 8000 feet up in the High Atlas, begun only a century before, and intended to be the most fabulous in the world (it was called 'The Palace of a Thousand and One Nights') fell into disuse, still unfinished. Sixteen years later we found a desolate ruin, starkly silhouetted against the majestic snow peaks of the Atlas, their lower slopes shot with rainbows. The labyrinth of halls and apartments was deserted but for a solitary guide and some storks nesting in the decaying towers; above, in a burnished blue sky, soared vultures and birds of prey. Walls and battlements were crumbling but in some rooms, roofless and exposed to the elements, there were beautiful mosaics and carvings and in one a lovely fretted window. In a courtyard of painted tiles, overlooked by the harem, a cherry tree bloomed and the caretaker picked sprigs of blossom for us.

In other places we visited, the buildings were of *pisé*, or brown sun-dried mud, merging imperceptibly into the tawny sun-baked land – Agdz, where we were assisting housing projects; Tenerhir, whence we visited the towering gorges of Todhra; Erfoud and Rissani, again in the Sahara. On our return northwards, through Ksar es Souk to Midelt, we found snow at Ifrane, but lower down picked violets by a stream before traversing fertile plains and orchards to Rabat.

When the mineral survey began I took several journeys through remote parts of the Atlas. There were happy memories, of almond blossom sparkling in spring on hill slopes and rocky gullies, otherwise stark of life, and of ill-fated attempts to learn to ski. But nothing could compare with that carefree week spent by the four of us, two of whom are no more.

A week later the diplomatic chiefs of mission received the usual last-minute royal command to attend the inauguration of a dam near

Ksar es Souk, a six-hour drive across the Atlas. The King had one of his many palaces handily nearby, but no one had bothered to think where the diplomats would rest their heads. There was a mad scramble for rooms in the small hotel at Midelt. A pre-dawn start to the dam site culminated in a long, hot wait in a semi-desert landscape, an experience that years later was also to befall Queen Elizabeth II. The King, when he finally appeared, was swathed in a white djellaba and hood, looking more like a ghostly mediaeval monk than a reigning monarch among the hordes of brightly gowned Moroccan men who swarmed in from the surrounding hills.

The timing was unfortunate. An American friend of Paul Hoffman's was to arrive that day, with his wife, to inspect our textile factory project in Fez. Anxious not to fall further into my boss's disfavour, I dashed back across the mountains to Fez.

Fez is a mediaeval jewel, with its fairytale palaces, towers and minarets, and its ancient Medina, a labyrinth of narrow tunnelled lanes, burrowing down between tiny shops. An encounter with a loaded, panniered donkey is a traumatic experience, and you need a guide – usually a small boy – if you are ever to find your way out. You descend into the Medina as into a mine secluded from all daylight, or a nether world where time has been frozen. You can buy everything imaginable – gold and silver jewellery, crafts of every description, rugs glowing with colour in the dim light, copper pans, carved furniture, pottery straight from the kilns, a veritable Aladdin's cave of treasures, each in its own quarter. In a second-hand clothes shop I once saw two grey-headed Moroccan men, dignified in the flowing folds of their traditional attire, cannily examining a djellaba: one had stuck his head inside to see, against the faint light of the doorway, whether it had any holes, while the other held the garment over his friend's head like a tent. From every side your senses are assailed by a thousand odours, some agreeable, some distinctly not: the scents of a myriad spices mingle with the stench of human and animal ordure, the tang of Arabic coffee wafting out of darkened doorways, the sickly sweet fragrance of mint tea, and of perfumes being concocted there and then. Near the tanneries small boys sell you posies of mint leaves to stave off the nauseating stench. Now and then the network of winding alleys opens into a miniature square, where sunlight streams in from a pure blue canopy of sky, shimmering on the delicate fretwork of sculptured roofs and balconies and heavy studded doors of a small medarsa, where young men are initiated into the intricacies of the Muslim faith and the Koran. All human life is there in the Medina, pulsing with activity and boundless surprises. I always found it enchanting.

My visitors were not so impressed. Nor did the textile factory, our prize project, arouse admiration. For Americans they were extraordinarily taciturn. The drive back to Rabat passed in heavy silence. I dreaded the report that would go back to my boss.

I had carefully planned a dinner of Abdul-Khedir's most irresistible dishes, including his famed soufflé. The only other guest was Valentina Lim, my old secretary in Manila, now my personal assistant in Rabat. By a blazing fireside we plied them with drinks and forcedly cheery conversation, but even Nena's impish Filipino humour fell flat. Suddenly Abdul-Khedir appeared, 'Mademoiselle!' he lamented as soon as we were out of earshot. 'The cat has had kittens under the dining-room table!'

There was Never, cradling a little ball of fur, spitting fury at allcomers. This was the final straw. Now, to the list of my shortcomings Mr Hoffman's crony could add that of letting wild cats run uncontrolled in my house. There was no escape but to tell the truth. The response was astonishing. My previously glum guests became animated. The wife exclaimed, 'How lovely' and declared that the new mother was in no way to be disturbed. We rearranged the table and for the rest of the evening my two guests ooh-ed and aah-ed over this miracle of nature. Abdul-Khedir's soufflé was flat, to his great chagrin, but the atmosphere and conversation were most certainly not.

I never received a report on the textile factory, but Hoffman wrote a charming letter, thanking me for treating his friends so well.

10 July 1971

Jacko, still travelling incessantly, felt himself to be in the wilderness and our separation weighed on him. He was full of doom and gloom, concerned about his health, especially his heart condition, which he referred to as OQM – 'Operation Question Mark', an operation contemplated in Australia in 1967, but discarded as too dangerous. In Ethiopia he had told me his life expectancy was about two years.

In May 1971 he attended an FAO conference in Casablanca, after which we drove to England where I was to have an operation on my leg. We stayed in Granada and Salamanca, in whose austere university precincts I rediscovered the spirit of Unamuno, and spent a delightful two days in the Languedoc, sampling claret, before we meandered up the western coast of France. After my operation I stayed at a hotel in the Mendip Hills until I was sufficiently recovered to help my father. During a brief stay in Herefordshire with my mother's sister Margaret and brother Henry, I had a brief encounter with the man I had first met five years earlier. Our feelings were unchanged but there appeared no possibility of his becoming free. I was resigned to this, and he accepted my relationship with Jacko.

Nena was to drive back with me to Morocco and arrived at Pippins after spending a couple of days with the Gibsons. Saturday 10 July 1971 is a day I am unlikely to forget – one of those crucial junctures where several disparate threads come together, and determine one's future. Under the old cider apple tree in Pippins garden Nena handed me a note from Mary Gibson containing a letter sent through her by the wife of my great love, generously offering to set him free. I spent the next few hours in turmoil, only to be thrown into new confusion by other events. Jacko and Nena had taken my father out to lunch and brought the news that he had collapsed; Jacko had even feared for his life. By the time they returned he had recovered, and adamantly refused to have the doctor called, saying the attack was due to the heat and an unaccustomed Campari. And then, while we were still arguing, the BBC six o'clock news announced that an attempt on King Hassan's life had been made at his birthday party in Skhirat and a terrible massacre had taken place.

All lines to Morocco were blocked but I telephoned C. V. Narasimhan in New York and said I would fly to Rabat next day. Next morning I got news from Jean-Pierre Schellenberg who had represented me at the ill-fated feast. At about two o'clock, when some of the 800 guests were playing golf and others partaking of the customarily sumptuous banquet, parachutists appeared in the sky and loud explosions were heard. At first the guests thought that this was part of the extravaganza that usually accompanied the King's parties – an aerial display and fireworks. Jean-Pierre and Mohammed Echiguer, who had wandered off by themselves, found a live grenade, and realised that the drama was real. Soldiers stripped them to their underwear and frogmarched them back to join ambassadors, ministers, and other dignitaries, forced at gunpoint to lie face down on the tarmac drive, under a broiling sun. The Belgian Ambassador had already succumbed to a stray bullet and died in an arbour, attended by a few distraught diplomatic colleagues. Over 100 people were killed on that bloody afternoon, and 200 wounded. A few, among them Mohammed Benhima, escaped along the beach. The King had withdrawn to his throne room and managed to alert loyal troops before the rebels cut telephone lines. The revolt was ostensibly led by the Chief of the King's Military Household, General Medbouh – though, as subsequent events showed, he had a secret backer: General Oufkir, the sinister Minister of the Interior, whose eyes were always hidden behind the darkest of dark glasses. The coup was badly planned. Medbouh was slain and in Rabat attempts to set up a Revolutionary Council and a Committee of the Popular Army were thwarted.

Many hours passed before the surviving guests were released from their ordeal. Jean-Pierre arrived home late at night clad only in his underwear. My father was more concerned by the fact that I too would have been stripped, had I been there, than by more lethal implications. He was not mollified by my flippant reply that Driss would have fashioned something from the UN car flag, remarking, with some asperity, that it would be 'far too small'.

By Sunday morning the Government had the situation under control, so Nena and I embarked at Southampton that evening as originally planned.

The problems awaiting in Morocco made it difficult to think clearly about the astonishing offer made to me on the same day as the Skhirat tragedy. Two or three years before I would have accepted with alacrity. Now circumstances had changed, though my sentiments had not. Jacko had come to rely on me, we had a happy companionship, and he had instituted legal proceedings to enable us to marry. It seemed the height of disloyalty to abandon him. The other pair had been married for many years. Was it not better to maintain the status quo, even if two of the four might be less happy than they could otherwise have been? Moreover the problems affecting my parents were worsening, and I did not see how I could simultaneously cope with the upheavals that acceptance of the offer would bring. The logic pointed inexorably in one direction. I let my head rule a heavy heart. It was a decision I was to regret ever afterwards, but even looking back now I had little alternative.

My Father's Death

My premonitions about my family were all too soon proved correct. On 10 September I snatched a weekend at Pippins, en route to meetings in Geneva and Rome. On the Saturday evening I had my last real conversation with my father. Perhaps he had a premonition − or perhaps had had other attacks about which he did not tell me. From Rome I was to fly to New York to see Gabriel Valdés who was still trying to persuade me to go to Chile. I had decided to refuse but my father insisted that I should accept. As with all the other chapters of my career he had informed himself about the situation in Chile and was well aware of the attractions of the posting and of my frustrations in Morocco. More ominously, had I but read the signs, he showed me where to find the briefcase containing his papers.

In Geneva I caught a severe chill, which worsened in Rome. So I changed my plans and flew to Rabat to collect an overcoat. On Saturday 25 September, I was about to step into the car bound for Casablanca and New York, when the telephone rang. The message was stark and laconic: 'Your father has had a stroke, and both your parents are in Weston-super-Mare Hospital.' I thanked Heaven that, by a complete fluke, I was not already in New York and flew to Paris, where I caught the last plane to London and the last train to Bath, where neighbours met me and rushed me to the hospital. My father, paralysed and speechless, managed a crooked smile. My mother was in a state of shock in the adjoining room. He had been found unconscious on the kitchen floor, late on Friday afternoon, by the village butcher. My bedridden mother was ringing the Swiss cowbell I had given her in a vain call for help.

Christina came and we spent the next three days at the hospital. The doctors said my father would survive but would be paralysed. They advised me to find a nursing home where my parents could be together. On the Wednesday my father looked worse. I wanted to stay the night, but the doctor pooh-poohed the idea. 'He is in no danger, and you must conserve your strength for difficult days ahead.' My father falteringly forced out the words, 'Go home' – the last he ever said to me.

To my eternal regret I obeyed him and not my instinct. Next morning at 7 a.m. the phone rang. I flew down the stairs. It was the hospital to say he was failing fast. I drove the 16 miles to Weston-super-Mare like the devil, but arrived too late; he had died alone a few minutes before. I have never forgiven myself for not having stayed that last night or for not having obliged him to see a doctor after the first attack. In response to my bitter recrimination the doctor who had advised me to leave protested that his death was totally unexpected. Later, news was published that, around the time of my father's stroke, a number of unexpected deaths had occurred in local hospitals, due to defective saline drips. To this day I believe he may have been one of the victims.

On that sad day, 30 September 1971, we drove my mother back to Pippins. I had taken her to my father's room the day before, for a pathetic last encounter. Shortly after her return home a strange incident occurred. My father had trained a sparrow, called Bertie, and his female companion, Gertie, to feed from our hands and fly across the garden in response to their names. His pride and joy was a robin, who came into the kitchen for crumbs. One morning the robin flew through the kitchen, finding its way unerringly to my parents' bedroom. There he perched at the bottom of my mother's bed and gazed penetratingly at her as if to say, 'Where is he? What have you done?' My normally calm mother became hysterical. The robin flew out and never came back.

I was in a state of shock. I had had plans for my father when my mother died, it never occurring to me that he might go first. He was cremated on 4 October. Jacko flew back from Cairo to be with me. At my mother's wish the ashes were buried under the old Blenheim apple tree from which my father had loved to contemplate the garden they had created together from a meadow. I looked after my mother for some weeks, and then engaged a nurse-housekeeper but she did not work out. Christina, who had just retired, gallantly moved to Pippins to care for her sister. The doctors told us that she would soon die but still she clung to life, with the determination that had characterised her whole existence.

Last Days in Morocco

In Morocco I was finalising the Country Background Paper, as the basis for the first Moroccan Country Programme, supported by an excellent team, drawn from my staff and agency representatives. It was praised as a model of what should be done – a relief to me as co-designer of the new system. I was also trying to persuade the Government to embark on a rural development programme based on a broader use of UN system resources and expertise already in the country, in order to squeeze the maximum benefit in favour of the poorest people. My experts responded enthusiastically but the Government gave only lip-service and no practical support. Social and rural development were not high on their agenda, perhaps even considered dangerously subversive. The scare at Skhirat had not wrought any change in the autocratic policies by which Morocco was ruled.

On 14 December I arrived in New York for the discussions postponed by my father's death. As a condition for accepting a transfer to Chile I negotiated a commitment of frequent missions to Europe and New York, so that I could visit my mother. Since I cost the organisation far less than colleagues with wives and children this was not unreasonable but, as I should have foreseen, the promise was never honoured.

I spent Christmas and New Year at Pippins, a decidedly unfestive season, the first without my father. The next eight weeks in

Morocco were a hectic round of work, farewell calls, receptions and packing. In contrast to the reluctance with which they had greeted me, the Government seemed genuinely sorry to see me go and decorated me in a surprise ceremony with the Order of Ouissam Alaouite, with the grade of *Commandeur*.

It was hard to define my feelings on leaving Morocco. There had been professional frustrations in dealing with a government uninterested in pursuing development in the broad, humanistic sense, as opposed to the large-scale investment projects that they and the World Bank favoured, but I had made warm personal friendships. And I was enchanted by the vast and varied beauty of the country: from the crenellated snowy peaks of the Atlas mountains to the rolling dunes of the desert and the craggy wilderness of the Rif; the rich farmlands and flowering orchards nearer the sea; and the magnificent coastline stretching from the balmy waters of the Mediterranean to the crashing breakers of the Atlantic. I regretted that I had not taken more time to explore these wonders, instead of bashing my head fruitlessly on an impenetrable stone wall of autocratic government.

There had been glimmerings of openings towards a more liberal and democratic society, with a greater role for the opposition party, Istiqlal, but Skhirat led to a new clampdown. About the King my feelings were ambivalent. I was shocked by the profligacy and autocratic nature of his court. I had had similar reactions to the pomp and circumstance surrounding Emperor Haile Selassie, but this surpassed it. There were extenuating circumstances in the case of the Emperor, essentially a mediaeval monarch, without formal education. Hassan II had enjoyed a modern university education in France but liked to have the best of both worlds and was even more fiercely feudal than Haile Selassie. Yet one had to admire his political shrewdness in playing off one side against another, and the courage and cool-headedness that saved his throne at Skhirat. Those qualities stood him in good stead over succeeding years, though his once handsome visage became increasingly ravaged.

As I was leaving Rabat on 28 February, our doctor rang to warn me that my mother might not last until I got there. I found her still alive but very weak. Christina and I nursed her day and night. The weeks went by and she still survived. I postponed my travel to Santiago and the UNDP administration began to hassle me. I asked for leave without pay, but was curtly told that I must use up my accumulated leave first. I considered resigning but was dissuaded by the doctor.

The one bright spot in an otherwise dark panorama was that Jacko was given a worthwhile job. When he was staying at Pippins for Easter 1972 the new Secretary-General, Kurt Waldheim, asked him to take on the Bangladesh emergency operation. Mishandled in its earlier days, it presented a daunting and complex challenge, the kind of political and logistical tangle that he was superbly equipped to unravel.

After five weeks Christina and I were exhausted. I found the best nursing home in Bath, and with heavy hearts we took my mother there on 4 April. It was hard to make her understand what was happening and her look of bewilderment as she left Pippins for the last time was heart-rending. The house was to be let, to help defray nursing home fees. On 9 April I left for Chile.

My flight stopped over in Casablanca, very late at night, but Taibi and Marie-Thérèse Benhima were there and I was swept into the VIP lounge, where Dom Pérignon champagne awaited, for an emotional farewell. Restored to favour, Taibi had been appointed Minister of the Interior in succession to General Oufkir, who had been transferred to the Ministry of Defence, as part of the shake-up of the military establishment that the King deemed necessary in the wake of Skhirat. In Oufkir he had made a dangerously mistaken choice.

A few months later, on 16 August 1972, Benhima found himself in the firing line again, when the royal plane bringing the King from Paris was attacked by four Air Force fighter planes. Although hit several times, the Boeing 727 limped into Rabat Airport, where ministers were assembled to greet their monarch, with the exception of Oufkir. Hardly had the King passed into the *Salon d'honneur* when fighter planes strafed the airport and the reception line. There were several dead and seriously injured, among the latter my friend Mustapha Faris, the Planning Minister.

News was already being broadcast that His Majesty had been killed but he was unscathed and again behaved with valour and sangfroid. It was soon discovered that Oufkir had ordered the attack and it was Benhima who, with great presence of mind, saved the day by giving counter-orders and summoning loyal troops. He himself arrested Oufkir, whom he described to me as an 'old friend and former comrade-in-arms' in the blow-by-blow accounts he personally sent me in Santiago.

Oufkir did not survive long. Some said he shot himself with a revolver that someone pointedly left near him. But Benhima told me later it was the King himself who despatched him.

────── 15 ──────

Chile: Democracy Subverted

Salvador Allende and his Socialist Party had made successive attempts to win power through the democratic electoral process. Victory had nearly been theirs in 1958 and in 1964 was probably foiled by the large sums of money that the USA – alarmed at the thought of a leftist government in Chile as well as Cuba – poured into their opponents' coffers. In September 1970 Allende won 36.3 per cent of the vote. Since 50 per cent was required for outright election, a decision by the Chilean Congress was entailed, a dangerous seven weeks' hiatus during which the United States pulled out every stop to thwart Allende's election. President Nixon instructed the CIA to 'save Chile' from Allende (whom he referred to as 'that sonofabitch'), to 'leave no stone unturned ... to block Allende's confirmation' and to 'make the economy scream.'[1]

On the eve of the crucial debate in Congress the CIA instigated a botched attempt to kidnap General René Schneider, Commander-in-Chief of the Chilean Army, hoping the military would then seize power. Instead, the General was killed, the military closed ranks and General Carlos Prats became Commander-in-Chief. Two days later, on 24 October 1970, Allende was confirmed as President.

Despite drastic curtailment of US aid and credit to Chile and difficulties with the United States over the nationalisation of the copper mines, 1971 went better than expected. Keynesian pump-priming initiatives launched by Pedro Vuskovic, the Minister of

---

1. Nathaniel Days, former US Ambassador to Chile, *The Last Two Years of Salvador Allende*, Cornell University Press, pp. 6–8.

Economy, resulted in a 12 per cent increase in industrial output and a more far-reaching programme of land reform was also undertaken. In April 1971 the Unidad Popular ('UP' as Allende's supporting coalition was known), won municipal elections with a greatly increased vote.

Towards the end of 1971, however, inflation rose alarmingly. Worse still, world prices for copper, Chile's main export, began to decline. This may well have been the result of National Security Decision Memorandum 93 issued by Henry Kissinger in November 1970, which established a policy of pressure on Allende's government to prevent its consolidation and ordered a review of steps to drive down the price of copper.[2] Chile's reserves were depleted, and the Government called a moratorium on its external debt. A visit in November 1971 by Fidel Castro, who came for ten days but stayed three weeks, hardly reinforced either national or international confidence. Many basic consumer items disappeared from shop counters to fuel a growing black market, and 5000 middle-class housewives took to the streets in a cacophonous protest, banging empty saucepans. The economy was beginning to scream.

UNCTAD III

I was not in good shape myself when I arrived on 10 April 1972. I had postponed my arrival to the last possible moment before the opening of the Third General Conference of the United Nations Conference on Trade and Development (UNCTAD III), a huge affair involving delegations from every UN member state. It lasted six weeks and once all the grandees left I headed the UN delegation for this gruelling marathon. I had simultaneously to take charge of one of UNDP's largest programmes in Latin America. The deputy post was vacant and my assistant resident representative, Ramiro Paz, son of my old friend Víctor Paz Estenssoro, the former President of Bolivia, was a brilliant but unpredictable young man.

2. Idem, pp. 21–22.

I barely had time to present my credentials to the Foreign Minister, Clodomiro Almeyda, on 11 April, before Gabriel Valdés arrived, followed next day by Kurt Waldheim (who had become UN Secretary-General three months earlier), at 4 a.m. on 13 April, just in time for the opening of the conference. During the intervening hours Ramiro picked a fight with Valdés and resigned. Less than 72 hours after my arrival I had no international supporting staff.

My first encounters with Waldheim were hardly more auspicious. On Saturday 15 April the Minister of Planning, Gonzalo Martner, who had worked with me in Bolivia, invited me to a working lunch in Viña Del Mar where the President had sent him to take charge of reconstruction works after a recent earthquake.

I drove to Viña on the road that snakes its way down to the coast through tawny, cactus-spiked hills and hamlets of tile-roofed *ranchitos*, garlanded with dusty bougainvillea. Gonzalo was ensconced in some splendour in the presidential seaside palace. We lunched in similar style, waited on by presidential retainers, talked about the situation of the country, and walked by the roaring breakers of the Pacific. Tea was brought to us in President Allende's study high up in one of the turrets. Immediately afterwards I was to drive back to Santiago for an official dinner. Suddenly there was a commotion downstairs. Peering down on to the marbled entrance hall two storeys below we saw Waldheim being ushered in with someone Gonzalo identified as a senior Foreign Ministry diplomat – 'A *momio*', he added scornfully, using the derogatory term (mummy) applied in Chilean slang to right-wing opponents of the Government. The two unexpected visitors proceeded to partake of a leisurely tea, blissfully unaware of onlookers above. I had no problem about joining them but Gonzalo was adamant that under no circumstances would he meet the *momio*.

Time passed and my exit, increasingly urgent if I was to reach Santiago in time, remained blocked. Any explanation to my new boss of my sudden appearance from upstairs with the minister, which would have been perfectly natural in the first instance, became ever more implausible. Gonzalo said there was another way out by a back staircase, but it entailed crawling along a tunnel under the roof. I bowed to the inevitable and the minister, with the UN Head of Mission close behind, wriggled on their stomachs along the pitch-black tunnel, emerging dusty and dishevelled. The final challenge was to get to the car without being seen. I was greatly relieved to drive away, leaving Waldheim in happy ignorance of the drama played out above his head.

An issue that took up much of my time during UNCTAD III was the proposed creation, within UNDP, of a Capital Development Fund (CDF). The only public international source of capital was the World Bank group, usually large-scale and provided at interest rates many countries found hard to meet, even when they qualified for concessionary terms through the International Development Association (IDA). The CDF was a modest version of the original SUNFED idea, designed to provide grant capital for the small-scale projects that are often most effective in reducing poverty. I was a fervent advocate of the idea, which was supported by developing countries, but opposed by Europe and the United States. I was caught in the middle of this acrimonious debate, constantly called on to testify to one or other group. The most heartening happening was a meeting with some young Dutch Parliamentarians, led by Jan Pronk, later a prominent politician, who pressed a cheque into my hand for the as yet non-existent fund.

Otherwise I got nowhere, mainly because of strong American objections, vociferously expounded by their delegation leader who said it was a load of nonsense. Some years later, the same head of delegation went to Bangladesh as UNDP Resident Representative. On mission there as Assistant Administrator of UNDP, I found his programme peppered with successful small projects funded by CDF (which had meanwhile been created), and he proclaimed, without the hint of a blush, 'The CDF is a valuable instrument; I couldn't do without.' It was a telling example of the importance of practical experience, as opposed to ideological theory.

Salvador Allende

My first audience with President Allende took place *à deux* in his office in La Moneda Palace. Audience is too formal a word, for it was, from the start, a most cordial and relaxed relationship. Salvador Allende was rotund and rubicund, yet cut a very dapper figure by virtue of his erect bearing, crisp moustache, and clothes that, formal or casual, were always impeccable. You could see at once that he loved life, bringing boundless energy and enthusiasm to whatever he did, work or play. He was an unabashed bon vivant, though to my mind that was part of his attraction and in no way contradicted his determination to improve the lot of the many poor people in Chile through democratic and constitutional means. In fact, it increased his popular appeal, for most Chileans are noted – or were then, before tragedy hit – for savouring the good life, and for humour and sparkling jollity, however straitened their material circumstances.

Allende put me quickly at my ease, though I was disconcerted when his opening gambit was, '*Cómo es su gracia?*' – an elegant way of ascertaining my first name. I should not have been surprised, for his partiality for ladies was well known. Thus from the first moment I became 'Margarita'. He knew a lot about me, as I did about him from some of his ministers and other high officials who had worked with me in Bolivia ten years before. Over coffee we had a lively conversation about Chile's problems, and how the UN could help in improving living conditions and, more generally, relations with the rest of the world, where many countries were watching the Chilean experiment with misgiving and, in some cases, open hostility.

Whenever we met he always showed warm friendship and appreciation of what UN mission was trying to do. I came to admire his astute intelligence and genuine commitment to his ideals, and to like his exuberant and kindly personality.

Interlude in UK

Relationships with UNDP's administration were less easy. My promotion to D2 (Senior Director – another first for a woman in UN), delayed by rancour over my part in the Capacity Study, at last came through. But the commitments about travel to see my mother were never honoured. My home leave was due in June

1972 but Vaidyanathan informed me that I had used up all my leave in nursing my mother after my father's death and refused to allow me to take leave without pay. The bureaucracy was not prepared to lift a finger to help single women with responsibilities for infirm parents, even though we were the cheapest staff the organisation had.

I was desperate. My mother was counting the days until my arrival. I was exhausted after months of emotional strain, followed by grinding hard work in Chile, where New York had failed to provide any international supporting staff. A doctor certified that I must have two months' rest and I left for England. My leave was hardly restful. I travelled daily to Bath to see my mother and occupied the rest of the time preparing Pippins for tenants. Then Jacko came and we snatched a few days in Europe.

Return to Bolivia

When I returned to Chile the national holidays in September enabled me to spend a weekend in La Paz. It was seven years since I had left Bolivia and little of what had happened in the interim gave cause for rejoicing. Barrientos, the charismatic military usurper who had snuggled up to me on a journey into the jungle, had died in April 1969, in a mysterious plane crash. Elections due in 1970 had been forestalled by a military junta, led by General Ovando, the same who fled the palace in the 1964 revolution. He was overthrown a year later by a populist military President, General Juan José Torres, but that government succumbed to a far from bloodless coup in August 1971, led by General Hugo Banzer Suárez, who ruled with a rod of iron for the next seven years.

No one could understand why Víctor Paz Estenssoro, three times democratically elected President, had returned from exile to join Banzer's government. His friends, including myself, could only conclude that he feared he would never have another chance to exercise power. It was a mistake likely to damage his reputation as a statesman and I told him so over afternoon tea in a modest house on Calle 6 de Agosto. I was surprised by my own temerity and even more surprised when he agreed. By then he was disillusioned with Banzer and had broken with him.

The Dream Fades

Pedro Vuskovic's 'economic miracle' was collapsing in galloping inflation, scarcity of basic goods siphoned into the black market and a vertiginous decline in the value of the peso. The workers had undoubtedly deserved a better deal, but now they staged constant strikes, clamouring for higher wages still. Land reform was creating its own problems, with many peasants taking things into their own hands, while landowners formed pockets of resistance. In some areas internal order had broken down and armed groups from both ends of the political spectrum roamed the countryside.

I did not meet Pedro as often as I had expected, given our long friendship. He was a changed personality. In place of the tolerant, genially smiling man I had known in Bolivia, I found a dour fanatic pursuing ideological ends. Now in power, after years of advising others, he seemed fired with zeal to bring about maximum change with minimum delay. In a way he was right: there was a real sense of 'now or never' about this government, and half-hearted approaches were likely to get bogged down through skilful manoeuvring by powerful opposition forces. But Pedro went too far and I no longer recognised the friend of yesteryear.

One of the many ironies was that the Communist Party, which was a member of Allende's UP coalition, constantly urged a slower pace of reform, fearing that over-precipitate action would jeopardise the whole process. It was the far left of the Socialist Party, including Pedro, that insisted on rapid change, and was ultimately responsible, together with the extreme right opposition, for the fall of Allende. Allende himself always steered a middle course. Gonzalo, the Planning Minister, was more receptive of advice than Pedro. On Sundays we would drive into the country-side to see the problems in the raw. While we agreed on the aims of the Government's policies we had spirited discussions about how they were being implemented. Close friend and delightful companion as he was, I became worried that his feet were not always firmly on the ground.

Once again I found myself in a delicate political situation. The confidence placed in me by the highest levels of government made me an object of suspicion to their opponents. I had to work all the harder to preserve the objectivity and impartiality that must infuse all UN activities. My task was hardly facilitated by some politically sensitive projects and some UN experts less than punctilious about observing UN norms of conduct. An FAO project on land reform became a major *casus belli*. Our project manager was a brilliant American academic who believed passionately and uncompromisingly in his mission. Rightly or wrongly, he and his colleagues were perceived as unconditional allies of the government in some of its more headstrong actions.

This was child's play compared to the activities of a Spaniard named Joan Garcés. Before my arrival Gabriel Valdés had acceded to the President's pressing request for his services. Garcés was appointed by UNESCO to a project entitled 'Social Development', but in practice became Allende's speech writer and political adviser, a very grey area for a UN civil servant that did not go unobserved by the opposition. On numerous occasions I begged Garcés to circumscribe his activities within his job description and the limitations of a UN role. He was always courteous but immovable, a man with a mission who had been given a God-sent opportunity to carry it out. Nor was Gabriel himself any more successful in similar démarches to the President who insisted that Garcés was indispensable.

Garcés was by Allende's side in La Moneda on 11 September 1973 when the Pinochet coup took place. He escaped to find refuge in the Spanish Embassy. The Spanish Ambassador, Enrique Iglesias (the Head of the UN Economic and Social Commission for Latin America – ECLA) and I then had to pull all the strings at our command to obtain a safe exit for him, for he was the *bête noire* of the coup leaders. In 1998, 25 years later, I recognised a name among the instigators of the request for the British Government to extradite General Pinochet to Spain. It was Joan Garcés.

In October 1972, a national truckers' strike paralysed the country, sparked off by a government decision to establish a state enterprise for land, water and air transport in the southern provinces. With lightning rapidity the stoppage extended to other sectors and there was sporadic violence. It is hard to believe that such a complete blockade was effected without external support. US animosity towards the regime continued unabated, fuelled by bitter negotiations over the expropriation of US copper companies. In April–May 1972 there were several mysterious break-ins into the Chilean Embassy in Washington, though it was only much later that CIA involvement, long suspected, was documented. Now, in the midst of this nationwide strike, the Chilean peso, which had been dropping like a stone, suddenly rose in value, a highly unlikely phenomenon unless dollars were pouring in to support the strikers.

The strike was ended at high political cost. Senior military officers were brought into the cabinet, General Prats, the Head of the Army, becoming Minister of the Interior. Pedro Vuskovic's head rolled. He became Head of the Chilean Development Corporation, but was no longer the economic tsar. The October strike marked a watershed after which the slide into the abyss became inexorable.

My Mother's Death

An international consultation organised by the Canadian Development Agency outside Montreal allowed me to fly to England in early November to spend two days with my mother, whom I had not seen for three months. I went at my own expense. UNDP Headquarters even tried to forbid me to go to Montreal, although the meeting was of direct relevance to our work.

It was a very low period. The Chilean experiment in social reform into which I had put my heart and soul was failing, and my beloved mother had not long to live. I rarely saw Jacko and the prospects for our coming together permanently were in abeyance. Sir Ronald Bodley Scott had told Jacko in August 1971 that Barbara's cancer had returned and she was too frail for matters to proceed. Yet a few months later she had appeared in Santiago to address UNCTAD III, under the auspices of the Vatican, and had insisted on inviting me to tea, a very awkward occasion. I had no proper home. Too busy and tired to seek one, I had been staying with my friends from Uruguay, Valentina and José Ugarte, who were the soul of kindness, but I needed a place of my own. So I felt enormous relief when, through a chapter of coincidences, I found a furnished house I liked and could afford. I moved there in December 1972.

Villa Clara Rosa, hidden in the steep valley of El Arrayán in the foothills of the cordillera, was named after its owner, a Venezuelan millionairess reputed to espouse the Communist cause. Her current consort was a Chilean scientist, the brother of Carlos Altamirano, the ultra-left Secretary-General of the Socialist Party, a connection that caused grievous problems later. The house was in poor repair, but its beautifully laid out grounds covered four acres, and contained over 2000 rose bushes. Trees and shrubberies cascaded down to the River Mapocho, which rushed along one boundary, swollen with the melted snow of the Andes. There was a swimming-pool on its banks and across the river rose steep cliffs, merging into a sunburnt and cactus-spiked hillside, where mountain goats performed acrobatics among the pinnacled crags. Ramón, an elderly half-collie, came with the house, and whenever I took a bath a small owl peered through a skylight preening himself vigorously. It became a daily ritual to perform our ablutions simultaneously. The two gardeners had been born and bred in the village, the head one called Delicio, a name so appropriate as to imply that he had been intended from birth to tend this idyllic place.

I flew to England to spend Christmas with my mother. The flight was delayed and it was not until late on Christmas Eve that I reached Bath. Christina had taken a flat in a nearby village where Nena joined me. We spent Christmas Day with my mother, and Jacko arrived a day later. My mother's last message to me in Chile, scrawled with great difficulty, had been that she longed to see me. Perhaps she had waited for me to arrive for, early in the morning of 28 December, I was called to her bedside and found her unconscious. The doctor asked whether efforts should be made to resuscitate her. My instinct was that she should be left to go in peace, but it was a hard decision to take alone. I rang Christina, who also agreed. At about two o'clock that afternoon my mother breathed her last. For her, at least, I was there, holding her hand. She did not regain consciousness, but perhaps knew I was present. She died on Jim's birthday, her adored brother, killed in 1917.

The loss of both my beloved parents within a year hit me hard. I threw myself into the oblivion of work, arranging the funeral with what some considered unseemly speed. It took place in Bath, on New Year's Day 1973, on a cold, bright winter afternoon that my mother would have loved. Beyond the windows of the cremat-orium the Somerset countryside, where she had been so happy, lay spread in sparkling sunshine.

Life in Chile

When I returned to Santiago in early February, after briefings in Europe and New York, the southern summer was waning. María Angélica Jünemann, a Chilean member of my staff, had become a close friend and often stayed with me. My original housekeeper, a rotund lady called Victoria, had evaporated during my absence. Segundo Bugueño was recommended and I asked him to come for a trial weekend. Just as María Angélica and I were relaxing by the swimming-pool on Saturday afternoon a terrible turmoil erupted. Segundo came running down the steps, followed by the dishevelled figure of the Minister of Planning. It transpired that Gonzalo had decided to arrive unannounced but the defective bell at the entrance, at the end of a long avenue, failed to function. Undeterred, he had scaled the wall, topped by barbed wire, and broken glass and was impaled on these heights when Segundo, alerted by Ramón's barking, arrived on the scene, convinced that he was going to secure his future by capturing a would-be burglar. Disgusted by the outcome, he announced the distinguished visitor, muttering the while, '*Está más despistado que el mismo Presidente Allende*' (He's even more at sea than President Allende).

Segundo, although born in the humblest rural circumstances and illiterate, had worked in the best households and was an ardent ultra-conservative. He disapproved of my receiving Allende's Ministers, especially if they appeared over the wall, and could not understand why I advised a government so clearly bent on the perdition of the nation. Notwithstanding he served me devotedly for eight years and became part of my family.

I was concurrently the UNDP Liaison Officer with ECLA, and headed the UNDP delegation to its biennial meeting in Quito in March 1973, where 'the Chilean experiment' was the drama of the moment. In a recent much-acclaimed speech in Nairobi Robert McNamara, the World Bank President, had announced that agrarian and educational reform and fair distribution of resources were prerequisites for development and for World Bank funding. These were priority policies of the Allende government, but notwithstanding the Bank was withholding funds from Chile. I advised Gonzalo, who headed the Chilean delegation, to highlight this contradiction in a speech that would put the Bank on the spot, and perhaps obtain much-needed financial support.

The Latin American countries formed a common front, demanding a more pragmatic and generous response from the United States to the continent's development problems, in a document entitled 'The Quito Declaration'. A battle royal ensued over the draft, with the Americans opposing key clauses. This was the occasion when the Cuban Minister, Carlos Rafael Rodriguez, got into the act, recalling Lewis Carroll's connections, as earlier mentioned.

In Quito I had my second encounter with Kurt Waldheim. He asked me to accept, from 1 June 1973, a seven-month secondment to UN Headquarters in New York as Deputy to Jacko in the Bangladesh relief operation, The intensity of the work had told on Jacko's health, and he had been given the additional task of organising UN Emergency Assistance to Zambia. On the personal front this had the attraction of being near to Jacko and working with him was professionally stimulating, while our programme in Chile was bogged down by the political and economic crisis. Nonetheless, I had serious qualms about leaving so fraught a situation.

There were lengthy consultations between the Secretary-General, UNDP and the Government. In Chile the matter went up to President Allende himself, and it was not until early May that he agreed to a compromise: I would retain my responsibilities as resident representative, visiting Chile every two months.

Meanwhile, there was one happy interlude in April, when Gonzalo Martner invited me, and some of my staff, to accompany him to southern Chile. We visited UNDP projects and explored with the provincial authorities a new initiative in regional planning and development. This was to go hand-in-hand with greater devolution and decentralisation, and Gonzalo had adopted my idea, originally attempted in Morocco, of drawing on the mass of international experts in the country to help, in addition to their normal job descriptions. This would also link existing projects more closely into the overall pattern of government policy. Like so many good ideas of that time, it was doomed by subsequent events.

The week-long trip took us to Talca; to the valley of the River Maule, with its port of Constitución; to Concepción, where I had experts working in a steel mill, and Talcahuano; to the coal mines at Lota and Schwagger; to Los Angeles, and an FAO project for soil conservation and irrigation; to Temuco, and our large forestry project; and to Valdivia, where we were helping to set up an institute of dairy technology. Our visit to the coal mines involved descending 3500 feet and then travelling five miles under the Pacific Ocean, first in coal trucks, and then shuffling along dark tunnels on foot. True to form I fell flat on my face, and in the process dislodged the lamp on my helmet, so that afterwards I steered an even more unsteady course. We visited the beautiful lake of Villarica, with its symmetrical white volcano towering in the background and reflected in its pellucid waters. We laughed a great deal, ate in the local markets, and had a hilarious experience in Concepción when Gonzalo, intending a good deed, tried to give a lift to a passer-by, who, when we buckled a seat belt round him fled like a startled rabbit, fearing imminent kidnap. On another journey we crossed to the island of Chiloe, where fisher folk maintain old traditions and went as far south as Aysén, where the Chilean navy took us on a patrol through the fjords.

Even at the time these trips had a nostalgic quality. Nothing was ever to be quite the same again.

Bangladesh and Zambia

It was a wrench leaving Villa Clara Rosa in June, when the garden was still ablaze with autumn colours and the persimmon tree glowed like an unseasonal Christmas tree. I had an affectionate farewell meeting on 16 May with Allende, and was with him again on 29 May, when he gave a lunch for the President of the UN General Assembly. I little imagined that this was the last time I would see him alive.

In New York the pace was hectic. As Jacko's deputy I was fully involved in both the Bangladesh and Zambia operations and in charge of the office during his frequent missions. Typically, Jacko had been called in only when the first operation, UNEPRO, set up by the previous Secretary-General, U Thant in 1971, was in serious difficulties. In November 1970 what was then East Pakistan suffered a catastrophic cyclone. The dilatory response of Pakistan's central government, on the other side of the subcontinent, had major political repercussions, leading to the electoral victory, in December 1970, of Sheikh Mujibar Rahman and his Awami League and a demand for autonomy. Negotiations broke down in March 1971. At that point U Thant offered humanitarian assistance. Almost simultaneously civil war erupted and the suffering was compounded by hundreds of thousands of refugees pouring over the Indian frontier. In December 1971 war broke out between Pakistan and India over Bangladesh and, with the Soviet Union and China on opposing sides, the Security Council met in emergency session. There was stalemate until the Pakistan forces suddenly surrendered and the independent state of Bangladesh was born.

The earlier problems, on top of grinding poverty, were exacerbated by the ravages of the war. Ten million refugees were returning from India and 100 million people were in imminent danger of starvation, many without shelter, with the monsoon fast approaching. The ports of Chalna and Chittagong, vital for delivering humanitarian aid, were blocked by wrecked and sunken ships, the internal transport system was paralysed and telecommunications shattered. Seldom can a new country have started life in direr circumstances.

UNROD replaced UNEPRO in late December 1971 but initially was no more successful. As Sir Brian Urquhart's memoirs (*A Life in Peace and War*) make clear, the reason for Jacko being called in only when matters were in disarray was related to the Capacity Study. This 'telling study of the UN system,' he recalled, 'had much offended some of the Specialised Agency heads and, in particular, Paul Hoffman ... ' 'This,' he goes on,

> had discouraged U Thant, in spite of my repeated urgings, from assigning Jackson to the East Pakistan (now Bangladesh) problem earlier. Greatly to his credit, Waldheim overrode these objections, and Jackson was persuaded to take charge of the Bangladesh operation.

Urquhart noted that the international rescue operation called for 'extraordinary leadership and skill' and observed 'at long last we switched from quixotic amateurism to large-scale professionalism ...'

> Jacko's enormous experience was coupled with imagination, drive, a world view, and a comprehensive approach which covered politics, finance, availability of supplies, shipping, transport and communications, the weather, crop prospects, grain futures, and the morale of all the people he was dealing with. He gave himself totally to the task in hand and seemed to have no other interests.

In Bangladesh there was an urgent need for practically everything. Jackson first got salvage operations going in the main ports, even getting the Soviet Navy's assistance in Chittagong. He chartered the supertanker *Manhattan* for grain storage in the Bay of Bengal until we could provide inflatable warehouses. He procured mini-bulkers – tiny tankers – for internal transport. He made plans for the planting and harvest, worried about the monsoon, badgered the UN Specialised Agencies and the voluntary agencies into cooperating, pursued governments for contributions in cash and kind, and juggled vast quantities of commodities, including grain and rice, to take the maximum advantage of the best market prices. He set target dates and objectives and constantly urged the somewhat bewildered officials of the new state of Bangladesh to keep to them. He insisted on the United Nations system of autonomous agencies and programmes speaking, for once, with one voice and acting with a common objective.

With the exception of UNRRA, which Jacko had master-minded in the 1940s. UNROD was the largest relief operation the UN had ever undertaken and, after inauspicious beginnings, by far the most successful. The aid mobilised totalled some US$1.5 billion. Two-thirds came from bilateral funds and over US$100 million through non-governmental organisations, the balance being provided multilaterally through the UN, which called the shots. UNROD (which entered a third phase as UNROB in April 1973) was the prototype of the integrated manner in which a complex, emergency operation ought to be conducted. Jacko operated on the principle of 'three umbrellas': the first encompassed the UN system; the second covered the bilateral contributions from governments; the third, non-governmental organisations.

He brought this vast endeavour together by having a clear strategic plan, with well-defined objectives and priorities based on reliable assessments of needs. He also ensured a steady flow of information to everyone involved and his regular briefings of governments were legendary: frank, hard-hitting and breezy. Through similar tactics he hacked a path through the jungle of UN procedures and bureaucratic trappings. Never had contracts been signed or staff recruited with such speed. Yet he had a tiny staff at Headquarters: two professionals, and three secretaries, plus occasional advisers. Jacko shuttled tirelessly between New York, Dacca and various capitals. The Capacity Study principle of maximum delegation was applied and there was a running dialogue by code cable – in colourful non-UNese language – between Dacca and New York. At Headquarters he engaged the enthusiastic cooperation of everyone even remotely involved. Weekly lunches in his conference room brought under secretaries-general cheek-by-jowl alongside the clerk who ensured that we received urgent code messages in the middle of the night, the nurse who gave field staff their shots and even the man who cleaned the office and filled the water jugs. The present secretary-general, Kofi Annan, then a junior official, was often there. On trips to Dacca, Jacko went laden with basic necessities for field staff and helped resolve their family problems. It was a team effort par excellence and everyone, however humble their role, felt they had a stake in UNROD's success.

When UNROB was phased out at the end of 1973, it had achieved its objectives against formidable odds: 100 million people had been saved from starvation; the wrecked transport system restored; and the country helped towards a viable future. One of my last acts in UNROB was to write a memorandum for the Secretary-General on the lessons to be learned from the experience. No action was ever taken on it. Yet the handling of the Bangladesh operation should be the model for managing the many complex emergencies that have arisen since the Cold War. They present the same combination of civil strife and populations stricken by natural and man-made disasters and require the same integrated response by the international community: simultaneous political and humanitarian action and an evolution from relief and rehabilitation to normal development coopera-tion. Like the Capacity Study, the Bangladesh experience is still relevant.

Zambia was a different emergency. President Kaunda asked for assistance under Article 50 of the UN Charter, which allows such requests from member states facing economic problems as a result of carrying out measures decreed by the Security Council – in this case, sanctions against Rhodesia. It was the first time the article had ever been invoked, but Zambia became a precedent. We had to assess the economic cost to Zambia of applying the sanctions (no easy task), estimate the aid required to offset it; and advise the government on alternative routes, bypassing Rhodesia, for its imports and exports.

In July 1973 I spent ten days in Lusaka estimating the economic cost to Zambia before Jacko joined me for discussions with the Government. He approached the task with customary pragmatism, insisting that we visit a supermarket to see whether forbidden goods were sneaking their way across the frontier. In a corner we discovered some bottles of Cointreau. 'Ah, but look,' said Jacko, 'they are thick with dust and must predate sanctions.'

At a working lunch with Kaunda and his ministers my place could not be found at the table, and it was Kaunda who solved the problem: it had been assumed that I was a man. Before lunch started Kaunda not only said grace, but then switched on a small radio for the BBC News and bade everyone be quiet until it was over. Afterwards tea was served, and it was Kaunda who played 'mother', wielding the huge teapot himself.

I was impressed with his intellectual grasp and personal simplicity and had reason to be grateful to him. The Zambian Ambassador to the UN began to make unpleasant noises about Jacko and myself being British. The main attack was on me. Considering how many hours I sweated on Zambia's behalf, and my 20 years as an international civil servant, I was bitterly hurt. Kurt Waldheim, ever ready to bend to the prevailing political wind, seemed likely to remove me. Kaunda was outraged and wrote a personal letter to him, clearly drafted by himself, in which he praised my work, adding that I enjoyed his complete confidence and that he would be happy to have me working in his own office.

I was saddened when Kaunda, unlike Nyerere in Tanzania, clung on to power too long, surrounded by sycophants who concealed from him the rumblings of popular discontent. Observing from afar, through the prism of the media, he seemed to become a different person from the modest man I met and liked in 1973.

From Lusaka we went on to Dar-es-Salaam to inspect one of the key ports. The Tanzam railway, still under construction by the Chinese, was another important element, as were the ports of Beira in Mozambique and Lobito and the Benguela railway in Angola. We completed our work in time for Jacko to report to the summer session of the ECOSOC in Geneva on 17 July.

Debacle in Chile

At the end of July I returned to Chile to find an even more alarming situation. In congressional elections, in March, the UP had gained six seats in the Chamber of Deputies and 43.4 per cent of the votes, compared to Allende's 36.3 per cent in 1970, and two seats in the Senate, giving it 40 per cent of the upper chamber. This apparently encouraging result actually worsened the situation, giving confidence to extreme leftists in the UP and making it more difficult for Allende to control them. It also increased the already dangerous degree of polarisation, fuelling the conviction among extreme opposition elements, including those military who had been plotting coups (three were rumoured in 1972 and early 1973), that there was no constitutional way out of the impasse.

There were more strikes, violence spread to Santiago, and paramilitary armed groups were formed by the extreme left and by an ultra-reactionary rightist group called Patria y Libertad. The latter plotted with restive military officers of the Second Armoured Regiment to mount a coup and kidnap Allende on 27 June. The plan leaked and the regimental Colonel, informed that he was relieved of his command, led his tanks and troops in an attack on the Ministry of Defence and the Moneda Palace. There was an incongruous orderliness about the affair: the armed column obeyed all the traffic lights in its advance and one tank stopped at a petrol station to fill up!

The *tancazo* was quickly suppressed by General Prats, but it marked the beginning of the end. In riposte, workers seized factories, more paramilitary groups sprang up and relations between the military and the President worsened. Three Cabinet reshuffles took place in two months. In the second of these, on 9 August, the military returned briefly to government, with General Prats assuming the portfolio of defence. On 23 August General Augusto Pinochet succeeded him as Commander-in-Chief, swearing allegiance to the President.

Allende was worried about the safety of General Prats, his constitutional bulwark among the military, whose strict adherence to legitimacy was eroding his support from other senior officers. I was electrified to learn from Gonzalo that, after the *tancazo*, the President asked him to request my permission for General Prats to live in Villa Clara Rosa during my absence, since it was near the President's heavily guarded estate in El Arrayán. Fortunately, Gonzalo shot this down and I was spared the embarrassment of telling the Head of State that I could not accept his Commander-in-Chief as a lodger.

When I arrived Santiago was agog with a new drama: three days earlier, the President's naval aide, Captain Araya, was shot on the balcony of his house in the middle of the night, in circumstances that could have been either political or a crime of passion. Tensions mounted and hopes for a peaceful outcome were pinned on negotiations between the Christian Democrats and the Government but they seemed to reach a dead end on 3 August.

On 9 August I hosted a dinner at Villa Clara Rosa, to which I invited several ambassadors – the American, Nathaniel Davis, the Italian and the French among them – as well as Gonzalo and other Chilean ministers. At the last minute the situation prevented the Chileans from coming. The situation could hardly be more grave, but we saw a glimmer of hope in the latest information: the Christian Democrats and the Government were talking again and might yet reach an agreement that could save constitutional government. I was impressed by Nathaniel Davis's even-handed approach. The US was painted as the villain of the piece by Allende supporters, and there could be no doubt, as was amply proved later, that powerful US forces had long been at work to bring Allende down. My instinct at that dinner was that Davis, a career diplomat, was not a party to all this, and his book on Chile shows that he did not know the whole truth.

During those days the weather was of an extreme and cloudless beauty, the garden banked in violets and spring flowers, magnolias, peach and cherry were in bloom, and plum blossom hung like snow outside my study window. The nights were cold, the garden frosted in moonlight. From my balcony I watched the shadows of the pine trees along the river bank and pondered the poignant contrast between this beauty and tranquillity and the ominous events unravelling all around.

The last Sunday was misty. Gonzalo came to lunch. He was steeped in gloom but, with María Angélica, we scrambled over the hills higher up the valley, catching fleeting glimpses of Andean peaks still capped in snow before returning to pisco sours by a blazing log fire. It is the only pleasant recollection of an otherwise grim time.

The Pinochet Coup

I had no option but to return to New York as Jacko was on mission, our other colleague on leave and another food crisis was threatening Bangladesh. On Tuesday 11 September 1973 I was in England, en route to Dacca, when a call came from New York. Christina and I were having tea at Pippins under the old cider apple tree. The caller was Gabriel Valdés with the dire news of a military coup, led by Pinochet. Would I please get back to Santiago immediately? I telephoned Jacko, and was taken aback by his angry reaction. It seemed to me self-evident that my place was in Santiago, where I was responsible for the safety of my large mission, but he was furious that neither Gabriel nor I had asked his permission. On calmer reflection I realised that he was worried about my safety. In my experience Latin American revolutions followed a rather civilised pattern. I was therefore stunned to learn from Mary Gibson at Heathrow that Salvador Allende was dead. I had known that he was doomed to be deposed but never dreamt that he would lose his life.

My journey acquired a nightmare quality. My flight was delayed, owing to a reported sighting of a man suspected of perpetrating bomb outrages at London railway stations the previous day. He was not on board but I missed my connection in New York. I went into Manhattan for hurried consultations in UN and UNDP, reduced my luggage to one small bag and tried unsuccessfully to placate Jacko. At ten o'clock that night I boarded a flight for Santiago. Gabriel had preceded me the previous evening amid reports that the military would ask him to become interim President. All Chilean frontiers, ports and airports were closed but rumour had it that Santiago Airport would open shortly. On Thursday morning we waited hours in Lima for news. Eventually we continued southwards but the captain's requests for permission to enter Chilean territory were refused and we landed in Buenos Aires, where Gabriel was also stranded. By the time we had talked it was 2 a.m. on Friday morning – 7 a.m. in England – and since Tuesday I had had only two hours in bed.

When another 24 hours passed without any call for Gabriel, we decided that it would be impolitic for him to hover in Argentina and he returned to New York, enjoining me to reach Santiago as soon as possible. The country had been hermetically sealed by the military, for what dire purposes one could only speculate. Such rumours as did filter through lent a terrible credence to the most gruesome conjectures.

I installed myself in the UNDP office and went daily to the airport but there were no flights. All forms of communication were restricted but I managed infrequent 'conversations' by telex with Enrique Iglesias, in ECLA. By Sunday (16 September) I was desperate enough to contemplate taking a night bus to Mendoza and negotiating my way across the frontier. Enrique vigorously dissuaded me: it was dangerous, he said, and the frontiers were likely to remain closed.

In Buenos Aires I had found Sergio Molina, a prominent Christian Democrat, also trying to get back to Chile. Sergio entrusted me with his passport, so that if I found a solution I could make reservations for us both. That Sunday Sergio was lunching at the Chilean Embassy, while the resident representative, Miguel Albornoz, was lunching with the Argentine Defence Minister. Minutes after my conversation with Enrique, Miguel called.

'Have you got Sergio's passport?' His urgent tone immediately alerted me.

'Yes.' I replied. 'Why?'

'I'm sending a driver to collect it.'

Experience had taught me that Miguel was adept at not revealing his hand. 'Why?' I enquired, no doubt with maddening repetition.

'Never mind,' came the reply. 'It's important.'

It could mean only one thing: plans were afoot for Sergio to get to Santiago without me. My intense irritation enabled me to think quickly. 'It's back at the hotel,' I lied. 'Anyway I won't give it to anyone except Sergio.'

I sped back to the hotel where Sergio soon appeared with the Chilean military attaché. The new government had asked him to become Director of the Budget and to fly to Chile on a military plane being sent specially to Buenos Aires.

'I will give you your passport on condition that I get a seat on this plane,' I said. 'We were in this together, and you can't desert me now.'

Sergio and his companion were embarrassed but, short of physical force, could not wrest the passport from me. We agreed to go to the airport together and they would try to negotiate my passage.

More hours of suspense followed. The plane turned out to be a small Beechcraft, holding ten passengers. Other Chilean officials were also passengers but I was squeezed aboard. It was 8 o'clock at night when we took off, our flight delayed by bad weather over the Andes. Less than two hours by commercial jet, this one took over four. Our little craft hedge-hopped over the cordillera, buffeted by a prodigious storm. I found myself regretting my blind determination to board it, especially when the pilot flashed his lights, like the headlights of a car on a dark night, to make sure where the mountains were. It was bitterly cold in the unpressurised plane at 20 000 feet and I was shivering in the travel-stained clothes in which I had left England five days before.

At last the lights of Santiago speckled the darkness below. It was an eerie sight for no one moved in the curfew-bound streets. We landed after midnight at the military airport. Our passports and faces were scrutinised by unsmiling military officers, and there was an ominous confabulation when it was discovered that I was not Chilean.

We were bundled aboard a dilapidated bus, which groaned its way through the deserted streets where the only other sound was an occasional explosion or sporadic burst of fire. Soldiers armed with machineguns crouched at the windows and we were ordered to keep our heads down. We were taken first to the Ministry of Defence and then, after another long wait and more suspicious enquiries, the bus trundled off to deposit us at our homes. Eventually I was the last person aboard.

Villa Clara Rosa was too far away and El Arrayán a suspicious address, being near Allende's country retreat, so I opted to go to ECLA. The UN security guard was understandably alarmed at the sight of an antediluvian vehicle, bristling with guns, hurtling straight towards the gates at 2 a.m. as if to ram them. It must have been a welcome anticlimax when the monster disgorged my bedraggled figure, clutching my small case. I was ushered into Enrique's office, where a stiff tot of whisky warmed my frozen limbs and the guards rustled up bacon and eggs. I was ravenously hungry, having eaten nothing since breakfast the day before.

I dossed down on Enrique's sofa and as soon as it was light cleaned myself up in the ladies' toilet, drying myself on paper towels. Enrique, amazed to find that I had got into the country, gave me a car to my own office. As I walked in I said '*Buenos días*' to staff struggling to deal with a crowd clamouring for help in the entrance hall. My harassed staff returned my greeting without looking up, but when they recognised my voice, their jaws dropped. It was the only amusing moment in an otherwise horrendous period.

An inflammatory statement by the military junta's Interior Minister that the main enemies of the state were 'extremists (communists), foreigners and criminals' had instantaneous and terrifying repercussions: people were denounced on the slenderest of pretexts, neighbour turned on neighbour and countless unfortunates were arrested for no other reason than a foreign passport. It was a veritable reign of terror that took everyone by surprise in a country renowned for its high level of civilisation and culture.

Working closely with Enrique Iglesias I found myself dealing with a frenetic sequence of crises, completely cut off from the rest of the world. Some months earlier we had made a joint recommmendation for the installation of a UN radio to safeguard our contacts with New York. Our request had been rejected by the Under Secretary-General for Administration and Finance as alarmist and costly. When events tragically vindicated us, Headquarters reversed its decision but the Pinochet Government refused permission for the radio to be installed.

I was responsible for the safety of many UN personnel and families, including fellows studying in the country and I had to establish relations with the new Government. As the senior UN representatives Enrique and I had to try to ensure that international norms of justice and human rights were maintained and refugees protected. In New York, Under Secretary-General Roberto Guyer, an Argentinian, did not make my task easier by commenting to the Secretary-General that UNDP had been too close to the Allende Government. According to Jacko, who was furious at the allegations, Guyer had attacked me personally.

I had no time to worry about malicious gossip, being too concerned with the plight of our UN personnel, some of whom had acted foolishly, while others, who had not, were nonetheless in grave danger. Pinochet and his military junta were no respecters of persons or international agreements and the United Nations was the object of deepest suspicion. The most dangerous case was that of Joan Garcés, already described. The manager of the agrarian reform project was fortunately out of the country, and I got his wife and family out on that first UN plane. The most vociferous of the experts clamouring for me to spirit them and their families out of the country were precisely those – few in number, I am glad to say – who had been most cavalier about their UN oath and taken overt political positions. When the moment of truth came they proved armchair revolutionaries, anxious to save their skins, and taking up time that I would prefer to use helping thousands of others endangered through no fault of their own.

One who behaved with dignity was Raul Maldonado, an expert in foreign trade. With UN permission he had, quite correctly, advised government trade missions but his name appeared in a military proclamation listing people who should report to the authorities. Many who responded were never seen again or subjected to torture in the infamous football stadium. Maldonado was arrested, but, after strenuous interventions by Enrique and myself, was detained in his residence. I arranged for him to be recalled for another mission and on 23 September sent him to the airport, armed with exit papers, and escorted by my deputy. Nonetheless, the airport authorities tried to prevent him boarding the plane. I called the chief of international airport police, protesting that he was protected by the UN Convention of Privileges and Immunities, but it was only after consultation with the military junta itself that Maldonado was allowed to leave, on my assurance that he could be recalled to give information. None of us breathed until the plane was safely in the air.

Our days were full of such heart-stopping moments. Seventeen people connected to the United Nations had been arrested. Thirteen were attached to the Latin American Faculty for Social Sciences (FLACSO). After lengthy negotiations, we obtained agreement for the release of eight of them. I spent the morning of

Saturday 29 September, at the stadium extracting them, an experience I am unlikely to forget. Most had suffered severe beatings and some had been tortured. Through the door of the stadium I caught glimpses of the thousands within, awaiting an uncertain and almost certainly tragic fate. The man in charge of this monstrous improvised prison, Colonel Espinoza, was surly and reluctant to let any of his prey escape his clutches. Short, bullet-headed, with cropped hair, he looked type-cast for the role of a Nazi gauleiter in a film. Years later he was behind the ruthless assassination in Washington of my friend, Orlando Letelier, who had been Allende's Foreign Minister. Years later still, he was brought to justice in Chile, together with General Manuel Contreras, but only after much international pressure.

I took my group out of the stadium under military escort, and we arranged their safe departure. Others were not so lucky. Two Bolivian fellows of FLACSO were killed. Jorge Rios, arrested on 12 September and shot, was identified in the morgue on 19 September. The other, Ignacio Soto Rodriguez, arrested on 26 September, was said to have jumped from a third-floor window during interrogation. Enrique and I protested to the Ministry of Foreign Affairs, but no explanation was ever given. I did achieve the deportation of Soto's widow, who was before a military court and in danger of summary execution.

Six thousand political exiles from the authoritarian regimes that dominated most of Latin America who had taken refuge in Allende's Chile were at risk in the indiscriminate mayhem that followed the coup. Secret police from Argentina, Bolivia, Brazil, and Uruguay swarmed into the country and found ready allies among the new military authorities in pursuit of their prey. Most of these terrified, hounded people looked to the UN for help. The UN High Commission for Refugees had no local office and their regional representative could not get into the country. The ECLA building was far out of town, and so they poured daily into my office, itself very vulnerable, on the ninth floor of a government building, protected only by large notices I had put up, proclaiming them UN premises. During the first days there was little we could do. There were heart-rending scenes: as curfew hour drew near grown men would fling themselves to their knees, clasp my legs, and beg not to be turned out into the street but I had nowhere safe to keep them.

On 19 September when a UN chartered aircraft was about to take off, somebody's papers were claimed not to be in order. I dashed to the Foreign Ministry to sort things out, and then to my office to telephone the airport to hold the plane, as the pass was on its way. In my crowded entrance hall I glimpsed a small man, with a phalanx of others behind him. It was Hernán Siles Zuazo, former President of Bolivia. His companions had been ministers in various Bolivian Governments, all, like himself, political exiles in this now dangerous territory.

'We know you love Bolivia,' he began. 'We consider you to be Bolivian and we want you to be the protector of the Bolivian community.' The most I could promise was that I would do my utmost for them, as for all others at risk. Don Hernán behaved with his usual high courage. His tiny flat became crowded with makeshift beds, for he took in the most vulnerable to stay with him. Every day we were in contact to coordinate our actions, which safeguarded numerous lives.

On my first day back, Monday 17 September, Iglesias and I met the new Foreign Minister, Admiral Huerta, to press home the imperative need for the junta to fulfil international conventions signed by previous Chilean governments to respect UN personnel and premises, protect refugees and observe human rights. The minister agreed to issue certificates for UN personnel and premises (they proved of little effect with over-zealous military authorities), but on refugees and human rights we met a blank wall. Incredibly, Admiral Huerta denied that there was any problem and, as proof, cited the Chilean national anthem:

> O la patria será de los libres
> O el asilo contra la opresión

(The fatherland will be the country of the free, an asylum against oppression.)

Therefore, he concluded triumphantly – following logic we could not comprehend, and found exasperating even to contemplate – refugees could not exist in Chile, and there was no room for concern!

Fortunately I found resolute and resourceful allies in an ecumenical group headed by the remarkable Cardinal Archbishop of Santiago, Raúl Silva Henríquez, who became a close friend. A Lutheran bishop, Helmut Frenz, was another prominent and forceful member. Together we pressured the Foreign Minister and eventually obtained agreement to set up a national committee to help the refugees and to establish safe havens for refugees at risk, under the UN flag, with full government guarantees. These negotiations were not concluded until 29 September.

While some members of the mission clamoured for protection my old friend Miguel Soler, now working in Chile with UNESCO, said simply, 'How can I help?' I asked him to register the daily flood of frightened people until safe havens could be established. This service began on 18 September with a team of UN experts who worked voluntarily. The mere fact of registering refugees made them less likely to disappear without trace, and some practical problems (many had only the clothes they wore) could be solved. Over 1000 people were helped in a few days, but there were heart-rending stories of missing relatives arbitrarily arrested in the middle of the night.

The extreme delicacy of the refugee negotiations obliged Enrique and myself to resort to 'secret diplomacy' until the junta's agreement was obtained. The international press had a field day, accusing the UN of doing nothing to succour the victims of the terror, and Kurt Waldheim sent us a spate of agitated cables. One of these asked us to search for a young American, Charles Horman, who had disappeared after the coup. Our efforts were fruitless for, as later depicted by Costa-Gavras's film *Missing*, he was already dead.

By 26 September, I felt the negotiations were sufficiently advanced for me to brief the diplomatic corps in a meeting called by the Papal Nuncío. Even this was ticklish, for I was aware of the presence among my audience of representatives of governments – notably military dictatorships in Latin America – only too pleased to see Allende topple, and little exercised by the plight of the victims. A notable absentee was the Swedish Ambassador who was known for courageously upholding human rights in dangerous situations. Our dismay and indignation can be imagined when, on 29 September, the *New York Times* published an interview with the ambassador in which he roundly accused us of doing nothing. Waldheim's dismay was even greater, reflected in a joint cable to Enrique and myself demanding explanations.

On Sunday 30 September, Enrique and I, together with Oldrich Haselman, the United Nations High Commission for Refugees (UNHCR) Regional Director, who had now arrived, called on the ambassador and pointed out that his comments did not correspond to the facts. When he blusteringly waved our explanations aside, I could contain myself no longer. To the consternation of my male colleagues, I exploded. Did he not realise that we had been working round the clock, in circumstances of extreme hostility, precisely in order to protect the refugees? Did he really think this could be achieved by grandstanding to the press? Could he not, as a seasoned diplomat, understand that, in extreme crises, when the voice of reason was absent and xenophobia rampant, secret diplomacy was the only possible channel? And why – the point that incensed me most – if he was so passionately interested, had he not bothered to attend the briefing I gave to the diplomatic corps? If he had, he could have avoided misrepresentations to the press that could jeopardise the whole process.

The ambassador was a brave and principled man, but he was arrogant in his self-righteousness. The incident was a sobering example of how do-gooders, treading the high moral ground, in dangerous liaison with mass media only too happy to propagate the worst, can wreak much harm.

Fortunately the refugee sanctuaries began to operate that same Sunday. Despite difficulties they worked well overall and provided safe haven for many terrified people, with the help of the churches and a volunteer corps of UN personnel. Next day we told the media what was really going on. On 2 October the *New York Times* published a detailed account of the UN role and even the Secretary-General was mollified.

The refuges could receive only foreign nationals. Any attempt to help Chileans was regarded by the junta as an infringement of national sovereignty. Many ministers and high officials of Allende's government were imprisoned on the remote and inhospitable Dawson Island, where they suffered great hardships before being released into exile. Vast numbers of ordinary Chileans were also relentlessly sought by the authorities. Those who escaped their clutches crowded into foreign embassies. Traditionally the right of diplomatic asylum was confined to Latin American countries, but many other embassies opened their doors and were soon bursting at the seams, with the overflow camping in the gardens. The UN had no premises suitable for offering asylum, but there were several clandestine operations in which Chileans were smuggled into an embassy, hidden in the boots of UN cars. An exception to the rule was the British Embassy. The Heath Government had decreed that no one should be admitted unless in imminent danger of death. A black joke was soon circulating, 'Don't even think of trying the British Embassy unless you are bleeding to death ... ' It is surely an irony of history that it was in Britain, a quarter of a century later, that General Pinochet was arrested.

One day I was visited by two unknown men. They had come, they said, as emissaries from Gonzalo Martner, the Planning Minister, who was in hiding, and wanted me to go to him and help him to safety. I was torn between loyalty born of 13 years of friendship and dire suspicion of their motives. If it was a trap and I fell into it then I would endanger our efforts to reach agreement with the junta on the refugees. Equally likely, my visitors might (erroneously) think I knew Gonzalo's hiding-place, and were using this ploy to get me to reveal it. I let my head rule my heart and told my visitors that they must convey my regrets to Gonzalo that I could not help him.

It was an immense relief to learn later that Gonzalo was in the Venezuelan Embassy, and to hear from him that I had done the right thing. He had never sent any emissaries, and my visitors' intentions could only have been sinister. Never renowned for punctuality, Gonzalo had overslept on the day of the coup and been on his way to the Moneda, very late for a meeting with the President, when the radio announceed that the palace was under attack. He had gone to an outlying *barrio*, where workers had hidden him, moving him from house to house to thwart daily searches by the military. Disguised as a *campesino*, Gonzalo had taken a bus to the centre of the city and vaulted over the embassy wall. Occasionally the Venezuelan Ambassador would invite me to lunch, after which I would converse with Gonzalo and other ex-minister friends in the basement. By happy chance I was on mission in Venezuela soon after Gonzalo's release months later. It was an emotional encounter, almost like welcoming back someone given up for dead.

Despite the general obloquy in which it held the UN, the junta discovered that it needed us. Within hours of my arrival I was hurried before the four members of the military junta, in session under the dour chairmanship of General Pinochet. They wanted immediate UN food aid; reserves of oil, sugar, wheat, flour, rice and powdered milk for the general population were estimated to last only a few days. The requirements cited were alarmingly high. I explained the World Food Programme's supply difficulties, and the limitations of UN resources, but promised that we would do our best, acting as intermediary with other donors. Ultimately WFP provided food for four emergency projects of US$1 million each and, as a quid pro quo, I extracted a reluctant request for US$20 000 worth of WFP commodities for refugees in our safe havens.

Contrary to their suspicion that all UN supported projects were hotbeds of leftist revolutionaries, the new authorities discovered that the majority addressed areas of major relevance to Chile's development. Even the agrarian reform project, which the junta appointed a special 'interventor' to investigate, was continued, in modified form. In a conversation I had with Admiral Huerta, the Foreign Minister, on a flight to New York on 4 October, he was visibly taken aback to learn the scope of our programme and its almost exclusively technical nature, remarking that the only projects of which he knew were the controversial ones in agrarian reform and social development (Joan Garcés).

One morning I was electrified to see on the front page of the vituperative newspaper of the extreme right-wing organisation, Patria y Libertad, a picture of the gates of my house, with the caption: 'From mansions like these Carlos Altamirano preached revolution'. Another photograph was of a house occupied by a Peruvian diplomat. Both residences were owned by Clara Rosa

Otero de Altamirano, sister-in-law of Carlos Altamirano, Secretary-General of Allende's Socialist Party, probably the man most hated by the Junta, and the only prominent figure to have avoided capture.

I wrote to Admiral Huerta pointing out that the article was an explicit incitement to violence and requesting assurances that the property, which was UN territory enjoying diplomatic immunity, would not be attacked. I added that Altamirano had never visited me there. The minister responded that *carabinero* guards would immediately be posted at my entrance but they never appeared and on 4 October Enrique Iglesias and I were summoned to New York by Waldheim. María Angélica was staying in Villa Clara Rosa, together with Valentina Lim, now assistant resident representative in Paraguay, who had been sent to help my office. I gave them strict instructions as to what to do if anything happened: 'Inform the Foreign Ministry and keep the UN flag flying. Emphasise that these are UN premises with diplomatic immunity, but *do not resist.*' I stressed the last point because María Angélica, as a Chilean, was highly vulnerable.

The attack, when it came, was shrewdly planned for a Sunday, 14 October, when the Foreign Ministry was closed. The house had been surrounded the previous night and through half-drawn curtains the military had spied on the two women as they (somewhat injudiciously) listened to the songs of protest of Victor Jara, who had been executed in the stadium, his hands, that had played such inspirational music, having first been cruelly destroyed. Next morning María Angélica found an army captain demanding to search the house. She explained that it was the residence of the UN Resident Representative. Questioned as to my whereabouts, she said that I was in New York. As she tried to convey the normality of the house, Valentina floated in, in clouds of crêpe-de-Chine negligee, impervious to María Angélica's desperate signals to keep out of the way. The Captain's eyes bulged: an *Asian* in the house? Clearly a very suspicious set-up. He insisted on the search. It was clear they were looking for Carlos Altamirano. They took away my parents' letters, the last memento I had of them, because 'they were written in English', though they could hardly have been less political; the Allende Government's development plan, described as 'subversive literature'; a book on Cubist painting, no doubt associated in their minds with Cuba; and the scimitar given me by the Sultan of Assayita in Ethiopia, now rusted in its scabbard, but pounced on as 'a dangerous weapon'.

My bedroom was searched and my closets ransacked. At length a private soldier cried out in triumph to his corporal: 'Look! Cartridges! – *Hundreds* of cartridges.' The corporal fixed María Angélica with a baleful, accusing eye. What the private had chanced upon was my six-month reserve of Tampax, unobtainable in Chile. When María Angélica explained the corporal flushed with embarrassment and, quite unfairly, tore a strip off the unfortunate private. Crestfallen, the search party withdrew.

The news of the forced search of my house caused a furore in New York. Waldheim vigorously protested to Admiral Huerta who replied that he had no control over the DINA (the secret police). The Chilean Chargé d'Affaires in New York was sent to apologise to me. I told him I would be satisfied only by the return of my personal possessions and in due course the military school handed them over, with noticeable reluctance. The incident, though fortunately without untoward consequences, was typical of the total arbitrariness of the new regime.

It is hard to convey the trauma of those days, the like of which I had never experienced before. It was an intolerable burden to know that the fate of human lives in some way rested in my hands, and that there were overwhelming odds against my being able to save them. Every day was a nightmare of frenzied activity during the all-too-scarce hours between the lifting of the curfew at dawn and its reinstatement at nightfall.

Soon, the privileged classes began to hold parties *toque à toque*, beginning when the curfew started and continuing all night until it was lifted. Many of them were not unhappy about the train of events; Allende's government had been a threat to their entrenched prerogatives. While they celebrated, many thousands spent the hours of darkness in fear, and some did not see the dawn.

Enrique and I had been given safe conduct passes but one or two frightening experiences led us to use this supposed privilege after curfew only in dire emergency. Enrique was once spread-eagled against a wall at rifle-point, and body-searched. As I drove back to Villa Clara Rosa one night – at 10 km. per hour with the inside lights on and the UN flag flying – a young soldier sprang out from behind a tree, fiercely brandishing his gun. He was excited, barely literate, and had never heard of the United Nations. His orders were to shoot first and examine papers afterwards, and he was only with difficulty dissuaded from carrying them out.

On most evenings I would be cloistered in El Arrayán, anguishing over the day's events and the horrors being perpetrated under cover of darkness, overwhelmed by a sense of helplessness. Even telephoning Enrique and other friends could not overcome this dire sense of isolation, for our telephone lines were tapped. Occasionally we overcame this problem by Enrique spending the night at Villa Clara Rosa, or I at his house.

The spring weather seemed heart-breakingly callous, early mists giving way to airy, sunny days in which the enchantment of my garden shone to its best effect – clusters of purple and white violets, banks of azaleas and rhododendrons tumbling down to the river, bright camellias glowing in the dark shade of the eucalyptus groves. The contrast with the grisly events of every day – corpses floating down lower reaches of the same River Mapocho, as I drove to the office, and countless scenes of human misery – was unbearable. One could hardly imagine a more telling demonstration of Nature's indifference to human suffering, or of the inanity of the 'pathetic fallacy', so beloved of nineteenth-century Romantic poets, that I had imbibed at Cambridge.

Jacko was clamouring for me to return. I was torn between my two obligations, both of which involved grave humanitarian considerations. It was finally agreed that I should stay in New York, so that Jacko could travel to Bangladesh and that Anthony Balinski, recently retired, would assume charge of my office until I returned at the end of 1973. The two months in New York were not easy. The future of Jacko and myself still hung in the legal balance. When he returned to New York he collapsed dramatically and publicly at a restaurant one Saturday, and I had to rush him to hospital, where for two weeks he underwent extensive tests, with no clear diagnosis.

I was itching to get back to Chile and I was shaken to the core when Gabriel told me it was no longer safe or appropriate for me to continue there. Instead he wanted me to become his Deputy Regional Director for Latin America and the Caribbean in New York. It was a great compliment but I had always resisted going to Headquarters, and refused earlier offers of promotion there because I loved working in the field. I felt that Gabriel's decision was influenced by the fact of his being Chilean, and a leading member of the Christian Democratic Party, which Pinochet's junta was treating with the same olympian disregard as all other democratic institutions. In vain I pleaded that my work for the refugees, though not likely to endear me to the junta, was exactly what the UN Charter and the UN Convention of Human Rights were all about; and that my transfer could be interpreted as admission of wrongdoing. Gabriel remained adamant.

I was hurt to discover that Balinski had advised him that I should not continue, on the familiar grounds of having been 'too close to the Allende Government'. Yet there was never any request from the junta for my withdrawal (flattering as that might have been in other respects). It was hard to believe that Balinski's advice was disinterested. He had not wanted to retire, and enjoyed Santiago. He was an old-world diplomat, a Polish count in permanent exile. What the Allende Government had tried to do was anathema to his deepest beliefs, the traditions in which he had been bred, and, while I am sure he did not condone the junta's excesses, I do not think he grasped the full extent of their perversity. The main sadness for me was that, though our opinions had differed, I had always prized his friendship.

On 22 December I returned to Villa Clara Rosa, where Jacko joined me, to complete his convalescence. María Angélica was there, Segundo attended to all our needs, and Delicio and Juan tended the garden in all its exuberant summer flowering. Ramón was joined by a gangling young German Shepherd puppy from a neighbouring *parcela*, whom we nicknamed 'Tontón' because he was endearingly foolish, and incorrigible in eating anything and everything.

We lived briefly in an enchanted enclave, a summer dream encapsulated within the walls of Villa Clara Rosa. I was all too aware of the awful reality going on outside and yet, devoid of official responsibility, felt myself floating in a state of suspended animation, frustrated because I was not allowed to help. We read a lot, swam, and in the evening had barbecues on the terrace, listening to strains of Andean music floating out on warm night air, perfumed with scents from the garden, and watching for the bright star of Halley's comet, flickering far off in the lower Mapocho valley. The roses bloomed and every day we picked figs, peaches and apricots, warm from the trees.

I was not sorry to see the end of 1973. It had begun with my mother's funeral, other friends and relatives had died during the year, and in its last four months I had been caught up in the maelstrom of calamities that devastated Chile.

I had wrung one concession from Gabriel: that I should reassume my functions for a few weeks before the junta was advised of my transfer, in order to avoid misinterpretations. On 1 February 1974 I went back to my office and embarked on a round of visits to all our projects; and farewell calls, including on General Pinochet.

I left Chile on 11 March. Gabriel and Enrique had asked me to undertake a study on the UNDP regional programme of technical cooperation in Latin America, with a view to relating it more closely to the work of ECLA, a mini-Capacity Study, developing recommendations of the earlier work. It would bring me back to Santiago periodically, and so I postponed the heart-wrenching prospect of leaving Villa Clara Rosa.

During those quiet weeks over the New Year of 1974 I realised that Chile had been a watershed in my life and that I would never be the same person again. Some layers of innocence had been stripped away for ever. Not that I had been naive about the ultimate fate of the Allende government. The denouement had been inevitable for months, caused by the pressures on Allende, haplessly caught between the forces of the extreme right, diametrically opposed to his policies, and of the extreme left, ironically members of his own Socialist Party, passionately convinced that radical solutions must be pushed through without quarter. In an international context, the pattern of events had followed a tragically similar course to the earlier attempt at social change that I had witnessed in Bolivia a decade earlier, both countries dramatically affected by the Cold War being waged far away.

What had shocked me to the core in Chile was the brutal manner of the military takeover. Nothing in my long experience of Latin America had prepared me for this. Traditionally, a special plane bore the ousted President into exile and his ministers sought asylum in friendly Embassies. That this devastating breach with tradition should have occurred in Chile, arguably the most cultivated and civilised country on the continent, was almost inconceivable. The Chileans had a highly developed sense of humour, and constantly laughed at themselves, surely an unequivocal indication of maturity, and they had apparently well-rooted democratic institutions. How could they perpetrate the dreadful deeds against one another that I had witnessed?

Although I had always prided myself on being an international official, a citizen of the world, I realised now that whenever I had seen sanguinary events a small voice in the depths of my consciousness had consoled me: 'This could never happen in *England.*' Now this residue of chauvinism, a psychological shield against awful realities, had been blown away for ever. It came home to me with painful clarity that it was only necessary for a certain convergence of circumstances, interests and personalities to occur for uncontrollable human passions to be unleashed. What had happened in Chile could happen anywhere – even in England.

PART SIX

New York

16

New York 1: UNDP
Headquarters 1974-78

UNDP - 1974-5

I took up my assignment as UNDP Deputy Director for Latin America on 1 April 1974. Gabriel left the day-to-day running of the regional bureau to me. He was a delightful boss, bursting with imaginative ideas and fired by boundless enthusiasm. A superbly gifted politician, he was on first-name terms with many major Latin American statesmen. A succession of dignitaries processed through his office, among them many Chileans, some exiled, some having been imprisoned and tortured (one university student had been tied up naked, smeared with some substance and attacked by savage dogs). Gabriel tried to help them, giving those who were qualified professionals short UNDP consultancies.

One day he arrived in a state of excitement, having been warned by the United States Mission to the UN of an assassination plot against him by the Pinochet régime. The idea seemed extra-ordinary but when General Prats and his wife were murdered in Buenos Aires on 30 September 1974 and when, in 1976, the former Foreign Minister, Orlando Letelier, was blown up in Washington, in a car in which Gabriel's son should also have been travelling, it became all too plausible. The Americans advised Gabriel to stay away from his office window and vary his daily routine. Since Gabriel's habits were notoriously unpredictable this became our private joke. Every day an FBI man, clad in the regulation dirty mackintosh, came with titbits of information as to how and where his assailants might pounce. Fortunately they never did.

At Headquarters I enjoyed the discussions of policy matters, and the opportunity to provide practical field experience (many at Headquarters had none) but I missed operational work. Rudolph Peterson, the administrator, advised me to delegate more, now that I was in Headquarters, sound advice that he took too literally himself, being frequently away in California, still associated with the Bank of America. He appointed two deputies, one from a developing country, the Indian I. G. Patel, for programme matters, and Bert Lindström of Sweden for administration and finance. While politically correct, it was hardly a good arrangement managerially. I. G. was a brilliant theoretical economist (he later became Head of the London School of Economics), Lindström a banker. Neither of them had ever run a far-flung operational programme of develop-ment cooperation. When Peterson was there he was crisp and decisive, but when he was not things became fuzzy.

I. G. chaired a weekly policy meeting of senior officials at which I tried to push some key concepts of the Capacity Study, particularly that of rolling Indicative Planning Figures (IPFs). As explained in Chapter 13, the Governing Council had modified our proposals for a flexible rolling system enabling programmes to synchronise with each country's development plan in favour of a rigid system, under which they would operate within a fixed five-year cycle applicable to all. I argued that this would discourage governments from making the country programme an integral part of their national development plan and overburden the Govern-ment Councils, as all programmes would come forward for approval simultaneously. Worse it could lead either to the accumulation of unused resources, or to a financial crisis if funding did not achieve expected levels. I. G. decided that there should be a public debate between me and an Indian diplomat, earlier renowned for his abrasive interventions in the Governing Council, whom he had recruited for UNDP. The encounter was bruising but a number of people thought I had made my point. Nothing whatsoever happened to change the situation.

Another bone of contention was I. G.'s pet idea of 'national experts': that UNDP should recruit nationals of the country concerned to provide technical assistance rather than international experts. A corollary of this was 'government execution', whereby the recipient government would manage the external input, instead of a specialised agency. My concern was that, if UNDP funded local personnel in preference to outside assistance, then this would undermine its whole *raison d'être*: the provision of know-how unavailable in the recipient country and training national personnel. Its special contribution would become simple budget support money, not know-how. The uniqueness of UNDP's role, particularly in distinction to the World Bank, whose main business was providing money, would disappear and it would risk losing its way.

My warnings again fell on deaf ears but were vindicated by subsequent developments. In 1975, UNDP suffered an acute financial crisis – in essence a cash flow problem that would have been averted by a system of rolling IPFs. Later the system of national experts and government execution led to practical problems and even abuses. UNDP, its original focus lost, has long been seeking a new role to justify its existence.

Jacko's personal situation being still unresolved, we sought an apartment where we could live together, still a bold move at that time for senior UN officials. On 1 July 1974 I moved into Waterside Plaza, a complex of towers built on land reclaimed from the East River at 25th Street and rubble from war-bombed Bristol. The apartment was on the thirty-seventh floor and I called it The Eyrie. After much vacillation Jacko took the one-bedroom apartment next door, and the two were connected by an arch. Segundo joined us in early 1975 and over the next 12 years we entertained many friends and colleagues there.

Our windows covered a sweep of nearly 360 degrees, looking up East River to the 57th Bridge, the UN and the skyscrapers of central Manhattan; across the river to the chimneys and docks of Brooklyn, transformed at night into a fairyland of lights; and, from the back, to the Empire State Building and a glimpse of the Hudson River. East River was a busy waterway: day and night tugs plied up and down, nosing along barges laden with gravel, or refuse; oil-tankers sailed past; and helicopters zoomed in and out like bombing mosquitoes. In summer yachts added a touch of elegance to the water traffic, narrowly avoiding the seaplanes, which nipped in to land neatly under our windows. Seagulls would fly past at eye-level and we could observe their acrobatics far below. At night the river was garlanded with lights; bridges became tiaras of blue diamonds; F. D. R. Drive a moving ribbon of coloured streamers, and the dark expanse of water below was starred by the twinkling lights of water-craft. A full moon rising over Brooklyn would turn the black waters into silver and lend a marble sheen to Manhattan's towers and tenements. Every Fourth of July we had an unsurpassed view of celebratory fireworks bursting over the city and later, on the occasion of the bicentenary of America's independence in 1976, the cavalcade of tall ships from all over the world sailed majestically beneath our windows.

Final Farewell to Chile

Meanwhile my connection with Chile continued and my team and I finished our regional study on 31 December 1974. The document was far-reaching, laying out the practical application of many of the concepts of the Capacity Study at the regional level, but there was no action on it, partly because of the financial crisis and partly because – as I was beginning to discover the hard way – lack of follow-up was par for the course for UN reform.

In Chile horror stories still poured in, compounded for me by tragic news of a bloody coup in another country I loved, Ethiopia one year to the day after the Pinochet takeover in Chile on 11 September 1974. It was impossible to put these things out of mind during our last Christmas at Villa Clara Rosa. We loved the place so much that we thought of buying it but in the end decided we could not live in that haven of peace and beauty when dreadful deeds were being perpetrated outside our cloistered walls. We saw the new year in from my balcony under a starlit southern sky, the only sound the thunder of the Mapocho River echoing back from the dark, pine-shadowed cliff on the other side of the gorge, and spent New Year's Day swimming under the tall shade of the eucalyptus and basking in midsummer sun.

I was heartbroken to leave that oasis in the Andean foothills, and especially Delicio and Juanito who tended the garden with such love and skill. The day before my departure in January 1975 was darkened by yet another tragedy: Tontón, the young German shepherd who had adopted us as a gangling puppy, was found dead, victim of a senseless spate of dog-poisoning in the village of El Arrayán. Tontón's going, and the manner of it, were a sadly symbolic coda for a period throughout which intense beauty and deepest tragedy had been constantly intertwined.

International Women's Year 1975

1975 was declared International Women's Year (IWY) by the UN General Assembly, its culminating point the UN Women's Conference in Mexico. IWY provided illuminating insights into many misconceptions. Most men considered that it was a woman's affair, to be resolved exclusively by women. Rudolph Peterson was dumbfounded when I declined his offer to head the UNDP delegation to the Mexico Conference, explaining that the assumption that the delegation should be entirely composed of women was totally at odds with reality, since only 12 per cent of UNDP's professional posts were occupied by women, none senior enough to implement the conference's recommendations. I was, however, unable to convince him that the occasion was important enough to demand the presence of the administrator himself. Apart from the Secretary-General, no other organisation in the UN system considered the conference significant enough to merit the presence of their highest official. But at least the UNDP delegation was headed by a male assistant administrator.

Two interesting offshoots of the IWY were the scramble by male-dominated organisations to get a woman on board; and the ubiquitous flowering of the hideous appellation 'Ms'. I was inundated with invitations to speak at conferences and offers of employment, while our male colleagues appeared to think that if they called women 'Ms', they would no longer seek promotion or a greater say in the organisation – a brazen example of tokenism. I was amused to see in the *New York Times* that an American woman academic felt much the same way, pointing out that 'Ms' was unpronounceable, the nearest approximation being 'the sound of a bumble-bee breaking wind'.

One invitation came from Amadou M'Bow, the Director-General of UNESCO, who asked me to join a panel of counsellors to advise UNESCO how to respond to the major problems of the world. Myself apart, it was composed of well-known intellectual luminaries, among them Yehudi Menuhin. The panel was chaired by an eminent French moral philosopher. His thoughts and manner of expressing them were so recondite (though in French he sounded magnificently sonorous) that none of the rest of us could understand what he meant, though we politely forbore to say so. He produced an incomprehensible draft report that reflected his own impenetrable vision of the world. To my horror I, the only woman, was voted into the chair to sort out the mess – a typical male ploy, I found, whenever things went wrong beyond redemption. The moral philosopher stalked out in high dudgeon, back to the Sorbonne. By dint of burning the candle at both ends I pulled together a report acceptable to my colleagues. I never heard whether it helped UNESCO wrestle more effectively with global problems. It seems unlikely.

M'Bow, who was introducing major reforms and enjoying the good reputation of a new broom, also tried to headhunt me as UNESCO's 'Inspector General'. I went to Paris for discussions but ultimately declined because the job description and degree of authority assigned to this supposedly powerful office were unclear. In the light of the subsequent disrepute into which M'Bow and UNESCO fell, it was as well that I did not accept.

Following the Mexico conference, I went to Asunción to give a lecture to the Paraguayan National Women's Association. General Stroessner, the long-standing dictator, received me and the UNDP Resident Representative at 6 a.m. one morning, as was his eccentric wont. Our conversation went well until, in praising the Paraguayan National Women's Association, I sparked off a furious tirade about the dangers of Marxism and Communism, themes evidently closely intertwined in the presidential mind with the women's movement.

UNDP 1975–78

With the onset of the financial crisis, Rudolph Peterson departed; he had been chosen to swell the UNDP's coffers but the reverse had occurred. His successor was Bradford Morse, a former US Congressman, then Under Secretary-General for General Assembly Affairs. He did not know much about development either but he had a quick mind and boundless energy and was totally committed.

Brad had organised the meeting of US Senators and Congressmen to whom Jacko and I presented the Capacity Study on Capitol Hill in 1970. He greatly admired the study and, months before he took over UNDP on 1 January 1976, began consulting us about the steps needed to put UNDP back on the right track. Brad's opening speech to the UNDP Governing Council in January was crucial. He asked me to prepare it in total secrecy and our code word, 'Phoenix', denoted UNDP rising from the ashes.

The speech was unlike any ever given before by a UNDP administrator. Its radical ideas were enthusiastically received by some delegations, more reticently by those nervous of change. Brad also announced that he was setting up a small Administrator's Unit for Special Assignments to help him handle the financial situation and all aspects of UNDP's programme. This, coupled with my appointment to head this unit, caused a flurry among UNDP dovecotes, especially the regional bureaux that previously operated as virtually independent fiefdoms.

My unit was to be temporary and I was on loan from the Latin American Bureau. My team was small. Since we were required to advise on every document crossing the administrator's desk, as well as all major policy issues, our task was onerous and far from a popularity contest. But it was a rewarding experience, not least because our little group operated as that rare thing, a real team. In July 1976, with UNDP's finances stabilised, Brad disbanded our group. He asked me to stay as Assistant Deputy Administrator – rather a tongue-twister, since I had previously been a Deputy Assistant Administrator – and continue to advise him on policy issues.

Jacko and I entertained a lot, and he was none too pleased that I invariably dashed in to change when the guests were already sipping their pre-dinner drinks. At the time Brad was between marriages and his main life was in the office, which he was always loath to leave. Maddeningly, he would keep me and Tim Rothermel, his executive assistant, sitting for hours at his desk while he carried on interminable telephone conversations. When I could not plead a dinner engagement and Jacko's impending wrath I rarely managed to get away before 10 or 11 o'clock. During 1976 I did not visit a single developing country – a gap without precedent in my 24 years with the UN. In contrast Jacko was still dashing round the world as Under Secretary-General and chief troubleshooter.

In May Mary Gibson came to visit. With Jacko, we spent a wet weekend in Huckleberry Cottage at Lake Mohonk, before driving on to Sugar Hill in New Hampshire. Hardly had we installed ourselves in a comfortable log cabin when Waldheim summoned Jacko back to New York for a meeting. Always a stickler for duty, he insisted on answering the summons. I drove him 90 miles to the nearest airport, only to find that planes were grounded owing to iced wings. He travelled to New York in a rackety night train from White River Junction, and we returned to our cosy log fire.

Next day Mount Washington radio announced 'variable cloudiness and some sun' so Mary and I set off along the Appalachian Trail running through Franconia Notch, an expedition that narrowly avoided disaster when we got lost in thick forest and torrential rain. The lowest point came when, dripping from head to foot, we stood eating wet bread and cheese, and Mary asked in her best conversational tone, as in an opening gambit at a cocktail party: 'Do you suppose there are bears here?'

'*Bears??!!*' I exclaimed incredulously (as we struggled along I had imagined every possible calamity, from falling into the river, to sprained ankles, broken limbs, and hypothermia but not that).

'Jacko said there were,' went on Mary. Then, seeing the expression on my face as this new peril was added to my list and constant nagging fear, that through my carelessness, her children would be left motherless, she added hastily, 'But only if one leaves the trail' – and tried to look round reassuringly at the tangled undergrowth surrounding us.

On the last lap we had to wade through a river, returning like drowned rats to the cabin. Hardly had we revived ourselves with hot baths and whisky, when Jacko rang to say that he would return by an overnight train, arriving at a station at 6.30 a.m. which he alleged was much nearer than White River Junction. Next morning I dragged my aching limbs from bed before dawn and drove an unconscionable distance, along winding roads in thick fog. Eventually I located the 'station', a railroad siding lost in the middle of Vermont, the only sign of life a disconsolate figure walking up and down, peering at early morning bird life. I frostily expressed the hope that the meeting had been worth all this. It was some hours before Jacko confessed that it had been cancelled!

Bears and bad weather figured large in a similar excursion in October of that year, with my Aunt Christina. We hoped to enjoy autumn foliage, but the season came early. At one point we were actually *snowed* in! But this time we saw the mountains, incredibly beautiful under fresh snow, and walked and drove through wild scenery, devoid of tourists. I got lost several times when walking alone, but fortunately for my peace of mind it was only on our last day that our landlady cheerfully remarked that one of her guests had come face to face with a bear on the Iron Mountain Trail where I'd been walking only a few hours previously.

In 1976 I suddenly found myself the official HMG and EEC candidate for the post of Controller of the Inter-American Development Bank in Washington. I went to Washington for interviews with the President in September 1976 and two days later received an official offer. The job was a challenging one, with considerable scope for new approaches in the evaluation of the socio-economic impact of development loans. Moreover, there were then no senior women in the Bank. But my main consideration was whether it was right to leave UNDP when it was in difficulties and, at Brad's request, I declined the offer.

One of Brad's persuasive arguments was that he was contemplating changes at UNDP Headquarters. Announced on 15 November they included my appointment as Assistant Administrator heading the Bureau for Programme Policy and Evaluation (BPPE). For the first time a woman was appointed to a post at the Assistant Secretary-General level, in a substantive, line post of a general nature. It was unusual, even for a man, for anyone who had come up through the ranks to reach that level, normally filled by political appointment. I now had the same rank as the assistant administrators heading the regional bureaux.

My first great test would be my performance at the UNDP Governing Council in January 1977 when many appraising eyes would be upon me. Not all my fellow assistant administrators, especially those in charge of the regional bureaux, had received my ascent into their ranks with unalloyed joy (Gabriel Valdés, ever generous, was not among them). My previous roles in the Capacity Study and at the right hand of the administrator had filled them with unease.

I was therefore nervous when my agenda items came up at the council. Presentation of the papers was not difficult. The real challenge came when I had to respond spontaneously to a lengthy debate. I was acutely aware not only of 48 delegations watching me, or of the administrator beside me on the podium, but also of my colleagues listening on sound-boxes in their offices. One of them, not always friendly, had the grace to concede to me afterwards that I had 'done really rather well'.

That baptism of fire bolstered my self-assurance and I came to revel in the cut and thrust of council debate. A major decision of that first council was to undertake another review of UNDP's future role and activities at a ministerial-level meeting during their next session in Geneva in June. Preparing this major policy document involved consultation with specialised agencies and other UN organisations. Governments insisted on having the document six weeks in advance, allowing us less time to write it than they demanded merely to read it! Our 'Role and Activities' paper was full of radical ideas. In Geneva the proposals were very well received, especially by the more forward-looking delegations, but once again the final compromise took some of the heart out of a proposal conceived as an integrated whole. Nonetheless the follow-up of that paper became a constant theme during my two years at the helm of the bureau.

Brad was concerned that the World Bank was encroaching on UNDP's bailiwick, providing ever greater amounts of technical assistance, as the Capacity Study had foreseen would happen. More personally he was sensitive about the pre-eminence of his fellow American, Robert McNamara, the World Bank President. Added to this, major donors wanted to reduce UNDP assistance to developing countries whose per capita income had significantly increased. This was vigorously opposed by the countries affected and there were fraught debates in the governing council, fuelling discussion as to where we were headed. Some at Headquarters, especially those without field experience, argued that UNDP should do more intellectual research into development issues. Others, including myself, considered that it would be fatal if UNDP lost its operational focus and that it was not equipped to compete with academic institutions.

Brad's own response was to burst into my office proclaiming enthusiastically 'M. J. A., I want UNDP to be *the* world authority on ...' – whatever the flavour of the month happened to be – integrated rural development, public administration, new and renewable sources of energy. It was usually something on which the World Bank had taken a lead, often building on UNDP's ideas and experiences (integrated rural development was a case in point). I tried to persuade Brad that we did not have the capacity to become a 'world authority' on these things and that where we *should* aspire to such a role was in the theory and practice of technical cooperation, UNDP's *raison d'être*.

This was the thesis of the 'Role and Activities' document, applied in practice during my stewardship of the bureau responsible for UNDP's policy. Rather than setting up a large research outfit, I kept our specialised staff small and built up relations with universities and institutions engaged in development research. I also developed closer substantive links with the specialised agencies, principally through a 'Technical Advisory Panel' staffed by agency representatives seconded to my office. This, a tardy realisation of one of the Capacity Study's recommendations, greatly helped to ensure a more coherent approach by the UN system.

At the June Governing Council of 1978 I had papers to present on virtually every item of the agenda and spent my time running between the Plenary, the Budget and Finance Committees and working groups, drafting decisions. This won me the joke prize within the secretariat of 'Best Speaker', in the form of a framed certificate bearing the ironic citation "Who is eloquent even when remaining silent'. My rise in prominence aroused less charitable reactions elsewhere. One male colleague warned me that I had better be careful, otherwise something disagreeable could happen to me.

Field Missions

I was once again travelling all over the world on many varied missions. In May 1977 I led an integrated rural development mission to Bolivia under World Bank auspices. General Banzer was still the military dictator. We thought we had sown the seeds for a rural development programme, based largely on the 1964 plan abandoned after the military coup, but another opportunity to bring a better life to the *campesinos* of the *altiplano* was let slip.

That same year I attended three regional meetings of resident representatives in Ecuador, Sri Lanka and Qatar and had a crowded three-week tour to the Pacific. My ports of call included Australia, Western Samoa and Papua New Guinea where I had an exciting trip up the Sepic River, visiting UNDP-financed crocodile farms in the heart of the jungle. In New Zealand I had the difficult task of persuading the Finance Minister to stop withholding the country's contribution to UNDP and to pay it in convertible currency. It was a bizarre negotiation, conducted in the minister's box in Parliament, where he was attending an acrimonious debate on abortion. We reached agreement at 3.00 a.m. just as an agitated MP below us was brandishing a foetus in a bottle, after which I telephoned Brad, so that he could clinch the deal with the Foreign Minister who was attending the general assembly in New York.

The most important meeting that year was the UN conference on Technical Cooperation among Developing Countries (TCDC) in Buenos Aires, which had been organised by my bureau. TCDC was based on the premise that technical assistance should not be exclusively North–South, since South–South interchanges based on similar experiences, that were easier to assimilate, could also

be valuable. In spite of many elements of North–South confrontation at the conference, an acceptable consensus was reached.

On my way to Buenos Aires I stopped in Chile for the first
time in three years. The situation had improved a little, but
there were still gross abuses of human rights. Villa Clara Rosa
had been sold. It was sad to find the furniture piled up for
auction. The weather was tantalisingly good, the cordillera
shimmering against a blue sky, camellias and violets in bloom
among the eucalyptus and magnolias beside the front door. On a
later visit I was devastated to find that the new owners had dug
up the thousands of roses to install a conventional swimming-
pool in front of the house, instead of the charming pool down by
the river bank.

I also spent ten days in Bolivia, inspecting projects in Santa
Cruz and Cochabamba. General Banzer had at last agreed to give
up the reins of power in favour of a transition to democracy and I
found myself visiting an interim President, General Pereda Asbún.
Two of the main contenders for the presidency were my old
friends, Hernán Siles Zuazo, and Víctor Paz Estensorro. Bolivian
politics were as complex as ever. My aim was to ensure that
whoever assumed power would concentrate sufficient resources
on rural development, and I felt that I achieved this. Before the
year was out, however, there was another coup ...

My most exciting trip that year took me to Nepal and
Afghanistan. In Nepal I was involved in developing an innovative
rural health project, which would combine modern methods with
ayurvedic or traditional medicine. I flew on the UNDP plane with
the Secretary of Health to visit health centres in Bharatpur, in the
hot dry plains south of Kathmandu. One of the casualties I saw
there had been mauled by a tiger when collecting wood in the
forest ... The UNDP plane was used to ferry supplies and
personnel into remote mountain valleys. I was taken on one of
these flights to the landing point nearest to Mount Everest, a
minute stony strip high in the Himalayas, onto which our Porter,
Pilatus made a heart-stopping right turn, after flying like a small
bird up an immense white-walled corridor, with Everest looming
at its northerly end and a majestically dazzling view of the
Himalayas.

The night before I was to fly on to Afghanistan, news came of a *coup d'état*. Later, news filtered through that Prime Minister Daoud had been assassinated and a Communist Government installed. Incredibly, however, I received a cable confirming my seat on Ariana (Afghan) Airlines from Delhi to Kabul. I spent a frustrating two and a half days in Delhi waiting for Kabul Airport to reopen, making daily trips to the airport, reminiscent of my efforts to get into Chile five years previously. When the crew finally announced our imminent departure a panic arose as to whether the new Government would honour my visa but authorisation for my entry was radioed to the Ariana pilot, who bundled me aboard at the last moment.

Kabul was remarkably quiet. There were no bomb craters in the runway, as had been rumoured, though there were signs of recent strife: the palace tower, half blown away, leaning a little drunkenly over the top of the surrounding trees; tanks and armed troops everywhere. But the gun turrets and bayonets were festooned with flowers and alongside one tank, parked outside the shattered window of the British Airways agency, the driver happily squatted, boiling a kettle for his tea. Otherwise business seemed to be proceeding normally and I transacted most of my own, but was unable to see our rural development projects outside Kabul.

Problems reappeared when I tried to leave. Iran Air (on which I was to go to Teheran for an official lunch and thence to London) failed to arrive. This was a disaster as Brad had told me to represent UNDP at an important inter-agency meeting in Geneva, and made clear that if I didn't get there in time, I needn't bother to show up in New York. There were hours of anguished waiting at the airport, bristling with heavily armed troops. Should I go by land to Pakistan, risk the Aeroflot plane taking off in an hour for Moscow, without a Russian visa, or take my chance of returning to Delhi on an Ariana plane thought to be somewhere between Frankfurt and Kabul? Somewhat anticlimatically, I found myself flying back to Delhi with the same Afghan crew as had brought me in, who insisted that I fly in the cockpit with them. At the time it was hard to envisage that I had witnessed the beginning of a long and horrendous sequence of war and terror for the Afghan people.

Personal Developments

Jacko's travels were in different areas of the world but we usually managed some days together in Geneva in June, after the governing council, when we visited old haunts around Trélex, climbed to St Cergue, and took the little train on to Nyon, picnicked and wandered through the woods to savour a Pernod at our favourite bar in Givrins.

Pippins was another haven, to which we repaired whenever possible. For someone who had lived almost entirely in hotels Jacko revealed a surprising penchant for domesticity. Our tasks were neatly apportioned: he did the shopping, and cooking and I the gardening. Unfortunately neither washing, ironing or cleaning held any charm for him and so fell to me.

This division of labour almost gave rise to traffic accidents at Easter 1977. I was digging in the garden while Jacko prepared a lunch of roast beef and all the trimmings as we were expecting his son, now in his last year at Oxford. I was also awaiting the tanker bringing oil to keep the central heating going. Seeing the huge vehicle arrive I dashed across the garden, gripping my muddy spade, to warn the driver not to turn into my narrow drive. The street was chock-a-block with cars all honking their horns. I could understand the drivers' irritation but not the goggle-eyed expression on their faces. Then I perceived that Jacko was directing the traffic, a tall, elegant figure wearing one of my frilly flowered aprons, and brandishing a wooden spoon. The tanker driver nearly drove into a wall and indignantly enquired, 'What's this then, a reversal of roles?'

On another visit, in October 1978, we had days of glorious autumn sunshine. There was a harvest of apples such as I have rarely seen and a magnificent cock pheasant, whom we nicknamed Pharaoh, paraded around the garden, his brilliant plumage competing with the autumn colours. One afternoon Jacko strolled across the lawn to where I was working. His only contribution was to bowl a windfall apple over the garden wall with the self-consciously beautiful action of a seasoned cricketer. He was inordinately pleased with himself, but not for long. By mischance his hand also held his spectacle case, and his gold-rimmed spectacles executed the same splendid parabola as the apple. Jacko, crestfallen, disappeared into the impenetrable thicket of blackberry bushes in my neighbour's garden and searched for several days, coming out only for meals, bloody and distinctly bowed. He recovered his sense of humour sufficiently to describe the loss of his glasses to the insurance company as similar to the flight of a 'woomera', kindly elucidating to the uninitiated in Australian lore that this was the opposite of a boomerang – the thrown object does not return. The insurance men were so amused they framed the claim and paid promptly.

In 1977 we spent Christmas in Jamaica at Negril, then still a long crescent of seven miles of palm trees and uninterrupted white sand. It was a very necessary respite. We had reached a watershed, professionally and personally. Jacko's long innings with the United Nations had seemed to come to a formal close at the end of 1977. He was 66. Waldheim poured fulsome praise on him at a farewell luncheon and many remarked that his departure signified the end of an era. For him it was a terrible rupture and he continued to be dogged with health problems, mainly because he drove himself so hard.

There had been other disappointments. Barbara, her health improved, had in 1977 agreed to allow their judicial separation to be converted into divorce. Our long wait seemed to be over. And then Robin suddenly announced his engagement. Barbara decreed that it would not be seemly for the family to have a divorce and an engagement in the same year, and the legal proceedings were once more shelved.

Robin and Carlie married in July 1978. It was a lovely country wedding at Stow-on-the-Wold. But afterwards discussion of divorce between Robin's parents seemed to have been postponed *sine die*.

In June 1977 Jacko and I had done some house-hunting in the Jura but having looked at several properties, he once more came to no decision about a permanent home The only homes he knew were those with which I had provided him in New York and at Pippins. He undertook some voluntary assignments but they did not present a challenge commensurate with his capacities and experience. Still possessed of enormous energy he filled his time with more cooking and the cultivation of house plants. Matters were not made easier by the fact that, while his international career seemed to be at an end, I was constantly being headhunted.

New Challenges

In September 1977 I was offered the post of Secretary-General of the International Planned Parenthood Federation (IPPF) in London. It was looking towards a more broadly based development role and I would be following in the footsteps of two UN colleagues whom I greatly respected, David Owen and Julia Henderson. A London base might also have been timely, given Jacko's new circumstances. I was subjected to a gratifying degree of persuasion by the IPPF board. One of their members, a distinguished Colombian doctor, invited me to Colombia where I was amazed to see what he had achieved in a country where, two decades before, you hardly dared reveal that you were not a Catholic, much less even breathe the phrase 'family planning'. Now I was shown clinics in coffee plantations, accessible to even the poorest rural workers, who could also buy contraceptives cheaply at the local store. I was tempted to accept the post but Brad pleaded with me to stay with UNDP to see through my initiatives in BPPE.

I was not allowed to do so for long. In 1978 the main UN Secretariat went through one of its periodic restructurings. The huge Department of Economic and Social Affairs was split into two departments, one dealing with policy and research, the other responsible for operational programmes. The latter was called the Department of Technical Cooperation for Development (DTCD).

In July 1978 the Secretary-General asked me to accept a new post of Assistant Secretary-General, as deputy to the Under Secretary-General heading DTCD. The new department was to be the operational arm of the UN, carrying out technical cooperation projects funded by the UN regular budget, UNDP (it was UNDP's second largest executing agency), the UN Fund for Population Activities, and funds-in-trust from individual countries. It covered natural resources and energy, development planning, public administration and finance, population, and some social aspects and included recruitment and purchasing units. It was now the largest department in the UN, with 600 personnel at Headquarters and twice that number in the field.

Brad and I both reacted negatively. The UN was more hamstrung by bureaucratic and political restrictions than UNDP and was considered one of the least effective of UNDP's executing agencies. The appointment of the Under Secretary-General to head DTCD, Issafou Djermakoye, who had until then been Under Secretary-General in charge of the Department of Trusteeship, had been made on political grounds. Waldheim was dismayingly frank in confiding to me that Djermakoye must have a competent deputy who would run the department. For convoluted political reasons he wished this person to be British, because he had been unable to fulfil a promise that a British nominee would head the World Food Council. Two candidates from Whitehall had been presented but Waldheim had found them unsuitable. Hence, the mantle had fallen on me, who had the right background and was British to boot. I pointed out to Waldheim that this was hardly likely to satisfy my compatriots. Unless I was replaced in UNDP by someone British, which seemed unlikely, they would not be getting the promised additional Assistant Secretary-General post.

There was a more immediate problem. Djermakoye, who could be charm itself, could also be arrogant and irascible, as no doubt befitted a tribal chief from Niger. He had once vented the full force of his rage on me. I did not think I could work with him, carrying the responsibility for the department but not the authority.

Waldheim remained insistent. I went to see Ivor (now Lord) Richards, then the UK Permanent Representative to the UN, hoping that he would let me off the hook by insisting on HMG's right to an additional Assistant Secretary-General post, but he said that there would be no objection if I acceded to Waldheim's request. This was typical of the British Government's hands-off approach to posts in the UN. Their attitude was correct but, while they played cricket along gentlemanly lines, everyone else was playing hard ball.

Brad and I came to the conclusion that it was difficult to withstand Waldheim's wishes. He derived some comfort from the fact that someone enjoying his confidence would be running

UNDP's second largest executing agency, but told Waldheim that the arrangement would never work unless I was given carte blanche in the management of DTCD, leaving Djermakoye to play a political and representational role. Waldheim sent a letter to that effect to Djermakoye, who to our amazement signed on the dotted line without demur. As soon as the pact was sealed Djermakoye took me out to a sumptuous lunch and plied me with charm and his favourite champagne – Roederer Cristal. Any uninformed onlooker might have concluded that we were celebrating our betrothal in a personal rather than professional sense.

17

New York II: The Department of Technical Cooperation for Development (DTCD) 1978–87

Trials and Tribulations

B rad Morse had originally insisted that I should not take up my new functions until 1 February 1979 so that I could attend the governing council's January session but because of the urgency of the problems facing the new department he released me on 1 December 1978, on condition that I continued to help UNDP on policy matters.

My first priority was to weld the many units thrown into the new department into a coherent whole and by early March we had refined a plan for the management and integration of the department. A simultaneous challenge was the improvement of the department's performance in delivering technical assistance.

To my agreeable surprise, I was getting on famously with Djermakoye and my reorganisation proposals were approved successively by Djermakoye, the Under Secretary-General for Administration and Finance, and Waldheim himself. I was riding on the crest of an exhilarating wave, blissfully unaware of the hidden shoals ahead. Djermakoye was away on mission when on 16 April 1979 I unveiled my grand design to the department's 600 staff in the ECOSOC Chamber. Djermakoye was to sign the official circulars on his return on Monday 23 April. I would be away, as Waldheim had asked me to represent him at a ministerial meeting of ECLA in La Paz. I left for Bolivia in a state of euphoria. Rarely has pride come before a greater fall.

I enjoyed my week in Bolivia to the full, unaware of dire developments taking place on the other side of the world. Djermakoye was spending that weekend in Paris. Waldheim was in London, returning from a visit to China, and it was to London that he summoned the equally unsuspecting Djermakoye to inform him that he must immediately cede his post to the People's Republic of China. Poor Djermakoye was to be shunted back to the moribund Department of Trusteeship and Decolonisation. China had demanded an Under Secretary-General post and had rejected the trusteeship vacancy as unworthy of a permanent Security Council member. Waldheim wanted a third term as Secretary-General and the Chinese had almost thwarted his election for his second term, lifting their veto only at the last moment. To ensure their support for his re-election Waldheim gave them DTCD. The futility of this political move, taken without consideration for good management, came home with a vengeance two years later, in 1981, when the Chinese again vetoed him and this time did not relent.

If Djermakoye had been badly treated, I had been sold down the river. Waldheim, who had persuaded me, against my will, to take the DTCD job, did not even bother to inform me of what had happened. I knew nothing until I returned to New York. Even worse, the Chinese had demanded that my reorganisation plans be put on hold and there was to be no gentlemen's agreement about my management role. Morse was furious and asked me to go back to my old job. I was tempted but declined, rashly optimistic that I could salvage my plan.

For the next eight years I was to live, during office hours, in what I can only call a Chinese enclave. The Chinese had little notion of an independent international civil servant. My new boss, Mr Bi Jilong, lived in the Chinese Mission, as if a diplomat in the employ of his national foreign service, as to all intents and purposes he was, except that he was being paid by the UN, and had sworn an oath to accept instructions from no government. Mr Bi did not come alone: an astute Chinese official was made head of his office. He also had a huge car provided by the Chinese Mission, driven by a very small Chinese chauffeur who could barely see over the bonnet, and wove an erratic course through Manhattan traffic as if on a bicycle in Beijing. Fortunately for my nerves I was not often a passenger in that vehicle, as Mr Bi laboured under the delusion that I, too, had a car, provided by the UK mission, another indication of how little he understood of the way in which the rest of us lived and worked.

I decided to cancel an imminent round-the-world trip to Tokyo, Manila, Bangkok and Dacca, primarily organised around the UNCTAD conference in Manila in May 1979, in order to be on the spot to safeguard my proposals. Mr Bi insisted that I maintain my travel plans, a distinctly disturbing omen.

On my return I invited Mr Bi and his assistant for a day-long session to my apartment, plying them with facts, figures and arguments, and one of Segundo's splendid lunches. My most devastating discovery was that, two months into the job, Mr Bi laboured under a misconception as to which department he had been appointed. He criticised my proposals as 'too operational', placing insufficient emphasis on research and targets for the UN Third Development Decade. When I pointed out that our department was the UN's operational arm, and that those missing features were the responsibility of our sister department, he seemed genuinely disconcerted. It became painfully clear that Mr Bi and his assistant were preparing a different blueprint and I was excluded from the exercise. He evidently considered me an imperialist reactionary, despite my long years of service in developing countries.

When I apprised the Under Secretary-General for Administration and Finance and the Secretary-General of these disturbing developments, contrary to the conditions of my appointment, they simply wrung their hands, and pleaded with me to be 'a good soldier'. Waldheim came near to apologising, perhaps realising, tardily, what havoc his overweening political ambition had wrought in the UN's biggest department. The Chinese plan did not emerge until December 1979, which did nothing for staff morale.

Meanwhile I threw myself into the business of improving the department's operational performance. Mr Bi was not interested in the day-to-day operations, which were DTCD's *raison d'être* – indeed, our bread-and-butter, since our overhead earnings from UNDP and other funding organisations, which financed many of our staff, were calculated on our rate of delivery. My office walls were soon covered with charts, enabling me to detect weak points while comparative graphs fomented a healthy sense of competition.

The results were gratifying. In short order the department's delivery rate shot up, and soon became the best of all UNDP's executing agencies. In my first year, 1979, we delivered a worldwide programme 20 per cent higher than the previous year, some US$100 million, representing 70 per cent of our project budgets, which totalled US$145 million. In 1980 and 1981 we did even better: our budgets increased to US$165 million and US$173 million respectively, and we achieved delivery rates of 81 and 82 per cent. In barely three years DTCD's activities increased by over 80 per cent, and we gained the reputation of being a reliable and expeditious executing agency for UNDP and the UN Fund for Population Activities (UNFPA).

There were other favourable offshoots: after the Mexico Women's Conference the heat was on the UN to increase the proportion of women in professional posts. Having a rising budget from overhead earnings I was able to recruit new staff and in one year increased the percentage of professional women in DTCD from 18 to 28 per cent. We did not use quotas, but simply gave preference to women when they were either better than, or equal to, their male competitors.

Then in 1982 voluntary contributions from governments to both UNDP and UNFPA dropped, due partly to economic recession and partly to 'aid weariness' among major donors. Our programmes had to be reduced by 25 per cent, successful projects had to be cut and developing countries relying on our assistance suffered acutely.

I had the unpleasant task of cutting our Headquarters staff by almost 40 per cent over 18 months, requiring another major restructuring of the department. I had accumulated an emergency reserve fund and from this redundancy settlements were paid. The one advantage of the crisis might have been the opportunity to lose less efficient staff but the Under Secretary-General for Administration and Finance insisted that the lay-offs should be voluntary. It was they who clung on hardest, while many of our more capable staff left.

Those were dark days but we came through. Ironically, the decline in multilateral funding was accompanied by an increase in bilateral programmes, because donor countries saw them as bringing more direct and tangible benefits to their own economies and therefore as being more in their interest than contributions to multilateral aid. I therefore sought bilateral funding. I persuaded Italy, for instance, to fund large projects for execution by DTCD, but considerable strings were attached. This was contrary to the concept of untied international aid but was the only way to keep assistance flowing to developing countries.

We began to break even during 1984 and by the end of 1986, my last full year in the post, our budgets and delivery were higher than they had ever been.

Mr Bi intervened in personnel matters, and other facets of management, in ways not always conducive to the efficient execution of our programmes. There was an insidious little coterie around his office and I was conscious of shifting sands even dealing with people supposed to be my subordinates. Mr Bi was succeeded by Mr Xie but the change made little difference.

I put everything in writing, partly to have the record straight, and partly because I was never sure how much Mr Bi understood of what I said. On one hilarious occasion I went into his office and said: 'Mr Bi, X has telephoned from Addis Ababa on a matter on which we must react immediately.'

We agreed on a course of action but as I rose to go Mr Bi stopped me, saying, 'I'd like to discuss another matter. This morning X telephoned from Addis Ababa ... ' and to my astonished disbelief repeated the same message.

For once the deadpan diplomacy I always tried to exercise with him deserted me and I blurted out. 'But, Mr Bi, that's what we've just been discussing.' And fled, to spare his discomfiture.

My memos to Mr Bi received three kinds of response: an immediate 'Yes', if the issue was simple. If it was more complicated the 'Yes' came after three weeks. You did not need to be a genius to realise that this gave time to consult Beijing through the Chinese Mission. The third kind of memo never got a reply. Clearly the answer was 'No', but nobody was going to say so. I did not let my Chinese masters off lightly and sustained a relentless flood of follow-up memos. This did not overcome the stonewalling at which the Chinese were so adept, but it gave me an outlet for my frustration.

One of my reminders to Mr Bi began, 'I am sorry to badger you about ... ' (whatever it was). Unbeknown to me, it caused consternation. 'What did "badger" mean?' the Chinese enquired of everyone except me. As usual they consulted the Chinese mission. After due interval for referral to Beijing the answer came: 'A voracious carnivore that goes straight for the jugular.' Small wonder that my every move was regarded with suspicion.

Field Missions

Since DTCD's programme encompassed all regions of the developing world, I had a gruelling schedule of travel, but these journeys provided an invigorating reminder of field realities as well as respite from the daily battles in New York. There were emotional re-encounters with friends and haunts I had known long before, some in grievously changed circumstances. The Cold War was still at its height and, having experienced its impact on countries in which I had served, I was intrigued by my first experiences in communist countries.

Communist Countries

In 1979 I paid my first visit to the Soviet Union. They paid their contribution in unconverted roubles that could be used only to finance Russian experts and equipment and fellowships in the Soviet Union. Their field experts were usually of good quality, but those sent for Headquarters' posts were less so; all lived in the

Soviet Mission and had to give 50 per cent of their salary to their government. Arranging contracts and buying equipment was a nightmare of bureaucracy.

I travelled alone and had some bemusing personal experiences. Hardly had I arrived in a Moscow hotel room that appeared to have microphones but no bed when the telephone rang. A guttural male voice announced that it was calling from reception and would I like a young lady sent up to attend to my needs? On discovering I was the wrong gender for his purposes he hastily rang off. Evidently there was no parallel service for official female guests!

Soviet officials had a funny way of going about business. We would be in the middle of an official meeting when I would be whisked away, without warning, to see the Tsar's jewels *NOW*. One peremptory summons purported to come from Mr Jacob Malik (the long-serving Deputy Foreign Minister), who wanted to see me right then. To judge by the look on his forbidding countenance he would have given a great deal never to have seen me at all, a sentiment that I reciprocated after half-an-hour of his relentless tirade. Then there was the unending procession of men who would appear from behind potted palms at a critical juncture in our negotiations, to delighted and pseudo-spontaneous cries of surprise, 'Ah, here – quite by chance – is Mr X, who has just dropped in from Omsk, or Tomsk (or some other far-flung outpost of the Soviet Empire) and is deeply interested in joining your department.'

Thereupon I would be expected to interview the chap under the gimlet eyes of my hosts, despite my protests at the incorrectness of the procedure. At length, exasperated, I said 'You would stand a far better chance if you presented women candidates.'

A shocked silence ensued, broken by a nervous laugh from the chairman, 'Ah, Miss Anstee, you are a very funny lady ... ' an opinion confirmed by obedient chortles from his cohorts. I quickly disabused him about my sense of humour on this issue, pointing out that the Soviet Union frequently proclaimed that professional women had greater equality there than anywhere else. It was to no avail. I understood: from my hotel window I had seen women clambering about the rooftops cleaning the gutters.

My request to contact my former deputy, Georgy Kozhevnikov, gave rise to similar evading action. I did not summon up courage to request to see my former Foreign Office boss, Donald Maclean, much as I had longed for years to ask him why he had done what he did. It would have been refused anyway. Years later, when I revisited Moscow in more favourable circumstances, Donald was dead.

Domestic tragedy struck in September 1980. I was about to leave for China when our faithful Segundo suddenly collapsed. Leukaemia was diagnosed but despite doctors' assurances that he would last five years he hovered at death's door. On the eve of my departure we said goodbye in his hospital room, both sensing that it would be the last time after eight years together. Two weeks later, from Beijing, I authorised his return to Chile, on a stretcher accompanied by a special nurse.

On 1 December 1980, Segundo died in Viña del Mar. AIDS had not yet been discovered publicly, but as information emerged I realised that Segundo had borne all the symptoms. By taking him to New York and a better material life I had exposed him to temptations that were his undoing.

In October 1980 China was already changing but was only just opening up to travellers from the West. I felt I already know quite enough about China from my experiences over the previous two years in New York but Mr Bi was adamant that I should lead a group of 20 senior officials from developing countries responsible for programmes of rural development on a mission financed from China's non-convertible contribution. We were to spend a month visiting People's Rural Communes in four regions – around Tianjin, Wuxi in Jiangsu Province, Shanghai and Guangzhou (formerly Canton).

I spent two days in Beijing, for talks with the Government on our substantial technical cooperation programme. The emphasis was on natural resources, especially mineral exploration, but we had also embarked on our largest programme in the whole world: a US$15 million computerisation project in support of China's national census of its one billion people. That project was to cause me political headaches later when I had to intervene at the highest levels with the US and French Governments, who opposed the export of the computers to China for different but characteristic reasons: the USA, because supply of equipment with defence applications to a Communist country was forbidden under COCOM[1] regulations; the French, because one of their diplomats had been expelled from China on account of an affair with a Chinese lady ... ! Eventually, the census was successful and the department played a major role.

The Chinese were attentive but surprisingly inefficient hosts and some of the high-ranking members of my group were hard to please. Our large Chinese escort, headed by a senior man from the Ministry of Agriculture, was all male, except for two interpreters. My group was also heavily masculine, apart from myself and a young Ecuadorian. Our hosts waxed enthusiastic about the liberalisation of China's economic policies, especially the permission for peasants to produce some crops for private gain. I was unpopular when I suggested that inflation might result, and was sternly reminded that inflation did not exist in a Socialist state; later events proved me right.

Our Chinese companions were kept separate for meals and accommodation. Our arrival in remote villages whose inhabitants had seldom seen a European face, and never set eyes on a black person, invariably caused a sensation. People hung perilously from the top of compound walls to watch us eat. This was embarrassing, as their need for food was obviously greater than ours and several weeks of Chinese fare were quite enough for me. On our last dinner in Guangzhou the lethal Chinese drink, *mao tai* was served in quantities and our normally retiring Chinese leader got uproariously drunk and ended up under the table.

We were impressed by the frugal efficiency of the communes which managed to feed an immense population, admittedly at great social and human cost, but it was difficult to see how it could be done otherwise. We saw no case of hunger or malnutrition. My

1. COCOM is the acronym for a Cold War committee that controlled sales of sensitive military-related equipment to communist countries.

abiding impression of the countryside was of a landscape of stooping figures (often to the accompaniment of Chinese opera blaring across the fields, an incongruous example of 'music while you work'). We were fascinated by the ingenious ways in which resources were exploited to the maximum (even railway banks were used to grow cabbages), by the dovetailing of rural industry and agricultural production and the use of appropriate technology and organic methods of pest control. The key to the whole process was the abnegation and discipline of the Chinese peasants, especially the women.

The winds of change were blowing through the country exceedingly fast, in order to sweep away the excesses of the Cultural Revolution, and the people's thirst for contact with the world, from which they had so long been excluded, was striking, as was the number of them who sidled up, not to eavesdrop, but to practise long-rusty English.

Although arrangements for our tour had been under negotiation for two years, few advance bookings had been made and when there was prior planning it was rigid and unrealistic. On the long train journey from Tianjin to Wuxi, sleeper bookings had been made by dividing our number by four. This meant that the four women would have to share a compartment something the Chinese policy of strict social apartheid would not countenance. The only alternative was for the Ecuadorian girl and me to share a compartment with my two male subordinates. Our hosts huddled in corners for days anguishing over which solution posed lesser moral dangers. Interestingly, concerns over mingling the sexes prevailed and with evident trepidation they allowed the two interpreters to join María and myself. One of them, Lai Lai, gave us fascinating insights into the Cultural Revolution and became my fast friend to this day.

My role increasingly resembled that of a Cook's tour operator and a series of cliff-hanging experiences and the resultant clamours from my charges took their toll of my nerves. I felt overwhelming relief when our train from Guangzhou steamed over the frontier into the New Territories. I recalled that in 1954, my husband and I had been pulling all the stops to get into China. Now I was only too glad to leave.

Earlier in 1980 I had visited another Communist country facing very different circumstances – Mozambique. Only six years after independence the government had to contend not only with widespread poverty, but also with a civil war supported by South Africa. There were many other obstacles to development. There was, for example, not a single Mozambican geologist in a country with significant mineral resources. Angola had been the colonial flagship on which Portuguese investment and settlement had concentrated, Mozambique the poor relation. It is ironic that 20 years later, Mozambique has relative peace, and a burgeoning democracy, while Angola still struggles to recover from savage civil war.

DTCD was already giving considerable aid and in my conversations with ministers we agreed on further projects, some very innovative. Mineral and oil exploration was a priority but we no longer had access to funds on the scale needed for such operations. Gritting its ideological teeth, the Government had decided to grant concessions to Western multi-national corporations. Sensibly recognising that they had no experience in negotiating with such enterprises, they turned to us for help. We provided two groups of highly qualified experts, one in mineral resources, and the other in petroleum, to advise on the technical specifications for concessions, the selection of companies, contract terms and the oversight of the execution of the operations, to ensure that the chosen firms were fulfilling their obligations. Low in cost, those projects were of incalculable value to a struggling developing country.

These programmes brought me back to Mozambique 15 months later. My itinerary was supposed to take me on to Angola, but my visit was cancelled at the last moment. I had to wait another 11 years before visiting Angola and then in very different circumstances.

In 1985 I visited two Communist countries considered international pariahs – Vietnam and Cuba – where outside aid was given only by the UN and some Scandinavian countries.

My mission to Hanoi in January 1985 was occasioned by a meeting of the interim Mekong Committee, which was developing multipurpose, multinational projects to exploit the resources of the Mekong River for the benefit of the riparian countries, Kampuchea,

Laos, Thailand and Vietnam. These countries were deeply divided politically and ideologically, yet cooperated well in this joint endeavour, as I had witnessed when I first attended a meeting of the committee in Laos in 1980. Virtually all the studies had been completed, in large part thanks to quiet technical work by the United Nations over many years, including DTCD. The Mekong project was an interesting example of how economic and technical cooperation can contribute to the solution of political problems.

Jacko also attended Mekong meetings but in 1985 when we landed in Hanoi, it was to learn that, because of strained relations with Vietnam, the Thai Government had decided not to attend. That was unprecedented, since member countries had always been careful to treat the Mekong Committee as a purely technical body. After frantic consultations it was agreed to adjourn substantive proceedings to a later date, so Jacko returned to Bangkok. I stayed on to visit our projects and have discussions with the government. In Ho Chi Minh Ville (formerly Saigon) we were involved in developing repair workshops for a power station equipped with American plant, for which spare parts were unobtainable, and for the railway, a vital link to the north. The railway yard reminded me of an international cemetery of locomotives, of all vintages and diverse origins: French, American, Russian and even Indian. One day was devoted to visiting a water drilling project, for land settlement purposes, in the Plaine des Joncs, a name familiar from the days of the Vietnam War, when it was an area of entrenched guerrilla activity.

One of my escorts was a local UNDP staff member, Monsieur Kien, a wiry little man who had been a Viet Cong colonel, a military past he found hard to live down. I was quite worn out by several days of having orders barked at me in an enclosed space. Once, in his anxiety to get me somewhere on time, Monsieur Kein gave me a hefty shove into the back of the usual ancient black car. These were ubiquitous and uniform, and that one was already occupied by Russian dignitaries who gazed in paralysed alarm as an unknown female was jet-propelled onto their laps. But Monsieur Kien's gruff demeanour hid a heart of gold as well as enormous integrity. On my last morning he presented me with a Vietnamese hat, the varnish still wet. It was not the easiest gift to carry and I cut a striking figure in frosty Europe, sporting a conical straw hat on top of an overcoat!

I was impressed by the high quality of Vietnamese engineers and other senior officials and by their ingenuity in solving almost insuperable problems of shortages of resources and spare parts. What they most wanted from us was modern equipment, on which we could help only marginally, not only because of limitations of funds and mandate, but also because of opposition to aid for Vietnam by some members of the UNDP Governing Council. My visit left me with a complex mixture of feelings. There were many things to criticise, but it was hard not to admire the stalwart way in which the Vietnamese were tackling their development problems. I was able to accelerate our projects and although I never returned, I frequently saw ministers and high officials when they visited New York and helped them in their negotiations.

Later in 1985 I was invited to Cuba to inaugurate a pilot plant for producing nickel from laterites, that we had helped to set up. It was located in a huge industrial complex in Moa, at the other end of the island from Havana. The Government flew me there in a special plane and as soon as I cut the ceremonial ribbon the first lorry load of laterites hurtled into the plant and the processing began.

The Cubans had many achievements to show. In Havana I was taken to a huge hospital, Hermanos Amejeiras, which had ultra-modern equipment, and to the Biological Research Centre, which was producing interferon — Cuba was the only developing country to do so. I also visited a rural community where it was a pleasure to see well-nourished children bursting with health and energy, in contrast to the pathetic sights I had observed in other developing countries. The literacy rate nationwide was an astonishing 99 per cent. A cynic might claim that I had been taken to a 'showcase' but this was patently not the case: the official driver first took me to another village by mistake, where my unheralded arrival produced consternation but the same welcome sights of happy, robust children.

While the restrictions of the Cuban regime laid it open to criticism, one had to recognise that the grinding poverty so evident in other parts of the world had been eliminated. Moreover the Cuban people – helped perhaps by a generous climate – retained all the spark and humour characteristic of their race, that ineffably Latin combination of irreverence and nonconformity that renders preconceived labels irrelevant and breaks traditional moulds. Cuban Communism was very different from the kind I had seen in Soviet Russia.

Asia

In 1979 I paid my first visit to Bangkok. A few months later, Waldheim asked Jacko to take on the mammoth task of co-ordinating humanitarian relief for the Kampucheans, both those in the country and the thousands of refugees from the atrocities of the Pol Pot régime camped on the Thai border. Fraught with political minefields, as well as enormous logistical problems, the job was just up Jacko's street. His frustration ended, he threw himself into the work with boundless energy. From the end of 1979, however, it meant long separations as he set up his headquarters in Bangkok where I briefly visited him whenever my travels took me nearby.

In 1986 I went to Chiang Mai, that city of glittering pagodas in the north of Thailand, thronged with colourful hill tribes, to represent the Secretary-General at another Mekong Committee meeting. Afterwards I visited Thai and UN geologists at an off-shore tin drilling project in the Bay of Phuket. Phuket was rather subdued after violent riots two days before culminated in the burning down of the tantalum plant – a telling demonstration that environmental concerns are not limited to developed countries. A narrow wooden boat ferried us to the drilling sites where, drilling at greater underwater depths than probably ever before, the project had identified rich tin deposits, ironically just when the tin market had collapsed. This exemplified a difficulty inherent to development cooperation: projects of this kind take a long time to produce results and in the meantime the value of the resource that you are trying to provide can suffer a severe decline.

My UN passport and the projects DTCD was supporting enabled me to travel to Rangoon in 1980, when it was almost impossible to get a visa. I found what I thought was another fascinating case of a country unfolding after long seclusion. The process was more tentative than in China – as one minister said to me, 'We are like a tortoise emerging from the shell, cautiously putting forth first the head, then one leg ... and so on ...' As has since transpired, even that description was over-optimistic. Burma was a tantalising enigma, with its strange mixture of socialism, Burmese style, and devout Buddhism, of soothsayers and fortune-tellers and engineers and intellectuals. The people I met were disarmingly open and at the time I rashly wrote that, though the transition to democracy was painfully slow, it was on the way. Twenty years later I have to eat those words.

I went on to Pakistan, spending two days in Karachi with the Sind Government before going on to Islamabad, which looked particularly lovely in the autumn light of November, poplars gleaming pale yellow against the stark surrounding hills. My visit included Peshawar and on through the Khyber Pass, where we lunched with the political agent in his bungalow only a few yards from the Afghanistan border, on which fraught subject the Pakistan Foreign Minister was then addressing the general assembly in New York. There was no vehicle movement across the frontier but there was a constant stream in both directions of men and heavily veiled women laden with large bundles. The thought struck me that if I donned a *chador*, I too could slip undetected into Afghanistan.

My main purpose was to visit camps housing over a million Afghan refugees, then the largest concentration in the world. I saw small boys (no girls!) learning by rote under a tent, and I visited the women's quarters. At the time I wrote,

> There is a long tradition of providing refuge and mutual help among the Pathan tribes which straddle the border, beset by centuries of strife, but one cannot help wondering how long it will stand the strain exerted on local resources if the exodus grows as seems only too likely.

On that, at least, my prognosis proved correct.

On my second mission to Pakistan, in July 1986, a visit to Quetta was cancelled because of political disturbances but I flew to Lahore, to visit our programmes with the Administrative Staff

College and the Water and Power Development Authority. I was impressed by Lahore's wide avenues and parks, its magnificent imperial buildings, and the pervading aura of dusty, faded grandeur. The city exuded a general air of *capital manqué*, which it presumably might have been, were it not so near the border with India. That visit coincided with an extremely interesting time politically, with Miss Bhutto and her supporters holding rallies up and down the country (she was later imprisoned). The Shariya laws were being hotly debated in Congress, with the mullahs encamped outside, and everyone speculating about the future path to democracy.

A trip to Peshawar to visit a project on precious gems was cancelled at the last moment on account of a command performance to call on the President, General Zia ul-Haq. We talked for an hour at his office in Rawalpindi about the prospects for Pakistan's economic and social development and the ways in which the UN could help and I was struck by his detailed grasp of the subject. Not long after, he died in an aircrash.

The Middle East

At the end of 1981 I spent nearly a month in the Middle East, visiting Egypt, Jordan, Saudi Arabia and what was then North Yemen.

For Saudi Arabia, where it was almost unheard of for a woman to go on official missions (Margaret Thatcher was a notable exception), I had armed myself with long dresses and scarves. Panic struck when that suitcase went missing between Cairo and Amman and was returned only just in the nick of time. Some male colleagues had expressed reservations about my visiting Saudi Arabia, but the Government had officially welcomed my visit, and made me feel welcome from the first meeting with Prince Talal. At my next, the minister said I was the first woman ever to enter his ministry (a fact evident from the expression on the faces of the porters when I crossed the threshold). As a woman, I was also allowed access to the female university students working in our community development project at Dirayah, outside Riyadh, with whom our experts could have contact only through closed-circuit television. One girl, on vacation from Leeds University, told me how bizarre she found the contrast with the swinging lifestyle of her Alma Mater. In Jeddah I talked with women teachers so forthright in their opinions that the tape recorder was turned off out of prudence. I was, however, *not* allowed to swim in the pool of the opulent hotel in Riyadh, even though it was dark and there wasn't a soul in sight.

That notwithstanding, I was given privileged treatment. Less fortunate were the wives of our experts with whom, to the surprise of their menfolk, I insisted on having a meeting in the interests of the general morale of our mission. Most were professional women but they were not allowed to work or drive. When one Indian woman's husband had a heart attack during the night she could not even rush him to hospital. The solution was for everyone to live in a UN compound, as foreign diplomats did, but the Saudi Government refused to permit it.

There were signs of change. One vice-minister began our meeting by enquiring, 'Why are you all wrapped up like that?' I struck an immediate rapport with another, Dr Nasser Al-Saloum, who was responsible for the huge highway project on which we were working. He gave an all-male dinner in my honour in Jeddah and arranged a tour of construction sites. At the dinner the Mayor of Jeddah invited us to tea at his beach house. While I had eschewed long skirts while clambering among cement mixers I felt I had better revert to them for the tea party but when we arrived at the magnificent seaside villa the only others sporting long robes were the men, their wives being attired in short-skirted models from Paris, flashing huge emeralds and dimpled knees. Doug Sturkey, the Australian Ambassador in Jeddah with whom I was staying, told me that it was the first time he had been to a mixed party in a Saudi Arabian home and that he had never met so many Saudis as with me, so perhaps I had a novelty factor.

Initially sharply critical of our assistance, Vice-Minister Al-Saloum came round full circle when I resolved the main problems. In September 1982 I flew to New York with him on Concorde (at the request and expense of the Saudi Arabian Government), so that we could have a mid-Atlantic discussion on the project.

On my second visit I was received like an old friend, even by a porter at one of the Ministries, who had been greatly exercised on the previous occasion about the propriety of my entering the hallowed male bastion of which he was the guardian. Clearly my status as 'an honorary man' was well established. Nasser Al-Saloum sent me to see rural road projects in the south. This time I got over the problem of trailing through cement mixers by wearing a borrowed *abaya* (a long black silk cape) over slacks, though there were moments when I feared I might suffer a similar fate to that of Isadora Duncan. After a long day the roads director took me to his house for Arabic coffee and sweetmeats and I talked to his wife in her own quarters. The young woman fingered my slacks and said wistfully, 'I used to wear trousers like these in the United States.' She and her husband had gone straight from their wedding ceremony to California, where he had qualified as an engineer and they had led a westernised style of life. Now back in a fiercely traditional area she led a prison-like existence. When I left she embraced me and wept. It was a sharp reminder of just how lucky Western women are.

In Jeddah I was seen off from the opulent VIP pavilion by Nasser Al-Saloum, who installed me near the plane's emergency exit. Not for long: when my imposing entourage departed I was rooted out by an officious steward, who explained to me loftily, as to the dim-witted, that women were (of course) not allowed to sit there. Instead, he shepherded into my erstwhile place a decrepit old man, who looked far less capable than I of heaving open the door. Another sharp reminder of the lowly female state ...

My visit to North Yemen was particularly happy because both the Planning Minister, Fuad Mohammed and the Resident Representative, Toshi Niwa, had worked with me in New York. I fell in love with Sana'a and the country. The people were warm and friendly and their fascinating culture and history were evident everywhere, in Sana'a's multistorey earthen houses, with their elaborately carved porticoes and lintels, a living relic of mediaeval times. I went on a three-day trip to Taiz, the Tahama region and Hodeidah to visit rural development and agricultural programmes.

Abu Dhabi, my next port of call, was a dramatic contrast, with its highways and skyscrapers. Yet here, too, ancient tradition was far from being effaced. Sheikha Fatima, the ruler's wife, received me during a ceremony at a girls' school. I sat on the ground, amid schoolgirls and black-robed ladies in wooden masks, the same garb as worn by the Sheikha. She talked to me of the work of the Women's Association of the United Arab Emirates. It was hard to equate such scenes with the promotion of women's rights.

Oman, where I went in December 1984, is one of those marvellous places where you find the past vividly woven into the present at every turn. The sun-mellowed walls and aged turrets of the forts in Muscat, the tangle of masts and high-prowed silhouettes of traditional boats in the port, even the faintly swashbuckling air afforded to Omani dignitaries by their flowing robes, and the ceremonial dagger flashing in a silver-sheath at the waist, combine to create a romantic aura of high adventure, of voyages of discovery, still lingering from the days when Oman was a sea power to be reckoned with. It is still a seafaring nation and when you observe the harsh hinterland of sweltering mountains falling sheer into the sea, it is not hard to see why the gaze of the inhabitants should have turned to the ocean.

I found in my dealings with the Government a refreshing directness in addressing some delicate matters. Perhaps this is what distinguishes them from other inhabitants of the Arabian peninsula – men of the sea rather than men of the desert.

I went on to Kuwait, a very worried city after violent bomb explosions only a few days before, armed tanks guarding government offices and embassies. The sequel was the tragic drama of a Kuwaiti airliner hijacked to Teheran. We were still providing technical cooperation to Kuwait, but it was all paid for by the Government. Kuwait also provided financial and technical cooperation for developing countries so I discussed how we might develop joint activities in various parts of the world.

Africa

Our largest programmes were in Africa, the poorest continent, and I undertook many missions there. During an enforced seven-hour wait at Maputo Airport in January 1980 I had a long talk with Robert Mugabe, who was sending the first batch of his followers to Salisbury, prior to the elections that were to transpose Rhodesia into Zimbabwe. When we next met, 15 months later, he was Head of the Government. I was then attending the Zimcord Conference, at which the fledgling Government requested assistance for its development plan. My department was involved in many projects in different sectors and the Finance Minister was my long-time friend and colleague, Bernard Chidzero. I continued to be closely associated with Zimbabwe over succeeding years and am saddened to see the auspicious beginnings turn into the tragedy we are witnessing today.

Julius Nyerere, in contrast, knew when to step down. Unfortunately, his idealistic vision for Tanzania did not meet with practical success. He had the imaginative concept of relocating the capital not only in the centre of the country, but also in one of the poorest regions, Dodoma, and making it a pole of development. DTCD was charged with town-planning aspects and the integrated development of the surrounding area. I visited Dodoma in 1980, flying there from Dar-es-Salaam in a small plane. A few months later I was telephoned at 5 a.m. with the news that the self-same plane had crashed with the loss of eight UN colleagues. The visionary plans for Dodoma also failed to survive.

On that same mission I was received by the self-styled Life President, Dr Hastings Banda in Malawi. A small, unimpressive-looking man, once a Liverpool doctor, he nevertheless ruled his people with a rod of iron. The meticulously swept streets were safe to roam at the darkest hour of night, and regimented ranks of colourfully dressed women sang his praises and swayed in unison at every public event. It was hard not to laugh at the sheer Ruritanian fantasy of it, or to be shocked at the undemocratic nature of this paternalistic state, but the system provided order and stability for a number of years in a manner not often achieved in Africa.

Later in 1980 I travelled to the Sudan, flying from Addis Ababa in a small UNDP plane that climbed to a chilly 17 000 feet to cross the mountains. A few days later the same plane took me to Juba, in the south, where we had many successful projects. The tensions between north and south had not yet erupted into the vicious civil war that still rages today. In Juba I met Abel Alier, President of the High Executive Council for the Southern Region, an impressive and reasonable leader who was also the Vice-President of the Sudan. Sadly, this is another case where these early hopes were misplaced and our work was swept away by strife.

In the following year I visited Benin twice. The first occasion was a Donors' Round Table in which my speech came at the end of a long series of discourses, and I felt embarrassed at inflicting more verbiage upon the long-suffering audience. So it was all the more surprising when my gloss on the Government's motto 'the struggle continues ...' by declaiming *'La lutte pour le développement du Bénin continue'* merited a standing ovation and a public kiss from President Kérékou. Later, when we met in his office, he began the conversation by asking *'Alors, Madame, la lutte continue ...?'*

On the second mission I had a hair-raising trip up country to Natingou and Parakou to visit gold mining and water projects in an ancient DC-3, of which one of the windows blew open soon after take-off. There was no glass either in the window of the hut assigned to me in Perma where the wooden bed collapsed and a torrential tropical downpour treated me to an un-bargained-for cold shower in the small hours.

Latin America

In Central America we had several innovative projects, particularly in geothermal and other sources of energy. It was also a very troubled region and security as well as technical considerations took me there in the spring of 1980. I first went to Mexico, where I met many old friends, including Chilean exiles. Pedro Vuskovic was among the latter but he now shunned even his compatriots. I never saw him again before his death in Mexico a few years later, a disillusioned and embittered man.

I went on to Guatemala, a country of stunning beauty that made the brooding violence overshadowing it all the more tragic. The tragedy was brought home to me even more potently when, in September, the planning minister who had entertained me in April was gunned down in the street. Within a year five of the seven men who had sat with me round that cheerful lunch-table had been brutally murdered. A more fortunate survivor was General Ydígoras

Fuentes, that most vivid character who was Guatemala's Ambassador in London when I was a third secretary and who challenged the Vice-Marshal of the Diplomatic Corps to a duel. Now in heavily guarded retirement, his views were as trenchant as ever.

After considerable debate about the dangers involved I travelled by road to El Salvador, which had been in a state of undeclared war for many months. The Resident Representative, Tim Painter, who had worked under me in Bolivia, had taken elaborate precautions to keep me incognito, especially my rank, for fear of kidnapping. (The South African Ambassador had been captive for months and was later killed.) I found myself the only woman in a hotel of 180 rooms with only six guests, all the others journalists.

The United Nations was the only large foreign group left. Many embassies had closed and the bilaterals had abandoned their programmes. It is politically very difficult to withdraw a UN programme and I admired the equanimity of our experts and Tim's handling of dangerous incidents, the occupation of the office by dissident groups and death threats. Both nights and days were punctuated by gunfire, and I visited the place where Archbishop Romero was ruthlessly gunned down. Here at least there has been a happier denouement. In 2002 I revisited San Salvador for a peace-keeping training exercise and found a capital in peace and a military force ready to share its experience of conflict resolution elsewhere in the world.

International Conferences

One of my responsibilities that I least liked was representing DTCD at international conferences: two international women's conferences, in Copenhagen in 1980 and Nairobi in 1985; the Conference on New and Renewable Souces of Energy, also in Nairobi, in 1981; and immediately afterwards the first Conference on Least Developed Countries in Paris, for which I had chaired preliminary meetings in Ethiopia. We also organised many more closely focused technical meetings all over the world.

I considered it essential to highlight women's issues but in a practical manner. Not a great supporter of conferences, so many of which generate more heat than light, I found that the Nairobi conference *did* achieve something. It demonstrated that a network of women of all countries, classes and callings was building up, especially in the parallel forum attended by 16 000 women. Every day the campus of Nairobi University took on the aspect of some vast, almost mediaeval fair, milling with women dressed in a wide array of international dress, from blue-jeans to saris, even the black *chadors* of the Iranian group (proclaiming their right to cling to the veil) and one day I ran into a bowler-hatted *campesina* from the Bolivian *altiplano*. Workshops on every conceivable subject were held under trees, with women sitting on the ground in rapt attention.

In DTCD we attempted to adapt even the most technical projects to women's needs. A water project in Mali, for instance, included training for women in well maintenance. Neglect of wells was one of the main failings of the programme and women had the major interest in keeping the wells operational. Another innovative approach in Burkina Faso was the invention of a wheelbarrow that enabled women to carry four water jars over rough ground instead of one on their head. It was cheaply made of scrap metal and one discarded motorcycle wheel. It was on show at Nairobi but we never found the lady from Burkina Faso who was to demonstrate its use and somebody nicked the wheel ...

Just how far we had to go in obtaining recognition of women's roles was tellingly demonstrated to me when I visited our geothermal power project at Olkaria during the Nairobi Conference on New and Renewable Sources of Energy. When I presented myself the plant superintendent looked anxiously over my shoulder and enquired, 'Are you the advance party?'

'No,' I replied, 'I *am* the party.'

'Oh dear' he said, plainly disappointed. 'We were told the Assistant Secretary-General was coming but I suppose something happened to prevent him?'

Overview

Looking back on my eight years in DTCD I have a sense of achievement, despite the frustration of working with a politically appointed boss with a different agenda. The experience made me realise the extent to which the Cold War was impeding our efforts to bring about improvements in the living conditions of poorer people in the developing world. The East–West confrontation constantly prevented a positive resolution of the North–South debate that would have been so much more effective in ensuring a more stable world. These constraints had thwarted many of the efforts in which I had been engaged in the field in earlier years, notably in Bolivia and Chile, but the extent of their perverse effect came home to me much more clearly during those years in the eye of the storm in New York.

I had chosen to work with the United Nations because I believed the organisation could make a difference and I wanted to be part of that effort. I still believe that DTCD, in those years, did make a difference in a myriad different ways, some involving overall development policies, others the day-to-day life of ordinary people, albeit not as great a difference as would have been possible had the international political circumstances been different. Subsequently, however, as part of the perennial reform and budget-cutting initiatives so beloved of member states, the department was eliminated along with its good work.

18

Special Missions and Thwarted Ambitions

The World Food Programme

In January 1982 Javier Pérez de Cuéllar succeeded Kurt Waldheim as Secretary-General. Waldheim's burning desire for a third successive term had been foiled – irony of ironies – by repeated Chinese vetoes in the Security Council. It was not the ambassador but the hapless Mr Bi, who was sent to tell Waldheim, obstensibly his boss, that they would persist in opposing him. I was unaware of the reason why, pleading illness, Mr Bi asked me to represent him at the private meeting of the Administration Committee on Co-ordination in October 1981. When I presented Mr Bi's excuses the Secretary-General, white with anger, almost shouted: 'A diplomatic illness, no doubt.'

Waldheim left unresolved another matter that affected me adversely. The post of Executive Director of the World Food Programme (WFP) in Rome was to become vacant and, to my gratified surprise, the UK Government decided to present my candidature, the first time I had ever received their political support. The reaction to their soundings with other governments was encouraging. It would be the first time a woman headed a major UN organisation and I had run WFP projects in the field as well as frequently representing the Secretary-General at WFP's governing body in Rome. There was a snag: the FAO Director-General, Édouard Saouma, had a say in the selection, although the final decision rested with the Secretary-General. Saouma favoured an autocratic style of management and kept WFP firmly under his thumb. We got on well, but he could have no illusions about my independence of mind, which my supporters thought was one of my main assets.

All seemed to be going well until a bombshell fell. The Australian Mission in New York had been enthusiastic about my candidature but when Canberra was consulted the authorities decided that, as a large food exporter, Australia should have its own candidate. They presented Jim Ingram, head of Australia's bilateral development cooperation proramme. Waldheim characteristically wrung his hands, 'What can I do?' he asked me almost reproachfully, 'I want to appoint you, but now I have *two* names from Group B countries' (the group comprising developed countries). He hinted that I should solve his problem by withdrawing but I was not disposed to oblige.

We were in this impasse when Ingram, who was making a campaign trip to Rome, Washington and New York, as well as key developing countries, came to see me on 11 November 1981. Without preamble he launched into a virulent attack: if I had any sense of decency I should withdraw my candidature immediately.

'You are completely unknown, whereas I am well known everywhere, and have the support of Washington, and developing countries to which Australia has given aid under my direction'.

'I can't withdraw,' I replied. 'First, the UK government submitted my candidature, so only they can withdraw it. Second, as a woman I could not possibly do so. This is the first time a woman's hat has been thrown into the ring to head a UN organisation and my female colleagues would be enraged if I chickened out.'

Ingram then played his trump card. 'But you have no chance of winning. Saouma has just given me his unconditional support!' He glared at me triumphantly.

I found myself gripped by a sustained cold rage and retorted, 'You are aware, I suppose, that what Saouma wants is a "yes-man"?'

I could not have scored a more potent bull's eye. Ingram flushed bright puce, and for a moment I thought he might hit me. Instead he stormed from my office.

Predictably, the new Secretary-General chose Ingram. Pérez de Cuéllar told me he hoped I would understand that he could not afford to fall out with the FAO Director-General at the beginning of his tenure. He also told me I had been his first choice to be his Chef de Cabinet, an Under Secretary-General post. He had, however been dissuaded by one of his senior advisers that this was inappropriate as I was 'from a NATO country'. The Cold War was still at its height, but I thought I had won my spurs as an international civil servant by working my way up through the ranks without government support (Pérez de Cuéllar himself said that he considered me 'as a Latin American').

A few months after Ingram's appointment I ran into Saouma in Charles de Gaulle Airport in Paris. He invited me to a drink and without more ado said, 'I have to apologise, I made a terrible mistake', both admissions I had never expected to hear from his lips. 'Ingram is impossible and I so much wish that I'd chosen you.' This tardy revelation was scant consolation.

Ingram – perhaps goaded by my words – was seeking greater independence and he was right, for WFP was completely dominated by FAO. The Secretary-General, foiled of his hopes for a quiet life by choosing Saouma's candidate, had to step in. Incredibly he asked me, who had been pipped at the post, to arbitrate the quarrel between the two men, together with Patricio Ruedas, Under Secretary-General for Finance and Administration.

Our work lasted eight months. Meetings of the Committee on Food Aid (CFA), WFP's governing body where I continued to represent the Secretary-General, were the scene of virulent debates. To cool the atmosphere our group met elsewhere, including once in London, where I chaired the meeting. Ruedas had recently described to me the pitfalls for the unwary foreigner in distinguishing between the short 'i', and the long 'ee' in English. Arriving late at a diplomatic reception his wife had apologised with the explanation, 'It is shitting (sheeting) down with rain.' At our London meeting the FAO Finance Director, a Pakistani, was being difficult about the documents that would emerge from separating the two accounting systems. The WFP Deputy Executive-Director, a normally gentle Bangladeshi, became exasperated: 'It is quite simple! All you have to do is add another shit! Just add another shit.' I forbore to remark that that was just what I did *not* need any more of.

I presented our report to the CFA in May 1985. For once, the United Nations system had healed itself; there was a significant delegation of authority from FAO to WFP, leading to more effective delivery of multilateral food aid but Ingram never thanked me for my pains.

The UN High Commission for Refugees

There were more disappointments over the next five years. Pérez de Cuéllar's antidote was to shower me with special missions. These assignments demonstrated his confidence in me, but could not assuage the frustrations of constantly being passed over for promotion on grounds of nationality or gender, and sometimes both, I became the longest serving Assistant Secretary-General, and there was still no woman Under Secretary-General.

In 1984, the tenure of the UN High Commissioner for Refugees (UNHCR) was coming to an end. At discussions about a possible successor in the European Union the British Foreign Secretary, Francis Pym, put forward my name. Initial reactions were positive, but in the end the ever cautious Secretary General opted to extend the incumbent.

When the post next became vacant in 1985 my name again came up. This time the U.S. was pushing Jean Paul Hocké, a Swiss official with the International Committee of the Red Cross (ICRC). Jacko had known him on the Kampuchean relief operation and thought well of his field work, but did not think that he had the right qualities to become high commissioner. Pérez de Cuéllar told me that I was his preferred candidate but that he had been advised that the post could not go to a woman 'since most refugees are Muslims'. I suggested that he ought to make the equally spurious riposte that it could not go to a man because most of the refugees were women and children! I pointed out that I had served in one Muslim country, and successfully visited and negotiated with several others, including ultra-conservative Saudi Arabia. Pérez de

Cuéllar would not take up the cudgels on my behalf, but asked me to talk to the Arab ambassadors.

No one wished to offend the United States or imperil American funding to the UN refugee organisation and Hocké was chosen, but Jacko's judgement proved correct: after many administrative problems and allegations of extravagance, Hocké had to leave the post long before his tenure was up.

This time Pérez de Cuéllar appointed Thorvald Stoltenberg, former Norwegian Foreign Minister. He was excellent but his term was also short-lived. After only 11 months his Prime Minister called him back to reassume the foreign relations portfolio. The organisation had suffered from so many changes in leadership and a 'safe pair of hands' was needed. Pérez de Cuéllar gave me to understand that those hands could be mine. The story of how yet again the UNHCR post slipped from my grasp comes later.

Special Representative of the Secretary-General for Bolivia

After General Banzer decided to hold elections in Bolivia for the first time in 14 years in 1978 a troubled period ensued of brief civilian presidencies interspersed with military coups. In elections held in 1980 Hernán Siles Zuazo emerged the victor, but the military would not allow him to assume office. Subsequently the situation deteriorated so much that they threw in the towel. In October 1982 Siles Zuazo inherited a country mired in debt, and an economy in desperate crisis.

On 30 November the new President appealed to the General Assembly for international support. He simultaneously asked Pérez de Cuéllar to appoint a special representative to help restore the country's fortunes and international image, and requested that I be that person. Nothing like this had ever been done before, but the Secretary-General agreed with alacrity, and instructed me to go to La Paz forthwith. I could not postpone a mission to Australia and do not recommend a one-week round trip from New York to Australia, followed by immediate departure to Bolivia. For virtually the only time in my life I suffered severe *sorojche* (altitude sickness) and wondered, my head bursting, whether I could make any sense with President Siles.

The problems facing Bolivia would have befuddled even the clearest head. Democracy had been restored, but the situation remained desperately fragile, politically, economically and socially. I went back to New York two days before Christmas with a plan of action agreed with the Government. It had not been easy to devise. The IMF, the World Bank and bilateral donors were adamant that they could not help, adopting a 'wait-and-see' attitude. The onus for resolving this situation fell on the UN, but we had no funds for such purposes. The only solution was to play an indirect, catalytic role, and try to mobilise support from other sources.

The fledgling Government had inherited an enormous external debt, but did not know how much they owed, to whom, or on what terms. Within two weeks I had hired consultants with the limited funds DTCD could spare, to sort out this problem. In the longer term the twin pillars of my strategy were to be two Round Tables on International Cooperation for Bolivia, under joint government and UN auspices. I had insisted they be held in Bolivia, so that the participants would see the desperate straits of one of the poorest populations in Latin America at first hand rather than pontificate about them amid the fleshly comforts of Washington, Geneva or Paris.

The first meeting aimed to outline the Government's strategy, and the broad requirements for external cooperation. At the second the Government would present its medium-term development plan and projects needing outside finance. The first meeting, which I chaired, was held 20–22 April 1983 and scored an initial success although it was a miracle of improvisation. The only building available was the opulent new Central Bank, built by one of the military régimes, but never used. At the opening meeting the interpretation and communications system failed and I suddenly felt someone tickling my legs. I could not believe that my neighbour, President Siles, was the cause. It was, in fact, a mechanic weaving his way on all fours and desperately unplugging and replugging wires. Outside the miners seized the state mining corporation and *campesinos* blocked all the roads. It was speculated that these actions were meant to attract the attention of a captive international audience. Fortunately this latter phrase did not acquire more than metaphorical significance, despite a strong rumour that the Central Bank would be occupied.

A cabinet crisis made it necessary to postpone the second round table meeting planned for September 1983. The internal ructions in the Cabinet revolved around the economic dilemma: without stringent economic measures international financial support would not be forthcoming, but these would penalise an already hard-hit population, which had naively believed that democracy would bring better days. I knew President Siles well enough to say bluntly:

> Your Cabinet should not be arguing *whether* or not to go to the IMF. I have my own concerns about some of their policies but unless they support you the rest of the world won't want to know. What the Cabinet *should* be discussing is *how* to negotiate the most favourable treatment possible from the IMF.

Some economic measures were introduced, causing popular protest and labour unrest. Democracy, paradoxically, made it possible for these to assume vigorous and sometimes violent expression and rendered it more difficult to govern the country. We re-scheduled the round table for April 1984.

In 1984 I went to La Paz four times, and made three visits to Washington, as well as to Brussels and Bonn, in my efforts to get the Government to bite the economic bullet and the international community to provide support. It was an experience at times bright with hope, at others dashed with despair, foiled by a lethal combination of political and economic factors.

The Government circulated its four-year development plan for 1984–87 and the projects requiring external funding to all donor countries and organisations. Unfortunately international sympathy towards Bolivia had declined, owing to the Government's perceived indecision in tackling the economic situation, and the round table was again postponed. We were having to deal simultaneously with three interrelated issues: the economic crisis and the short-term measures needed to resolve it; the renegotiation

of the external debt; and the financing of longer-term development. The critical economic crisis monopolised the Government's
attention at the expense of development programmes, which were
indispensable to *any* lasting solution of current problems and the
repayment of the debt. This recurring pattern became a series of
vicious circles: donors would not give assistance unless the
Government took *prior* economic adjustment measures; while the
Government found it impossible to impose further belt-tightening
on people already enduring great hardship unless they could
assure them of international support.

The dilemma was epitomised in Washington. I had asked to see the
Secretary of the US Treasury to ascertain whether bridging finance
could be provided for Bolivia but I was received by a bumptious
young official, who looked at me pityingly from a great intellectual
height and said, 'Bridging financing is subject to two conditions,
neither of which Bolivia fulfils. The first is that external debt must be
so great as to endanger the international monetary system.'

I could not help retorting, 'So should I advise President Siles to
borrow as much as possible to meet that criterion?' My sarcasm fell
on deaf ears.

'The second condition,' the young man went on unsmilingly, 'is
a low budget deficit and Bolivia's is sky high.'

Since the United States had a whopping deficit this was too
much. Assuming the role of idiot child, in which he had evidently
cast me, I enquired, with all the innocent amazement I could
muster: 'Ah ... so budget deficits *are* important are they?'

The young man had the grace to blush, but my arguments got me
nowhere.

It had always been envisaged that the Secretary-General would
inaugurate the second round table after visits to Panama and Lima.
When the La Paz commitment was cancelled, he invited me to
accompany him to Lima in the Panamanian President's private jet.
There were communication problems and an unscheduled refuelling stop in Guayaquil and when at last we arrived at Lima Airport
President Belaúnde and all the assembled dignitaries and troops
had been drawn up for an hour under the broiling sun.

We were lodged in the Country Club, surrounded by a
formidable display of security, Sendero Luminoso (Shining Path)

being then at the height of its destructive powers. As the most senior staff member I accompanied the Secretary-General to his meeting with President Belaúnde, and all the other ceremonies. Marcela Pérez de Cuéllar, his elegant wife, had her own programme. On the last day the social page of a major Lima newspaper effusively extolled her grace, beauty, elegance, her qualities as a hostess, and generally portrayed her as a well-known and unique figure on the Peruvian scene. There was only one problem: the photograph was of me! Marcela was very gracious. The Secretary-General mumbled gallantly that he felt 'very honoured', while I wished the ground would swallow me up. This was the second time that I had been taken for the wife of the Secretary-General (the first being with Hammarskjöld in 1959), hardly an auspicious way of ensuring further advancement.

On the night before my departure for La Paz, Roberto Jordán Pando, the Planning Minister, came with a personal message for the Secretary-General from President Siles, advising him that the Government had adopted a stringent economic package likely to satisfy the IMF. As Roberto and I landed in La Paz, the President was broadcasting to the nation. But by the time we had got down into the city Roberto, who was one of the main architects of the measures was, for political reasons, no longer minister.

Once the measures were announced, bridging finance became even more urgent. In an unprecedented move, I chaired a meeting in the World Bank in Washington in early May 1984, under the auspices, not of the Bank, but of the UN Secretary-General. It brought together the major international financial institutions, the US Government and the EEC, to whom a team of Bolivian Ministers presented the Government's economic programme. A meeting of UN member states followed in New York, opened by the Secretary-General. We obtained commitments for more than half the US$240 million needed to cover the expected balance of payments gap until agreement was reached with the IMF.

But before the package was finalised, the situation had fallen apart in Bolivia, owing to the vociferous opposition of the Central Oberera Boliviana (COB), the powerful labour confederation, and a crippling strike at the Central Bank, leading to the resignation of the Finance Minister. The April measures and negotiations with the IMF were suspended, and the rescue package went into the freezer.

On 30 June 1984 President Siles was kidnapped in the middle of the night from the Presidential residence in a botched attempt at a coup. He was held prisoner for ten hours but was rescued unharmed. I heard a first-hand account of this drama at a lunch with the President and his family in July. Don Hernán, with customary unruffled calm, said that since he could do nothing about his incarceration he had simply gone to sleep. This revelation incensed his wife and daughters for, while he slumbered, they had been distraught with anxiety.

During that July visit we agreed that the second round table should be held early in 1985 and that meanwhile we should negotiate development finance for specific programmes and projects. Unfortunately, this timetable also proved impossible to maintain, and when I returned to La Paz in November hyperinflation had set in and opposition parties were clamouring for the President to resign. I sent a memorandum to the Secretary-General, calculating that the 1984 inflation rate would be between 60 000 and 120 000 per cent, adding that, with that number of noughts, the difference was negligible. In the event inflation reached 24 000 per cent, exceeding the spectacular German rate after the First World War.

The country was paralysed by a general strike, and it was rumoured that the COB intended to kidnap me in order to exert more pressure on the beleaguered Government. This news was relayed to me en route, with the suggestion that I postpone my trip. After some hours of suspenseful telephoning from Puerto Rico, the green light came from the Secretary-General himself. This turned out to be the right decision for my mission took place at a critical moment.

Political tension was lowered a few days after my arrival by Siles Zuazo's offer to hold elections in June 1985 and step down one year early. This was a typically courageous act but did not solve the grave economic situation. Decisive action became even more difficult in a pre-electoral period. Without external financial help the democratic experiment would founder but such support could not be justified on the basis of the IMF's criteria. Any such decision must be a political one, linked to the preservation of democracy.

The Secretary-General asked me to discuss the situation with Jeane Kirkpatrick, the US Ambassador to the UN, and in the State Department in Washington where I met the Deputy Secretary, Mr Kenneth Dam (No. Two to Secretary Schultz) on 29 November. Next day the State Department issued an unequivocal statement of support for democracy in Bolivia, which I hoped would give pause for thought to would-be coup-makers.

Against all odds the fragile democratic process in Bolivia survived until the elections in June 1985. It was only in the early hours of 5 August that the Congress elected Dr Víctor Paz Estenssoro as the new President. At 1.15 p.m. that day the Secretary-General instructed me to attend the next day's ceremonies. I had less than two hours in which to get a ticket, pack and leave for the airport. Pulling a few strings I got a seat on a Lloyd Aéreo Boliviano flight leaving Miami that night. It was hardly a restful flight for the plane was packed and we stopped at Caracas, Manaus and Santa Cruz.

We landed at El Alto Airport at 9.00 a.m. and I just arrived in time for the Te Deum Mass in spite of an over-officious palace guard, who tried to impale me on his lance because I arrived in a taxi from the wrong direction. Afterwards there was a parade of the armed forces, which we watched with President Siles from the balcony of the palace, together with the Presidents of Argentina, Colombia and Uruguay. It was a heady Andean day, sparkling like champagne, and as the band marched off down narrow cobbled streets, overhung by the tiled eaves and wooden balconies of old colonial houses, their red jackets and white breeches gleaming under the blazing sun, one was almost transported back into the nineteenth century. In the afternoon the formal transfer of power to the new President took place, followed by another parade and an evening reception. When I eventually tumbled into bed at midnight I had been on the go for nearly 48 hours.

I stayed a week for discussions with the new authorities, most of them well known to me since the 1960s. During a long talk on his first day of official business, President Paz Estenssoro asked that the Secretary-General continue his support. The new Government moved fast. Three weeks later, on 29 August, Supreme Decree 21060 promulgated stringent measures of economic stabilisation, immediately welcomed by international financial pundits. Serious negotiations with the IMF could at last begin. My responsibilities took on renewed impetus because such negotiations were notoriously slow and Bolivia needed money to tide it over.

Victor Paz dealt decisively with the labour unrest that greeted his package but the tense situation prevented him from attending the UN General Assembly. There was another reason: though full of vigour he was 80 years old and confided to me that he was suffering early symptoms of Parkinson's disease for which reason (never made public during his four-year term) his doctors had advised against travel outside La Paz. In his stead, Vice-President Garrett went to New York where I organised a programme of intensive lobbying, supported by personal representations by the Secretary-General to virtually every Head of State or Foreign Minister. On 18 October 1985 as a result of this, and of an initiative by President Lusinchi of Venezuela, we launched an emergency fund of US$150 million in swap loans to tide the country over. We raised US$105 million immediately and in December, in Washington, I sought the support of the IMF Managing Director, Dr Jacques de la Rosière, the State Department, the World Bank and the Inter-American Development Bank.

De la Rosière's intervention was particularly important. The IMF teams sent to Bolivia were playing the game strictly according to the book. The Secretary-General and I persuaded him that the Bolivian operation was not a financial and accounting exercise but involved major political issues affecting the stability of a country lying at the geopolitical heart of South America. De la Rosière was quick to grasp the strategic significance of the Bolivian negotiations and weighed in to ensure a more liberal approach.

But fate was unkind and a series of external factors worsened Bolivia's situation. Hardly was the ink dry on Supreme Decree 21060 when the International Tin Council collapsed and with it the tin market. Bolivia had left the council earlier but the drastic fall in tin prices was a serious blow. Another fell in January 1986 when petroleum prices declined and decimated Bolivia's earnings from natural gas (tin and natural gas constituted nearly 90 per cent of the country's export earnings). At each setback the IMF did its sums again. The negotiation of the stand-by agreement dragged out for nine months and was eventually signed in May 1986.

Social unrest reached fever pitch and the government survived largely because of the dogged determination of Victor Paz and his ministers. The bridging finance we raised was also helpful, as was the fact that much of the population lived on subsistence farming and their lot was no better or worse. The brunt fell on miners, factory workers and town dwellers, all politically vociferous. Paradoxically, the element that probably did most to save the situation – and democracy – was the influx of drug dollars, not through the Government, which was determined to curtail the drug trade spawned by corrupt military dictatorships, but through informal channels. The success of the daily currency auctions that played a key role in reducing inflation and stabilising the exchange rate was facilitated by drug dollars coming in at a time when external funds were scarce. Total exports fell from US$1 billion a year to US$500 000, but the balance of payments showed, under 'errors and omissions', the large figure of US$400 000, which, it had to be assumed, came from the illegal export of drugs outside the Government's control.

In April 1986 the Secretary-General at last made the official visit to Bolivia cancelled two years earlier. Because of the UN's growing financial crisis his stay lasted less than 24 hours, but was perceived by opponents of the economic stabilisation programme as a heaven-sent opportunity to make their objections dramatically known. Another cancellation would constitute a grave political blow for the Government; but it was essential to avoid events that might impede the Secretary-General's departure. After consultation with everyone from the President down I nervously gave the green light, only hours before his scheduled arrival. Fortunately, there was no untoward incident, mainly thanks to an impressive display of security forces and by changing the announced itinerary. But I didn't breathe easily until I waved off the Secretary-General's plane.

We had a private dinner at the President's residence, and next morning met with him and his full Cabinet. Agreement was reached on the assistance the Secretary-General should seek from the international community, notably contributions to an Emergency Social Fund to help offset the social impact of the stabilisation programme and the fall of commodity prices. I later arranged for the Secretary-General to chair a donors' meeting in New York at which the Foreign Minister, Guillermo Bedregal, and the Planning Minister, Gonzalo Sánchez de Lozada (today President of Bolivia for the second time) officially presented this programme, for which generous support was forthcoming.

A few days later I was awarded Bolivia's highest honour, the Condor of the Andes, with the rank of Dame Grand Cross. Previously I had been refused permission to accept it by the UN but this time Victor Paz's Government decided to take the law into their own hands and sprang a surprise ceremony on me.

I was anxious to use that visit to Bolivia to establish a permanent home there. Fed up with the frustrations of working with the Chinese and of constantly being passed over for senior appointments I was bracing myself to leave the UN at the end of 1986. I was the longest-serving Assistant Secretary-General, at that level for ten years. In 1984 the possibility of my becoming the coordinator of relief efforts for the Ethiopian famine had fallen through. In the same year I had declined an offer to head the UN Centre on Transnational Cooperations without promotion.

After a peripatetic life, over 40 years outside my land of birth, and with no family left except my aunt, I decided that Bolivia was the best place to settle. I loved the country, had many friends there, and could continue to work usefully there after retirement on issues close to my heart.

In 1984 I located a rocky promontory on the shores of Lake Titicaca on which to build my retirement home. On one side it commanded a superb view of the Cordillera Real, on the other the Great Lake, beyond the Straits of Tiquina, where the legendary islands of the Sun and the Moon float on the horizon. Roberto Jordán Pando had recommended the services of an engagingly witty lawyer whose bohemian, breezy approach to life tended to spill over into his business dealings. Two years later the land was still not mine but my visit cleared up one basic misapprehension: the negotiations with the local *campesinos* by my incorrigible intermediary had been directed at the wrong plot of land! That corrected, I was assured that the matter could be settled 'within a month'. It was to take 18 ...

I did manage to finalise my residence papers, another process that had been dragging on for years. Not that anyone made difficulties. Everyone from the President down proclaimed it a marvellous idea. It just never seemed to materialise – one of those daunting situations when everyone chants *no hay problema*! (no problem), a sure sign that one must steel oneself to a long struggle against the impalpable.

The Mexican Earthquake

In September 1985 Mexico suffered a horrific earthquake. I was in London, en route to Rome, when the Secretary-General instructed me to mobilise and co-ordinate international assistance. I travelled at once to Mexico and spent ten days talking to the President and to ministers, visiting disaster sites, and assembling the vast mass of requirements into some logical order of priority (the total damage we estimated at US$4 billion but reconstruction would cost much more).

The sights in the affected part of the city were appalling – huge buildings that had housed flats or offices, hospitals, schools and hotels all reduced to a mass of rubble or leaning drunkenly over the sidewalk. The most gruelling experience was to witness desperate attempts to excavate a small boy buried for many days. I arrived just as the tunnels burrowing towards him collapsed and the weary rescue workers gave up hope of getting him out alive. There was something ghoulish about the hordes of reporters and television crews hovering around. Indeed there was something almost surrealistic about Mexico City, one zone pervaded by death and destruction while in the rest of the vast metropolis life went on with apparent normality.

The pathetic debris of human lives scattered in the ruins – a wedding photograph, a framed diploma, scraps of clothing – somehow made the tragedy more real. President de la Madrid asked me to accompany him in his plane to Ciudad Guzmán, in

Guadalajara, the worst hit town outside Mexico City. Thirty-eight per cent of the modest adobe houses had been destroyed and again there was something very affecting about patios, stripped bare of walls, but still with a purple bougainvillea or pot of flowers bearing witness to the care expended to make them attractive.

Everywhere I heard stories of bravery and abnegation. Everyone tried to do something, however modest. I had a touching example on leaving. Owing to a sudden strike I was bidden to present myself at the airport on the off-chance and found that a Mexicana flight would leave shortly for Philadelphia, where I could find a connection for New York. But my ticket had to be changed and a huge queue reduced my prospects of catching it to nil. Then my porter looked at me closely, 'But aren't you *Margarita*? I've seen you on television – no problem!' he said, marching me to the front of the queue, while announcing grandly to all and sundry, 'This is the lady sent from the United Nations to help Mexico. Now we must help *her* get back to New York to raise the money we need.' It was due to him that I got back on time on 12 October to throw myself into the task of organising the first donors' meeting, which was opened by the Secretary-General and the Mexican Foreign Minister. The documents were ready only just in time; we were all strewn about the floor stapling them until the small hours because a Mexican Airlines plane bearing 500 copies failed to arrive. Our efforts were rewarded by pledges of assistance from 40 countries.

In January 1986 I visited Mexico again to finalise the list of reconstruction projects – schools, hospitals and telecommunications – requiring external funding. These were presented at a second donors' meeting but the outcome was disappointing. It is a sad fact of life that, while people and governments respond generously in the immediate aftermath of tragedy, it is much more difficult to sustain that interest during the long haul of rehabilitation and reconstruction. Logically the justification for continuing international support ought to have been reinforced by the fact that Mexico was already grappling with an enormous debt burden and that to all this was added, in early 1986, another kind of 'earthquake', the vertiginous decline in the price of oil, its principal source of export earnings and internal revenue. Perversely it tended, instead, to overshadow the whole issue. Since money devoted to repairing earthquake damage would reduce resources available to pay the debt, I argued that the best way of assisting Mexico resolve part of its financial difficulties, without creating a precedent for debt relief (of which everyone was at that time wary), would be to contribute generously to the reconstruction. The logic of the argument was conceded in many quarters but the tangible response was negligible.

With the acquiescence of the Mexican Government I set about organising a meeting for which there was no precedent: a small informal gathering in New York, bringing together, under UN auspices, representatives of the international financial institutions and from Wall Street to discuss with the Mexican authorities the possibility of setting debt-servicing payments against post-earthquake reconstruction. A prominent Peruvian banker, Pedro Paul Kuchinsky, whom we sent to Mexico to pursue the idea came back enthusiastic but at the last moment the Government had cold feet, fearing that the mere fact of holding a meeting on debt matters, however low-key and informal, could damage their international financial standing.

I explored other possibilities. Plácido Domingo had lost an aunt in the earthquake and taken part in fruitless efforts to rescue her so I wrote to him, suggesting that we join forces in arranging a major benefit for reconstruction projects. I never received a reply.

In April 1986 I represented the Secretary-General at the biennial Ministerial Meeting of ECLAC in Mexico. A recurrent theme was the need to find new approaches to the all-pervasive problem of debt, which was slashing living conditions in debtor countries and undermining their political stability. In my speech, I referred to the Mexican case, compounded by the earthquake, and to Bolivia, as prototypes of the terrible dichotomy between debt and development. I pointed out that smaller indebted countries did not have access to bridging finance during the lengthy negotiations preceding agreement with the International Monetary Fund, because they did not endanger the world monetary system, though their dearth of reserves made them and their adjustment programmes very vulnerable. I pleaded for special measures to provide immediate assistance to courageous adjustment programmes until traditional mechanisms could be put into place.

At the meeting I was delighted to find Raúl Prebisch, who had just celebrated his eighty-fifth birthday in a joint party with Thomas Meseric, the veteran of the UN Press Corps. Raúl was in tremendous form, straight as a ramrod and bubbling with ideas. We had a memorable lunch, reminiscing about our long acquaintanceship of nearly 30 years. We discussed the main themes for his speech, delivered, as always, without a single note, cogent, intellectually stimulating and gripping the undivided attention of the audience. There were other ways in which the passage of years had not changed him: a pretty girl passed by our table, and for a moment I totally lost Raúl's attention ... I saw a lot of Raúl during those days. I had a government car and ferried him about but had to leave him at an open-air gathering one damp night for another appointment. With a chill of premonition I learnt that Thomas Meseric had suddenly died. Raúl flew to Chile on Friday 25 April. I returned to New York and on Monday learned, with disbelieving shock, that Raúl too had died earlier that day – a heart attack, following a cold caught in Mexico. Latin America had lost a great spirit and I a much-loved friend and mentor.

At that same meeting the Mexican President called for a special Latin American ministerial-level meeting on debt and development, in January 1987 to which I accompanied the Secretary-General. He arrived from a whirlwind tour of Central America, in the company of the Foreign Ministers of the so-called Contadora Group and the Secretary-General of the Organisation of American States (OAS), in a last-ditch attempt to bring peace to the area. They gave pessimistic impressions of prospects for a settlement at a working dinner given by President de la Madrid. The outcome of the conference was not very encouraging either, although I did detect the glimmerings of greater understanding of the competing claims of debt and development by some industrialized countries.

Other Special Assignments

In my Bolivian and Mexican assignments I did not achieve all that I would have liked but I felt I had 'made a difference'. One senior

UN official remarked that in Bolivia the UN had achieved the consolidation of democracy and cited it as an example of the major benefits that the organisation could bring about in a quiet way and with minimum expenditure of funds. Such achievements, because difficult to single out and measure, go unrecognised.

Similar satisfactions were not forthcoming for some of the other special missions Pérez de Cuéllar asked me to undertake. While I was juggling with Bolivia and Mexico in 1985 he appointed me as chairman of a group to review and improve the operations of the World Food Council. The other members were former Ministers of Agriculture: Sartaj Aziz of Pakistan, and Abdelatif Ghissassi of Morocco. Our work involved meetings in Rome, Washington, Paris and New York and consultations with the governments and other institutions. Our report was well received but with the financial situation of the United Nations worsening no follow-up action was taken by the governments that had mandated the review.

From 1982 to 1984, at the Secretary-General's request, I chaired the UN Appointments and Promotions Board. The promotions system was cumbersome and largely ineffective, mainly because performance reports were misleading. Since staff members who got less than an 'outstanding' rating launched lengthy appeals, their bosses took the easier course of giving the highest marking, which lost all validity. I felt deeply committed to the UN policy to get more women into professional positions but the resistance of some managers, even in the case of women of proven merit, was as regrettable as the insistence of some women that they must have preferment simply because of their gender, irrespective of qualifications or competence. With the board members I developed measures to make the system simpler and fairer but no action was taken.

During 1982 I also chaired an inter-agency body, the Consultative Committee on Substantive Questions (Operational). That year we analysed the causes of the shortfall in resources for multilateral development, and proposed a programme of remedial action. Our report went to the Administrative Committee on Co-ordination in November 1982, but support for multilateral aid continued to decline.

UN Reform

Just before my home leave in July 1986, the Secretary-General asked me to orchestrate follow-up action on the UN special session on Africa held in May 1986, and mobilise funds for the long-term development of that desperately poor continent. During my leave, however, he telephoned to say he would prefer me to co-ordinate the implementation of the recommendations of the Group of Eighteen – a body of High-Level Inter-Governmental Experts which, in August 1986, presented its report on 'the efficiency of the administrative and financial functioning of the United Nations'.

The growing financial crisis of the UN had come to a head when the USA announced that it would pay only part of its 1986 contribution unless certain conditions were met. These included the introduction of 'weighted-voting', which would have entailed renegotiating the UN Charter. Since the USA accounted for 25 per cent of the budget the impact was enormous, and was further accentuated by the Gramm-Rudman law to reduce the US deficit by an across-the-board cut in budget appropriations. It was the worst crisis the organisation had ever faced. The Group of Eighteen was a compromise solution: if the group came up with a reasonable programme of reform that was acted upon, then the USA would reconsider its position.

On 15 September 1986 my appointment as Special Co-ordinator, working directly with the Secretary-General, was announced. I was released from DTCD until May 1987, when he had to report to the General Assembly. The Group of Eighteen report was an uneven document, the product of a committee composed of 'experts' chosen for geographical representation rather than technical competence, and so prone to political compromise rather than logical analysis of the problems. Its recommendations gave rise to considerable controversy in the General Assembly, which could not reach agreement on what should be done until just before Christmas 1986. Meanwhile we had already started work on contingency planning and structural reviews of all the major areas covered by the organisation – political, economic and social sectors, conference services, public information, finance and administration. Once the General

Assembly gave the green light, we undertook consultations in various parts of the world.

My energies were again being torn in different directions. On 26 November 1986 the Secretary-General announced sweeping changes in the top levels of the Secretariat, responding to member states' demand for rationalisation and a 25 per cent reduction in the higher echelons of staff. I was appointed Director-General of the UN Office at Vienna (UNOV), the third Headquarters of the UN (after New York and Geneva) with the rank of Under Secretary-General, and with effect from 1 March 1987. Together with a Canadian woman, a political appointee who was to head the Department of Public Information, we became the first women Under Secretaries-General. The Director-Generalship in Vienna had been a largely ceremonial and administrative post, with no substantive responsibilities. Now I was to be, concurrently, Director-General of UNOV, Head of the UN Centre for Social Development and Humanitarian Affairs and Co-ordinator of all UN Drug-related Activities. I would take over functions that had previously occupied one Under Secretary-General and one Assistant Secretary-General full-time in Vienna, and part of the time of two Under Secretaries-General in New York. For policy reasons my assumption of these new functions could not be postponed until I finished my major reform job in New York and so on 1 March I flew to Vienna for an initial visit of two weeks, and for the next three months juggled my two responsibilities.

In early May the Committee on Programme Co-ordination (CPC) began consideration of the Secretary-General's first report on the implementation of the reforms. In writing it I had been careful to avoid UN jargon and to present the reforms and budget cuts, not as ends in themselves, but in the context of the key political, economic and social functions that the UN is called upon to fulfil. Gratifyingly, the CPC gave us a good reception, as had key people in the US Congress whom I had briefed in Washington two weeks earlier.

What had we achieved? As a result of our work, the Secretary-General carried out all the most important changes requested. The Committee on Policy Co-ordination was modified to meet US complaints about the way in which budgets were voted, and so ensure zero growth. Headquarters' structure was streamlined, some departments being merged to achieve the target of slashing posts at Assistant Secretary-General and above by 25 per cent and the rest of the staff by 15 per cent. Among other major measures was a new vacancy management system, which made the manner of filling posts and granting promotions much fairer, thus permitting a rational career pattern for the most able.

Yet the measures adopted gave rise to objections from the very member states most vociferous in demanding reform, particularly if they affected positions occupied by their nationals. A farcical situation developed over our proposal to establish a small office directly reporting to the Secretary-General to keep a watching brief on emerging crises in the world, so that the organisation would be better prepared to react promptly and effectively to emergencies. In Washington, headlines blazoned that the UN was setting up a KGB. In Moscow there was a simultaneous outcry that the UN was creating its own CIA ... ! It was a typical 'no-win' situation in which the UN often finds itself, when a rational arrangement can be given paranoid interpretations, aided and abetted by the media.

The United States obtained everything it had demanded but Congress still blocked payment of US contributions. Crippling debts continued almost to the present day, with devastating effect on the efficiency and staff morale of the UN. No one can expect managers to perform with vision when every day they have to worry how to meet the next day's expenses. It is rather like an old-fashioned husband saying to his wife, 'You are not running the household efficiently and economically, and I'm going to stop your housekeeping money until you do better'.

Yet still, all these years later, the clamour for 'broad reform and reductions' continues. For myself, my experience in 1987 destroyed any lingering faith I had in across-the-board reform, because of political compromise and the inconsequential attitudes of member states.

Personal Life

Jacko's appointment by Waldheim, at the end of 1979, as co-ordinator of the Kampuchean operation made it harder to synchronise our movements. In 1981 he had spent less than three months in New York, and in 1983 we spent barely two and a half months together, anywhere in the world.

He was struggling heroically with an almost intractable problem and had become emotionally involved with the plight of the Kampuchean people. Incredibly the genocidal Pol Pot regime, one of the most inhuman and despicable that history records, still occupied the Kampuchean seat in the General Assembly, and was de facto recognised by the international community. This blatant hypocrisy infuriated Jacko. He performed his customary miracles – already by mid-1980 he got adequate food and seed into the country before the monsoon started – but was in constant anguish that he could not do more.

His health suffered. In 1980 and 1981 he had to take periods of rest and in September 1984 there was a real scare. He received an emergency operation for an accumulation of fluid in the lungs and around the heart – a severe case of pericarditis. He made a remarkable recovery but was bruised psychologically by Pérez de Cuéllar's decision to dispense with his services in 1984, partly because of the manner in which it was conveyed, but mainly because he felt passionately that the job he considered a kind of crusade was far from finished. His mind and remarkable operational capabilities were as sharp as ever, but were never again to be put fully to the service of the international community or the destitute of the world.

Jacko again found it almost impossible to adjust to a quieter life, though he worked tirelessly for various organisations on a voluntary basis. Always a complex personality, prone to bouts of depression and self-doubt, he became more withdrawn. We continued to enjoy mutual companionship and we never stopped consulting one another on professional matters, but something intangible had changed. One factor was the lack of any formalisation of our relationship, even after Barbara Ward's death in 1981. This was a source of mystification to our friends and indeed to me who had given up the love of my life in 1971. But it was a subject that could not be broached.

Had Jacko and I married I would have left the UN years before. As it was, I was anxious to ensure that when I did leave I would have a proper home. At intervals Jacko announced his intention of buying a house, but it never came to anything. That was why I had started to make my own arrangements in Bolivia, and there were other developments.

In 1979 I had spent Christmas with Christina. Christmas Day was a crisp, frosty day of brilliant sunshine, the hedgerows and trees hung with hoarfrost like glittering silver decorations. While everyone else was indoors, we had the snow-covered hills to ourselves. The highlight of that walk was the sight, from the top of Knill Garraway of the walled garden at Knill, brilliant in sunshine and the bright reflections of snow. We became acquainted with the owners on another day, when we peeped in for a closer look at this idyllic spot, enclosed on three sides by old walls of rosy bricks and on the fourth by the vivacious Hindwell Brook (really a small river), with a vista beyond of water meadows and the steep escarpments of Knill Garraway and Herrock Hill. I was enchanted. This was the countryside where I had wandered as a child, and my mother had spent her childhood in those hills. Christina was enchanted too, but the property was not for sale. It was not until seven years later that Christina was able to acquire this dream abode. The sale was completed in March 1987, but then nine months of renovation and reconstruction ensued.

That summer I sold Pippins. It was a wrench for me, since my parents had created the garden, but Wedmore was marred by the advent of a motorway nearby. More intangibly, the sale signified a realisation that it was no use my waiting any longer for Jacko to take decisions that would ensure our joint future.

Figure 1 Visiting an Andean Indian family on the *altiplano*, Bolivia, early 1960s.

Figure 2 Rural development mission, China, 1980.

Figure 3 As Director-General of the UN Office at Vienna, and Coordinator of all UN drug-control related programmes, visiting agricultural projects for alternative crops in Northern Thailand, 1989.

Figure 4 Visiting a gold mining project in the jungle in Benin, 1981.

Figure 5 Portrait in Montevideo, Uruguay, 1959.

Figure 6 UN Day, Addis Ababa, 1967. With Robert Gardiner, Executive Secretary of the UN Economic Commission for Africa, and Diallo Tello, Secretary-General of the Organisation of African States (later executed in his own country).

Figure 7 With Javier Pérez de Cuéllar at a UN conference in Vienna, 1988.

Figure 8 With UN Secretary-General Kofi Annan, Vienna, 1998, just after we received the news that my successor in Angola, Maître Beye, had perished in a suspicious plane accident, along with other UN colleagues.

Figure 9 Jacko (Sir Robert Jackson) at Trélex in 1969 with Thomas, the Capacity Cat, who tried to prevent the Study being written by sitting on it – the only cat ever to appear in an official UN report!

Figure 10 Official UN photo of Jacko during the Bangladesh operation, taken in the early 1970s.

Figure 11 Hanging of Jacko's portrait in the Palais des Nations, Geneva, 1997.

Figure 12 With the then UN Secretary-General Boutros-Ghali, 6th February 1995.

Figure 13 First meeting with Vadim Bakatin, Mikhail Gorbachev's Minister of the Interior, Moscow, 1989.

Figure 14 Visiting Lenin's study in the Kremlin with Minister Bakatin, 1989.

Figure 15 With Fidel Castro at the end of the 8th UN Crime Congress, Havana, 1990.

Figure 16 With Foreign Minister Eduard Shevardnadze, Moscow, 1991.

Figure 17 With Prime Minister Li Peng, Beijing, 1991.

Figure 18 With President Jimmy Carter, Vienna, 50th anniversary of the UN Declaration of Human Rights, 1998.

Figure 19 Finale of World Congress of Women Moscow, 1987.
[Mikhail Gorbachev in centre, myself second to his right, then Mrs Papandreou and next to her Mrs Gorbachev.]

Figure 20 'Indeed, "negotiating the labyrinth"!' – my Chef de Cabinet noted, on this tête-à-tête with Italian Foreign Minister, Giulio Andreotti, at the Pío Manzu Foundation Symposium with that title in 1987. We were discussing the problem of co-ordinating drug questions with his protégé, di Gennaro.

Figure 21 Touching the damaged reactor at Chernobyl 'with a distinctly nervous smile', 1991.

Figure 22 Assessing earthquake damage in Mexico, 1985, with Ambassador Jorge Montaño.

Figure 23 As Special Representative of the Secretary-General for Angola after presenting medals to a departing UN military contingent at UNAVEM Headquarters, 1992. (UN photograph).

Figure 24 Inspecting the burning oil fields in Kuwait, 1991, after the Gulf War.

Figure 25 Taking possession of my land on the shores of Lake Titicaca, Bolivia, 1988.

Figure 26 Villa Margarita, when completed, my home on Lake Titicaca, 1991. There has been further development subsequently.

Figure 27 Villa Clara Rosa, El Arrayán, Chile, 1972–4.

Figure 28 A special birthday celebration, 25th June 1996, at The Walled Garden, with itinerant Bolivian musicians from Potosí.

Figure 29 The Walled Garden, Knill.

Figure 30 'Kidnapped' during a peace-keeping training exercise for US and Latin American troops, Honduras, 2000 (US army photo).

Figure 31 Investiture at Buckingham Palace, 7th March 1994 (International Women's Day).

Figure 32 A tense moment during the Angolan Elections, 29th–30th September 1998. This picture hangs in the UN. (UN photograph).

PART SEVEN

Vienna

19

In Vienna Woods 1987–92

The UN Office at Vienna

The year 1987 was to prove a watershed for me, both professionally and personally. I was naturally chuffed that I had at last broken through the glass ceiling that had previously prevented women from attaining the topmost rank of UN officials. The British government also seemed pleased. Prime Minister Margaret Thatcher sent me a warm letter, together with an offer of support in my new functions.

My arrival in Vienna on Sunday 1 March coincided with a heavy snowstorm which blanketed the city. From my hotel room, I had a view of snowy roofs, towers, turrets and cupolas, as well as of couples of all ages waltzing expertly on the ice rink next door, a romantic and typically Viennese scene. On Monday morning I installed myself in my palatial but sombrely panelled office, with a UN security guard saluting at the door and at 10 o'clock addressed the Commission on Social Development. The speech was important because my advent marked the beginning of a new strategy for the UN Office at Vienna (UNOV).

UNOV came into being in the 1970s when Kurt Waldheim was Secretary-General. The Austrian Government wanted to improve Vienna's international and neutral status, taking advantage of its strategic location between Eastern and Western Europe, at a time when the Cold War was still at its height. It offered to construct a custom-built headquarters to house the International Atomic Energy Agency (IAEA) and the UN Industrial Development

Organisation (UNIDO), which were already in Vienna, and units of the New York secretariat.

A huge complex of massive towers arose on the other side of the Danube, dominating Vienna's southern horizon. The UN Centre for Social Development and Humanitarian Affairs (CSDHA) had been transferred there, but still came under the Department of International Economic and Social Affairs in New York, an arrangement that made no sense. All UN programmes relating to narcotic drugs were also transferred to Vienna from Geneva and New York: the UN Division for Narcotic Drugs (DND), the International Narcotics Control Board (INCB), and the UN Fund for Drug Abuse Control (UNFDAC). The first Director-General of UNOV, whom I succeeded, had a mainly representational and administrative function and no jurisdiction over substantive units. I had much wider responsibilities. Full command over all the UN entities in Vienna was transferred from New York to me. The Assistant Secretary-General post in CSDHA was abolished and I became its head. I was also appointed the Co-ordinator of all UN drug-related programmes.

The strategy was to make the Vienna Headquarters the nucleus for all UN activities relating to social policy and social development but, in true UN fashion, innumerable obstacles arose in practice. Certain aspects of social policy formulation had remained in New York in DIESA, the former parent department. The Secretary-General agreed that they should come to us, but the Under Secretary-General in charge of DIESA, a jealous guarder of his turf, refused to comply. Twice Kofi Annan, then Assistant Secretary-General for Personnel, assured me affably that the posts would be transferred, but nothing happened. The fight continued unresolved for the next five years.

A more pernicious difficulty arose with the Assistant Secretary-General heading UNFDAC. Guiseppe di Gennaro was infuriated by the decision to put anyone over his head. He had hitherto answered to an Under Secretary-General in New York, but he was comfortably remote, and now I was on the spot. Guiseppe was passionately committed to stamping out the illicit consumption and trafficking of narcotic drugs but he had to be the king-pin and had strong political support from Giulio Andreotti, then Foreign Minister of Italy. As soon as my appointment was announced in November 1986 he engineered a draft resolution opposing it in the Commission on Narcotic Drugs (CND). Simultaneously, Foreign Minister Andreotti protested to Pérez de Cuéllar. Geoffrey Howe, then British Secretary of State for Foreign Affairs, had to intervene personally with his Italian counterpart before Andreotti's grudging acquiescence was obtained — to a decision wholly within the Secretary-General's prerogative as Chief Executive! The matter was never really settled. Pérez de Cuéllar did not take a strong stand with di Gennaro because Italy was the largest contributor to UNFDAC.

I was at pains to emphasise to di Gennaro that I intended to handle my role as drug co-ordinator with a very loose rein, and had no intention of interfering in UNFDAC's day-to-day work. It was to no avail; at the UN International Conference on Drug Abuse and Illicit Trafficking (ICDAIT) in Vienna in June 1987, he engineered another attack on my authority from the floor. This coincided with my birthday — unequivocally a *cadeau empoisonné*, obliging me to make a spirited response from the podium. The revolt died down but constant sniping was to be par for the course.

Two or three years earlier Jacko and I had gone out of our way to help di Gennaro who had been our guest. In a curious way, our relations continued cordial on a personal plane in Vienna: once, when his roof was leaking, he asked if I could offer him a bed for the night! He would have fought anyone put over him but the fact that I was a woman was the last straw. Some years later Guiseppe wrote a book. Predictably, he treated me unkindly but, much more unforgivably, he attacked Andreotti (who had fallen on hard times, and was under criminal process), the man who for decades had been his benefactor.

The ICDAIT Conference had other problems. The Prime Minister of Malaysia, Mahathur, and the Foreign Minister of Bolivia, Guillermo Bedregal, were locked in struggle for the conference presidency. At the eleventh hour, as I was about to escort the Secretary-General to the podium to call for a vote from the floor, a compromise was reached whereby Malaysia got the Presidency, and Bolivia the chairmanship of the main committee. Despite all the inauspicious circumstances, the conference reached an international consensus on priority measures to combat drugs and gave a greatly increased mandate to the United Nations.

The continuing UN financial crisis was to dog my whole five years as Director-General. The problem was double-headed: on the one hand the acute cash-flow difficulties caused by non-payment of assessed contributions (especially by the United States, the largest contributor); on the other, the continued pressure to reduce future budgets. In Vienna, we were struggling to provide increased programmes requested by member states but were not allowed to increase our budget nor even to recruit staff to fill vacant posts (because of the cash-flow problem). Recently created, UNOV was a lean, rather than fat, cat but we were still required to reduce our staff by 15 per cent (because of the budget problem). We were not being asked to do 'the same with less', but '*more* with less'. The drug budgets were laughable: the UN regular budget for the Division of Narcotic Drugs and the International Narcotics Control Board, at US$4 million, was less than the price of one suitcase of heroin at Heathrow Airport! Even the US$60 million voluntary funds financing UNFDAC's operational projects in developing countries were peanuts compared to the drug traffickers' billions.

I was constantly criss-crossing the Atlantic, fighting the budget battle in every possible forum and making myself pretty unpopular with some New York colleagues. I had staunch support from *all* the ambassadors accredited to my office in Vienna (these numbered some 110), and the Commission on Narcotic Drugs passed an unprecedented, unanimous resolution urging that the drug pro-grammes should not be cut. None of us was able to get our message clearly enough across to our opposite numbers in New York to prevent the axe from falling (ironically, very heavily on drugs).

During the ICDAIT Conference, I represented the Secretary-General, on 22 June, at the opening of the World Congress of Women in Moscow. Those of us who were to sit on the praesidium learned that General Secretary Mikhail Gorbachev was to open the Congress and, just minutes before he arrived with his wife Raisa, I was casually informed that there would only be two speeches, Mr Gorbachev's and mine! As we all trooped out behind Mr and Mrs Gorbachev, under a blaze of television lights, into the immense hall of the Kremlin, packed from floor to ceiling with 7000 women, from 150 countries, it became agonisingly clear to me that the Secretary-General's message that I was to read was totally inadequate.

Mr Gorbachev set matters of concern to women in the context of a major policy speech, embracing wider issues. Apart from the welcome indication that he considered women to be an important audience it was long enough to permit me to jot down hurried notes for an ex tempore personal speech to add to the dry official message. Once I had negotiated steps and a wide expanse of slippery parquet without falling flat on my face, I found the experience exhilarating. There were women from every walk of life, and most political persuasions, ranging from rural African women to a svelte lady, sophisticated in bright red and a huge black hat, and a group of anti-nuclear protestors from Greenham Common, waving banners. Afterwards, I was given two photos – one of Mr Gorbachev delivering his speech with me intently listening behind, the other of me making mine, but only half of Gorbachev's face in the background. I never managed to get that rectified.

Among the many technical meetings over which I presided in 1987, the most difficult was a conference of ministers responsible for social issues, held in Vienna in September 1987. This innocuous-sounding event had become a pawn of the Cold War. There had been a long controversy, with East–West connotations, over the conference agenda, and even suggestions it should not take place, lest it degenerate into a political wrangle. ECOSOC gave the green light barely two months before documents had to be issued. Financial restrictions making it impossible to use consultants, all the work was done in-house, and the conference must have beaten all records for the shortest lead time and lowest cost. Even more satisfactory was the praise heaped on the quality of the analyses by the delegations – a much-needed morale-booster for my staff.

People from nearly 100 countries, including many ministers, attended the conference. The debate almost entirely avoided political controversy, largely due to restraint on the part of Eastern European countries, a clear indication of their changing approach. The emphasis was on the critical importance of resolving social issues too long neglected everywhere, and common to all countries, cutting across the arbitrary frontiers of East–West and North–South. An international consensus began to emerge. 'Guiding Principles' were adopted both for member states and ourselves. This document expanded our mandate but once again the extra tasks were to be undertaken 'within existing resources'.

A more unusual experience was a symposium organised in Rimini in October by the Pio Manzu Foundation on the subject of 'Negotiating the Labyrinth' (the labyrinth being the current state of our world) at which I represented the Secretary-General. The opening ceremony was presided over by Foreign Minister Andreotti and broadcast live over Italian national television. There was a very eclectic collection of distinguished personalities, but so few women that I couldn't resist reminding the audience that it was Ariadne who extricated Theseus from the labyrinth. With Gary Hart, the former US Democratic presidential hopeful, who had been forced to retire owing to scandal over his private life, I had several interesting conversations about the impact of the media on presidential campaigns – and candidates – and was amused to discover that his traumatic experiences had in no way dimmed his capacities as a charmer, or his aspirations as a ladies' man. Most importantly I had a tête-à-tête with Andreotti during which I explained my concept of my role as Drug Co-ordinator, and requested his support in persuading di Gennaro to cooperate. His response was positive, but di Gennaro remained hell-bent on pursuing his own agenda.

I still retained my functions as Special Representative of the Secretary-General for Bolivia. Frequent visits were no longer necessary, but I had promised the Government to go before the end of 1987 and did so in November. It was an important country for our drugs programme and I spent two days visiting coca-producing areas. The Government deserved credit for launching a new and vigorous onslaught on drugs, given their limited resources, but there needed to be greater understanding abroad of the complexities that they faced and greater material support from the international community. The Secretary-General's appeal for the Social Emergency fund had met with a good response and we now needed to concentrate on resolving Bolivia's external debt problem. I was touched when the President and his wife gave a dinner for me, for Victor Paz shunned social occasions.

I flew on to Lima, for talks with the Peruvian Government on social and drug issues. During a short stopover in New York I briefed the Secretary-General and returned to Vienna in good spirits, unaware of the cataclysmic blow that was to fall a week later.

A Tragic Development

Jacko did not want to live in Vienna and initially decided to stay in New York and visit me often, while I travelled frequently to Headquarters. We spent our leave in July organising renovation and extension work at The Walled Garden for Christina and in August 1987 had a few days together in Vienna, and again in New York in October. I flew to London on his birthday, 8 November, which we celebrated at a dinner with his son and daughter-in-law, and my friends the Gibsons, after which he left on a long round-the-world trip. It was the last time I saw him in an apparently healthy physical state.

Jacko returned to New York on Friday 18 December and was to travel on to the UK on the Monday to spend Christmas with us at Knill. There was a dreadful fatality about that weekend I had arranged for our housekeeper to cook his lunch on the Saturday and for Valentina Lim to visit him. As he had a meeting Jacko cancelled both arrangements, and asked Valentina to come instead on Sunday evening. When we spoke on Friday morning, he sounded cheerful and said he would ring me on Saturday night. When by midnight, Vienna time, he had not rung I called but there was no reply. On Sunday my half-hourly calls met with a persistent engaged signal. At 2 a.m. on the Monday morning (8 p.m. Sunday in New York) I phoned again. Valentina answered. She and another UN colleague had just broken the security chain on the door and found Jacko lying in the hall, paralysed by a severe stroke. As we pieced the story together, it seemed that this had occurred in the early hours of Saturday morning, so he had been lying untended for nearly 48 hours. He had dragged himself to the telephone and heard my call on the Saturday evening but could not unhook the instrument. Later he managed to call the emergency services, but, his speech being slurred, they evidently thought he was drunk, and hung up. He was unable to replace the phone.

I could not leave immediately because my aunt badly needed help at Knill. I was assured that Jacko was being given first-rate care, and his life was not in danger. I even managed to speak to him by telephone. Fortunately Robin was able to fly immediately to his father's bedside, though for only 24 hours. Immediately after Christmas I followed. Every day I spent 14 hours at Jacko's bedside, holding his hand, reading to him, and helping him with his rehabilitation exercises. In between I ran my office in Vienna by telephone.

Jacko's one overwhelming desire was to get back to England and 'Sister Agnes' (the King Edward VII Hospital for Officers in London). He despaired of my being able to get him there but we managed it on 14 January, thanks to help from many quarters, particularly Robin who accompanied us, and British Airways, who made superb arrangements. Jacko was severely paralysed, so the move required minute logistical planning (worthy of the Bangladesh relief operation, I told him, which at least made him smile), ambulances at each end, stretchers and wheelchairs. The flight seemed interminable and I have never been so glad to see the lights of London twinkling below us.

A month later Jacko moved to a rehabilitation centre in Surrey, where he spent a weary eight months. I telephoned him every night and visited as often as I could. He recovered physically more than we had dared to hope but balance and a virtually useless left arm remained a problem. Fortunately his speech came back to almost normal, and in May 1988 he appeared, in a wheelchair, on a BBC TV programme, *Panorama*, dealing with Kampuchea.

I did not manage to find a settled home in Vienna until June 1988, because Dr Mock, the Austrian Foreign Minister, had told me, on arrival that the Government wished to provide me and my successors with an official residence as the Swiss Government did for the UN Director-General in Geneva. So I had flitted from one temporary abode to another, rather like Beethoven, except that I don't play the piano, either too loudly or at all, and I *did* pay the rent! After many months Dr Mock told me regretfully that the Government could not fulfil its promise. Eventually I was established in an apartment in the nineteenth district in Nüssdorf, with large balconies and marvellous views over the city in one direction and vineyards on the other. All the familiar furniture from New York was there and I had an excellent housekeeper, Elisabeth Hejny, 'Sissy'. I wanted Jacko to join me but this unrivalled world traveller now refused to leave England. We installed him with a housekeeper in a pleasant garden flat in Roehampton, near the airport, so I was able to stay with him on my way to other destinations.

After a time Jacko's physical recovery hit a plateau, and he lost heart. His mental agility, his great interest in current affairs, and his capacity for righteous anger at the misdemeanours of the UN remained unimpaired, but this only exacerbated his frustration. In November 1988, having to address a meeting in the House of Lords, I was in London for Jacko's seventy-seventh birthday and cajoled him into coming to lunch at the Oxford and Cambridge Club, with the strong-arm help of his son and my Chef de Cabinet. That was his last outing, except to visit doctors. He never went back to Knill and never saw finished the renovations that we had supervised in the summer of 1987. Fortunately many friends visited him, and he kept in close touch with the outside world. But it was a sadly diminished life.

Social Programmes

Meanwhile, I was trying to keep UNOV afloat. Few people realise that political activities constitute only about 10 per cent of the UN budget, and that the rest goes to economic and social programmes, of relevance to people the world over. This was certainly true of the issues we were dealing with in Vienna. Three areas that I was responsible for – the disabled, the aging and youth – had been the subject of global conferences and ambitious plans of action. Political commitment had not been matched financially, and all three were run on shoestring budgets and skeleton staff. None of this exempted us from criticism that we were not doing more and I had to find innovative ways of raising extra-budgetary funds.

I scored an early success by contriving to establish, outside the budget, a post of Special Representative of the Secretary-General for the Disabled, in the person of a distinguished Norwegian, Hans Hoegh, formerly Secretary-General of the International Committee of the Red Cross (ICRC). More help appeared in the person of Sir John Wilson who, blind himself, had for years done sterling work for the sightless. He urged me to support an initiative to raise money for the disabled in developing countries through televised shows, contribution dinners and the like. The aim was to obtain financial sponsorship by large corporations for specific projects.

We worked hard for months on this but encountered insuperable problems, partly the lack of seed-money to finance professional impresarios but because the UN Legal Department's refusal to allow the use of the logo for the UN Decade of the Disabled by sponsoring corporations. I thought that the appearance of the symbol on, say, a bottle of Coca Cola in the American mid-west, indicating that the firm was funding projects for the disabled in poorer countries, would not only produce money, but would publicise the needs of the disabled and the little-known work of the UN. One of their more arcane arguments was that the UN had survived for 40 years without resorting to such tactics, to which I responded that government contributions from public sector funds having diminished we, like everyone else, must resort to the market. They also maintained that if member states did not provide the means to carry out the mandates they had given us then we had no obligation to do so. Such nihilism was entirely foreign to my nature but, after a long struggle, we had to abandon the venture.

Parallel endeavours to set up a world foundation of aging – the Banyan Fund, (named after the long-lived banyan tree) – to help older people in developing countries realise their full potential came up against the same obstacles and, after a promising start, had also to be abandoned by the UN. The powerful American Association of Retired Persons (AARP) took the fund under its wing.

Sometimes we received gratifying support from small countries, putting wealthier states to shame. One such was Malta, which established the International Institute on Aging, in affiliation with my office, for research and training. I accompanied the Secretary-General to its inauguration in April 1988 and was made chairman of the institute's board of governors.

The institute was the brainchild of the President of Malta, Dr Vincent Tabor, and on one of my visits in October 1989 I was to present him with a testimonial from the Secretary-General for his pioneer work on aging. Unfortunately, due to a slip-up in Vienna, neither I nor my colleagues actually *had* the testimonial. A splendid formal ceremony had been arranged with military band, Prime Minister and Cabinet, diplomatic corps, church dignitaries, etc. Frenzied calls to Vienna revealed that there was no way of getting the missing scroll to Valletta in time. The Institute on Aging came to the rescue and forged a replica. Luckily, the President suspected nothing, and triumphantly held the testimonial up for the TV cameras. When the real thing reached him he was so tickled that he hung them both up together! Another diplomatic pitfall loomed: in Malta ladies wore hats at ceremonies taking place in the morning. Mine, like the testimonial, were in Vienna but I acquired a natty little black number in a hasty sortie along the cobbled streets of Valletta.

The Social Dimensions of Development

Our fund-raising activities were adversely affected by the prevailing economic climate, but it is also true that social issues are the last to be considered. The oft-lauded market, left to its devices, simply sends them to the wall. This was a central theme of my statement to the spring session of the Economic and Social Council in 1991. I linked it to the inconsistency and dilatoriness of governments in giving any real support to UNOV, despite the expressed wish of the General Assembly, in 1987, to give new prominence to social problems; these, I argued, were the great *political* challenge of the 1990s, in every region of the world, especially the developing countries. The speech was criticised in some quarters as being too hard-hitting for a mere member of the Secretariat but the Secretary-General supported me.

414 NEVER LEARN TO TYPE

The unquestioning enthusiasm for liberal economics and swingeing stabilisation programmes had begun to be tempered by a growing realisation that the social consequences could be disastrous. The Emergency Social Programme in Bolivia had been a pioneer in introducing attenuating measures and was imitated elsewhere. More generally UNICEF's 'Adjustment with a Human Face' had significant impact. A lot of meetings on this theme blossomed.

One such conference, entitled 'Human Dimensions of Africa's Recovery and Development', was held in Khartoum in March 1988. Although the full horror of the Sudanese tragedy was not yet apparent I found Khartoum sadly deteriorated. Now Juba and the South were inaccessible. Poverty was everywhere. Even the goats roaming the bare dirt streets could find nothing to scavenge except paper and plastic bags. It was hard to believe that the situation could get worse, yet it has, with one of the worst wars of recent times, until recently unnoticed by the rest of the world. The desperate plight of most of Africa 15 years later, riven by barbaric civil wars and unimaginable human suffering, gives a distinctly hollow ring to the recommendations of that particular gathering. The same might be said of another meeting, to which I spoke, a conference on sub-Sahara Africa development, organised by Jan Pronk, the Dutch Minister for Development, in Maastricht in July 1990.

In September 1990 UNDP invited me to give a paper at a round table in Amman, Jordan, on 'Development: the Human Dimension'. A number of radical thinkers present sat up most of the last night producing a draft 'Declaration of Amman' that contained some volcanic proposals, including a recommendation that developing countries should jointly refuse to honour their external debt. Discussion next morning was circumscribed by the imminent arrival of Crown Prince Hassan. I argued that some of the recommendations were unrealistic and premature in the current climate but even the amended document was ahead of its time.

Then the Administrator of UNDP rose to speak. William Draper III was a close friend of President George Bush, a conservative thinker, imbued with the current economic orthodoxy. He had decreed that no UNDP project could be approved unless it contained a 'private sector component', a condition difficult to meet in many countries. In Amman he expressed pleasure that this subject so close to his heart had figured prominently in the declaration, evidently not taking on board the fact that most of the declaration was anathema to the private sector. Draper did promote the cause of women but whenever we met he would bang me on the back in a great bear hug and bellow, 'Hi yah, kiddo!' Seething inwardly, I restrained the impulse to ask him how many other Under Secretaries-General he greeted in this fashion.

The social downside of the market economy became a frequent theme in my presentations for the UN Commission on Social Development, to ECOSOC, and to the Second and Third Committees of the General Assembly and was a major subject for discussion on my visits to many countries.

In May 1989 I was invited to China. In view of the growing crescendo of protest in Tiananmen Square, I called the Chinese Ambassador in Vienna and suggested a postponement. He was appalled by the very idea; the visit was fixed, the programme arranged, and everything perfectly normal in Beijing – a typically Chinese reaction. 'Nonetheless, I think you should check,' I urged. On the day I was to leave, the ambassador called, requesting I postpone my trip, as if our earlier conversation had never taken place. Had my visit gone ahead, it would have coincided with the bloody denouement of the tragedy.

Two years later everything was under strict control. My most interesting meeting in Beijing in April 1991 was one of 40 minutes with the Prime Minister, Li Peng. This was an extraordinarily formal set piece: the two of us sat on a dais, each with an interpreter, not facing one another but looking out towards an audience of Chinese officials and other hangers-on. It was hardly conducive to what in diplomatic language is termed 'a frank exchange of views', but we had a good discussion on the importance of social policy, on which there was a remarkable level of agreement. Greatly daring, I steered the conversation towards the relationship between human rights and social development. Li Peng was unfailingly affable, apparently acquiescent, but inscrutable. The wounds of Tiananmen were still raw.

At any rate the Chinese were anxious to show me that they were concerned for the social welfare of their citizens. I was taken to a centre for the aging, where some elderly ladies gracefully modelled dresses they had made; played croquet in the pouring rain with another group of enthusiastic seniors; and visited a cosmetics factory, staffed by disabled people. I came away laden with mysterious beauty products (their qualities exclusively described in Chinese) and industrial quantities of a slimming cream (a nice diplomatic touch), reputed to be infallible, but which did not produce results in my case, mainly because it had such a pungent smell that I couldn't use it without risking public ostracism.

I had not been in China since 1980. Then a car had been a rare spectacle. Now there were traffic jams. Bicycles were still plentiful but corralled in special lanes. The weather was grey and chilly, but forsythia and cherry blossoms gave promise of spring, and China seemed in the throes of change.

Chile was once again trying to tackle social problems after long years of dictatorship and exclusive emphasis on the market and orthodox economic policies. It was a joy to go there in August 1991, my first visit after the restoration of democracy, and to be reunited with many old friends basking in the new freedom. The Government gave me a very clear message: they wished to make up for lost ground in the social area but could not afford to do so at the expense of the economic growth that Chile had achieved in recent years. They faced the same dilemma as many other developing countries. Nonetheless it was heartening to see Chile managing so well, so far, the other precarious balancing act of returning to democratic rule. On that same trip I found that social programmes were also a high priority in Colombia for President Gaviria and his ministers. Alas, it was too late for those caught in areas already overrun by the widening internal conflict.

One of my initiatives to focus more attention on social issues was to set up a social development forum in UNOV. It was informal, bringing together ambassadors, academics and NGOs and met whenever I could find a provocative speaker. We had lively debates on matters such as the imperative need to bridge the widening gap between North and South and the economic and social dimensions of security, the consolidation of which, it was becoming ever clearer even then, was not assured by military and defence measures alone but required tangible improvements in the standards of living of poorer people all over the world. General Ansegun Obasanjo of Nigeria, then candidate for Secretary-General, took as his theme the relationship between 'Democracy and Good Government'. Now, poor man, he is finding how difficult it is to put his ideas into practice as President of his own unruly country.

Another innovative idea was to bring together ministers responsible for economic and social policy in Eastern Europe and Latin America. This fascinating encounter took place in Vienna in February 1991. We shut them up together for two days with no agenda except to compare experiences. I was delighted to find that this exchange confirmed my conviction that Eastern Europe countries undergoing drastic change could gain much – *mutatis mutandis* – from Latin America, and the lessons of Bolivia's programme were brilliantly expounded by Enrique García, then Planning Minister. There was unanimous agreement that the most difficult aspect of economic change is its social dimension – the one to which least attention is paid.

In Vienna we were among the first to highlight the wider implications of AIDS, originally regarded primarily as a medical problem. We produced a groundbreaking study of its impact on women in 1988, and in meetings with Dr Jonathan Mann, then heading WHO's AIDS programme, we emphasised its economic and social consequences, as well as the relationship with drug abuse.

I served for three years on WHO's Global Commission on AIDS, which had its first meeting in Geneva in March 1989. I found myself in an impressive constellation of scientific, medical and academic luminaries, including the American and French scientists disputing the honour of being the first to identify the virus. At one of our sessions we witnessed the deplorable spectacle of a public row between the Japanese Director General of WHO, Dr Nakajima, and the brilliant and dynamic Dr Mann, which led to the latter's immediate resignation. He was a great loss. Afterwards he continued his work in the United States, until he and his wife were tragically killed in the Swissair disaster off the coast of New England.

Women's Issues

For the first time I had direct responsibility for programmes related to women. The Division for the Advancement of Women was part of the Centre for Social Development and Humanitarian Affairs and serviced the UN Commission on the Status of Women, which met annually, sometimes in New York, sometimes in Vienna. Throughout the year numerous expert groups worked on subjects such as domestic violence, women in public life and government, etc. The commission was a forum for women of great distinction from all over the world. During the Reagan presidency, the US delegation was led by his daughter Maureen Reagan, and no one could quite believe their ears when, during a debate on domestic violence, she revealed that she had been a battered wife.

We strove to ensure that women's issues permeated all UNOV's programmes. I had a world map showing the incidence of women in parliaments and every ambassador who came to call was shown how his country stood in the ratings, not always a comfortable experience – for most of them were men. Before the Berlin Wall came down, the communist countries of Eastern Europe made a much better showing than Western Europe but as democracy pervaded Eastern Europe the proportion of women declined precipitately. There was an interesting sidelight in one of our expert groups. The Soviet Representative had served longer than anyone else on the Commission and had for years patronised the other delegations, endlessly extolling the total equality afforded to Soviet womanhood. Now she stunned everyone by proclaiming that the position of Soviet women was scandalous, discrimination was rife, women were given the most menial of tasks, and all earlier claims had been window-dressing she had been obliged to disseminate.

During a public panel held one International Women's Day, the Indian Ambassador protested that quotas were unfair: women should take their chance on merit alongside men. He was quickly silenced by an Argentinian woman diplomat who recounted that in Buenos Aires girls had done so much better at university entrance exams that quotas had to be established for boys to avoid their being reduced to a small minority!

CEDAW, the committee set up to monitor compliance with the Convention on the Elimination of all Forms of Discrimination against Women, comprised well-qualified women who subjected their victims to ruthless cross-questioning. Woe betide anyone who did not take the exercise seriously, as evidenced by the ordeal of a hapless African diplomat, male and francophone. Already incensed that his government had not sent the woman in charge of women's affairs, the CEDAW members were goaded to fury when the unsuspecting man began ingratiatingly 'Mes très chères Mesdames ...' and proceeded to throw cloying compliments in all directions. They made mincemeat of him, and I wondered whether I would not have to order a stretcher to carry the distraught man from the room.

I frequently addressed women's meetings in various parts of the world. One of the most interesting was the International Forum in Brisbane in July 1988, as part of Australia's bicentennial celebrations. Its theme was 'Future Directions by Women in Public Sector Administration'. All the speakers were prominent women: ministers, politicians, civil servants, judges, lawyers, bankers and professors. Some men present said it was one of the most stimulating forums they had attended.

In 1989 I was invited to Women's Day in Japan, which they celebrate on 31 May It was the first time that a foreigner had been asked to speak at an occasion hitherto exclusively Japanese. I was a member of a three-person panel, the others being one of Japan's very rare women ambassadors and a woman journalist. There was a huge audience of over 1000 Japanese women. Our subject was stereotypes, and as an example of how they might be changed, I told a story about the small boy in Pakistan who announced that he wanted to be an engine-driver and, when pressed as to whether he shouldn't aspire, say, to becoming Prime Minister, replied dismissively – 'Oh no! That's *women's* business.' I was treading on delicate political ground, since the cabinet was in crisis and the opposition socialist party was led by a woman – Miss Doi. A few weeks later, it was the women's influence (not my joke, I hasten to add) that led to Miss Doi's unexpected success in the elections and the toppling of Prime Mininister Uno. Senator Moryama, a very able woman member of the ruling party, with whom I had a working breakfast, was appointed to the key ministerial post of Secretary to the Cabinet.

We had planned a 'mini' UN Women's Conference to be held in Vienna in 1995, followed by a big one for the millennium in 2000, when out of the blue the Chinese announced that they wanted to have the 1995 conference in Beijing. Coming so soon after Tiananmen Square this raised all sorts of problems. I tried to persuade them that it was in their interest to host the major conference in 2000, but the Chinese remained unmoved by arguments that they would have to bear significant costs and admit all and sundry, including human rights groups. Despite American opposition the Chinese offer was accepted by member states. This was the first UN Women's Conference I did not attend. News of it reached me from afar, including grumbles by NGOs that their forum was located at such a long distance from the main conference. But perhaps it was not such a bad idea to hold the conference in Beijing and a steep learning curve for China.

Crime Prevention and Criminal Justice

In the crime field, apart from servicing the UN Committee on Crime Prevention and Criminal Justice, our main activities concerned the Eighth UN Congress on the Prevention of Crime and the Treatment of Offenders, of which I was the Secretary-General. In 1989, during a brisk three-month period, we organised five regional preparatory meetings, in Bangkok, San José, Addis Ababa, Helsinki and Cairo. The congress itself was supposed to take place in Vienna in 1990, but two years beforehand the Cuban Minister of the Interior offered Havana as the site. I was appalled at the political shoals looming ahead. and likely to obscure the technical importance of the congress. I warned the minister that his Government, already suffering great economic strains owing to the decline in Soviet aid, would have to defray estimated costs of US$1.4 million. The minister swallowed hard, but acquiesced. I pointed out that the Government must allow in all organisations recognised by the UN, some holding views not palatable to the Government, but the Minister insisted there would be no problem.

The Americans lobbied hard against the Cuban invitation but when it came to the vote the European Union countries went along with the developing countries and Eastern Europe, leaving the US isolated. This meant that an important member state would probably boycott this key event. Over the intervening months I did my utmost through every conceivable channel to persuade the US administration to attend, but without success.

The meeting, held from 27 August to 7 September 1990, was an enormous event of some 1200 delegates from 127 countries and over 400 non-governmental organisations. I had over 300 UN supporting staff from Vienna and New York. More than three years of work by UNOV had gone into the negotiation of the many instruments, model treaties and guidelines adopted by the congress. They covered issues ranging from international organised crime, drug trafficking and terrorism, to corruption, environmental crime, alternatives to imprisonment, the prevention and handling of juvenile delinquency, domestic violence, and human rights in the administration of justice. The creation of an international criminal court was also debated, though not agreed for nearly another decade.

The Cubans were magnificent organisers. The premises were imposing and the logistical organisation went off like clockwork. They lived up fairly well to their undertaking to let in all people and organisations whom the UN deemed qualified to take part though I had some difficult discussions with the authorities. One or two participants alleged later that they had been harassed, but not all of them had behaved with decorum, some using the occasion to make propaganda or stir up trouble. The United States not only refused to participate but threatened to withdraw the passports of any interested American associations and individuals who did so. A few hardy souls came nonetheless, but Americans were few and far between. It was sad to see the world's strongest bastion of democracy proving less tolerant of free expression than the country they had so long declared beyond the pale.

My Chef de Cabinet, my Special Assistant and I were housed in a government guesthouse surrounded by a tropical garden, with its own swimming-pool. I was even provided with my own hair-dresser, a lady trained in Moscow, who insisted that, as Secretary-General of the Congress I must have a different style every day.

These privileges were not without perils. I discovered, in my pre-dawn daily swim, that I was sharing the swimming-pool not only with large, amorous frogs but also with even larger tarantula spiders. When I developed an abscess in my ear (swiftly dealt with by the excellent Cuban medical service) and swimming was prohibited, I had a valid, if painful, excuse for no longer proving my valour. Then, one Saturday afternoon, exploring the end of the garden I was suddenly threatened by a decidedly unfriendly armed man. Fidel Castro, it transpired, was my neighbour.

El Comandante visited the congress frequently. At the inaugural session he spoke for only 20 minutes, probably his shortest speech ever. He hosted a reception at the Government Palace and stayed until 1 a.m at the one I gave for over 1000 people. We planned a walkabout but had to desist as people mobbed him and I nearly had my beautiful Cuban dress torn from my back. Seasoned diplomats from the most unlikely countries behaved like teenagers in the presence of their favourite rock star.

Castro wished to attend the final session but this was delayed by a controversial debate over the abolition of capital punishment. Castro was restlessly pacing up and down in the anteroom behind the podium where his Minister of the Interior was presiding, with me at his side. Every so often he sent a minion to haul me out and brief him on progress. The debate lasted so long that we could not have a formal closing ceremony. Instead the Interior Minister and I held a meeting of Cuban and UN staff to thank them for their support. To everyone's amazement Castro insisted on addressing them in a brilliant speech that won hearts all round. I know of no other occasion where a head of state has addressed support staff or followed a conference so closely.

I had a long private talk with Fidel, mostly about the Gulf crisis and the role of the UN, Cuba then being a member of the Security Council. We had daily contact for nearly three weeks but I was still amazed when, three years later, in August 1993, we unexpectedly met in the crowded throng at the Palacio Quemado in La Paz, during the inauguration of President Sánchez de Lozada and he at once asked, 'How is your house on Lake Titicaca?' The many instances of his charisma during that Congress made it easy to see why he still had many devoted followers, among them my hairdresser.

The day after the conference a chartered Cubana plane flew UN staff to New York. Our plane was sent to a far corner of Kennedy Airport and boarded by immigration officials who questioned each one of us as if we were common criminals or drug traffickers.

Narcotic Drugs

The ICDAIT conference in June 1987 set an ambitious framework for our work on drugs and in November 1988 another major conference marked a new milestone — the adoption of a far-reaching convention on illicit trafficking of narcotic drugs and psychotropic substances. I was the Secretary-General's Representative for the conference, which was presided over by Guillermo Bedregal, Bolivia's Foreign Minister. Over 800 delegates attended the conference at which many countries immediately signed the new convention. It tackled key issues such as extradition, money-laundering and bank secrecy, as well as reinforcing international cooperation and mutual legal assistance. International vigilance increased significantly as a result but unfortunately illicit drug production and trafficking also grew exponentially. The reasons lay outside the scope of the convention, among them the harnessing of sophisticated technology and communications to the service of international crime and the corruption fostered by the high gains to be obtained from the deadly but astronomically profitable trade.

I had many discussions with governments around the world about drugs. During a particularly important visit to Washington in March 1990 I talked with the State Department, addressed several meetings and made a dinner speech on Capitol Hill to key US Senators and Congressmen. Reagonomics and the primacy of market forces were still very much in vogue. I argued that these principles were equally applicable to drugs, which are a tradable commodity like any other, and so long as there was demand, there would be supply. It was therefore as much incumbent on consumer countries to resolve the problem as the producers, on whom the main burden of blame and remedial action fell. My argument encountered very deaf ears.

In 1988 President Virgilio Barco and I reviewed the appalling situation faced by Colombia as a result of the combined problems of drugs and guerrilla action, which together were tearing the country apart. An even more terrible turn of events in Colombia in 1989, when the front-running presidential candidate was assassinated, brought international concern over drugs to fever pitch. The UK proposed that drugs should be considered by the Security Council, as a direct threat to international peace and security and drugs became the dominant theme of the 44th General Assembly and other UN bodies. At the Consultative Group Meeting on Bolivia, held in Paris at the end of October, the World Bank set up a subgroup, which I chaired, on the implications of coca production for the country's economy. This 'brainstorming' showed a remarkable consensus among donor country representatives that the drug problem could not be isolated from issues such as the overall development of the country, the raising of living standards on the *altiplano*, and the provision of markets and reasonable prices for alternative, legal produce substituting the coca crop. But these views were reflected in the official policies of only a few governments.

The proposal for a security council meeting foundered, and a substitute proposal for a Special Session of the General Assembly was adopted in its stead. Prime Minister Manley of Jamaica suggested a multilateral 'strike force' under UN auspices, but this idea was hotly contested by other countries. Held in February 1990 in New York, the special session adopted a political declaration and a global programme of action. It gave a high political profile to the drugs issue but suggestions for a wider UN role in law enforcement and interdiction of drug trafficking did not prosper, nor did any practical proposals for increasing funding. Once more the cry went up from member states that miracles must be achieved 'within existing resources'. We had hoped that ECOSOC and the Committee on Programme Co-ordination (CPC) would subsequently review our System-wide Plan of Action for Drug Abuse Control, an innovative tool that we had developed for the coordination of all drug programmes and allocate adequate resources for its implementation, but both bodies dealt cursorily with the plan and sidestepped the issue of money.

My work on drugs was not only theoretical. In Bolivia I took part in drug seizures in the Chapare regions and visited projects there and in the Yungas. Other field missions took me to northern Thailand and Turkey where UNFDAC also supported important government programmes of drug control. Di Gennaro continued to wage a relentless war against me in public, despite all my conciliatory efforts. In private he was almost ingratiatingly courteous. Some time after Geoffrey Howe, the British Foreign Secretary, had tried to resolve this impasse with di Gennaro's protector, Andreotti, I was taken aback when passing through London, to be torn off a strip by Timothy Eggar, then Junior Minister in the Foreign Office, for my 'less than adroit handling of di Gennaro'. I was doubly furious, first, because I had done my utmost to get on with di Gennaro and, second, because the allegation could only have come from the British Ambassador, who had never mentioned such concerns to me. That incident blew over but was typical of an ambivalent attitude on the part of HMG.

Later I wrote to Mrs Thatcher reminding her of her promise of support, with very positive results. In June 1988 I was invited to London as an official guest of HMG, one of the immediate outcomes of which was the secondment to my office of a Foreign Office official, to assist with the drug programmes. After another visit to London in March 1989, I obtained a grant of £500 000 to strengthen the staff of our Division of Narcotic Drugs and the International Narcotic Control Board. I also had a meeting with Mrs Thatcher's Principal Private Secretary, Charles Powell, at which I expounded my idea that the UK should convene an international conference on the reduction of demand for drugs – that much-neglected aspect of a multifaceted problem.

In the autumn of 1989 I was in New York when Mrs Thatcher addressed the General Assembly and the Secretary-General asked me to attend his private meeting with her. Bending her penetrating gaze on me she said, 'Since Miss Anstee is here, let us begin with drugs.' Thereupon she launched into a monologue, the gist of which was: 'I am a chemist. There are some extraordinarily effective herbicides nowadays. Spray the crops and you will eliminate the lot.' Avoiding the eye of Don Javier, who hated anything resembling an argument, I pointed out that it was not quite that simple; there were problems of sovereignty, of poverty and lost livelihood, not to mention the extraordinary power of the drug cartels and traffickers. The Prime Minister was not to be persuaded but the Secretary-General was looking ever more agonised and so she said, 'Next time you are in London, come and see me.'

That meeting took place in January 1990. It was a ding-dong dialogue between the two of us, with Charles Powell sitting quietly in the background. I enjoyed the cut and thrust of our exchange, especially as I felt I had made headway in persuading the Prime Minister of the economic and social complexities of the drug issue. Two months later, in April 1990, Mrs Thatcher opened the first, and so far only, Global Conference on Reduction of Consumption of Narcotic Drugs in London under the joint auspices of HMG and my office. She was followed by Dr Virgilio Barco, President of Colombia, and the Secretary-General. Some 126 countries were represented, and the UK Home Secretary, David Waddington, presided over the plenary. As he was much distracted by the Strangeways Prison riot, David Mellor, his Junior Minister, played a larger part and proved a quick-witted partner at press conferences.

Princess Anne spoke at the conference, going to the heart of the matter with plain talk, and I was intrigued to see, as I sat by her side, that the speech was written in her own hand. Two memories stand out from the reception that Mrs Thatcher gave at No. Ten: the Prime Minister perched on top of something that raised her head and shoulders above her assembled guests, suddenly interrupting a homily on drugs to point a Kitchener-like finger to 'Miss Anstee, over there', where I cowered in embarrassment by a fireplace; and an encounter with her husband, Denis, who admired a brooch I was wearing, and on learning that it was an Australian opal (one of Jacko's last presents) exclaimed, 'I must get one like that for my sweetie.' The epithet hardly sat easily with his wife's public image.

The conference was unusual in that it did not consist merely of speeches by ministers but included audiovisual presentations by people who dealt daily with problems of drug abuse and addiction, resulting in a sharing of practical experiences. It marked a milestone in political thinking about the drug problem but unfortunately there was no adequate follow-up.

A parallel UK initiative was less felicitous. HMG proposed yet another restructuring review of the UN drug units, this time with the assistance of management consultants. In my January meeting at No. Ten I had told Mrs Thatcher that I was greatly concerned by this development: the drug units had been restructured less than three years previously, such a study would tie up our limited staff for months, and the management consultants would absorb money (I recall a sum of half a million pounds) better spent on drug control activities. Mrs Thatcher agreed whole-heartedly. 'A waste of time and money!' she exclaimed, adding, 'It will simply provide funds for even more opulent furnishings for the offices of the management consultants.'

Here Charles Powell intervened to warn: 'But, Prime Minister, the Foreign Office has already taken a decision on this.'

The Foreign Office prevailed and a month after the London Conference the group began its work. It was supposed to be composed of 'independent experts' to advise the Secretary-General, who was then to make his own recommendations to the General Assembly. Things went awry from the first day. The most valuable expert, the only one who had confronted the problem in real life – a former Colombian Justice Minister then serving as ambassador in Prague – refused to take part, declaring the study a distraction from the real issues. A very courageous man, he had earlier been sent as ambassador to Hungary to protect his life when he left the justice ministry, but the drug traffickers had tracked him down and shot him in the head. Only three weeks later he had presided over the UN Committee on Narcotic Drugs in Vienna, heavily bandaged, a dramatic personification of the horrors of the drug trade.

The consultants were a group from McKinsey, led by Henry Strage, who had done good work in the UN earlier; his team spent several weeks preparing a presentation for the opening session. To everyone's amazement, at that first meeting the Moroccan 'expert', who seemed to have undergone a personality change since we had enjoyed an amiable personal and professional relationship some years earlier, launched an incoherent attack on me and demanded the dismissal of the McKinsey Group. The other 'experts' were stunned but seemed inexplicably cowed by his vehemence. The McKinsey Group was summarily dismissed and not even allowed to make their presentation (though presumably the UK and other donors had to pay them compensation). Thereafter the group relied on its own counsel, meeting behind closed doors, and calling on myself, di Gennaro and other senior staff members to answer questions. The most vociferous were diplomats or politicians with no real understanding of the issue.

Their first draft proposed the unification of the three existing drug units under a single head, something with which no one could disagree. The controversial element was that it was to be a totally *separate* programme, taken out from UNOV, and the close co-ordination with social and crime programmes that I had developed since all these programmes had been consolidated under myself as Director-General in 1987. In his comments the Secretary-General endorsed unification, but stressed the need to retain the multidisciplinary approach to the drug phenomenon and the integrity of UNOV. Notwithstanding, the group's final proposal insisted that the new structure must be independent, and report directly to the Secretary-General. Conveniently overlooking the fact that they themselves were mandated to report to the Secretary-General, they arranged for their report to reach governments, and become the subject of inter-governmental meetings, before it was presented to him.

The Secretary-General's recommendations to the General Assembly were therefore prepared in extremely difficult circumstances. His report envisaged a unified programme under an Assistant Secretary-General, preserving the overall control of the Director-General of UNOV. Several key governments insisted, however, that the post should be at the Under Secretary-General level, which made independent status inevitable. A resolution to that effect was adopted by the Third (Social) Committee and endorsed by the Fifth (Financial) Committee. Consequently a new drug programme, divorced from the social programmes, was set up on 1 January 1991. This was contrary to the same major governments' insistence, only four years before, that proliferation of programmes must be curtailed, multidisciplinary and co-ordinated approaches fostered, and the number of Under and Assistant Secretaries-General reduced by 25 per cent. No one raised an eyebrow when the same delegation insisted in the Third

Committee on a new Under Secretary-General post for drugs, while berating the Secretary-General in the Fifth Committee for failing to meet the 25 per cent reduction!

The Times of London published an unpleasant article highlighting the difficulties between di Gennaro and myself, that someone had obligingly leaked, giving the impression that our relationship was the nub of the problem. That certainly needed sorting out, but major and costly restructuring was not the answer. What was needed, if UN drug programmes were to have any chance of success, was a stronger mandate and more resources, neither of which was forthcoming from that expensive study. Moreover, the way in which the 'experts' sidestepped the Secretary-General and ignored his recommendations constituted gross interference into his responsibilities. I was appalled that the UK should have taken a lead role, not only in launching the idea but also through its representative in the group. Several other members of the group confided that they were not in agreement with the report's recommendations, but they were outvoted by stronger personalities, swayed more by political considerations than technical and substantive reasoning.

Di Gennaro nursed high hopes that he would head the new programme, but he was to be disappointed and left, a bitter and disillusioned man. Another Italian was appointed to head the programme to placate the Italian Government, UNFDAC's largest contributor. I continued as Director-General, in charge of social programmes, including crime prevention, but the Secretary-General's proposals to transfer to Vienna the social policy functions and staff remaining in New York, and so consolidate the concept, had been turned down by the General Assembly in 1989. This was another example of micro-management by member states, undermining the very reforms they had urged the Secretary-General to undertake. In this case they were aided and abetted by secretariat officials in New York who lobbied against the transfer.

In 1992 the new Secretary-General, Boutros-Ghali, once more combined the post of Director-General of UNOV and head of the drugs programmes and decreed that the New York posts that had so long been a bone of contention should go to Vienna. It was back to square one and March 1987. In far-off Angola I rejoiced at the news – but not for long. Before action could be taken the decision was rescinded for reasons never clear to me. Instead the Centre for the Social Development and Humanitarian Affairs was transferred back to New York, with the exception of the crime branch. The other parts of CSDHA were split up among various departments in New York. The focus on social issues was fragmented at the moment when most needed, as the adverse social impact of market economy measures became ever clearer. I felt I had little to show for five years of hard struggle in Vienna.

Ceremonial Hazards

There were lighter moments. My functions as Director-General involved receiving the credentials of new ambassadors. When an Iranian Ambassador was appointed, my punctilious Polish Chief of Protocol came to me in distress. 'The embassy say he can't shake hands with you, as you are a woman.'

Irritated, I nonetheless instructed him to say I understood.

Shortly after he was back, even more embarrassed. 'Now they say he wants to hand them to me while you stand by.'

At this I exploded. 'Would they like me to wear gloves? Tell them that, as the Secretary-General's representative, I must accept the credentials personally. Our hands need not touch. Otherwise there's a simple solution – he doesn't present his credentials.'

That was a clinching argument: without the official presentation of his credentials the Ambassador could not attend any UN meetings.

A splendid annual occasion, in true Viennese style, was the UN Charity Ball in the magnificent Rathaus, at which the Mayor of Vienna and I opened the dancing. Mayor Zilk was an able Socialist politician but, surprisingly for a Viennese, not a good waltzer. Tragically, some years later, his hands were badly damaged by a letter-bomb, sent by a right-wing fanatic. Some 2000 people attended the balls, which fostered a rare intermingling between Vienna and the 'international city' on the other side of the Danube.

In 1988 UN peace-keeping forces were awarded the Nobel Prize. Austria had supplied 27 000 peace-keeping troops over 28 years; one in every ten peace-keeping soldiers was Austrian, and 24 had given their lives. We had a military ceremony to celebrate the award, with a military band, and a contingent of Austrian 'Blue Helmets' from Cyprus. It was my first experience of inspecting troops, together with the Ministers of Defence and Foreign Affairs. The December day was raw with snow looming and a gusty wind. I hung on to my hat with one hand and my speech with the other as I held forth to the assembled troops (not a hope of ad-libbing since I spoke in German) but I had not allowed for the cold making my nose run. Dilemma: not having a third hand, should I put hat and/or fluttering pages of speech at risk by using my hand-kerchief? How long could I hope that the rivulet coursing down my upper lip would pass undetected by the assembled dignitaries and the TV cameras? In the end, early training prevailed and I mopped up Niagara between gusts of wind, luckily without untoward consequences. We were all chilled to the bone but were quickly revived by a military field kitchen, which dispensed tea, laced with rum, and hot goulash soup.

During all of my time in Vienna Waldheim posed a delicate political problem. When I arrived he was concluding his first term as President of Austria, as the storm broke out over his allegedly Nazi past during the Second World War. Jacko and I had both suffered from the political expediency that guided so many of his actions when he was Secretary-General but we thought the attacks unfair. He had certainly concealed his past, but I could not help thinking that the attacks would not have been so aggressive had he been head of a larger state. When Jacko came to visit me in September 1987 he met Waldheim, and we were invited to lunch.

Despite the international furore – or, more likely, because the Austrian electorate was incensed by the campaign against him – Waldheim was re-elected in 1988. He was the President of our host country but his attendance at official functions in UNOV created uncomfortable situations with representatives of other nations. I felt sorry for Waldheim. His life had all the elements of a Shakespearian tragedy: he had achieved his two burning ambi-tions – to become UN Secretary-General and President of his own country, only to find these brilliant achievements turn to ashes.

Professional Disappointments

By the end of 1990 I was feeling rather low. I had had some acute disappointments, not least the collapse of the strategy for UNOV established by the Secretary-General in 1987 and endorsed by the General Assembly. There was even a push to make the crime programme independent as well. I was dismayed at the inconsistencies of governments and wondered whether I had not been right when I once described the UN as 'an impossible management challenge' – I feared that social issues would continue to get short shrift, a situation equally dispiriting for my staff, whom I had driven as hard as myself.

There was still the option of accepting some other challenge in the UN system but here too there were disappointments. In 1989 the Secretary-General asked me to head the troubled UN Disaster Relief Organisation (UNDRO) in Geneva. I felt that UNDRO's days were numbered and refused. I was right, for shortly afterwards a new post of humanitarian relief co-ordinator was created in New York and UNDRO became a subsidiary office. For a while it seemed I had a good chance of getting that new post but an appointment was made on political and nationality grounds.

In late 1991 the post of high commissioner for refugees, for which I had been a front runner three times, unexpectedly became vacant again. Pérez de Cuéllar, conscious of his own imminent departure and that I had had a raw deal in Vienna, told me that I was his prime candidate. A little later, however, he said that he had also to find a niche for his Chef de Cabinet, Virendra (Viru) Dayal; he would therefore put Dayal's name forward first and if that did not run, (which he recognised it might not) he would nominate me. My heart sank. Traditionally the High commissioner post was filled by someone from a developed and major contributing country. My premonitions were quickly realised: uproar erupted among some of the most influential member states, and was blown up into a major row by international media.

Late at night, listening to the BBC World Service, I heard Viru, normally so calm, and diplomatically discreet, bitterly denouncing discrimination and racism. He was clearly not going to get the job, but I doubted whether my name would now go forward. In that I was right too. Governments took the matter into their own hands. The vacuum was filled by Mrs Sadako Ogata's candidature, bolstered by the promise of hefty Japanese financial support. She proved an excellent high commissioner and it is an immense satisfaction that a woman should have won plaudits in a job that I had been told, only a few years earlier, no woman could do. But I would not be human if I did not regret that Pérez de Cuéllar had not proposed my name first, in which case, I would probably have got the job to which I had so long aspired

Jacko's Death

These disappointments took second place to grievous personal loss. On 12 January 1991 Jacko died. We had had a joyous evening together on New Year's Day. Jacko drank wine and champagne, which he had not done for a long time, we laughed and reminisced, and for once it was like old times. I did not say goodbye for he was asleep when I left for Vienna early next morning.

During our daily telephone conversation on Thursday 10 January, I told him that I was leaving on the annual Ministry of Foreign Affairs skiing trip (at Bad Hofgastein, an hour's drive beyond Salzburg), and that I might be unable to phone again before Sunday evening. He cheerfully replied that he looked forward to hearing from me then.

I never heard his voice again. He was taken ill on Friday evening. I had been meticulous about leaving phone numbers but a perverse fate decreed that I should not be found in time. Protocol changed my hotel at the last minute, and although I phoned details to my office, they did not reach Sissy, who was out. It was after midnight before Jacko's housekeeper managed to call her. Then Sissy had to ring all the hotels in Bad Hofgastein until she located me at 3.00 a.m. Had it been possible to contact me earlier, I could have driven back to Vienna with the Foreign Minister, and caught the first plane to London on Saturday. Instead I had to get to Vienna from a remote mountain village in the middle of the night. That entailed negotiating in German with security guards who could not work the hotel switchboards and so could not contact the Chief of Protocol. Ironically, I could telephone London, but was made even more desperate by learning that Jacko was constantly calling for me and that I must hurry. I could only send my love and a message that I was doing my best.

The Chief of Protocol, at last located at 5 a.m., put the ministry's car at my disposal and I reached Vienna at 9 o'clock. There Sissy had worked out possible flights, and my driver was waiting with the car. I called London and was told Jacko was still alive. But a little later Mary Gibson rang to say he had just died. She met me at Heathrow and drove me to the flat where I took a last farewell.

I stayed in the flat for ten days helping Robin to make the funeral arrangements, and responding to tributes and messages of sympathy that poured in from all over the world. There were long obituaries in the main newspapers.

After the funeral, in Putney on 21 January, I flew to New York to attend scheduled meetings. Friends there seized the occasion to organise a gathering in memory of Jacko, held on 24 January in the Trusteeship Council Chamber, decorated with spring flowers. It was presided over by the Secretary-General, his presence secured only after some argument. Viru Dayal had called me to say that the Secretary-General, who had sent a message of sympathy to Robin but not to me, would not have time to attend. It was then my turn to blow my top, and time was found.

I had feared that I would be unable to keep my composure but found myself laughing at reminiscences of Jacko's habit of confounding a succession of Secretaries-General with cricketing analogies and naval repartee. The Secretary-General, Viru Dayal and Brian Urquhart spoke and a message was read from Brad Morse. Tributes to his formidable achievements were paid by the Ambassadors of Australia and Bangladesh. I spoke last. Afterwards I lunched with the women who had organised the event. We sat at Jacko's table in the Delegates Dining-Room, and drank a bottle of his favourite champagne. I think he would most emphatically have approved.

In April 1991 Robin and Carlie took Jacko's ashes to Australia, where I joined them. There was another memorial at Jacko's old school at Mentone, near Melbourne. Many of his oldest Australian friends were there, including Dame Elizabeth Murdoch (the mother of Rupert) who gave a dinner in the evening. Next day, we went to the family grave plot where Jacko's ashes now lie on a grassy knoll, under eucalyptus trees. We saw his boyhood home which he had so often described to me, recalling summer nights when he slept on the verandah, surrounded by the scent of freesias, flowers which remained special for him until the end of his life.

I now felt very much alone, professionally and personally.

20

Debt, Development, Democracy and Disasters

Bolivia and the Paris Club

During my time in Vienna Pérez de Cuéllar continued to give me challenging additional assignments, most of them related to disasters, national and man-made.

My responsibilities as his Special Representative for Bolivia continued, though UN help was now needed only at critical moments for negotiations with multilateral financial institutions and the international community, especially to relieve the crushing burden of servicing and repaying external debt. With UN support the commercial debt was repurchased but bilateral debt with other governments could only be handled through the Paris Club, to which Bolivia could not present its case until it had the International Monetary Fund's seal of approval.

The first meeting with the Paris Club took place in November 1988. It was an elite body of treasury officials from the major economic powers that admitted no UN organisation other than the IMF and the World Bank. UNCTAD was allowed in on sufferance to provide advice in the wings to developing countries but played no official part. So it was something of a breakthrough when I was given a seat at the table to support Bolivia in the name of the Secretary-General, both on that occasion and at subsequent meetings in March 1990 and January 1992.

A bizarre game of hide-and-seek followed the opening session. The club met behind closed doors to discuss what terms they would propose, while the Bolivian delegation waited with me and my UNCTAD colleague in another room. When the French chairman marched in with the first offer, the two of us scuttled out, only to dash back when he emerged, to advise the delegation how to respond. My UNCTAD colleague, well versed in terms accrued to other countries, provided valuable suggestions. The Bolivians then made their counter-proposals, while we again made ourselves scarce. Baleful glances thrown in our direction by the chairman and his entourage showed that our efforts were not entirely appreciated by the creditors. This pantomime went through several 'reprises' until the Bolivians obtained the best deal possible.

Before the first meeting the Secretary-General had written to all Paris Club members pointing our that conditions in Bolivia were on a par with those of the sub-Saharan African countries, for whom special arrangements had been conceded at the Toronto summit of the G7. We were unsuccessful in persuading them to give Bolivia the Toronto terms on that first occasion. Nonetheless we helped the delegation to obtain better conditions than would otherwise have been the case.

At the second meeting the Paris Club agreed to apply Toronto terms, the first time that a non-African country received this special treatment. Bolivia's exemplary economic and financial performance, combined with alarming social indicators, were important factors but I think a clinching argument related to drugs. In my statement I pointed out that Bolivia was making strenuous efforts to fulfil its international obligations to substitute the cultivation of the coca plant; if it was successful, and was not helped by the international community – through assistance on trade access and commodity prices, support for overall development and debt concessions – then its economy would collapse and it would be even less able to pay its debts, a clear example of international demands cancelling one another out.

Our third visit to the Paris Club was even more successful, for by then the World Bank and the IMF had come to recognise that social development was directly relevant to the debt issue and the sustainability of economic reforms. Our success, combined with the development finance that we obtained from the annual World Bank Consultative Group greatly helped Bolivia's recovery efforts.

In August 1991 I made what was to be my last visit as special representative. There was a gratifyingly encouraging panorama to review. Bolivia had maintained its economic stabilisation policies through a change of political leadership and a different party, under the presidency of Jaime Paz Zamora, elected in 1989. It had attained the lowest inflation rate on the whole continent, relaunched economic growth to a remarkable 4 per cent of GNP in 1991, developed a social programme used as a model by many other countries and strengthened the democratic processes by peaceful changes of government through free and fair elections. In this the UN had played a crucial, catalytic role.

In 1988, after five long years of negotiation, I had finally managed to purchase the land on Lake Titicaca and in 1990 President Paz Zamora, at his own initiative, signed a supreme resolution according me Bolivian citizenship. The saga of the land was by no means over. The ceremony of acquisition involved placating the Pachamama (the Earth Goddess) with libations of alcohol and rolling over my new property under the gaze of several former owners. The subsequent task of building an adobe house at long distance gave rise to many misunderstandings, some of them hilarious in retrospect; but in August 1991 the house was finished, eight years after I first sighted my promontory. It was still unfurnished and without electricity or water but it was an emotional experience to spend my first night in my new home. I woke to a chilly dawn to see the fiery red light of a new day seeping over the serrated contours of the Andes and the lake below my balcony flush to rose. I went for a walk before breakfast, down to my beach, then climbed the steep, stony fields above the house. Later friends came for a picnic of *salteñas* and drinks on my incipient terrace. I had no idea that I would not see my house again for over two years, or that I would be lucky to be alive to do so.

Special Representative of the Secretary-General for Peru

Peru's economic situation had declined disastrously, exacerbated by the armed insurrection of the Sendero Luminoso (Shining Path) guerrillas, as well as by President Alan Garcia's refusal to honour Peru's external debt and summary treatment of foreign oil companies. Only the strongest measures could restore international confidence and the flow of foreign aid. In early 1990 the authorities asked the Secretary-General to exercise his good offices, as he had done in Bolivia, and to send me to Lima. My mission was extremely sensitive because a presidential election was in full swing and this was the Secretary-General's own country. My first visit took place after the first round of the election, when two presidential candidates were still in the ring, and the Government had several months to run. We wanted to make clear that the cooperation was being extended to the country and not to any political party or personality.

During four days in April 1990 I met the current government authorities, and the two presidential candidates, Mario Vargas Llosa, the writer, then the favourite, and the surprise outsider, Alberto Fujimori, an agronomist of Japanese parentage. They could not have been more different. Vargas Llosa was supported by the Peruvian establishment and the business community and had announced his intention to restore financial orthodoxy and regain the favour of the international financial institutions. He and his wife received me in an apartment that was the epitome of cosmopolitan elegance in a fashionable suburb overlooking the Pacific. Fujimori was pursuing a populist campaign, promising that the country's woes could be solved without resorting to the stringent policies demanded by the IMF. I visited him in his modest house, literally barricaded by journalists. Inside the furnishings and pictures were almost entirely Japanese, the one anomaly a row of the largest bottles of Scotch whisky I have ever seen. With both candidates I discussed the problems they would have to confront, if elected, and explained the support that the Secretary-General could provide. I also met the Diplomatic Corps. They were uniformly pessimistic about what could be done, as were the bishops and non-governmental organisations.

Peru was also in the thrall of drought, but diplomats disillusioned with previous aid experiences in Peru told me categorically that humanitarian assistance would not be forthcoming unless we could guarantee its distribution outside government channels.

Broader support for the economy as a whole — the main purpose of my mission — was out of the question, they stressed, until government economic policy forthrightly addressed the problems. That could not be expected until a new President took over three months later. Yet seven million people, nearly one-third of the population, were not getting enough to eat — a terrible statistic that was receiving no publicity outside Peru.

I opted for a two-stage approach: the first, of an emergency nature, to offset the impact of the drought; the second, broader in scope, to be developed in the light of the economic measures taken by the new Government. I obtained guarantees from the Government and both presidential candidates that all emergency aid would be handled through an organisation composed of church authorities, NGOs and private sector representatives and I arranged the immediate dispatch to Lima of a UN inter-agency mission, to assess the exact needs. As a result, on 8 June 1990 the Secretary-General was able to launch an appeal for US$85 million for food, seeds, fertilisers, medical supplies and water projects. The initial response was swift, but ultimately we only obtained US$25 million.

Alberto Fujimori won the second round of the election. His success was attributed to disillusion with traditional parties and his campaign claim that Peru's economic ills could be cured by gradualist, non-painful means. Fujimori's message, while music to the electors, was not likely to charm open the coffers of international funding.

On 20 June I was back in Lima for two days of discussion with the President-elect, working closely with the Peruvian economist, Hernando de Soto. The immediate outcome was that I organised a working lunch, hosted by the Secretary-General in New York on 29 June, to enable Fujimori to meet the heads of the International Monetary Fund, Mr Camdessus, the World Bank, Mr Conable; and the Inter-American Development Bank, Enrique Iglesias. The message to Fujimori from the heads of the world's most powerful financial organisations was unequivocal: persist in your campaign policies and Peru will remain an international outcast; no one will provide funds unless stringent economic measures are taken. Fujimori proved a quick learner.

He immediately gave a press conference, at which he said all the right things to quell the doubts of the international community. I was then amazed to find myself in a meeting with him and his closest advisers to discuss the composition of his cabinet. Another outcome was the creation of a group of advisers, including Hernando de Soto and myself, to assist in building new international bridges. This was unfortunately short-lived, because of discrepancies about policies which caused de Soto to resign.

I returned to Peru on the first day of the new administration and hammered out a strategy with the new Prime Minister, Juan Carlos Hurtado Miller. Our plan envisaged presentation of the new Government's programme to the annual meetings of the IMF and World Bank in September, followed by an appeal to the UN General Assembly. The Government announced a stringent economic programme on 27 August. On my recommendation it envisaged a parallel emergency social programme, based on the Bolivian experience. The Prime Minister presented this programme to donor countries in New York on 3 October 1990 at a meeting presided over by the Secretary-General. The latter's appeal concentrated on the social programme – US$100 million in 1990 for the emergency, and US$300 million annually thereafter for the development phase. The reaction of donor countries was enthusiastic, a great change from the negative atmosphere I had encountered in Lima in April, but the influx of actual money moved slowly.

My next meeting with President Fujimori took place in strange circumstances. When I visited China in April 1991, the Chinese diplomats escorting me let slip the information that Fujimori was also staying in the Foreign Ministry compound, after an Inter-American Development Bank meeting in Japan.

'What a wonderful coincidence,' I exclaimed. 'I am his adviser, and it will be an excellent opportunity to meet'.

The Chinese did not share my enthusiasm. After two days they grudgingly agreed to tell Fujimori I was there, reporting back, with ill-disguised surprise, that he was anxious to see me. The meeting, at ten o'clock at night, took place in the palatial mansion reserved for heads of state, near my own more modest villa. Fujimori appeared in his shirtsleeves, his arm in a sling, broken, he explained, by slipping on the steps to the podium when about to make his speech in Japan. The Peruvian Ambassador was hovering, but was waved away peremptorily, with a hint of the autocratic manner I had previously only glimpsed, but that became characteristic of his presidency.

With me he was, as always, affable and attentive. We sat incongruously at one end of a vast hall, lined with parallel rows of empty brocade sofas. That coldly formal setting made him appear a lonely and austere figure in his white shirt, while the sling heightened the impression of someone fighting against heavy odds. Peru's problems at that stage seemed almost insuperable. I was worried that the emergency social programme had not started and warned that unless social issues were tackled, the economic policies would never work. Fujimori agreed, and assured me that the matter would be resolved.

Nevertheless, there was little progress, for political and other reasons, and I deferred my next visit to Peru to August 1991, when I had several meetings with Fujimori and – with the Prime Minister and Foreign Minister – officially launched the social development programme that should have begun a year earlier. Our talks centred on the remaining moves for Peru to be fully reinstated into the international financial community: agreements with the International Monetary Fund, the World Bank, and the Inter-American Development Bank; debt-rescheduling negotiations with the Paris Club; supporting actions by the Secretary-General; and measures to strengthen the still precarious social programme. The local media took great interest in my activities, erroneously thinking that I was some kind of *éminence grise*.

In September 1991, Peru presented its case for the rescheduling of its bilateral external debt to the Paris Club. I had advised the Peruvian authorities on the strategy to follow and had addressed appeals by the Secretary-General to the main creditor governments. I accompanied the delegation, headed by the Economy Minister, Carlos Boloña, to the meeting, where UNCTAD again helped. After two days and nights of intense negotiation, lasting into the small hours, Peru was granted exceptional preferential treatment, second only to that accorded a few months earlier to Egypt and Poland.

I flew from Paris to New York to be present at a meeting between Fujimori and the Secretary-General. There was room for mutual satisfaction for, in the space of one year, Peru had been reinstated in the international community. In addition to the Paris Club success, the President had just signed agreements in Washington with the IMF and the Inter-American Development Bank. As in Bolivia, it is doubtful whether Peru would have been able to achieve all this without the technical and political support provided by the UN Secretary-General.

That was my last formal contact with Fujimori. After my transfer to Angola in early 1992, I observed from afar how he grew in presidential stature by defeating the Sendero Luminiso and restoring Peru to internal peace and economic stability. Sadly he became ever more authoritarian, succeeding himself in the presidency, changing the rules of the constitution, and introducing other measures at odds with the concept of democracy. The man who fled in disgrace to Japan in November 2000 was very different from the one I had met in his modest home ten years earlier.

The End of the Cold War

From Vienna I had a unique view of the dramatic changes in Eastern European countries as a result of *glasnost* and *perestroika* in the Soviet Union and the fall of the Berlin Wall. UNOV had come to be considered as 'their' United Nations, nearer to their interests than New York, and we were soon called in to play a role in the vertiginous transformation.

On 1 September 1989 the Secretary-General asked me to represent him at a meeting, in Warsaw, of mayors of peace messenger cities (cities ravaged by war), which coincided with the fiftieth anniversary of the German invasion of Poland. Dramatic changes were evolving. President Jaruzelski and the new Prime Minister, Mr Mazowiecki, were present at the inaugural meeting, at which I spoke, and sat side by side at the commemorative concert in the opera house where Leonard Bernstein played a major role.

Next day, I had a long conversation with Jaruzelski, ranging over all aspects of the Polish situation, including its grave economic problems. I noted certain similarities with the Bolivian case: both countries emerging from a long period of authoritarian rule, and facing complex problems requiring drastic action difficult to take in a democratic context, especially when the mass of the people harbour excessive expectations from the restoration of democracy. Poland was in a more difficult position, its population more sophisticated and politically articulate, and no cushion of a subsistence economy, nor influx of narco-dollars. I urged the necessity of adopting social measures to offset the adverse impact of economic liberalisation and was surprised by Jaruzelski's apparently sincere commitment to democratic change.

I had received a pressing invitation to Moscow in April 1989 from the Minister of the Interior, Mr Vadim Bakatin, who was close to Gorbachev. The visit was postponed until October because of the elections. The minister met me at the entrance to his office with a huge bouquet of flowers. He was handsome, charismatic and intelligent but what most struck me was his frankness. We could communicate only through interpreters but an almost immediate rapport sprang up between us. What he said was extraordinary, coming from the lips of a highly-placed Soviet official: 'We have a terrible problem of crime and drugs, denied for years, but now, as a result of *glasnost* and *perestroika*, increasing by leaps and bounds. We need United Nations help.'

He wanted the kind of technical cooperation the UN provides only to developing countries, and I could only assure him that we would urge Western countries to assist bilaterally. That same evening the minister sent me on his plane to Tbilisi, the capital of Georgia. A large delegation, headed by the Georgian Minister of the Interior, received me with armfuls of flowers. Late as it was, a huge dinner followed at the state guesthouse. 'You will sleep in the same bed where Mrs Thatcher slept,' my hosts proudly announced, with a reverence that suggested the sheets had not been changed since. By then I was so dog-tired I would have slept anywhere.

A similarly large group, and a similarly groaning table, were awaiting at breakfast, including lashings of fiery Georgian brandy that I had difficulty in refusing without causing offence. The packed programme that followed was a salutary reminder that the USSR encompassed a vast continent and conglomeration of peoples. Tbilisi is a melting-pot of cultures, where Europe and Asia meet, and the softer influences of warmer southern climes hold sway. It was, as I said in one of the innumerable impromptu speeches I made that day, a land of poetry and song, music, wine and roses. By the end of the day the car was knee-deep in flowers, which were piled into the plane when I left.

Lunch was another Gargantuan feast in an ancient inn in Mtskheta, hewn from surrounding rock. Our host was the local Communist Party secretary, an unlikely role for a man who looked like an English squire, with his immaculately tailored suit, and equally immaculate moustache, and who greeted me with a large bouquet of unmistakably Queen Elizabeth roses. He was the toastmaster and, toasts in Georgia being serious matters, I became nervous for his health and, indeed, for my own, to which he so constantly drank. He was also extremely gallant, and his ardent proposals of marriage multiplied thick and fast as the toasts wore on. In case I should be too carried away, one of my companions from the Interior Ministry warned me that my suitor was already married. Mrs Thatcher had left a string of admirers, among whom he was the most eloquent, though it was not clear whether he had proposed wedlock to her also. The coincidence of our first names, gender and nationality conjured up a special link and my hosts insisted on giving me presents to pass on to her (which I duly did). Lunch ended with deep-throated singing by three Georgian men, fortified by large quantities of wine, and looking like amiable buccaneers.

We had to be torn away for a meeting in Tbilisi with the Council of Ministers, where crime and drugs were the main topic. On the way, I saw people carrying banners. I realised that it was some kind of demonstration but not that it was sparked by my presence. Whispered consultations during the meeting revealed that the demonstrators wished to present me with a petition to the Secretary-General for Georgian independence. It was a delicate moment. The authorities urged me not to see them, but that would be an infringement of human rights and the right to free expression. We persuaded them that a refusal would damage their public image as well as ours and agreed on an informal encounter in the street. An unshaven and not very prepossessing-looking man, supported by his followers, presented me with a tattered document. Contrary to the Government's fears, it was all very calm. I duly sent the Petition to the Secretary-General but as it was in

Georgian we never knew exactly what was in it. The man who gave it to me was Ghamzakurdia, recently emerged from prison. After Georgia's independence he became President and later sparked off a civil war, ultimately meeting an untimely end, in dubious circumstances, in Chechnya.

My visit culminated in the signature of an agreement by Minister Bakatin and myself providing for close cooperation with UNOV in crime prevention and criminal justice, at a state guesthouse in the forest outside Moscow, celebrated by another dinner. That day the railway had been reopened between Azerbaijan and Nagornyy-Karabakh who were virtually at war with one another. I was amazed to hear Bakatin, in his speech, compare that achievement and our agreement, as equally important historic events. Next day he took me around the Kremlin and we visited Lenin's apartment, untouched since his death. At the Foreign Ministry, the the vice-minister expounded to me the Gorbachev Government's new policy towards the UN, which he asked me to convey to the Secretary-General. The message was one of close cooperation, including a pledge not to resort to the veto in the Security Council – a complete volte-face to the traditional Soviet attitude. The contrast with my visit in 1979 could hardly have been more marked.

My final press conference was presided over by Minister Bakatin and attended by two or three hundred journalists. The most penetrating and direct questions came from the Soviet journalists. Did I think the Government was sincere in its intentions? As one example I pointed out that, for the first time, the UN Standard Rules for the Treatment of Prisoners were being applied in all USSR prisons and police academies – a good illustration of how seemingly theoretical UN activities can bear fruit.

This was the start of close cooperation over two and a half years. In January 1990 Bakatin came to Vienna as official guest of the Austrian Government. I was able to inform him that I had obtained offers of bilateral assistance from the USA and the UK, as well as sending advisers from my own staff. The Austrian Foreign Ministry's request that I give a dinner for Bakatin put me in a quandary. Sissy was a wonderful cook, but my apartment was small, and interpreters had to be invited as well as the other guests. Contrary to my custom I made it a 'stag affair'. The Western ambassadors I had invited were bowled over by the minister's openness, and his wide intellectual grasp of many issues. As the evening wore on they were sitting on coffee tables and even the floor, in animated discussion about the momentous changes taking place in the Soviet Union, and the severe risks entailed. Most riveting of all was Bakatin's account of relations with Boris Yeltsin, who had hit international headlines by claiming that the authorities had thrown him into the Moscow River. 'Pure fabrication,' said Bakatin 'He wasn't pushed. He was drunk and fell in.' Given Yeltsin's subsequent reputation this seemed quite possible. The party broke up at 2.00 a.m. Next day I faced a barrage of questions from ambassadors' wives as to why their husbands had returned so late. I assured them there was safety in numbers.

Convinced that the UN could best help by strengthening exchanges between the Soviet Union and the West, I urged Bakatin to attend the World Ministerial Summit to Reduce Demand for Drugs in London in April 1990. He was unable to do so but sent a delegation. I also persuaded him to offer Moscow as the venue for the first European meeting of Heads of Narcotic Law Enforcement Agencies (HONLEA). We had held these meetings in every other region, but none had been possible in Europe during the Cold War. I argued that a Soviet Union offer to host the very first encounter between police and judicial authorities from Eastern and Western Europe would demonstrate their new openness, improve international cooperation in pursuing drug traffickers and criminals across increasingly open frontiers, and provide valuable contacts with bilateral sources of technical assistance. Bakatin liked the idea, but foresaw logistical problems and consulted Gorbachev. At the London Drug Summit, the Soviet delegation announced their invitation for the HONLEA meeting in November 1990.

Police and judicial authorities came from Canada and the USA, as well as from Western Europe. The difficulties Bakatin envisaged had increased with the worsening economic situation. My staff were in despair: even notepads and pencils were difficult to obtain. Most surprising of all was the lack of organisational skills on the Soviet side. Bakatin was beside himself, and thanks to his dynamic intervention the meeting was successful, despite some practical hiccoughs. Technical discussions in the working groups were especially useful, as were the bilateral meetings to develop closer cooperation with Western countries. Everyone recognised that the incidence of crime and drugs would worsen as the rouble became fully convertible. *Glasnost* and *perestroika* brought problems as well as hope.

The minister placed a plane at my disposal to take me to Leningrad (now St. Petersburg again) where the Deputy Mayor told me food supplies were desperately tight. Even as I discussed crime and drugs with the Chief of Police two convicted murderers seized hostages in the prison, and killed a fellow convict. It was resolved swiftly by storm troopers with no further injury to the hostages; one murderer was killed, the other wounded.

I returned to Moscow for the last two days of the meeting and a reception given by the Dynamo Sports Club of the Ministry of the Interior, which took place on the night of Mrs Thatcher's resignation. My Russian hosts were appalled: 'How could you *do* this?' they asked me, almost accusingly, as if I were personally responsible for the ditching of the Prime Minister. They had long made me aware of their admiration for Mrs Thatcher, and thought it a compliment to dub me also as 'the Iron Lady'.

The reception was attended by former Soviet Olympic gold medallists including Gennady Korponosov, who had won his in ice-skating and ice dancing. To my dismay he swept me onto the floor for a dramatic solo tango. I love dancing, but the tango is not my forte, and I had visions of ending up sprawled on the floor in front of the several hundred men attending the meeting, of which I was the Secretary-General. I need not have worried. After the first few steps I discovered that I was being held in an iron grip by a powerful fist pressed into the small of my back, and could not go wrong if I tried.

Bakatin was greatly perturbed by the rapidly deteriorating situation in the Soviet Union. Several Western economists were advising the Government and stringent measures had been taken to liberalise the economy. My concern was that the transformation from a centrally planned economy to one determined by market forces was going too fast. I was also amazed by the almost ingenuous conviction of my Soviet contacts that capitalism would resolve all their problems. I tried to warn them that capitalism also had flaws and that, although their own system of communism had not worked, not all of it should be jettisoned: the social safety net, for one, provided low-cost housing, health services and food. My constant message was, 'Don't throw the baby out with the bath water.' If they did, I argued, the social consequences would be devastating, and could cause a political backlash, imperilling *glasnost, perestroika*, and the incipient birth of democracy. In a dinner conversation with Bakatin I mentioned my work in Bolivia and Peru, to offset the negative social impact of economic liberalisation.

I left Moscow on a Saturday morning, seen off by officials of the Ministry of Interior. We were all surprised when the minister suddenly appeared in the VIP lounge. 'I have been thinking about our talk,' he said, 'and I am convinced that we need a UN programme like those for Bolivia and Peru. Can you please help?'

I was dumbstruck. 'It's hardly the same situation,' I ventured at length. 'There's a vast difference of scale ... And the Soviet Union is not a poor, developing country.'

But the minister insisted, 'Please see what you can do.'

For the rest of the weekend I put on my thinking cap, but the process was rudely interrupted when I heard on the BBC World News on Sunday evening that Bakatin had been replaced as Minister of the Interior ...

Two months later in January 1991 I visited Moscow to speak at a conference on 'The UN towards the year 2000'. It was incredibly cold. One night the temperature sank to −36 °C, and on no day did it rise above −18 °C. When you stepped outside the very act of breathing seemed to be cut off, as if your lungs were also frozen.

I saw Bakatin who, it was rumoured, had been eased out of the Ministry of Interior for being too liberal. He was still close to Gorbachev, advising him as a member of the National Security Council, among other things on social policy. We met in the Kremlin and, in response to his earlier request, I offered to send a high-powered mission of Western academics, senior government officials and ministers experienced in social policy to advise on the formulation and practical implementation of policies to mitigate the social effects of economic transformation. Bakatin called in Evgeny Primakov, then also a Kremlin adviser to Gorbachev. Both received my proposal with enthusiasm, and thought it would please Gorbachev, whom they would immediately consult. Notwithstanding, some time elapsed before I received an official response, and the delay was to prove fatal.

Bakatin's successor as Minister of Interior, Boris Pugo, gave me an official lunch. We agreed to continue all our joint programmes and the new minister asked me to strengthen our cooperation still further. Continuity seemed assured but I was in for a great surprise.

Chernobyl

Another link with the Soviet Union was developing. Breaking with their traditional 'go-it-alone' policy, the Soviet Union requested UN assistance in mitigating the effects of the Chernobyl nuclear disaster. The General Assembly adopted a resolution requesting the Secretary-General to mobilise international assistance and in January 1991 he appointed me as the UN Coordinator. The task was, as usual, to be performed 'within available resources', of which I had none to spare. So I stood out for two months until I was assured of two professionals and one secretary, who did not materialise until March.

I had an initial meeting with the people dealing with the Chernobyl issue in Ukraine, Belarus, the Russian Federation, and the USSR, during my January visit to Moscow and was alarmed to find they were bent on providing four different plans and looked to me as arbiter. I explained that this simply wouldn't do ('if President Gorbachev can't get you all to agree,' I said, 'how can I?') and urged them to prepare a joint plan, for which I sent them a suggested outline.

I flew to Moscow on 23 April 1991 with my small team and representatives of the Economic Commission for Europe and UNDP. My staff were screened before we left by the International Atomic Agency so that the amount of radiation in their bodies could be compared with that registered after visiting Chernobyl. I could not spare the time, and was only screened on return.

From Moscow we flew to Kiev where we met Mr Masik, the first Deputy Prime Minister of the Ukraine. In Chernobyl we visited the damaged nuclear plant and the affected areas, and were all assailed by a sense of brooding menace, of an unseen, yet palpable terror lurking all around, the danger all the more terrifying because unseen. On entering the 'Forbidden Zone' of highest radioactivity, we changed our cars for vehicles kept permanently inside and drove through woods barred by danger signs, and a countryside of deserted homesteads, abandoned fields and meadows of rank, waving grasses, crops gone wild, and heavily polluted.

We lunched in the staff restaurant called, with lugubrious humour, the Sarcophagus, before touring the installation. Three of the four units were still in operation. We tramped through miles of corridors until we reached, from the inside, the protective casing (the 'Sarcophagus') around the infamous Unit 4 which blew up on 26 April 1986, where there is a memorial to the engineer who stumbled into that blazing, lethal inferno to see what was wrong and never returned. I was secretly relieved when a suggestion that I should be photographed inside the damaged reactor was abandoned, and bemused by the fact that I was given the same 'protective' clothing that I had worn when visiting the cosmetics factory in Beijing two weeks earlier – a white overall, a cloth around my hair and rubber shoes. In Beijing this was to protect the *product* from contamination by me; in Chernobyl it seemed unlikely that such frail materials could defend us from radiation. I *was* photographed, with a distinctly nervous smile, touching the outside of the reactor.

We were taken to the most radioactive spot in Chernobyl, just outside the reactor, a huge, blackened, distorted hulk, roughly – and, by all accounts, insecurely – encased in its 'sarcophagus', which loomed over the dead landscape like a monument to man's folly and arrogance: humanity had lurched into an area it imperfectly understood and unleashed forces it could not control. That impression was heightened by the empty town of Pripyat, once the home of 50 000 workers, now a place of abandoned, decaying apartment buildings, untended squares and parks, long grass and children's swings swaying forlornly in the polluted wind.

Several thousand people still worked at the plant, commuting by train from a new town 50 kilometres away and undergoing an elaborate ritual of changing clothes and showering. I was awed by their matter-of-fact acceptance of this precarious existence, and by the courage of 'liquidators' who had undertaken the perilous clean-up operations. Untold numbers of them had died. The rest were scattered all over the Soviet Union, abandoned to an uncertain fate. Among those still working at the plant was a beautiful young woman engineer. Her husband also worked there and they lived in the new town with their two children. She said philosophically, 'I suppose it's only when our children's children are born that it will be possible to assess the full extent of what happened here.' We were all ashamed of our own nervousness in the face of someone so calmly facing daily exposure to incalculable danger.

We returned to Kiev to a working dinner, hosted by Mr Masik, and next day visited a clinic where many small children, fatally affected by radiation, presented us with drawings. The scarcity of adequate medical equipment was dramatic. At that time the international scientific community was sceptical of claims that the increased incidence of thyroid cancer in children had been caused by the accident. Latterly, they have had to eat their words.

We flew on to Minsk, the capital of Byelorussia, the area most seriously affected by radioactive fallout because of wind conditions. It was the fifth anniversary of the disaster and, after meetings with Ministers and technical experts, I attended a memorial charity concert – a moving televised performance of Verdi's *Requiem* – at which I read a message from the Secretary-General.

Next day a small plane took us to Bryansk in the Russian Federation. We drove through a grey, sodden landscape to a new village where people from a contaminated area had been resettled and a schoolteacher entertained us in her home. I met other resettled villagers, mostly women, very concerned about their children, the lack of medical facilities, and the radioactivity that they might all have absorbed. The new houses were of reasonable standard but the rutted streets were muddy and waterlogged and there were no schools, shops or community facilities. It was a sad and desolate scene.

Our next landing was at Novrosti, a town of 50 000, still a contaminated area with a level of radioactivity well above the safety level. We saw community leaders and a hospital where the facilities were pathetically poor. It was a dank, dark day, but the overhanging sense of doom was dissipated by the warm welcome accorded us by people who had so little, and even less to look forward to: girls in colourful traditional dress greeted us with the customary offering of a huge loaf of bread, and the community gave us large hand-painted wooden bread bins (the ignoble thought crossed our minds that they might be contaminated, like everything else in Novrosti).

Back in Moscow, I was disconcerted to find that the officials had not prepared project proposals and that those that were ready did not conform to the joint plan. I could not help reflecting that I had worked with more competent officials in Bolivia and Ethiopia, 30 years earlier, and wondered how the régime had conjured up such fear in the West during the Cold War when they could not even prepare a project.

That night I was emotionally and physically exhausted after listening to the experiences of 'liquidators' who had now formed a charity to help the children of Chernobyl. Expecting to sleep instantly, I found myself gripped by the Russian play *Sarcophagus* being broadcast by the BBC World Service to mark the fifth anniversary. It dramatically encapsulated all the experiences of our six intense days. After that sleep was impossible.

On our last day we met the commission on emergency situations of the USSR Council of Ministers, and agreed follow-up actions. At the Kremlin I met Bakatin and Primakov, who told me that Gorbachev enthusiastically endorsed the proposed mission on social policy. The delay in replying had been due to mounting political problems. I urged that we fix a firm date as soon as possible. I also saw the Interior Minister, Boris Pugo, with whom cooperation on crime and drugs was proceeding well.

Over the succeeding six weeks we moulded the numerous requests for assistance into a joint plan, signed by the Prime Ministers of the USSR and the three affected republics – no mean feat in an exceedingly difficult political situation. This the Secretary-General sent out to all member states with a personal plea for support. The plan contained 131 economic and social projects on health, social welfare, resettlement, decontamination of land and water and 'Lessons of Chernobyl' (radiological aspects were left to the International Atomic Energy Agency). External funding was estimated at US$646 million. I presented the plan to ECOSOC in Geneva in July and, with the Foreign Ministers of the three republics, gave extensive briefings to ambassadors, NGOs and the press. At the Pledging Conference in New York, on 20 September, chaired by the Secretary-General and myself, various Foreign Ministers spoke and the joint plan received much praise. But firm commitments totalled only US$7.5 million in convertible currency and US$3.4 million in non-convertible funds. A lively debate on Chernobyl in the General Assembly led to another supporting resolution but, once again, to words rather than deeds.

My team was disbanded for lack of funds but I strove single-handedly to keep the issue alive internationally, lobbying governments in all possible forums. I argued that there were overwhelming political as well as humanitarian reasons for providing assistance. But Western governments were slow to realise that Chernobyl provided a unique opportunity to give much-needed help to the Soviet Union without waiting for new political structures and economic reforms, and to do so within a co-ordinated plan of action, with the UN monitoring the use of the aid. Chernobyl was not just a human tragedy of unprecedented scale: it was a major determining factor in accelerating *glasnost* and *perestroika* and the disaffection of the three republics with the Soviet Union. The problems of Chernobyl could be effectively addressed only through cooperation from the West, which could have fostered a new, integrating process through the very medium that sparked the disintegration. It was no coincidence that Chernobyl merited a paragraph in the Minsk Declaration setting up the new 'commonwealth', after Ukraine's declaration of independence at the end of 1991.

Social Policy Mission to Russia

Our team on social policies for the Soviet Union was headed by the distinguished British economist, Sir Alan Peacock, and comprised a number of equally notable Europeans. After further delays due to continuing political upheavals, the date for our mission was fixed for early September 1991. Just as everything seemed set, the attempted coup to topple Gorbachev took place, and in the ensuing chaos we were asked to postpone the mission. Boris Pugo, the pleasant Minister of the Interior, turned out to be one of the main conspirators. Faced with imminent arrest, he shot his wife and committed suicide. Gorbachev must have bitterly regretted his decision to replace the loyal Bakatin by Pugo — a misplaced attempt to placate the conservative opposition to his reforms literally backfired. It was a double irony: they objected to his policies of decentralisation — a desperate measure to salvage the integrity of the Soviet Union — while the coup simply precipitated the very disintegration the plotters sought to prevent.

A shaken Gorbachev, restored to the Kremlin with the help of Boris Yeltsin, appointed Bakatin to head the KGB, with a mandate to disband it, or at least pull its teeth as a state within a state. Eduard Shevardnadze was restored to the Foreign Ministry. On Friday 22 November 1991 I received an urgent message to meet him in Moscow to discuss the rescheduling of the Peacock mission. I cancelled other commitments and hastily departed to Moscow on Tuesday 26. I had never met Shevardnadze before but we struck up an immediate rapport during an hour-long tête-à-tête. We discussed the general situation, as well as the Peacock mission and fund-raising strategies for Chernobyl. As Shevardnadze was meeting the US Secretary of State, James Baker, a few days later, I urged him to push the case of Chernobyl, expounding my thesis that, as one of the causes of the discontent of the three republics, it might also serve as an integrating force, provided that rapid Western support was forthcoming.

As my meetings proceeded, however, it became clear that the centrifugal forces at work had reached the point of no return. I found Bakatin in a huge mausoleum of an office in the dreaded Lublyanka, a place I had never thought to visit, just as I had never expected to meet the head of the KGB. He recounted his activities with some glee and particularly how he had shown the US Ambassador the exact location of the bugging devices in their embassy. On the general panorama I found him uncharacteristically gloomy: the central structures of the Soviet Union were collapsing and likely to disintegrate altogether after the independence referendum in the Ukraine, due to take place the following Sunday. He feared that the Peacock mission could not take place, since social issues must be tackled in a co-ordinated manner. I replied that I was disappointed to see that he, the father of the idea, now wished to bury it. Moreover, whatever the political structures, the rapidly worsening social problems must be addressed if the whole process was not to founder. My arguments proved persuasive and, in his usual decisive way, he picked up the phone and after a brief conversation with the Russian President, Boris Yeltsin, we were in business again.

I talked also with Mr Gavrilov, the Deputy to Mr Silayev at the Inter-State Economic Committee and Mr Shohin, one of Yeltsin's Deputy Prime Ministers, who was in charge of social issues. Everyone wanted the Peacock mission urgently and I evolved a formula whereby it would work simultaneously with the residue of the central authority, with the Russian Federation and the two other republics. Within days of my departure the Soviet Union had been dissolved and the new 'Commonwealth' created. We were nonetheless assured that the mission would be welcome in January 1992.

The desperate situation confronting the country was amply evident during my stay. Because of the penury of the central Government they could only accommodate me in a hotel an hour's drive out of Moscow, lost in the woods. As we entered that forest my Foreign Ministry guide remarked conversationally that we would be surrounded by wildlife: 'Rabbits,' he said (pause), 'and foxes' ... (longer pause for inspiration).

'Wolves?' I asked, helpfully.

'Yes! Wolves!'

'Bears too?' (pushing my luck a bit).

'Yes! Bears too!' Pause; hurried conversation in Russian with the driver, and then: 'Sorry, bears not available!' Further hurried conversation, and then sadly: 'Wolves not available either!'

It seemed an allegorical comment on Moscow, where nothing much seemed to be available, whether you were looking for food or for reliable information about what was happening.

In contrast plenty of entertainment was available. I was taken to a very long, very lugubrious, Mussorgsky opera at the Bolshoi but didn't last until the undoubtedly gloomy end. It was difficult to follow, the programme being in Russian, but my Foreign Ministry escort could not keep abreast of the story either. When some chap sang an interminable, doleful aria, he explained tersely, 'He is describing the state of the country,' which just about summed it up. Next night there was *Fliedermaus* in Russian, but I escaped *Hamlet* on the third night because of my meeting with Bakatin in the KGB. Business ended, he said he would like me to see the dacha he was building with his own hands. As it was snowing hard and winter dark had set in, that did not seem a very good idea. Instead he took me to his home, a pleasant, by no means luxurious apartment where his wife and a girl friend were eating supper in the kitchen. I was immediately made to feel a member of the family and we repaired to the living-room where drinks and snacks were rustled up, and some of their Siberian friends joined us. We had no common language but that difficulty was overcome by Bakatin's assistant, who turned out to be Molotov's grandson. As the evening wore on guitars were produced, they sang Siberian and Russian folk-songs, and I contributed the odd British one. I found myself mentally pinching myself: could I really be sitting in this warm lamp-lit room singing along with the KGB head and his family? But Bakatin was hardly a typical specimen of the breed. He had a fine voice and is also a considerable artist. When I at last tore myself away to embark on my long trek back to the forest, he was reciting Russian poetry.

I accompanied the Peacock mission to Moscow. Confusion still reigned but nonetheless Mr Shohin organised a comprehensive programme of meetings with ministries and the burgeoning private sector. One memorable encounter was with Mr Gorbachev, ensconced in his new Foundation, in the building from which he was later evicted. He was very relaxed and we had a long, lively exchange about the problems of transforming the economy, in which we agreed on the urgent need to take remedial action on the social front. In fact, everyone we spoke to was on the side of the angels, but the packet of measures presented very promptly in our final report was never acted upon. One reason was that the father of the project, Bakatin, was, by January, a private citizen and no longer able to ensure action. Another was the common problem that 'hard line' economists were so engrossed in translating their theories into action that they were not amenable to an injection of softer options, even though these did not divert the main thrust of the reform. Had it been possible to present the recommendations earlier the outcome might have been different. They came too late on account of the very unravelling of the body politic that we had hoped to prevent. The political backlash I had foreseen came through with a vengeance.

Another factor was the reluctance of the West to come to the Soviet Union's aid. They adopted the same 'wait-and-see' and 'show-us-first' attitudes invariably applied to developing countries in the throes of economic liberalisation. They failed to recognise that the Soviet Union needed help at an early stage, precisely in order to mitigate the political and economic turmoil that could put the whole process of liberalisation and democratisation at risk, or that it was in the West's own interests to encourage a stable and prosperous Soviet Union. When aid eventually came from international financial institutions and bilateral donors the die was already cast. And the failure of the Soviet Union to address social problems simultaneously with economic measures led to continued splintering of the political spectrum and the social fabric for years afterwards.

Burning Oil Wells in Kuwait

Whenever disasters struck it seemed that my name came first out of the hat. The Secretary-General again named me as his Special Representative when, in September 1991, the Kuwaiti Government asked the Secretary-General to appoint a senior official to undertake a 'Chernobyl-type' operation to deal with the impact of the burning oil wells and other environmental effects of the Gulf conflict on Kuwait and the region. Once again the job had to be done within the UN's exiguous 'available resources'.

A visit to Kuwait was squeezed into my schedule in early October. In the space of a few months, by a strange twist of fate I visited the two greatest environmental disasters mankind had so far managed to wreak on itself. There was much in common between Chernobyl and the Gulf. Both disasters transcended frontiers and were no respecters of national sovereignty and both entailed incalculable long-term effects on health and environment. But Chernobyl was caused by a terrible mistake, the result of a system that failed, while the torched oil wells and the unleashing of millions of barrels of oil into the Bay of Kuwait were deliberate acts. Chernobyl was a silent, dead landscape, imbued with brooding, sinister menace. The Kuwait desert was a blazing, roaring hell, the epitome of Dante's Inferno. In the Burgan oilfields, a few miles from Kuwait City, we drove until brought up short by an impenetrable wall of black smoke, belching as far as one could see along the horizon on either side and up into the sky, interspersed with huge tongues of flame. The noise of escaping gas was deafening and the desert a blackened crust, interspersed with great lakes of oil, which migrating birds mistook for water.

Next day I was taken by helicopter to oil wells north of the city where we were able to weave at low altitude between the plumes of smoke and flames, with the doors open. We flew over the Bay of Kuwait and saw the devastation of mined beaches, tangled barbed wire, abandoned tanks and military equipment, and the pipelines that poured oil into the sea. A particularly dreadful scene was the 'Valley of Death', the graveyard of countless tanks and hundreds of retreating Iraqi soldiers.

I was taken to a conference hall, only recently completed, that had been destroyed by the invading forces, and to the brand new Scientific Research Institute from which the equipment had been taken to Iraq and the building gutted. All books and scientific records had been burnt, a few loose pages blowing around our feet. The wanton destruction and vandalism was such that it was hard to know where to begin. An even greater concern was the fate of the thousands of Kuwaiti men who had been taken to Iraq. No one knew whether they were dead or in prison and I was plied with yellow ribbons.

I met the Emir of Kuwait, the Prime Minister and the Foreign Minister and worked closely with Dr Abdul Rahman Al-Awadi, a friend from years before, who was in charge of environment questions. On return to Vienna I helped the governments of the region to develop a plan of action, with costed project profiles, which we presented to donor governments in New York in December 1991. The total cost came to US$1 billion, excluding the astronomical expense of putting out the oil fires and clearing wrecks and mines. Profuse expressions of sympathy were forthcoming but little cash. Kuwait was considered a rich country, despite the ravages of war. Unlike the Soviet Union, the Kuwaiti government's expectations were not that high, their main concern being to sustain international interest.

The big challenge was to maintain that interest – all too likely to wane with the extinction of the last burning oil well – over the lengthy process of rehabilitation. Many thought that Iraq should pay the bill, and there was a UN Compensation Fund, but payment depended on the sale of Iraqi oil, which Iraq had so far refused to contemplate under the stipulated conditions.

As I left Vienna two months later, the continued mobilisation of assistance for Kuwait and Chernobyl was a task I had to leave for others.

Christmas Thoughts 1991

During Christmas 1991 at Knill I pondered what I had to show for my five years in Vienna. The original concept of UNOV as the nucleus for social policy and programmes dealing with narcotic drugs had collapsed, owing to the meddling of governments, and indecision in New York, but there were still some achievements, notwithstanding tremendous financial and bureaucratic constraints.

Javier Pérez de Cuéllar with whom I had worked closely for ten years, left office on 31 December. In August I had written to him, requesting permission for a portrait of Jacko, that I would finance, to hang in the United Nations, alongside that of Governor Herbert Lehmann, with whom Jacko had worked in the 1940s in UNRRA. Whenever I saw him the Secretary-General assured me of his agreement, the last occasion being 18 December when I bade him farewell. On 31 December, his last day in office, he signed a letter to me refusing permission. On the same day he rescinded the Vacancy Management System that had been an important outcome from the UN reform team I had led in 1986–87. Conservative opposition to change had won again.

My own contract was to end in March 1992. Boutros Boutros-Ghali, the new Secretary-General, had seen the other Under Secretaries-General in New York in November but I had been unable to attend because I was presiding over a ministerial meeting on crime in Versailles. On 18 December Pérez de Cuéllar told me he had strongly recommended to his successor that he appoint me as his Chef de Cabinet. Judging by previous experience I thought it better not to entertain too many hopes.

At the end of the year I wrote to friends:

I am waiting for events to unfold. Earlier this year I felt that I would spend the rest of my life driving only with the rear-mirror. That perspective has changed but the windshield is murky and the road ahead looks a bit foggy.

PART EIGHT

Peace-keeping

────── 21 ──────

The Lands at the End of the World 1992–93

UNAVEM II – A 'Small and Manageable Operation'

At the end of January 1992 I met the new Secretary-General. Knowing that he was under pressure to cut posts, I hastened to say that I had no vested interest in staying on, but it was pointless for me to continue in Vienna unless the social development programme was fully integrated. If not, I was happy to retire. If I could be of service I would prefer an operational job and was ready to go anywhere.

I had many items to discuss but never got beyond the first: my efforts to help the Soviet Union and Eastern European countries. Full of my experiences in Moscow a week earlier, I said that the world community should, in its own interest, extend generous help, particularly to offset the dire social costs of economic transformation. If not, I foresaw grave economic and social problems that could lead to political backlash and instability, especially in the Soviet Union, with serious implications for the rest of the world. The West seemed oblivious to these risks and I urged that the UN and the Secretary-General take the lead in calling world attention to the problem.

Boutros-Ghali insisted, however, that all such help should go to developing countries, and we became locked in feisty argument, a radical change of style from his predecessor. I found our exchange intellectually stimulating, exhilarating even, but it took up much time and I felt less than exhilarated when the Secretary-General abruptly got to his feet and shook my hand, leaving much of my agenda unbroached.

Less than a week later, on 5 February, I was telephoned late at night in Vienna. The Secretary-General wished to know, within 24 hours, if I would accept the post of his Special Representative for Angola and head of the peace-keeping mission there – the UN Angola Verification Mission, UNAVEM II. I knew that a considerable gamble was involved and sought the advice of the man who had first aroused my interest in Angola 25 years before in Addis Ababa. I saw this surprise development as an ironic twist of fate, creating another bond between us, even though we might never meet again, and expected him to react enthusiastically to the prospect of my helping the Angolan people. Instead he said adamantly 'Don't touch it. It's an impossible mission and you'll only get hurt.'

His remarks proved prophetic but after hours of soul-searching, I perversely accepted the challenge. Marrack (Mig) Goulding, then Under Secretary-General in charge of peace-keeping, told me it was undoubtedly a difficult mission but not a totally lost cause. Others were less sanguine, and warned me that it would be dangerous.

Insofar as I was able to reason coolly the disadvantages were outweighed by other considerations. I longed to be back in the field and the tragic plight of the Angolan people made it hard to refuse. If the mission was successful, it would make possible the development of a potentially rich country and do much to assure political stability and economic prosperity in Southern Africa. The end of the Cold War and the Peace Accords recently signed between the MPLA Government of Angola (previously supported by the Soviet Union and Cuba) and the UNITA rebels (supported by the United States and South Africa) held out greater promise of a settlement than ever before.

This was also the first time that a woman had been asked to head a UN peace-keeping mission, with command over military and police components, as well as civilian elements. If I refused, the sceptics would say, 'It was offered to a woman, but she refused', while women would feel I had let them down. Yet the risks were considerable. Failure, which many thought likely, would entail the familiar search for a scapegoat, a role for which the UN seems particularly well designed. And if the senior official were a woman, then the aforesaid sceptics would have a field day.

The most persuasive argument was the echo of my mother's voice: 'Don't jib!' I decided that it was better to end my career with a bang (and how true that turned out to be!) than a whimper. Things moved fast. On Friday 7 February 1992, the Secretary-General announced my appointment, to last seven months, until multiparty general elections were held at the end of September.

Mig Goulding was supposed to lead a mission to Angola on 16 February to prepare the ground for my arrival, as well as plan for an electoral component to be added to the military and police operation, but he was called away on another mission. On 14 February I received another late-night call, asking me to replace him.

In Luanda I plunged into four hectic days of activity: briefings at Vila Espa, the UNAVEM camp; visits to the Government and UNITA delegations; attendance at a meeting of the Joint Political and Military Commission (known by its Portuguese acronym CCPM); and a flight to two troop cantonment areas (one government, one UNITA) in the rugged northern province of Uige. President José Eduardo dos Santos was unable to see me but Dr Jonas Savimbi, the UNITA leader, received me immediately, in some state, at his heavily guarded White House, surrounded by his 'Cabinet' and in the mediaeval court atmosphere that was his hallmark. An imposing and charismatic figure, Savimbi was all sweetness and light, promising full cooperation. But I detected that under this blandly smiling exterior lay a ruthless will of iron.

On the night flight back to Paris, I composed a personal letter to the Secretary-General voicing my concern about the immensity of the task in contrast to UNAVEM's marginal mandate and paltry resources.

Starting at the end of 1988, UNAVEM I, a purely military mission, had successfully monitored the withdrawal of 50 000 Cuban troops. Meanwhile Portugal, the Soviet Union and the United States had negotiated a peace settlement between the MPLA Government and UNITA, signed on 31 May 1991 in Bicesse,

Portugal. The UN had no part in the negotiation, except for a military observer present at the last stage.

The Bicesse Accords envisaged the cantonment of two rival armies, estimated to total 200 000, in assembly areas all over the country; their disarmament and demobilisation; and the formation of new, joint armed forces, numbering 50 000. A neutral police force was to be set up, the central administration was to be extended all over the country, and there was to be free movement of people and goods. The process was to culminate in multiparty general elections and a democratically elected government. UNITA wanted the elections in three months, the Government not before three years. In an arbitrary compromise the accords stipulated they must take place between September and November 1992. The supposition that 16 years of war could be restored in 16 months was over-optimistic, as was the assumption that elections would clinch the process, rather than mark a mere first step towards reconciliation and democracy. Moreover, no pre-conditions were established for holding the elections.

CCPM comprised only two members, the MPLA Government and UNITA, which alternated in the chairmanship, the thesis being that they would control one another. This arrangement naively presupposed a Boy Scout spirit, in circumstances hardly conducive to its evolution. Portugal, the Soviet Union (later the Russian Federation) and the United States, known as the Troika, had official observer status. The UN was only to be 'invited' as appropriate.

This extraordinary set-up was characteristic of the marginal role given to the UN at Bicesse. UNITA had wanted a strong UN presence, with armed 'Blue Helmets'. The Government had wanted the minimum, citing considerations of sovereignty, a somewhat illusory concept since they controlled only part of the country. In another compromise, the UN's role was restricted to observing and verifying that the two sides were doing what they said they were doing. This suited the negotiating countries, especially the two superpowers, who wanted a 'quick fix' now that the Cold War was over, when in fact the Cold War had exacerbated the Angolan conflict and armed both sides to the teeth.

The means given to the UN were not commensurate even with its limited mandate. On 30 May 1991 Security Council Resolution

696 established UNAVEM II with 350 unarmed military observers, 90 unarmed police observers and 80 civilians. It was to function until the day after the elections. Initially it was headed by a Chief Military Observer, with the rank of Major General. It was not until December 1991 that the Angolan government requested the Secretary-General to send electoral observers and it was decided to appoint a political head of UNAVEM II or Special Representative of the Secretary-General. Yet two more months elapsed before I was asked to arrive the day before yesterday.

An interesting sidelight came to my notice recently. When my appointment was announced the Portuguese observer, Ambassador Antonio Monteiro, expressed doubts to his minister, José Durão Barroso, about the wisdom of appointing a special representative to an under-mandated and under-resourced mission. The Minister found it an excellent development: it would get the Troika off the hook, should things go wrong. The UN – and hence I – was precast in the role of scapegoat.

When I assumed my post only seven months before the election date, no electoral preparations had begun and the military provisions of the Bicesse Accords were hopelessly behind schedule. Since October 1991 the Secretary-General had repeatedly warned the Security Council about the seriousness of this situation. The seeds of the eventual debacle were sown long before my arrival.

On 7 March 1992 I flew to New York to sort out budget and personnel matters. The Secretary-General's request for my small staff had been submitted to the Security Council on 3 March, but no action was taken until three weeks later. Approval of the budget – a mere US$118 million for 18 months – took even longer.

The Security Council, I was repeatedly told, wanted a 'small and manageable' operation. In vain I pleaded that Angola, as large as France, Spain and Germany combined, could hardly be considered small nor, from my preliminary observations, particularly manageable. There were difficulties also over obtaining civilian staff. Because of pressure to cut posts, outside recruitment was not allowed, and the tremendous increase in UN peace-keeping operations meant there was a dearth of people to choose from.

Moreover Angola was not a popular choice: the Secretary-General's report of October 1991 to the Security Council described conditions of service there as 'amongst the most difficult that have ever been faced by UN peace-keeping personnel.' Again the insistence on certain nationalities meant a less than optimum choice of incumbents for some key posts, for which I was to suffer later.

The Chief Military Officer from Nigeria, General Edward Unimna had been head of UNAVEM II until my arrival. Goulding had warned me that he was a difficult man but that it was politically impossible to remove him. In his own recent book, *Peacemonger*, Goulding records that he had welcomed my appointment but worried how Unimna would react, adding, 'He had not made a good impression when I visited Angola the previous year and I had received a number of complaints, then and since, about his short temper and autocratic management.' Later he describes him as 'a martinet, short-tempered, autocratic and even violent; he had been observed more than once to strike his driver. This was not the style of command which is needed in a multinational operation.'

Forewarned, I was at first able to develop reasonable relations with him. His unpopularity with his officers meant that they warmly welcomed me, even though a female head of mission was not what they had expected.

Things became complicated when my civilian deputy, Ibrahim Jobarteh, arrived. A long-serving UN official and clever administrator, he had a very mixed personal reputation, but there was no one else available. While he assured me he wished to improve relations with Unimna, it soon became clear they were making common cause to isolate me. They objected to my customary team approach of regular meetings with all the heads of individual components of the mission, to ensure that everyone understood the political context in which I was working and that there was appropriate interaction between them, especially between military and civilian units. They maintained that I should meet only with them and eventually boycotted these general meetings. Jobarteh had the gall to complain that I did not consult him enough, because I convened meetings at 8 o'clock and he never appeared until mid-morning, having hosted heavy drinking parties until the early hours. His aim was to run the show through direct contact with colleagues in New York behind my back, but soon found I was no Trilby needing a Svengali. Worst of all my special assistant, a young woman who performed well before his arrival, became part of his coterie and nightly gatherings. For the first time in my UN experience I could not count on loyalty from my immediate staff, except for a devoted Filipino secretary, Elizabeth Pantaleón, and my Chief Administrative Officer, Tom White. It became a very lonely job indeed.

I accepted to go to Angola for seven months but circumstances obliged me to spend 17. It was the most traumatic and heart-rending mission of my life, a story I have told in my book, *Orphan of the Cold War: The Inside Story of the Collapse of the Angolan Peace Process, 1992–3.*

I installed myself in the UNAVEM camp, 15 kilometres outside Luanda in order to be 'with the troops'. I had a tiny bungalow and shared another with the General as our offices. I had another office in an insalubrious building downtown. The majority of our staff lived and worked in what came to be known as 'Container City'. Conditions were crowded; water scarce; electricity, provided by an aged and noisy generator, was often cut; and communications at first very difficult, even with New York.

I had domestic help in the buxom shape of a lady with the appropriately statuesque name of María do Fátima, who sailed round the house like a galleon before a barely perceptible breeze, and in a generally becalmed state of mind. Fortunately I had decided to bring Sissy from Vienna at my expense (the UN does not provide such niceties). She arrived clasping a lugubrious teddy bear, almost as large as herself, and strung around with twice as much hand-baggage as any sensible person would carry or prudent airline allow. Sissy greatly helped my official work. With her arrival I was able to receive key people discreetly over a good meal in my little house.

There was a swimming-pool and at dawn I swam my kilometre before the rest of the camp stirred, undeterred by the fact that one of our Russian pilots drowned there, by green algae, or an invasion of frogs. The latter caused the Chief Administrative Officer to send a circular saying that the 'SRSG has complained about copulating frogs in the pool'. The Ghurkha guards whom we were eventually allowed to have under private contract (no one in the UN mission could carry arms) used to fish the offending amphibians out, but disconcertingly insisted on saluting me while I stood by, feeling foolish in a bathing suit.

UNAVEM was little less than a logistic miracle. Our scant personnel were spread over 84 locations: six regional head-quarters; 48 troop assembly areas; 18 police locations; and 12 critical points along Angola's long borders. Civilian and electoral staff were stationed in the provincial capitals. Even there, housing and sanitation were usually dreadful. The harshest conditions were endured by the military observers (UNMOs) in isolated assembly areas: teams of five officers, each of a different nationality, often with no common language, having to monitor several thousand disgruntled Angolan soldiers. At first they lived in grass huts, shaking snakes from the roof before they went to bed, but later we obtained tented accommodation.

Because of the remoteness of these sites and the devastated infrastructure UNAVEM's air support absorbed nearly 50 per cent of the budget. My fleet consisted of three fixed-wing aircraft and 14 helicopters, the latter, like their crews, contracted from Russia or Bulgaria, the cheapest international source. The helicopters were elderly, seemingly held together by wire, but the pilots first-class.

I flew the length and breadth of Angola, visiting provincial capitals and assembly areas, usually in the Beechcraft, changing to a helicopter wherever there was no landing strip. These demanding trips provided me with valuable information and boosted staff morale. We would leave at first light and come back late, the plane's lights extinguished to avoid unwelcome attention from the sharpshooters who abounded after dark, even around Vila Espa.

At assembly areas, I had to address several thousand soldiers, in the open air, without a microphone. I developed a parade-ground volume of delivery but at one UNITA area I asked the commander to bring the troops nearer. He barked an order and in seconds the men had surrounded me in perfect formation. I felt glad that it was a friendly occasion. The UNITA camps were better organised and their stored weapons, well-greased, looked all too ready to use.

I had a further demonstration of UNITA's rigid discipline on my visit, in April 1992, to Jamba, the mysterious non-town in the far south-east, unmarked on any map, that had for years been Dr Savimbi's headquarters. It boasted an international-class airstrip that had seen the passage of many prominent people, including officials from successive US administrations, but the town consisted of grass huts scattered in acacia scrub. I was received by dancing, chanting crowds in apparently huge numbers, until I discovered that they were being trucked from point to point. From this remote bush location Vorgan radio – the Voice of the Black Cockerel – broadcast UNITA propaganda as far as Europe. I expressed surprise that a clothes factory seemed only to produce dark green military uniforms, now that peace had been declared, and was blandly told that this was surplus stock to be worn by civilians ...

President José Eduardo dos Santos did not receive me until 2 April but any misgivings I had about the delay were dispelled by the cordiality of my reception. I developed good relations with both leaders. Their styles were very different: President dos Santos, modest and reserved, often only accompanied by his foreign affairs adviser; Dr Savimbi, ever flamboyant, flanked by serried ranks of well-rehearsed courtiors

CCPM took for granted that I would attend every meeting, and not just 'when invited'. I detected relief that there was another pair of shoulders on which to place responsibility. At UNAVEM's suggestion, cantonment and demobilisation were conducted simultaneously instead of consecutively and on 31 March, the whole of CCPM flew to Luanda for the first demobilisation ceremony. The troops were delirious with joy, and we felt a sense of euphoria.

My euphoria was short-lived. I returned to Vila Espa to receive a reprimand: the Secretary-General was displeased because the Portuguese Secretary for Foreign Affairs and Cooperation, Dr Durão Barroso, had expressed concern about the adequacy of UNAVEM's resources. The Swedes had spoken similarly. It was assumed, wrongly, that this was at my instigation, when the paucity of the means granted to resolve Angola's immense problems was plain for all to see. One European Ambassador in

Luanda referred to Angola as 'a footnote in the international agenda'. In CCPM, UNITA and the Government complained that Angola was being short-changed, a view supported by the Portuguese and US observers, whose governments had limited the operation in the first place! In New York the Secretary-General told the Portuguese Minister that the problems were the same everywhere, whether it was Cambodia or Yugoslavia, and his special representatives should not think they were *les seuls au monde*. Considering that Cambodia had a budget of US$2 billion and Yugoslavia US$600 million, compared to our paltry US$118 million, this was quite rich.

Security Council Resolution 747 (1992) of 24 March authorised the establishment of my small office, an electoral division and electoral offices in all 18 provincial capitals. We would have only 100 electoral observers, to be increased to 400 during the poll. The Angolans were to organise the elections, with UNAVEM II simply observing and verifying the process. My responsibility was to give a public verdict on whether the three phases – voter registration, the electoral campaign and the poll – were 'free and fair'. In a controversy that rumbled on for weeks Headquarters sustained that comparisons with electoral budgets for Cambodia and Namibia were invalid because in Cambodia the UN was *organising* the elections, and in Namibia had *supervised* and *controlled* them, while we were only to *observe*. I argued, without success, that the one to four difference in funding with Namibia was excessive, since Angola had ten million inhabitants and an estimated 6 million voters, compared to Namibia's population of 1.8 million and 6–700 000 voters.

My dwindling popularity in New York was not improved by the prominence given in international media to my quip about Security Council Resolution 747 – that I had been given a 747 Jumbo to fly but fuel sufficient only for a DC-3! Even authorised resources were slow in coming. Six weeks after my arrival I still had no secretary who could take English dictation. When an old friend did arrive for that function, she contracted cerebral malaria and typhus, very nearly died in my house, and was medically evacuated. My Chief Electoral Officer had to be medically evacuated after less than a month. Some delays were bureaucratic, others the effect of the strain placed on the UN by the upsurge in peace-keeping missions.

Free and Fair Elections

A UNDP team was to help the Angolans organise the elections. This project foresaw a transport element comprising four-wheel drive vehicles, and – astoundingly – 600 *motorcycles*, totally unsuitable for local conditions. Massive air support was essential if voters all over the country were to take part in the elections. The Angolan Government did not have the capability to provide this, much less incentive, since voters in remote areas were mainly UNITA supporters.

I concluded that the only solution was to seek contributions *in kind* from donors – transport (including aircraft), services, supplies and personnel. Initially even this approach received a cool response in New York. On 1 May the Secretary-General wrote me a letter that, despite expressions of admiration for my 'vigour and energy', was a thinly veiled rebuke. He instructed me to inform all concerned that member states would not approve increased resources for Angola and to discourage the Government from expecting any logistical support.

The matter was resolved only by my going to New York at the end of May. As usual I found much greater understanding when dealing directly with the Secretary-General than through written communication. I also managed to convince the Security Council, and was able to launch my 'lease-lend', 'make-do and mend' strategy. It was a huge gamble, but it worked. We eventually mounted the largest UN air operation in support of elections that the organisation had ever had anywhere, and all without any budget. We begged, we borrowed (we never actually stole!) and took every imaginative measure conceivable to ensure that the elections would reach all corners of Angola. Meanwhile, the Government was dragging its feet. It did not announce the election dates for 29–30 September until 2 April, nor appoint the National Electoral Council (NEC) and the Director-General of the Elections until 10 May, only 20 weeks before the election. Fortunately the

Director-General, Dr Onofre dos Santos, was an inspired choice. Brimming with ideas, he quickly re-ignited the flames of hope that had begun to flicker dangerously low.

Voter registration started on 20 May and was to end on 31 July but donors were slow in providing promised ground and air transport and by 30 June only 750 000 voters had been registered.

With government agreement, the process was saved by help from an unlikely quarter – the South African Air Force (SAAF) – formerly known in Angola only for its indiscriminate bombing in support of UNITA. This was a controversial move but seemed an encouraging sign of the new approaches gaining momentum in South Africa. Registration figures jumped to 4.3 million by 31 July. Thanks to an extension until 10 August, the ultimate result was 4.86 million eligible voters, or 92 per cent of an estimated voting population of 5.3 million.

The electoral campaign opened on 29 August. Twenty-five parties were legalised but there were only two real contenders, MPLA and UNITA. President Dos Santos, originally considered a poor performer on the hustings, grew into the part, presenting the calm demeanour of a moderate statesman preaching peace, unity and prosperity. Savimbi's speeches, in contrast, were fiery and colourful but his aggressive style was afterwards thought to have put many voters off.

While the electoral process was proceeding better than hoped I was greatly concerned about delays in the cantonment, disarming and demobilisation of troops. The Secretary-General's last report to the Security Council before the elections stated that only 45 per cent of government troops had been demobilised and a mere 24 per cent of UNITA's. Fear of an unknown civilian life was a factor for UNITA but our appeals to donors to fund reintegration programmes went largely unheard.

In another anachronism of the Bicesse Accords the UN was accorded no role in the formation of the new, Joint Armed Forces (FAA), but when things went wrong, we were brought in. Logistical problems played a role. I got agreement from the USA to supply tents, only to be rescinded later, because Congress had prohibited military assistance to Angola – as if tents were a lethal weapon! Portugal manufactured uniforms and airlifted them to Luanda.

It was not until June 1992 that I managed to persuade Headquarters and the Security Council to increase our police observers from 90 to 126. The establishment of joint police monitoring teams and the integration of UNITA personnel into a unified, neutral police force never got very far, despite intensive efforts by UNAVEM.

Two related crises rumbled on in CCPM, from April onwards. The government side voiced concern about UNITA's alleged 'hidden army' of 20 000 men. A joint investigation by government and UNITA representatives, UNAVEM and the Troika, failed to find any trace of it. Incomprehensibly the *Government* called off the hunt, while still maintaining their allegations. In early September the Foreign Minister painted me a dire picture of UNITA's intentions and demanded a large contingent of Blue Helmets – blithely forgetting that one of the main reasons why we did not have such a force was his government's opposition. Simultaneously UNITA accused the government's newly created anti-riot or emergency police force of being a 'parallel army'. My efforts to find a compromise by making it a neutral and transparent body, in which UNITA and other non-MPLA elements were adequately represented, were unsuccessful.

Another unresolved issue was the extension of the central administration. By mid-September many places remained outside government control. In others its presence consisted of one unfortunate man, dumped in an outlandish place, without offices, pay or food. There was an alarming degree of brinkmanship and cliff-hanging on both sides, though when the cliff-edge became vertiginously near, neither side wanted to take the fatal plunge while the elections were in the offing.

A major stumbling-block was the reluctance of the two leaders to meet each other. A 'summit', only the third since the Peace Accords, should have taken place on 24 August but Savimbi failed to appear. A deadly game of poker was being played out. When the meeting did take place on 7 September the two leaders agreed on a crucial encounter between 23 and 27 September, at which they must declare their armies to be disbanded and the FAA to be Angola's only armed force.

When I saw President Dos Santos on 23 September the date was still not fixed. Dr Savimbi was campaigning in the north and it was only on Friday 25 September that I managed to find him in Uige. I was kept hanging about for hours and then encountered a Savimbi I had heard about but never seen. He was aggressive, argument-ative, at times appearing to struggle with pent-up rage, at others rambling in a discourse consistent only in its vituperative accusations against the Government, the MPLA and President Dos Santos. He appeared impervious to my plea that he meet the President before the election. Back at Vila Espa I played my last card and, by 3.00 a.m., had arranged a satellite telephone call from the Secretary-General to Savimbi.

The next evening, Saturday 26 September, the meeting took place. Afterwards Savimbi made a conciliatory statement, much at variance with his tone the night before, which ended 'while many people think of war, we think of peace'. On Sunday a joint communiqué announced the disbandment of the two armies, and that the FAA would have *two* Chiefs of General Staff, one from each side. The new FAA was sworn in the next afternoon, barely 14 hours before the polls were to open. We were all moved by the sight of arms long raised against one another now raised in joint salute, the voices proclaiming their common allegiance to Angola, and the identical uniforms that made it impossible to detect who was government and who was UNITA.

Meanwhile, against all the odds, we had managed to set up a huge logistical support operation quite outside our mandate. A visit I paid to Washington, where I had high-level meetings in the Pentagon, the State Department, the National Security Council in the White House and both Houses of Congress, had greatly helped in this respect. Our greatest achievement was to assemble our air force. Both US and European donors ultimately decided the most cost-effective way was to provide cash, amounting to some US$10 million, with which we contracted Russian surplus military aircraft, the cheapest on the market. Huge Antonov-124s roared in over Luanda bringing in 40 M-17 helicopters. Ten fixed-wing planes followed. To these we added UNAVEM's own 14 helicopters and two fixed-wing planes.

Colonel Hank Morris was loaned to us from the El Salvador mission to orchestrate this mammoth operation. In all 25 000 people and 620 metric tons of materials and equipment were flown to and from 5800 voting stations from six hubs around the country but the airports could not handle the anticipated volume of traffic. At my suggestion New York asked a few countries to provide military air traffic controllers, and Argentina and Portugal obliged. We obtained Inmarsat sets to improve communications and set up a computerised control centre.

During the election days everything worked like clockwork. Luanda's airfield looked like a mini-Heathrow, with phalanxes of planes and helicopters, hastily painted white over military grey, and bearing either the UN emblem or the Angolan electoral symbol, a dove of peace. We had had our setbacks and tragedies. On three Saturdays running in September UNAVEM helicopters carrying electoral personnel crashed in the northern province of Uige. In Vila Espa it became a black joke that every Saturday we must mount a 'search and rescue' operation. Miraculously, in the first two crashes no one was killed, but in the third all but one perished.

On 29 and 30 September 1992 Angola had its two most peaceful days in 30 years. Of registered voters, 92 per cent turned out, many trudging for days through the bush, standing for hours under a hot sun, and waiting patiently through the night. Everywhere the ballot was witnessed by our electoral observers, representatives of the MPLA and UNITA and the other parties, and night-long vigil was kept over the ballot boxes. Many countries and organisations sent observers. In Sumbe I met two Americans who exclaimed, 'This is textbook, absolutely textbook. We have never seen anything that so scrupulously followed the rules.' A group of Dutch observers said the same.

There was one ominous exception to the general calm. On the pretext of an attempt on Savimbi's life, UNITA guards stormed the house of a government minister in Luanda. One unfortunate policeman was shot in cold blood in the garden of my Portuguese observer colleague, Antonio Monteiro.

Bullets not Ballots

Vote counting was slow. The main reason was excessive zeal: electoral officials and party representatives sat over more long nights, counting and recounting ballots, usually amicably. Two days after the election the two most senior UNITA representatives came to assure me they thought the elections went well.

Their encouragement left me unprepared for Savimbi's inflammatory broadcast next day, 3 October, attacking the MPLA and the National Electoral Council (of which UNITA was a member!) and alleging fraud. It was a rambling, muddled speech, sometimes repeating UNITA's commitment to peace, sometimes calling his supporters to arms. He proclaimed it was for Angolans, not foreigners or international opinion, to decide whether the elections were honest. On Monday 4 October, UNITA generals abandoned the FAA to which they had sworn allegiance a week before.

The timing was hard to understand, for the outcome was still in doubt. The quick count system showed the President winning 49.2 per cent of the vote, and Savimbi 38.2 per cent. If correct, that meant a second round, since neither had 50 per cent. I could not release these figures because this was the first time the technique had been used in a country so large and complex, and the President's vote fell short by only 0.8 per cent; the smallest margin of error would eliminate the second round. Nonetheless, it was of the utmost urgency that I tell Dr Savimbi that a second round was possible. But Savimbi had vanished. He had left Luanda, it was said hidden in a coffin. Meanwhile, we helped the NEC set up commissions to investigate all fraud allegations, composed of representatives of all parties, including UNITA, and Angolan and UN electoral staff.

Savimbi did not resurface until 8 October, and next day I flew to Huambo. The meeting was a superb piece of theatre: his lieutenants launched a torrent of invective, thus allowing him to intervene with a voice of apparently sweet reasonableness. To escape this well-rehearsed Greek chorus, I asked to see him alone. I stressed the possibility of a second round, but also recalled his great hero, Churchill, victorious in war, but defeated in an election, who yet came back to govern, and tried to convey the key role of a leader of 'Her Majesty's Loyal Opposition'. Moreover, the man elected President would have an unenviable task: a war-devastated country; an economy to be transformed into the market mould; and an electorate filled with unrealistic expectations. An opposition leader would have an excellent chance of being elected next time – democracies, I reminded him, did not consist of one election. Savimbi appeared receptive but no doubt his mind was made up.

The Secretary-General wrote to Dr Savimbi, recalling another hero of his, General De Gaulle and every plane brought more would-be mediators, among them four Permanent Representatives to the UN, sent by an alarmed Security Council; the senior members of the Troika, from Lisbon, Moscow and Washington; and Pik Botha, then South African Foreign Minister.

The arrival of the UN Ambassadors – from Cape Verde, Morocco, the Russian Federation and the United States – coincided with a large bomb explosion outside Luanda head-quarters of UNITA, who promptly took police hostages. Heavy firing continued for hours. It gave me perverse pleasure that my briefing of visitors more accustomed to deliberating in the padded confines of the Security Council chamber was interrupted by reports of incidents ever nearer our camp. The mission visited Savimbi in Huambo and met President Dos Santos and electoral officials. They left abruptly, ahead of schedule, and universally gloomy. US Ambassador Perkins exploded angrily, apparently unaware of the irony inherent in his words, 'This was a UN mission done on the cheap – a totally false economy.'

On their last evening we visited Pik Botha who, fortified by a glass of whisky, almost certainly not his first, would brook no interruption or counter-argument. Savimbi had given him 'proofs' of widespread fraud and 'as an African' (the Cape Verdean Ambassador winced visibly) he could not accept a different standard of democracy from 'Western colonialist countries' – 'We are not a pile of rotten cabbages to be buggered about.' It was my turn to wince when, patronisingly patting me on the knee, he intoned, 'This lovely little lady here has been doing her best but the UN resources were inadequate.' In that he was correct. Pik Botha's interventions only muddied the waters further. South

Africa was proposing a large role for Savimbi in a coalition government and the virtual scrapping of the elections. Fortunately, after a day of discussions with me, the Director-General of the Elections, and the Troika and some trying experiences with Savimbi, Pik Botha recanted, and South Africa subscribed to the international verdict that the elections had been free and fair.

The Security Council Mission had been wise to leave. The next night a huge ammunition dump, just outside our camp, exploded supposedly by accident, but later UNITA sabotage was suspected. Mortar bombs and ammunition rained down on us until dawn. I had been bidden to breakfast with Pik Botha, who had been up most of the night, watching the huge conflagration and who, ever gallant, had with difficulty been dissuaded from coming to my rescue. He had also sent his plane to Huambo in a vain attempt to bring Savimbi to meet the President.

On 16 October, the fraud investigation commission presented its findings. The unanimous conclusion, signed by everyone, including UNITA, was that there was no evidence of improper actions amounting to fraud. Everyone was relieved – until the UNITA representative insisted that he could not accept the report. As I had suspected all along, UNITA would not be satisfied by any other outcome than admission of widespread fraud.

On Saturday 17 October, the NEC announced that the MPLA had won 53.74 per cent of the vote, and 129 seats in the Congress, compared with UNITA's 34.10 per cent, and 70 seats. For the presidency, Dos Santos had obtained 49.57 per cent, Savimbi 40.07 per cent. Our quick count had been remarkably near the mark. That afternoon I declared that the elections, despite some irregularities, 'mainly due to human error and inexperience', had been 'generally free and fair', a judgement endorsed by the United States, the European Union and South Africa.

The situation could still have been saved by a second round but Savimbi would not retract. He constantly made new security conditions for meeting President Dos Santos. I readied a cordon of 'Blue Berets' to surround his aircraft and escort him but Hank Cohen, the US Troika member, and Pik Botha spent five hours in broiling heat at the airport waiting for the UNITA leader who never came. Botha reported that close colleagues of Savimbi had threatened to kill me and members of the Troika, and returned to Pretoria a sadder and wiser man. The Troika also left, after an unsuccessful visit to Savimbi. The big league of mediators flew off to the four corners of the globe, leaving us lesser mortals to wrestle with an intractable situation. The UN, originally given a walk-on part, not even 'bearing a spear', was now thrust to centre stage and I was the chief actor.

Formerly Dr Savimbi had called me 'the mother of the peace process'. Now Radio Vorgan attacked me viciously. I was without moral character, and had 'sold (my) honour and dignity for diamonds, industrial mercury, and for US dollars, from José Eduardo dos Santos.' The Secretary-General and the Security Council reacted angrily but the attacks continued, and a UNITA leader in Lobito was heard to declare that he was arranging my assassination.

Clashes were escalating everywhere but CCPM was still working. Two joint commissions were set up, one political, the other military. Savimbi sent his Vice-President, Jeremiah Chitunda, to Luanda, a relatively hopeful sign. But things were spinning out of control.

During the night of Friday 30 October, shooting erupted near the airport. A vital CCPM meeting was convened for Saturday but our patrols reported heavy fighting on the roads to the city. General Unimna inexplicably refused to accompany me and sent his Deputy, Brigadier Nyambuya, an excellent Zimbabwean officer. We set off in convoy and arrived safely. The meeting was one of the worst I had ever attended, both sides hurling accusations, the UNITA delegation chief, Salupeto Pena, like a man possessed, but it culminated in agreement to send joint military missions to all the areas in conflict. Each side was to order its followers to cease fighting.

The British Ambassador, John Flynn, had arranged a reconciliation lunch for the leaders of the two CCPM delegations, some ambassadors and myself. I had decided not to go, because of the deteriorating situation, but in view of the agreement changed my mind. Two ambassadors were already there, but the government and UNITA representatives never did arrive. I had not finished either my gin and tonic or my account of developments when a monumental explosion reverberated in the street outside. It heralded the sanguinary battle for Luanda.

I tried in vain to get an armed police escort or helicopter back to camp. Luckily the embassy had radio communication with all European Union embassies and with the Americans, who were in hiding in their compound near Savimbi's house, threatened by UNITA. Other ambassadors were taken hostage. The British residence was dangerously positioned between UNITA below us and government forces and the Ministry of Defence above. The horrendous racket of death and destruction thundered on for 48 hours. Sometimes the explosions were so near we feared that UNITA was advancing up the hill and might know that I was in the embassy, something we were keen to keep dark, as I was a prime target.

To contact my camp I had to dash out to the forecourt, under crossfire, to use the car radio. Luckily one of the military contingents, more concerned for my safety than New York, had provided me with a flak jacket. My frustration was all the greater because General Unimna disappeared off the airwaves. During almost three days in the middle of a battle I was unable to contact my military commander. The camp was not in danger but I was concerned about the morale of the UNAVEM staff – whom equally inexplicably, neither he nor Jobarteh convened during the weekend, nor did they send any reports to Headquarters. Knowing that everyone would be glued to their radios I said that I was 'somewhere in town, trying to negotiate a ceasefire'. I could not say more for our radios were monitored by UNITA.

John Flynn and I worked ceaselessly to obtain a ceasefire. The best chance was through international intervention. I was in constant touch with the Secretary-General, John with Foreign Secretary Douglas Hurd and both of us with the US State Department (the US Mission could not communicate with Washington). Miraculously, the problematic Luanda telephone system continued to work, so we could talk to the Government and to Antonio Monteiro, who was in touch with Lisbon. During Saturday night and all of Sunday the messages flew back and forth, the Secretary-General speaking several times to the President, everyone trying, without success, to reach Savimbi, hidden away in the central highlands.

None of us knew which side had the upper hand or how long the grim battle would last. When I lay down briefly in the small hours of Sunday morning I felt fear for the first time, convinced that none of us would survive. A knock at the door announcing a call from the Secretary-General at 3.00 a.m. was a welcome relief. Not so a briefing by the British military attaché on the game plan if the worst came to the worst. In the ambassador's office he said, 'This is where we make our last stand. The ambassador has a pistol, I have a pistol, and so does Sigi.' Sigi, a gentle giant, was my UN security guard, an Icelandic policeman who had never fired a shot in anger.

On Sunday morning Salupeto Pena, obviously deranged, was screaming murderous threats against the Portuguese, the UN and all white people. At last, at noon, we got through to Savimbi on his satellite radio. John did the negotiating, given UNITA's attitude to me. For over an hour Savimbi, rambling and incoherent, ranged over every subject under the sun – Munich, Churchill, Nasser and the Jews, the US election, his Bantu heritage, his childhood. He was obsessed with his own safety, oblivious to the hundreds of his fellow citizens being killed with every moment lost in this self-regarding exercise. John finally got him to accept a ceasefire. Savimbi, who did not know that I was beside John, asked him to 'tell Miss Anstee that I will apologise personally for the attacks on her ... what Vorgan said did not have my approval, I repudiate it strongly ... Those words upset me particularly for such a civilised lady ...'

Negotiations to get the Government's agreement went on for hours. The Secretary-General spoke to the President, who wanted a delay so that his generals could meet me. His most alarming condition was that I must personally accept responsibility for Savimbi's good faith, a tall order indeed.

The ceasefire was finally agreed minutes before midnight, but sporadic shooting continued through the night. It was not until early Monday afternoon that I could return to camp. An armed convoy took me to the Ministry of Defence, whence a government military helicopter flew me over the silent and devastated city. There had been a last moment of drama at the Ministry of Defence when a trigger-happy soldier had to be restrained because he thought I was Salupeto Pena trying to escape – a far-fetched case of mistaken identity. In fact, Salupeto Pena was already dead, killed, together with UNITA's Vice-President Chitunda, as they tried to flee.

Thousands more died on both sides during that dreadful battle, and mutual vengeance killings continued long after. A high-level meeting between the two sides was of extreme urgency.

I was in frequent touch with President Dos Santos and more sporadically with Savimbi, who tended to switch his satellite off, or claim he 'was too ill with flu to speak', when, if well-substantiated rumour was to be believed, he was in Zaire exploring possibilities of military assistance. His conversation was of the muddled 'stream-of-consciousness' variety, and he usually called in the middle of the night. He apologised eloquently for the attacks on me, which he described as 'faithless, baseless and undiplomatic', and again voiced concerns for his own security. His reiterated commitment to dialogue and peace had a hollow ring as UNITA was running amok all over the country, reoccupying municipalities everywhere.

The Secretary-General sent Mig Goulding to help me. On 7 November we met President Dos Santos who, in an extraordinary volte-face, stressed that only a much-strengthened UNAVEM, with a far-reaching mandate and 'Blue Helmets', could salvage peace. Our request to see Dr Savimbi being constantly put off, we took the initiative and flew to Huambo on Tuesday 10 November. We were left cooling our heels in the UNAVEM camp until, well after dark, a dilapidated car arrived with two UNITA Generals. Fearing a plan to take us hostage, as bargaining pawns, or to ambush us and blame the government, we organised a convoy of every available UN vehicle, each flying a large flag.

The UNITA Generals led this cavalcade far out into the countryside, where we found Savimbi surrounded by saturnine, heavily armed guards, in a dimly lit, malodorous cottage. An even stranger feature were shelves piled with pink-cheeked plastic dolls with piercing blue eyes and tinselly golden hair, beaming down on the grim scene, like a galaxy of misplaced cherubs. Our meeting went on for four hours. Savimbi was in discursive mood, and we were treated to a canter through ancient history, while

Churchill and De Gaulle were also given an airing. Mig said bluntly, 'You have two choices: war or dialogue.'

Savimbi replied, 'I will never lead a war. I prefer to retire. War solves nothing.'

Mig departed for New York with the message from both sides that a much stronger UN mandate and presence were required, including 'Blue Helmets'.

Negotiations to Restore Peace

By dint of further negotiation and another visit to Huambo I persuaded both sides to meet in Namibe, in southern Angola, on 26 November. Unimna and Jobarteh refused to accompany me, however, fearing failure and an outbreak of shooting. The meeting ended in bear hugs and a joint 'Declaration of Namibe' in which both sides reaffirmed the Bicesse Accords, their firm intention to honour the ceasefire, their wish that UNAVEM's mandate be enlarged and their desire to meet again as soon as possible.

But less than three days later, UNITA forces captured Uige and Negage, important northern towns. In the fighting a grenade landed on the UNAVEM camp and killed a Brazilian police observer. We were back to square one.

The Secretary-General called me to New York, where I arrived on 9 December. Dr Boutros-Ghali tried unsuccessfully to arrange a meeting with President Dos Santos and Dr Savimbi in Geneva, and on 22 December the President of the Security Council issued an anodyne statement, long on appeals but short on action. Meanwhile, instead of being strengthened, UNAVEM was dwindling as contingents completed their tour and were not replaced.

My own future was under discussion, as the seven months had now become ten. In the middle of 1992 the Secretary-General asked me to go to Mozambique after the Angolan election as his special representative there. I had agreed, provided the errors of inadequate mandate and resources that had undermined the Angolan process were remedied, and had provided Headquarters with specific suggestions. An acting special representative was sent to Maputo to hold the fort until I could leave Angola. In

December, however, the Secretary-General asked me to continue in Angola for another year. I explained that for personal reasons I could not accept a long commitment, but promised to remain until a replacement could be found. We agreed on 28 February 1993 as a target date. I never got to Mozambique, but my suggestions were acted upon, the Mozambique operation learned from the mistakes in Angola and was a success.

I had hoped to spend Christmas at Knill, but Christmas Day, a special anniversary for UNITA, was regarded as ominous. As it happened, there was a lull in the fighting. I organised a lunch for my closest collaborators, Sissy presented a sizzling hot turkey (a frozen one from Windhoek) on a sizzling hot day, and we shared a very small Christmas pudding and some mince pies. On New Year's Eve we had a party, but my best memory is of an hour spent on the Ilha watching the sun sink into the ocean and then, as the shadows deepened, a night heron fishing in the wavelets lapping the shore.

There had been progress in December over UNITA's withdrawal from Uige and Negage, and on Christmas Eve I gave the two leaders a draft proposal on UNAVEM's future role as the basis for a Security Council decision. My life was made easier by Goulding's decision to remove Unimna. His replacement was Brigadier Nyambuya of Zimbabwe with whom I had excellent relations. Together we recommended the immediate despatch of a Ghanaian company of 'Blue Helmets' that we knew to be available, to help meet UNITA's almost paranoid security concerns, but we were turned down by New York. The Government was now blaming the UN for everything. On 22 December the Foreign Minister told me aggressively that my reputation and that of the UN was at stake if we did not force UNITA to withdraw, something that was impossible without 'Blue Helmets', which he simultaneously declared were unacceptable.

Media comments about myself were laden with sexual innuendo. The *Jornal de Angola* named me one of the Top Ten Personalities of the Year, but in the caption below my photograph lurked a little bracket 'although it was rumoured that she was Salupeto Pena's mistress'. An even more amazing canard rumoured that the real reason for my visit to New York had been to have an abortion, the progenitor of the baby, it was whispered, being none other than Savimbi. On hearing these absurd slanders my Filipino secretary rolled her eyes in mock admiration: 'Miss Anstee, we are all wondering, how *do* you find the time?'

I met Savimbi in Huambo for two hours on Saturday 2 January 1993. I had rarely seen him in such an amenable mood, which caused me to speculate about the underlying motives. I returned to Luanda with some faintly encouraging proposals for high-level military contacts, as well as another Namibe meeting. In Vila Espa an urgent summons awaited me to see Foreign Minister De Moura. I was received with French champagne (pink, and profuse), and apologies for the inaccessibility of himself and the President over Christmas. The Government, too, wanted a Namibe II meeting, which I agreed to arrange for the next week.

But early next morning, Sunday 3 January, government forces attacked UNITA in Lubango. It was not until evening that I managed to locate the Foreign Minister who gave a long wail of despair, apparently unaware of what was afoot. The next day UNITA captured 200 FAA troops whom the Government had sent to Uige at our request.

During January war spread like wildfire. UNITA gained the upper hand and their forces were so close to Luanda that people began to think the hitherto unthinkable – the capital might be besieged. We launched démarches at every level, in a last-ditch effort to restore a ceasefire and new negotiations. We had also to protect our personnel. Slit trenches were dug in all our camps, reminding me of wartime schooldays, and contingency plans drawn up for evacuation. Those for the whole mission included a distinctly unappealing journey of several days by barge to the nearest port outside Angolan waters, if airports were closed. Embassies booked more comfortable vessels but we had to be 'the last to leave.'

Our plan for internal evacuation became quickly obsolete. Fighting escalated so rapidly that all our field stations and regional commands were in grave danger. Their withdrawal to Luanda and the coastal belt was achieved without loss of life in a superb air operation. The most dramatic exodus was from Huambo, where our camp was caught in crossfire. Several UNAVEM staff were injured;

one, with a bullet lodged dangerously near his heart, lay in an open slit trench, under torrential rain, for two days, without qualified medical attention. On 14 January a convoy of 29 UN vehicles, which also rescued NGO staff, managed to reach an airfield. One old lady, seeing the convoy leave, embraced the Regional Commander and, with tears in her eyes, said, 'Now our troubles will really begin.' Months later, UN auditors criticised us because much equipment remained behind. I could not resist the caustic comment that they should be asked to rewrite their report in a slit trench, under crossfire and pouring rain.

Savimbi continued to call me up late at night. In one of these kilometric monologues, on 6 January, he implored me to consider myself 'a mother', who should not abandon her children 'even when they break plates' (an odd analogy for thousands of deaths). He urged me to find a place where the military leaders could meet. We got agreement on Addis Ababa, but then Savimbi disappeared off the airwaves. On 20 January he broke his silence in a BBC interview in which he questioned my trustworthiness as a negotiator, yet another volte-face.

We were in an impasse until 22 January. At 2 a.m. a UNITA representative called to say peremptorily that the Addis Ababa meeting should take place from 27 to 30 January. There was no explanation of the long silence, or how they traced me to Lisbon where I unexpectedly had to spend the night owing to a flight delay.

Impasse in Addis Ababa

UNITA arrived late in Addis Ababa and then claimed they were 'too tired' to meet immediately. For vigorous men, inured to the rigours of bush fighting, they were remarkably prone to bouts of insuperable exhaustion at critical points in our negotiations. They were also aggressive and intractable. Their strategy was to play for time, as the military situation unfolded in their favour.

Just after midnight on the second day, when breakdown seemed imminent, I called in the two leaders and lent on them hard. In my exasperation I exclaimed, 'If either of your delegations included a woman, we might have a better chance of ending the senseless killing.' In all the negotiations I, the chairman and mediator, was the only woman at the table. The final communiqué reaffirmed the commitment of both sides to the Bicesse Accords, to maintain political dialogue leading to a ceasefire, and to meet in Addis Ababa on 10 February. My appeal for an interim truce went unheard.

The Angolan Ambassador gave a lavish alfresco lunch: tables groaning with the finest French and Angolan cuisine, aperitifs, wines and French champagne. Both delegations were in holiday mood, with much back-slapping, gales of laughter and regaling of news of family and friends on the other side. It was hard to believe 'there was a war on'. When it came to a toast, there was hesitation; they could hardly drink to each other's success. I quietly suggested, 'Peace'. I could not join in the apparently unclouded enjoyment of everyone else, haunted by the knowledge that the grim battle for Huambo was pounding brutally on, and the fighting, killing and dying were continuing unchecked all over Angola.

Next day the two delegations went back their separate ways, to war.

On 5 February when I was briefly in England, UNITA, with its customary eerie sense of timing and knowledge of my where-abouts, called me to say they could not return to Addis Ababa on 10 February 'for logistical and security reasons.' They continued their cat-and-mouse game, calling up with different demands interspersed by long periods of unnerving silence. In response to their insistence that UNAVEM transport them to Addis Ababa we drew up an elaborate plan, involving various aircraft, obtained guarantees from the Government, and assured UNITA they would be accompanied at every stage by senior UNAVEM military officers. After much chopping and changing UNITA agreed on the date of 26 February but at the last moment told me they were unhappy with the arrangements.

The Government insisted that we go ahead and we congregated in Addis Ababa on Friday 26 February. From there I was sporadically in touch with UNITA, who kept switching off their satellite radio. At 1.00 a.m. on Saturday morning UNITA tele-phoned, alleging the dangers were too great for the delegation to leave. Negotiations continued feverishly during the next day. President Dos Santos, who was in almost permanent session with his closest advisers, was very cooperative.

I could not reach Savimbi personally. In the end I was left with no option but to cancel the meeting and to point to UNITA's non-appearance as the cause. UNITA's protestations about security were patently a pretext. They wanted to take Huambo before resuming negotiations, so as to bargain from a position of strength, but government forces held out longer than expected. Huambo finally fell on 7 March, virtually destroyed by eight weeks of bombardment.

Hardliners now prevailed on the Government's side also. On International Women's Day, 8 March, when I was in New York for consultations, 2000 black-clad women demonstrated in Luanda, bearing a coffin with my name on it, and chanting, 'Margaret, you are a *bandida* (bandit), you are a criminal', for not having prevented the resumption of the war. I later learned that the event had been organised by 'elements' in the Government. I was sorry not to have been there to confront the women.

Next day, 9 March, in a triumphalist 'Address to the Nation', Savimbi virulently attacked several individuals, including the Roman Catholic cardinal, and myself, and demanded I be replaced by an African. Members of the Security Council came up to commiserate with me. As one of them said, 'If Savimbi had desperately wanted you to stay he could not have found a better way of ensuring it.' The UN spokesman reiterated that I had 'the full support and confidence of the Secretary-General'. I had been promised I could leave on 28 February but the Secretary-General, expressing disgust and indignation at Savimbi's remarks, said, 'I'm afraid you cannot leave now. I will not be dictated to.' He had a successor in mind, Sergio Vieira de Mello, an outstanding UN career official, and we agreed that, as his name could not be put forward for some months, his identity would be kept secret between us and not divulged even within the Secretariat. I accepted to continue only after receiving a firm commitment on this point, crucial to my credibility as a mediator.

On 11 March I briefed the Security Council, presenting five options for future action that I had previously submitted to the Secretary-General. They ranged from a major peace-keeping force of armed 'Blue Helmets' to a minimal presence, comprising only a small 'good offices' mediation mission. I adopted a frank approach which the council welcomed (Madeleine Albright, then US Ambassador to the UN, referred to us as 'sisters', because we were the only two women there).

Regrettably the forceful tenor of the council's discussions was watered down in Resolution 811 at US insistence. But whatever the council said, Savimbi simply pressed ahead, encouraged, I was sure, by the concurrent incapacity to get the Serbs in Bosnia to heed the Council's admonitions. It was becoming the done thing among rebels to cock a snook at the UN, and not at all far-fetched to detect a copy-cat phenomenon. The same resolution strongly condemned the verbal and physical attacks against myself. When I returned to Luanda the Government told me that they too deplored Savimbi's onslaught; they wanted me to stay on, and assured me I had their full confidence.

The onus was now on the Americans to demonstrate the leverage with UNITA that had led them to dilute successive Security Council resolutions, oppose sanctions against UNITA and defer US recognition of the Government, originally promised as soon as a legitimately elected administration was installed. They proposed further talks, under UN auspices, either in Rabat or Abidjan, in the hope that King Hassan II of Morocco and President Houphoüet-Boigny of Côte d'Ivoire, both long-time Savimbi supporters, could influence their wayward protégé. I preferred Morocco, since I knew the king and other influential men in the government, but at UNITA's insistence Abidjan was chosen. After a difficult bilateral meeting between the USA and UNITA it was agreed that negotiations would resume under my chairmanship on 12th April.

On 5 and 6 April, UNITA's Vorgan radio launched another vicious tirade, not only repeating all the old allegations but calling me a prostitute and threatening that a stray bullet would find me if I stayed in Angola. The BBC sent this edifying message whizzing round the globe on its World Service. The reaction of my aunt, who listened to it daily, was typically debonair: 'I don't mind about your morals, darling – though a prostitute might be a first in the family – but *do* be careful about stray bullets.'

Many others rushed to defend my virtue – and my life – among them the Secretary-General, the Security Council and the Troika, while the State Department read the riot act to the UNITA Washington Representative. UNITA unabashed, rebroadcast its venom, and declared they would not accept my mediation. President Houphoüet-Boigny upbraided his long-time protégé, Savimbi, saying that this was 'no way to treat a lady' and demanded that he make a personal apology to me before the talks began.

Humanitarian Disaster

Meanwhile human suffering was escalating. Security Council Resolution 811 enjoined me to mount a much larger humanitarian operation, adding the familiar caveat 'with the resources at her disposal'. NGOs and humanitarian agencies were greatly exercised about the participation of UNAVEM military personnel but nothing could be done without UNAVEM planes, UNAVEM communications and UNAVEM liaison with military commanders on the ground, especially those of UNITA. Our 'safety-first' policy of not undertaking flights or road convoys to combat areas without prior clearance by the Government and UNITA was not always understood. The shots most difficult to call ended up on my desk and involved agonising decisions.

We were caught between two fires. What the NGOs considered to be excessive caution, desk-bound officers in UN agencies, often without field experience, construed as recklessness. In a classic exchange the Executive Director of the World Food Programme (WFP) in Rome proposed that the Under Secretary-General for Humanitarian Affairs in New York, rather than myself, should clear all flights with the Government and UNITA and do so *30 days in advance* to facilitate WFP's planning. When I read this to the local agency representatives there was a universal guffaw. Everyone knew that UNAVEM obtained clearances on an almost hourly basis and that windows of opportunity were all too fleeting.

The courage and initiative of my colleagues gave succour in many fraught situations. A remarkable rescue was mounted, in atrocious weather, of Huambo refugees stranded in Caimbambo, where they had arrived weak and hungry after a horrendous trek over the mountains. In four days some 4000 were taken out by relays of UNAVEM helicopters, and another 2000 by road. I visited Caimbambo and can never forget a 15-year-old girl, who had staggered into the village the night before and given birth to a premature baby. Crawling with flies, they lay on the floor of a hospital wrecked by retreating UNITA troops, and yet the girl still smiled at me.

President Dos Santos told me that the Caimbambo operation had 'captured Angolan hearts'. UNITA jeered that it was evidence of my hypocrisy. Wilfully oblivious of the people who had fled from them in Huambo they said, 'She knows that Caimbambo is a war zone, and that there is no civilian population there.'

Marathon in Abidjan

On Easter Saturday 1993, President Houphoüet-Boigny sent a plane to ferry me and my small team to Abidjan. Both President Houphoüet-Boigny and Amara Essy, the Côte d'Ivoire Foreign Minister, for whom I developed great liking and respect, played an active part in our negotiations. Before the formal opening I had a two-hour meeting with the President. A tiny, myopic old man, steeped in time and wrinkles, he shuffled into the room supported by Minister Essy, and his immensely tall and ceremonial Lebanese Chief of Protocol. He gave me a lengthy soliloquy on his unsuccessful attempts in 1975 to reconcile Savimbi and the then President, Agostinho Neto, and his subsequent efforts to bring the two sides together. Angola was 'unfinished business' that he wanted to resolve in the little time he had left, convinced of his unparalleled influence with Jonas Savimbi. He described, almost with glee, the rebuke he had delivered to his protégé for the way he had treated me. I did not tell him of Savimbi's hang-dog apology, delivered by a discomfited UNITA intermediary the evening before. A formal apology and personal guarantees for my safety had been a prerequisite for the talks but they had been delivered perfunctorily and with ill grace.

True to form, the UNITA delegation arrived a day late, trotting out their usual complaint of utter exhaustion. In Angola their comrades shot at two WFP planes carrying humanitarian aid, and their delegation leader gave the usual glib explanation of 'accidental' firing. His assurances that 'UNITA had no animosity towards the Special Representative of the Secretary-General' were probably no more sincere, but on no occasion did UNITA raise any question about my chairing the meeting.

The meeting dragged on for seven weeks, spent drafting a 'Protocol of Abidjan', comprising 38 articles embracing every conceivable aspect: ceasefire; military dispositions; disarmament and demobilisation; law and order and the creation of a neutral police force; political arrangements for new elections and the establishment of a government of national unity and reconcili- ation; setting up democratic institutions and judicial systems; and human rights. UNAVEM was to act as arbiter and call all the shots. In short, the draft protocol sought to remedy the defects of the Bicesse Accords.

The Government was cooperative but UNITA followed their usual tactic of playing things out, requiring much time to 'study', arriving late, and refusing to work more than a limited number of hours (they would have done well in a radical trade union).

While they filibustered, the spectre of mass death was stalking the war-shattered countryside of Angola. Our efforts to help hundreds of thousands of people trapped in cities besieged by UNITA, or fleeing the battle zones, faced great odds. On 26 April a WFP Antonov-12, delivering food and medical supplies to Luena, was hit by a ground-to-air missile. The pilot crashlanded short of the airstrip, the plane burst into flames and the seven occupants jumped into a minefield. Rescue was impossible until next morning. One of the wounded died during the night, another lost his legs. It was hard to believe UNITA's protestations that this too was an 'accident'.

The government delegation went back twice to Luanda for consultations and Foreign Minister Essy flew to Huambo to see Savimbi. The UNITA delegation refused to accompany him; citing security reasons as usual. In the event, the danger came from their home side: when the minister's plane was circling over Huambo

UNITA gave the pilot incorrect coordinates for landing. The minister came back thinking he had obtained Savimbi's agreement to the protocol but this, too, proved illusory. President Houphoüet-Boigny intervened several times with both leaders but my heart sank when he told me that Dr Savimbi was applying his now familiar stalling tactic – 'Don't call me, I'll call you when it suits me' – even to his oldest and staunchest ally.

In early May the UNITA delegation left to meet Dr Savimbi who was 'somewhere at the front', where he remained consistently incommunicado. Characteristically, they stayed away for six days instead of three, while the rest of us cooled our heels in Abidjan, except one day when we were flown to Yamoussoukro, the President's phantasmagoric palaces and basilica in the middle of the jungle.

The Ivorean government, alarmed by UNITA threats, had surrounded me with burly Ivorean guards who slept outside my room and even accompanied me on my early morning swim. I also had my personal UN Security Guard. It was with this entourage that I went one evening for dinner with the British Ambassador, and they surged around me as soon as I reappeared. As I said goodnight I patted the Ambassador's dog which, flummoxed by all the commotion, promptly sank his redoubtable fangs into my left arm. Our departure became a rout, with crestfallen guards rushing forward to staunch the blood. News that I had been 'attacked' became something of an anticlimax when it was revealed that the aggressor had not been some zealous UNITA henchman but the British Ambassador's dog.

My task was made no easier by relentless public scrutiny and criticism. On the government side there had been a public recantation by a former Minister of Justice of his earlier vicious article in the *Jornal de Angola*, in which he blamed me for the renewed war, and urged me to grow old in a rocking-chair, lulled by the wails of Angolan children for whose deaths I was responsible; now his article was headlined 'Señora Anstee, forgive me'. In contrast, the May 1993 issue of *African International* (a franco-phone monthly) sported a full-page photograph of me, charmingly captioned 'Public Enemy No. 1'. The accompanying article concluded that I was a scapegoat, blamed unjustly for the failure of a UN mission under-mandated and starved of resources. But the headline was more likely to stay in the reader's mind.

My main problem was lack of backing from my own Head-quarters. I daily sent the latest draft of the Abidjan Protocol, which I negotiated in Portuguese, but which we painstakingly translated into English. I never received any comments or advice, and had to be dissuaded by my secretary from sending a code cable to Kofi Annan (who had succeeded Goulding as Head of Peace-keeping) enquiring, 'Is anyone there?'

On 7 May the Secretary-General asked me to accept yet another extension because, while the Government had accepted Sergio Vieira de Mello as my successor, UNITA had rejected him because of his Brazilian nationality. I was appalled that the UN had yielded to pressure that contravened basic UN principles but even more indignant that his candidature had been presented at all, contrary to my pact with the Secretary-General. Now the ground had been cut from under my feet as mediator by my own Headquarters, and UNITA could treat me as a lame duck. Later I learned that UNITA knew of the proposals for my successor even before the Abidjan talks began ...

Worse was to follow. The next day, someone in New York incorrectly told the media that I was to be replaced immediately by De Mello! Journalists had a field day speculating about the reasons, mostly derogatory to me. Deaf to my pleas that Headquarters issue a *démenti*, New York did nothing for six days, and then made a statement of typical diplomatic fudge that further weakened my position: while reiterating the Secretary-General's full confidence in me it stated that I wanted to leave, and that he would take a decision shortly. While that was true, it was crassly inept to make it public knowledge at a most sensitive juncture in the Abidjan talks. With exquisite timing the statement coincided with UNITA's return to Abidjan.

They arrived, unsurprisingly, 'too fatigued' to attend a meeting called to ascertain Savimbi's latest position before President Houphoüet-Boigny left for medical treatment in Paris next morning.

UNITA's refusal was a deliberate rebuff to him. I bade him farewell and watched the frail old man carried up the steps to the Concorde that President Mitterand had sent for him. He never returned alive, but died of cancer in France, deprived of his cherished goal of achieving peace for Angola.

UNITA's position had changed not one iota. A breakdown was staring us in the face but, noting some incipient cracks in the delegation's normally monolithic front, I persuaded them to ask Savimbi for new instructions. Since the weekend would be critical, I asked my main interlocutors in New York, Kofi Annan and James Jonah, for contact telephone numbers but received no reply. When I called on Friday night I could find no one.

Fortunately I had the Secretary-General's private number and on Saturday morning I asked him to speak to Savimbi. He took a pencil and paper and asked me to dictate what he should say. But Savimbi was again playing hard to get, allegedly somewhere 'at the front', and we resorted to a written message through the UNITA delegation. I was in constant communication with the Secretary-General, and again found direct contact more satisfactory than through those around him. At 2.30 a.m. (Abidjan time) on Monday morning, 17 May, the Secretary-General told me he had spoken with Savimbi, and deduced from his incoherent rambling that he wanted the talks extended for another week. I suspected more filibustering, but Boutros-Ghali insisted that we should agree. Foreign Minister Essy, who had undertaken a parallel démarche to Savimbi through President Houphoüet-Boigny, telephoned at 3.00 a.m. with a similar message.

There were two surprising developments during that extra week. First, the Government offered further concessions. Notwithstanding UNITA refused to budge. Second, the US Government announced its long overdue recognition of President Dos Santos's government. The timing at this crucial moment in the Abidjan talks was unbelievable, but I had long ceased to be amazed by Washington's policy towards Angola.

The protocol was predicated on political concessions on the part of the Government (a full role for UNITA in all levels of government and all aspects of national life), in return for military concessions by UNITA. The tragic irony was that the two sides agreed on all but a couple of the protocol's 38 articles. The main bone of contention was the requirement for UNITA to withdraw from the cities and regions it was occupying.

UNITA requested an assurance that one battalion of armed 'Blue Helmets' would immediately be despatched as a 'symbolic presence' to protect their withdrawing troops and the civilians left behind. I begged New York to authorise me to make this commitment, only to be told that the Security Council would not countenance the despatch of any Blue Helmets until I obtained the signature of the protocol and a ceasefire. In vain I pleaded that this was an absurd 'chicken-and-egg' situation, since I could not obtain either of those things unless I could promise the 'symbolic' battalion.

Even more dismaying were instructions to inform both sides that, even if the protocol was signed, current peace-keeping demands and member states' reluctance to provide troops and money were so great that *six to nine months* would elapse before UN troops could arrive. I did not impart this information, since it would have rendered the talks, and my role as mediator, pointless. I returned to the charge with New York about the symbolic battalion, without success. I realised that UNITA's demand could well be a bluff, made in the expectation that I would be unable to deliver, but if that were the case, I would have liked to be able to call that bluff. A mediator cannot succeed without leverage and of that I had been deprived.

On Friday 21 May, I declared the talks to be 'interrupted'. At the final meeting, Minister Essy, in a scarcely veiled rebuke to UNITA, recalled that many attacks had been made against me but that, after working with me for weeks he could only say '*C'est une grande dame.*' The two sides, who had been trading angry words for days, embraced with much back-slapping, and cries of 'My brother', before they went off to fight one another again. The rest of us were close to tears. I was described by *Le Monde* as having '*les traits tirés*', as I am sure they were.

The End of the Affair

I left for New York deeply depressed but determined that the world should not abandon Angola. I proposed to the Secretary-

General that the UN should combine an expanded humanitarian operation with a small 'good offices' mission that could monitor the military and political situation. The key element would be a small nucleus of armed UN troops (Blue Helmets) to ensure the security of the humanitarian operation. They would then be on the spot to monitor a ceasefire, if it eventuated; the only formality required being a security council decision to expand their mandate. In that way the dangerous hiatus between a ceasefire and the arrival of international support would be avoided. My ideas aroused the usual bureaucratic objections. Two of the three persons whom the Secretary-General asked me to consult were won round to my point of view — Kofi Annan and James Jonah — but it was the third, Ambassador Garekhan, who wrote a minute of our meeting. This, we discovered too late, gave the Secretary-General the impression that all three were opposed, instead of only one, himself. Much to the Security Council's annoyance I was not allowed to brief them, but only to sit in on their informal consultations. I threw decorum to the wind and privately informed as many members as I could about my idea. The response was encouraging, especially from Madeleine Albright, who said she would consult Washington.

At the council's informal consultations on 27 May, the Cape Verde Ambassador proposed amendments to the draft resolution, along the lines of my proposal, supported by Spain and Brazil. The US did not go along: Washington evidently had different ideas from Madeleine Albright. They also softened the criticisms of UNITA, still under the delusion that they could influence Savimbi, despite the Abidjan experience, which demonstrated that no one had influence with him anymore. Consequently Resolution 834, adopted on 1 June, was sadly short on decisive action. There was no mention of Blue Helmets.

Meanwhile, I had flown to Geneva to chair an appeal for humanitarian aid for the thousands of war victims. On 15 June I was back in Luanda for a last hectic two weeks. In New York the Secretary-General had told me that he had at last found a successor: Maître Alioune Blondin Beye, a former Foreign Minister of Mali.

I tried to ensure the safe delivery of aid through agreed humanitarian corridors. President Dos Santos accepted our

502 NEVER LEARN TO TYPE

proposal. UNITA did so 'in principle' but created difficulties that wrecked our plan. I also continued to plug my Blue Helmets proposal. President Dos Santos and the Government liked the idea. So did the new US Assistant Secretary of State for Africa, George Moose, who visited Angola. A strategy was devised whereby President Dos Santos would get the proposal included in a resolution on Angola to be adopted at the Organisation of African Unity (OAU) summit in Cairo in June. This would be endorsed by the Troika, meeting a few days later in Moscow, and submitted to the Security Council. But the President took no initiative in Cairo. I could only conclude that his initial enthusiasm waned because of his deep disillusion with the international community in general, and US policy in particular, grievances on which he waxed eloquent during our final encounter.

My request for a farewell meeting with Dr Savimbi in Huambo was not granted, but he sent a courteous letter in a decorative typescript. It ended with the prayerful wish that Almighty God would be with me and my family, which was rather better than a death threat.

On 19 June, Maître Beye asked me to delay my departure a day or two to brief him on my latest negotiations. I cabled New York for urgent approval but no reply came. On 25 June, which happened to be my birthday, UNAVEM threw a touching farewell party for me. Next morning a communications officer brought me a cable that, she nervously explained, she had withheld on the previous night because 'it would have spoiled your evening'. It was the reply to my cable, signed by Kofi Annan. Couched in terms more appropriate to a reprimand to a delinquent subordinate than a message between two Under Secretaries-General, particularly when the recipient was more senior, it curtly told me to get out of Angola on 28 June (two days before my original departure), report immediately to New York, and complete formalities for my final exodus from the UN on 3 July. This was the last official communication I received from the UN after 41 years of service. I was bitterly hurt by the tone and the unjustified assumption that I was trying to hang on. I replied, equally tersely, that I could not leave on 28, as I was giving a farewell reception, that I intended to take the many weeks of leave due to me before formally retiring and would arrive in New York on 14 July.

On 29 June, I flew to Namibia. During three days at a remote game reserve I went through something akin to the decompression process after a deep-sea dive. One night I slept under the stars in a clearing in the bush, the dark vault of the sky a blazing jewelled canopy, and moonlight filtering between the trees. It was a good memory to take away of the Africa I had long known and loved, overlaying the anguished, bloodstained months in Angola.

In Windhoek President Sam Nujoma and his principal ministers invited me to a working lunch. Nujoma, too, liked my idea of Blue Helmets but it was at this lunch that I learned, to my dismay, that President Dos Santos had not broached the matter in Cairo. Nujoma said that he would take the matter up with his Angolan colleague. Perhaps he did, but nothing came of it.

In New York I attended the Security Council's informal consultations on Angola and its formal session on 15 July, also attended by several African Foreign Ministers. The Secretary-General's report at last put the record straight on the reasons for my departure, saying that he had agreed reluctantly to accede to 'my wish' to be released. The surge of international opinion against UNITA was reflected in Resolution 851, which warned that the Council would clamp sanctions on UNITA if it did not accept a ceasefire by 15 September 1993. Ambassador Albright's statement was curiously nuanced. She talked of UN peace-keeping becoming a growth industry and warned of costs, a far cry from her eager reaction to my idea of an immediate deployment of Blue Helmets to Angola six weeks earlier.

Every speaker had some kind words for what I had tried to do, some very personal and moving. Next day the President of the Council, then Sir David Hannay of the United Kingdom, sent me a formal note, thanking me on the council's behalf.

No similar letter came from the Secretariat. Apart from a cordial farewell visit to the Secretary-General, no one was interested in Angola or in what I had to say. The man and the place of the moment were General Morillon and Bosnia, where the charismatic French General had just completed his mission. It was only as an afterthought that I was asked to brief Kofi Annan's daily meeting and invited to the General's farewell party.

In Washington my Blue Helmets idea was welcomed. I had meetings in the White House, on Capitol Hill, in the State Department, and the Pentagon, with the Angolan Ambassador, and with UNITA representatives. After seeing me, representatives of both Houses of Congress sent a bipartisan appeal to President Clinton and Secretary of State Warren Christopher, urging greater attention to Angola, and support for the immediate despatch of a contingent of Blue Helmets to carry out the functions I had described. I was rash enough to think that something might now happen. Later I learned that reference to Blue Helmets had been dropped, because 'it would cost money', an ominous echo of Madeleine Albright's remarks in the Security Council.

My last day with the United Nations was 31 July 1993. I had risen from being a local staff member in the Philippines in 1952 to the highest rank – Under Secretary-General. I had served in many different countries, in all regions of the world, and participated in virtually every aspect of the organisation's work. Privileged to have pioneered many new paths previously untrodden by women, I was the senior woman in the organisation, and possibly the longest-serving official of either sex, at any level.

It should have been a momentous day in my life. The only official acknowledgement of the occasion was a communication about pension and medical benefits. I left the tall building on First Avenue as I might have done on any day during the preceding four decades.

It was a strange feeling of anticlimax.

PART NINE

Postscript

22

Life After the United Nations

For years I had dreaded leaving the UN. Now I found the prospect less daunting. It was a very different organisation from when I joined it, full of ideals, in my youth – better in some ways, but worse in human environment and treatment of staff. No doubt that was inevitable in an institution that has become so vast; on which so many demands are made without giving it the wherewithal to meet them; on which so much criticism is heaped by member states for shortcomings that often stem from themselves; and where senior staff are subject to constant strain and overwork. But it did not make for a happy ship, especially at Headquarters.

For me, Bolivia called. The Secretary-General asked me to represent him at the inauguration on 6 August of the President-Elect, Gonzalo Sánchez de Lozada. It was an occasion full of hope, and a great antidote to Angola: for the fourth time in succession the Government was changing through due democratic process in a country that, not long before, had been a military dictatorship. The President asked me to act as an adviser and I agreed to do so, part-time and *ad honorem*.

In October I installed myself in the house on Lake Titicaca unseen for two years and which, during the darkest days in Angola, I had feared I might never see again. Asked by a minister how I was getting on, I replied, 'It's rather like Angola – no water and intermittent electricity. But at least there's no shooting.' Not to be left behind, the Bolivian Navy engaged in target practice at dawn next morning, with such brio that I started awake, groping for my non-existent radio. Then, with a flood of relief, I realised I was in Bolivia, and that here there was peace.

The house turned out to be poorly constructed, the wiring lethally amateur, and the colonial tile roof alternately leaked or was blown away by the wind, which also whistled through the badly fitting windows that framed such lovely views. It had virtually to be rebuilt. Too late I discovered that the considerable advances requested by the friend who built it had been used to pay his mounting debts. Two architects and ten years later I have a habitable, if modest, dwelling, and a rather less modest swimming-pool, heated by solar energy. My wild promontory has been tamed by Inca-style stone terraces, hanging gardens that cascade down to the lake shore. In much of it the natural vegetation of the original hillside has been left untrammelled, along with cacti and other plants that flourish on the inhospitable uplands of the *altiplano*. Roses, remarkably, do well at 14 000 feet above sea-level, and birds of many species flock to this small oasis.

Nearly 20 years since I first set my eyes and heart on the spit of land on which Villa Margarita now stands, I have a comfortable home in one of the most beautiful places in the world that is the envy of many. None of them, however, have followed my example, and I am still the only woman not wearing a bowler hat for many miles around. The locals regard me with tolerant amusement and the two villages between which Villa Margarita lies compete for my favours, under the illusion that I am immensely rich. From my bed I watch the sun rise over the Royal Cordillera of the Andes, sparking light from the dark waters of the Sacred Lake. I spend much of my time writing, and in the afternoon clamber breathlessly up the hills behind the house to watch the reflection of the setting sun suffuse those same majestic peaks in a mist of rose and gold. Most days I can lunch outside, while at night I need a blazing fire on my hearth. At weekends friends come from La Paz for a *parrillada*.

My work advising Sánchez de Lozada's Government took me frequently to La Paz. I was a member of the delegation to the World Bank's annual Consultative Group on Bolivia, and in 1996 and

1997 the Government asked me to canvass European Governments beforehand, in the guise of a roving ambassador. These whirlwind missions helped win support for Bolivia's development programmes and secure the country's inclusion in the IMF's and World Bank's programme providing debt relief for 'Highly Indebted Poor Countries' (HIPC).

In September 1994 I led an Inter-American Development Bank mission on socio-economic reform in Bolivia. One of the key areas addressed was the adverse social impact of liberal economic policies. Our independent report, published in February 1995, was hard-hitting, highlighting the dangers to long-term political stability of the widening gap between rich and poor and inadequate social spending. It defined narcotic drugs as a problem mainly of poverty and market forces (as long as demand existed – mainly in the developed countries – there would be supply). We argued that the problem would not be solved by current policies of pouring vast sums of money into 'alternative development' in coca-producing areas, but required sustained development investment in the areas of expulsion, on the *altiplano* and high valleys, where the poorest of the poor live, and in lowland regions not conducive to coca production, to which those living in highland areas incapable of redemption might be encouraged to migrate.

Our frank warnings of future social unrest should timely remedial action not be taken raised some hackles but the President welcomed our constructive criticism. Soon afterwards he asked me to help prepare a presentation for the World Bank Consultative Group meeting, based in the report. This took the form of an integrated rural development strategy – the third time I had tried to launch such a policy. Enthusiastically received by donor governments, it unfortunately had not got off the ground when the Government's four-year term came to an end.

In August 1997 a new coalition government, headed by General Hugo Banzer, the former dictator, now democratically elected, assumed office. My advisory role ceased until late 2002, when Sánchez de Lozada assumed his second presidency.

My commitments elsewhere have steadily increased. *Pro bono publico* work has taken me to many countries, lecturing, writing and attending conferences on development cooperation and finance, UN reform, Angola, humanitarian and disaster relief operations, peace-keeping and peace-building. I serve on the boards of several organisations concerned with related issues.

Much of my work has been with the United Nations. In 1993 I presented a paper on the lessons to be learned from the Angolan debacle to Boutros-Ghali, in the expectation that he would circulate it to senior staff. Unfortunately he kept it to himself. As I later chaired the Advisory Board of the Lessons Learned Unit of the UN Department of Peace-keeping Operations (DPKO) I was able to feed these findings into subsequent operations, as well as participate in useful work on many aspects of peace-keeping.

The training of troops for peace-keeping operations has proved a welcome opportunity to satisfy my preference for practical and operational matters. Peace-keeping requires different techniques from those traditionally inculcated into military forces, and mutual understanding between military and civilian elements is of crucial importance to effective peace-keeping. The British Army, with the Foreign Office, pioneered the idea of simulated practical exercises, based on a fictitious country riven by conflict and beset with every conceivable problem. I was privileged to take part in these from the beginning and have done similar work in Scandinavia, Africa and Latin America.

The Latin American exercises are organised by the United States Armed Forces for American and Latin American military personnel, with civilian role players provided by the UN. I play the part of the Special Representative of the Secretary-General (SRSG) that was mine in real life. My first involvement was in Paraguay in 1998, and I have subsequently taken part in similar exercises in Bolivia, Honduras, Ecuador, El Salvador and Argentina. I have been 'kidnapped' by masked guerrillas, amid simulated bombs and real red smoke, tied blindfolded to a tree, and returned, after due negotiation, slung over the shoulders of one of my captors, with a blanket over my head.

The most dramatic experience of all was a live NATO peace-keeping exercise in the Baltic in the Spring of 2002, involving 20 000 troops on the ground with their heavy equipment, air operations and a US warship and many other naval vessels. As SRSG I was given the equivalent rank of a four-star General.

A major lesson of UN peace-keeping missions in the 1990s was that traditional peace-keeping is insufficient to consolidate sustainable peace. In countries with a long history of internal strife it is essential to address its root causes and persuade the population that they have a stake in a peaceful future. Elections alone will not bring about democracy, and may even exacerbate the situation. This realisation led to the evolution of the concept of peace-building. The measures required vary from country to country but typically involve the creation of democratic and equitable access to power and resources; representative institutions; judicial and police reform; reconstruction; de-mining; vocational training and job-creation for ex-combatants; development of social services; and, ultimately, economic and social development programmes designed to increase living standards.

My involvement began with an international meeting I chaired in Austria in June 1995. My 'Chairman's Synopsis' of that meeting was circulated as a General Assembly document and subsequently I was asked to write two follow-up reports for two successive Secretaries-General, Boutros-Ghali and Kofi Annan, outlining the specific actions required of the UN system to implement these ideas effectively. In 2001 these were woven into a system-wide Plan of Action, by a small team and myself. All the measures proposed have been agreed in principle, but six years after I wrote the first report some key aspects have still not been implemented, partly through internal bureaucratic delays and partly through financial constraints. The wheels of the UN grind exceedingly slow.

I cannot free myself from Angola and seize every opportunity to publicise that forgotten tragedy. Writing my book, *Orphan of the Cold War: The Inside Story of the Collapse of the Angolan Peace Process, 1992–3*, was a cathartic experience, occupying two and a half years. I tried not only to give a faithful account of the events that led to the relapse into war but also to convey what it was like to be burdened by a huge responsibility for peoples' lives but deprived of the minimal resources to discharge it. The book was published in 1996, and a Portuguese translation followed in 1997. The public presentation of the Portuguese version in Lisbon, filmed on prime-time television, nearly became a riot. UNITA hard-liners attacked me, Angolans of a different persuasion defended me, and the two sides almost came to fisticuffs. While it made interesting publicity, it did not bode well for the Government of National Unity and Reconciliation that had just then been formed. The country soon plunged back into all-out war anew.

Ironically, the continuation of the war, despite the stronger mandate and increased resources provided to UNAVEM III and my successor, Maître Beye, led to kindlier judgements of the UN by some Angolans. At a conference in London in 1997, the Angolan Deputy Foreign Minister transfixed both me and his audience by his opening gambit; 'In 1992–3 some of us thought that the Angolan peace process collapsed because the UN sent someone who was British, white ... and female.' He paused for effect, then went on: 'For the last four years we have had someone who is African, black ... and male, and it still isn't working. So we have to look elsewhere for the true causes of continuing conflict.' This was handsome public recognition that UN Special Representatives become the scapegoats held responsible for events beyond their control. Tragically Maître Beye died in a suspicious crash of the UN Beechcraft in Côte-d'Ivoire, in June 1998.

In March 2000 I returned to Angola, after seven years, representing the British Angola Forum which we had set up in London in 1998. It was a highly emotional experience. There was a new spirit abroad: the Government claimed that the conventional war against Savimbi had been won, and new elections were promised for late 2001. My arrival, coinciding with action by the Security Council to make sanctions against UNITA more effective and progress towards agreement with the IMF, gave hope of renewed international interest.

I was given an extraordinary reception. I saw the President, key ministers, the Commander-in-Chief of the Armed Forces, opposition leaders, the cardinal and representatives of civil society. People in the street, road sweepers and vendors, gave the thumbs-up sign, as if my return symbolised a new beginning. All went out of their way to vindicate my efforts in 1992–93. The woman who had organised the coffin with my name on it in 1993 apologised and a prominent UNITA leader, now alienated from Savimbi, revealed that in Abidjan he had indeed disagreed with UNITA's position but was too frightened to speak. This time the worst thing that happened was that I got locked in a lavatory in Benguela!

In May 2001 I returned again, and had another long meeting with President Dos Santos. Savimbi was still cornered in south-eastern Angola and continued UNITA guerrilla activity gave cause for concern. And then, at last, on 27 February 2002 Savimbi was killed.

Military victory will not be enough to assure stable peace in Angola. The Government must govern the territories recovered from UNITA and show that its rule is oppressive but will bring a genuine peace dividend: reconstruction, democratic institutions and sorely needed public and social services. Only in this way can reconciliation be fostered and faith and confidence restored to people who for 30 years have known nothing but war. In my conversations with President Dos Santos I was delighted to find we had a meeting of minds on what needs to be done. The main burden must fall on the Angolans but they will need generous international support. The task ahead is vast. I suggested to the President that a pilot area should be chosen, as a testing ground for techniques that can later be extended to the whole country and a demonstration of what can be done. The Government has now selected two provinces, Kwanza Sul and Huambo (formerly Savimbi's stronghold), the UN is providing support and I have been asked to assist. It would be a dream come true to feel I could make some small contribution to lasting peace in Angola.

There has been pleasure as well as work. I sailed on three expedition cruises watching birds and wildlife in the Seychelles, in the islands around Britain and during a magical month in Antarctica. There I felt that the wheel had come full circle from those far-off days in the Foreign Office, when I cut my diplomatic teeth on Antarctic issues.

It was also agreeable to receive recognition from unexpected quarters. In 1992, while I was still in Angola, the Austrian

Government had awarded me Das Grosse Goldene Ehrenzeichen Am Bonde. Then in September 1993 the College of William and Mary in Williamsburg, Virginia, awarded me the first Reves Peace Prize. A few months later, Queen Elizabeth II honoured me, and the Universities of Essex, Westminster and London later gave me honorary doctorates. Two of the public orators could not resist the quip that this was the first time a doctorate had been given to someone pronounced a prostitute on the international airwaves (a reference to Savimbi's vituperative attack in 1993). A different kind of recognition came from a totally unexpected quarter in 2001 when the BBC televised a programme about me entitled *Nine Lives*, composed around nine individuals who had greatly influenced the course of my life.

I have spent part of each year in Knill with my Aunt Christina, writing, gardening and walking on the surrounding hills. Her death in 2000, a few weeks short of her ninetieth birthday, left a great void, but many happy memories. To the end she conserved her lively wit and positive outlook on life.

In 1996, when the garden was spick and span, ready for its summer opening, we decided to give a garden birthday party on 25 June. Our guests were a medley of farmers, country neighbours, diplomats, journalists and even two ambassadors – of Bolivia and Angola. Some came from near, others from very far.

The day dawned so foggy we could not see the crests of Knill Garraway and Herrock. Then the sun burst through and we had a perfect English summer day, sunny and warm, with a light breeze ruffling the trees and high white clouds scudding across a blue, blue sky. The garden shone at its best – roses, delphiniums and clematis against the rosy brick walls, long reaches of candelabra primulas blooming in the bog garden, and heavenly scents wafting on the breeze. The guests wandered through the gardens, drinks in hand, before lunch in a flower-decked marquee. Down by the river a small band of itinerant Bolivian musicians struck up in the shade of the weeping willows on their traditional instruments – quena, charango, *zampoña*. They wore the typical dress of Potosí: homespun trousers, round white hats, brightly garlanded, waist-coats and ponchos of rainbow hue. Their plangent Andean music blended perfectly with the gentle hills of the Welsh Marches, a landscape so distant and so much more verdant than the frugal vistas of the *altiplano* and the encircling snowy peaks that inspired it.

It was a magical day, bringing together so many of the myriad threads that have been woven into the fabric of my life. I reflected that, although I had not achieved all that I might have liked, I had led a wonderfully exciting life beyond the wildest imaginings of travel and adventure in which I had indulged in my country childhood. I was doubly fortunate in that my days were still full of new challenges and there was still so much to look forward to.

I liked to think that my parents, who sacrificed so much to make it all possible, might have concluded, had they been there, that, on the whole, I had not jibbed.

Epilogue

What does it all add up to? In my youth I first of all wanted to obtain an education, without much thought beyond that. Afterwards, caught up in the wave of optimism and new ideas that followed the Second World War, I was fired by the desire to contribute in some modest way to the process of bringing about positive change: an end to poverty and social discrimination; a new way ahead for women; and the establishment of conditions worldwide that would make peace and tolerant coexistence more attractive than war. The United Nations seemed the perfect channel for my aims and energies.

The echo of those youthful aspirations rings hollow in a world still rent by conflict and poverty, overshadowed by the insidious and all-pervading threat of terrorism and, as I write these words, teetering on the brink of war with Iraq. The Cold War that hampered so many of the endeavours with which I have been involved has ended, but its malign effects linger on. Paradoxically, the unipolar world in which we now live often seems more unstable and dangerous than during the precarious balance of power that went before. Yet, though the larger picture is depressing, I do see evidence of progress on the smaller scale. As I travel round the world I constantly run into people whose lives were transformed by UN programmes and find that projects on which we worked long ago have borne results. Unlike capital investment, the impact of technical cooperation is impossible to measure because it is inextricably interwoven with the many other threads of the process that we like to call progress. One thing is certain: 'development' has proved to be a much more complex and elusive concept than we ingenuously thought in the early 1950s. Yet without it, without the fairer distribution of the world's resources and the attainment of reasonable living conditions for those living under the poverty line, we and future generations are doomed to continue to live in an increasingly insecure world.

I have seen an enormous change for the better in the role that women play in the so-called developed world, and in some respects in developing countries. But in too many parts of the world women continue to be the down-trodden underdogs of society, condemned to drudgery and degradation at worst and, at best, severely limited in the scope of their permitted activities. So, although much has been achieved, there is still a long way to go.

As for the United Nations, it bears a much more tarnished image than in its heady early days when I first joined it. Now it is underfunded, constantly criticised for perceived lack of effectiveness and efficiency and sometimes bypassed by its most powerful member states. The brinkmanship that has taken place in the Security Council since the autumn of 2002 over the actions to be taken over Iraq have come alarmingly close to making the organisation a virtually irrelevant actor on the world stage.

Few people who criticise the United Nations realise that the Secretary-General and the international officials that serve him do not act unilaterally but as the servants of 191 member states. It is the latter who call the shots. More often than not national and regional interests prevail over logical actions for the common good. In such circumstances it is impossible for the United Nations to be fully effective in attaining the ideals so eloquently described in its charter.

The same limitations make it impossible for the United Nations to be fully efficient. Member states constantly call for reform. The organisation is so regularly overhauled that it is a miracle it functions at all. The basic problems remain the same. I was centrally involved in several of these exercises but, as I have tried to show in this book, it was often the very member states who had insisted on reform who undercut its effective implementation when they perceived it could affect their own vested interests. My starry-eyed conviction in the 1960s that logical, across-the-board reform was possible, received a rude awakening.

The present Secretary-General, Kofi Annan, was himself elected on yet another reform ticket and has made significant efforts to that end, but major reform is still bedevilled by the age-old problem: member states, even those supposedly like-minded, cannot agree on far-reaching changes, particularly the key issue of Security Council reform. National interests prevail, in yet another illustration of the paradox that bars effective international action at the start of the twenty-first century: sovereignty is still deemed supreme, although a shrinking and increasingly globalised world renders it daily more irrelevant.

Many people think that the Capacity Study, which Jacko and I wrote 30 years ago, is still relevant because its proposals were never fully implemented. If Jacko were alive I feel sure he would agree that the logical, across-the-board reform posited by the Capacity Study has no chance today. The UN is not a logical organisation, the vested interests of member states are too strong, and the more powerful countries do not want a forceful Secretary-General. The only way forward is through specific changes that would have a multiplier effect, such as a more rational way of selecting the Secretary-General, and executive heads of agencies, based on qualifications and experience, rather than political horse-trading; single, though longer, tenures for top officials, so that political jockeying for re-election would be eliminated; and a consolidated budget for the whole UN system that would reduce both duplication and the inordinate outlay of money on 'co-ordination', which simply creates new layers of bureaucracy. People – the best possible people, in the right place – are a surer recipe for success than the most elaborate organogram. But could governments agree on even this modest programme?

Nevertheless, I still believe passionately in the ideals and aims for which the UN was created, and in the indispensable need for it to exist. As Adlai Stevenson once aptly said, if it did not, then it would have to be invented. A globalised world needs a universal institution and the vast scope of the activities undertaken by the UN system embrace virtually every aspect of human life. Yet it is usually superficially judged on its handling of political issues that have been referred to it only when everyone else has failed to solve them.

I want to pay tribute to the many colleagues and others whom I have met over the years in so many parts of the world who continue to strive for the realisation of the ideals that led to the creation of the UN in 1945. Many of them work in harsh and sometimes life-threatening situations, undeterred by the many obstacles that confront the organisation at every turn. My dearest hope is that new generations will follow us in the long and difficult quest for 'social progress and better standards of life in larger freedom', in the eloquent words of the preamble to the UN Charter. Without that there can be no true world security.

List of Acronyms

ACC	United Nations Administrative Committee on Coordination
AIDS	Acquired Immune Deficiency Syndrome
ALALC	Latin American Free Trade Association
AVA	Awash Valley Authority
BBC	British Broadcasting Corporation
BPPE	Bureau for Programme Policy and Evaluation (UNDP)
CBI	Confederation of British Industries
CCPM	Comisāo Conjunta Política Militas (Joint Political Military Commission)
CDF	Capital Development Fund
CEDAW	United Nations Convention on the Elimination of all forms of Discrimination Against Women
CFA	Committee on Food Aid (WFP's governing body)
CIA	Central Intelligence Agency
CND	United Nations Commission on Narcotic Drugs
COB	Central Obrera Boliviana (Bolivian Labour Union)
CPC	United Nations Committee for Programme Coordination
DC3	Aircraft
DEA	Department of Economic Affairs
DERRO	Integrated Rural Development Programme for the RIF region in Morocco
DIESA	United Nations Department for International Economic and Social Affairs
DND	United Nations Division for Narcotic Drugs
DPA	United Nations Department for Political Affairs
DPKO	United Nations Department for Peacekeeping Operations
DTCD	United Nations Department of Technical Co-operation for Development

ECA	United Nations Economic Commission for Africa
ECLA	United Nations Economic Commission for Latin America
ECLAC	United Nations Economic Commission for Latin America and the Caribbean (Formerly ECA)
ECOSOC	United Nations Economic and Social Council
EEC	European Economic Commission
EPTA	Expanded Programme of Technical Assistance
FAA	Forças Armadas Angolanas (Joint Armed Forces of Angola)
FAO	Food and Agriculture Organisation (United Nations Agency)
FLACSO	Latin American Faculty for Social Sciences
GNP	Gross National Product
HIM	His Imperial Majesty (Emperor Haile Selassie of Ethiopia)
HIPC	Heavily Indebted Poor Countries (World Bank and IMF debt relief programme)
HMG	Her Majesty's Government
HONLEA	Heads of Narcotic Law Enforcement Agencies (meetings convened by the United Nations)
IADB	Inter-American Development Bank
IAEA	International Atomic Energy Agency (United Nations Agency)
IBRD	International Bank for Reconstruction and Development, also known as World Bank (United Nations Agency)
ICAO	International Civil Aviation Organisation (United Nations Agency)
ICDAIT	United Nations International Conference on Drug Abuse and Illicit Trafficking (1987)
ICETEX	Colombian Institute providing loans for students to study abroad
ICRC	Integrated Committee of the Red Cross
IDA	International Development Association (United Nations Agency)
ILO	International Labour Office (United Nations Agency)

ILPES	Latin American Economic and Social Planning Institute
IMF	International Monetary Fund (United Nations Agency)
INCB	International Narcotics Control Board
INSEA	Regional Statistical Training Institute for the Maghreb
IPF	Indicative Planning Figures
IPPF	International Planned Parenthood Federation
IWY	International Women's Year (1975)
KGB	Komitet Gosudarstvennoi Bezopaznosti (Soviet secret intelligence service)
LAB	Lloyd Aéreo Boliviano (Bolivian State Airline)
MNR	Movimiento Nacionalista Revolucionario (Nationalist Revolutionary Movement – Bolivian Political Party)
MPLA	Movimento Popular para a Lïberacāo de Angola (Popular Movement for the Liberation of Angola)
NATO	North Atlantic Treaty Organisation
NEC	National Electoral Council
NEDC	National Economic Development Council
OAS	Organisation of American States
OPEX	United Nations Operational and Executive Programme
OQM	Operation Question Mark
S.O.S.	Committee for the Security of Oil Supplies
SAAF	South African Airforce
SF	United Nations Special Fund
SRSG	Special Representative of the Secretary-General of the United Nations
SUNFED	Special United Nations Fund for Economic Development
TCDC	Technical Cooperation among Developing Countries
TUC	Trades Union Council
UK	United Kingdom
UN	United Nations
UNAVEM	United Nations Angola Verification Mission
UNCSDHA	United Nations Centre for Social Development and Humanitarian Affairs

UNCTAD	United Nations Conference on Trade and Development
UNDP	United Nations Development Programme
UNDRO	United Nations Disaster Relief Organisation
UNEPRO	United Nations East Pakistan Relief Operation
UNESCO	United Nations Educational, Scientific and Cultural Organisation
UNFDAC	United Nations Fund for Drug Abuse Control
UNFPA	United Nations Fund for Population Activities
UNHCR	United Nations High Commissioner for Refugees
UNICEF	United Nations Children's Emergency Fund
UNIDO	United Nations Industrial Development Organisation
UNIMOG	A four wheel drive German vehicle
UNITA	União Nacional para a Independencia Total de Angola (National Union for the Total Independence of Angola)
UNMO	United Nations Military Observer
UNOV	United Nations Office at Vienna
UNROB	United Nations Relief Operation, Bangladesh
UNROD	United Nations Relief Operation, Dacca
UNRRA	United Nations Relief and Rehabilitation Administration
UNTAB	United Nations Technical Assistance Board
UP	Unidad Popular (Popular Union) (Chilean Political Party)
US	United States (of America)
USSR	Soviet Union
VW	Volkswagen
WFP	World Food Programme (UN entity under the joint control of the United Nations and the Food and Agriculture Organisation)
WHO	World Health Organisation (United Nations Agency)
WMO	World Meteorological Organisation (United Nations Agency)
YPFB	Yacimientos Petroliferos Bolivianos (Bolivian State Oil Company)

Index